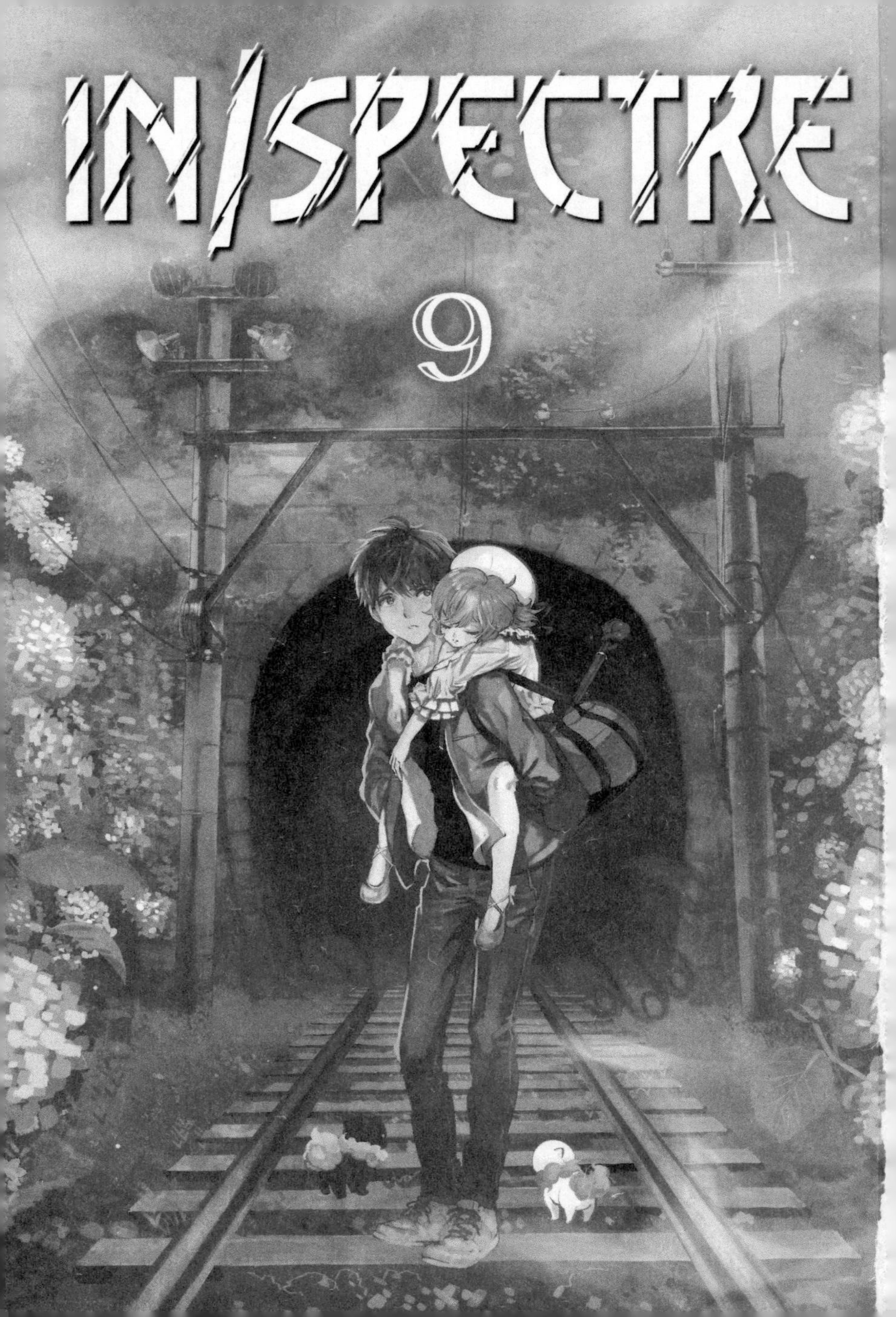
IN/SPECTRE
9

CONTENTS

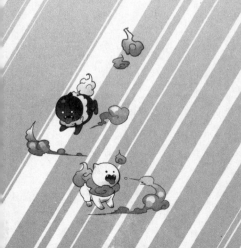

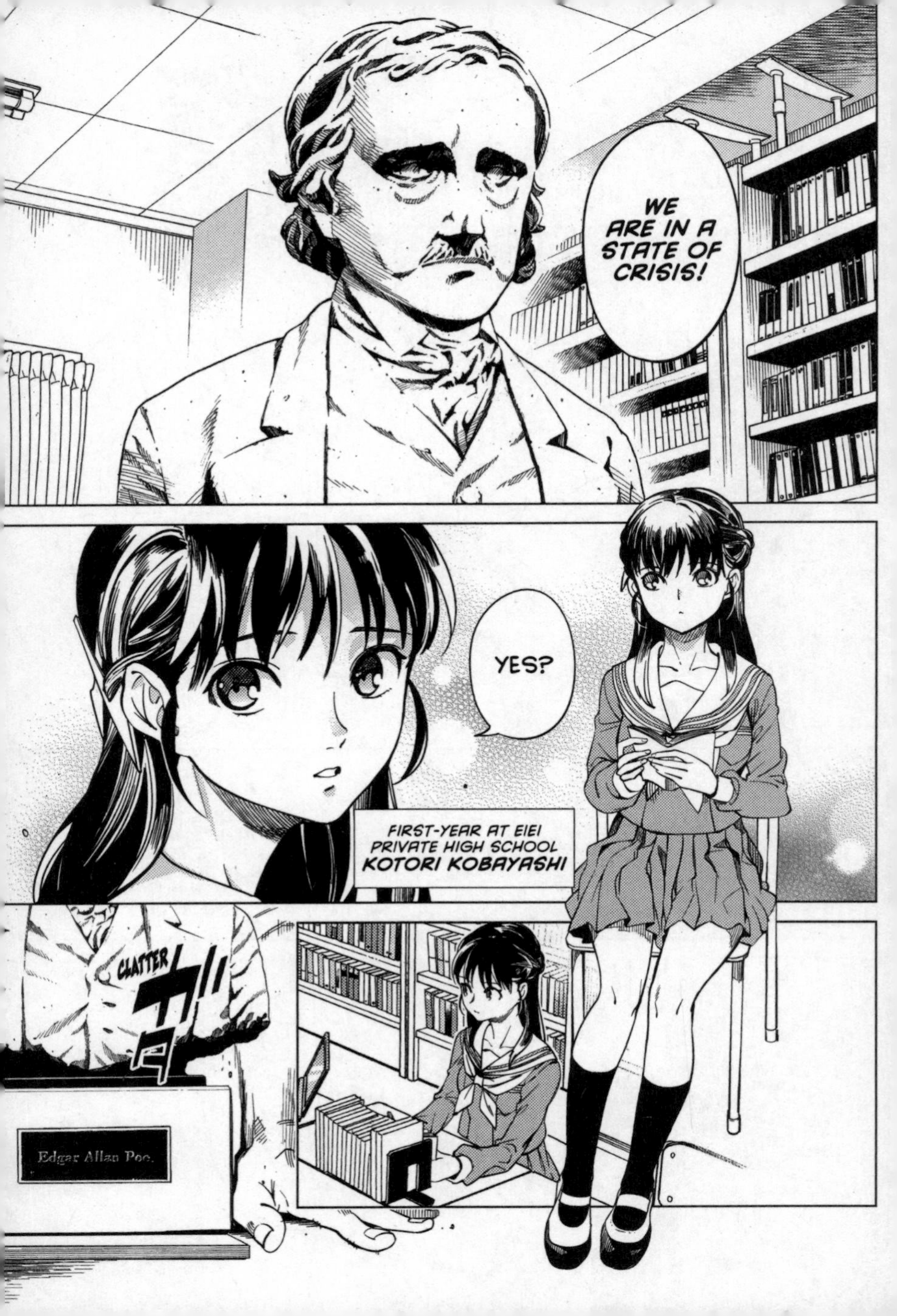
WE ARE IN A STATE OF CRISIS!
YES?
FIRST-YEAR AT EIEI PRIVATE HIGH SCHOOL KOTORI KOBAYASHI
CLATTER
Edgar Allan Poe.

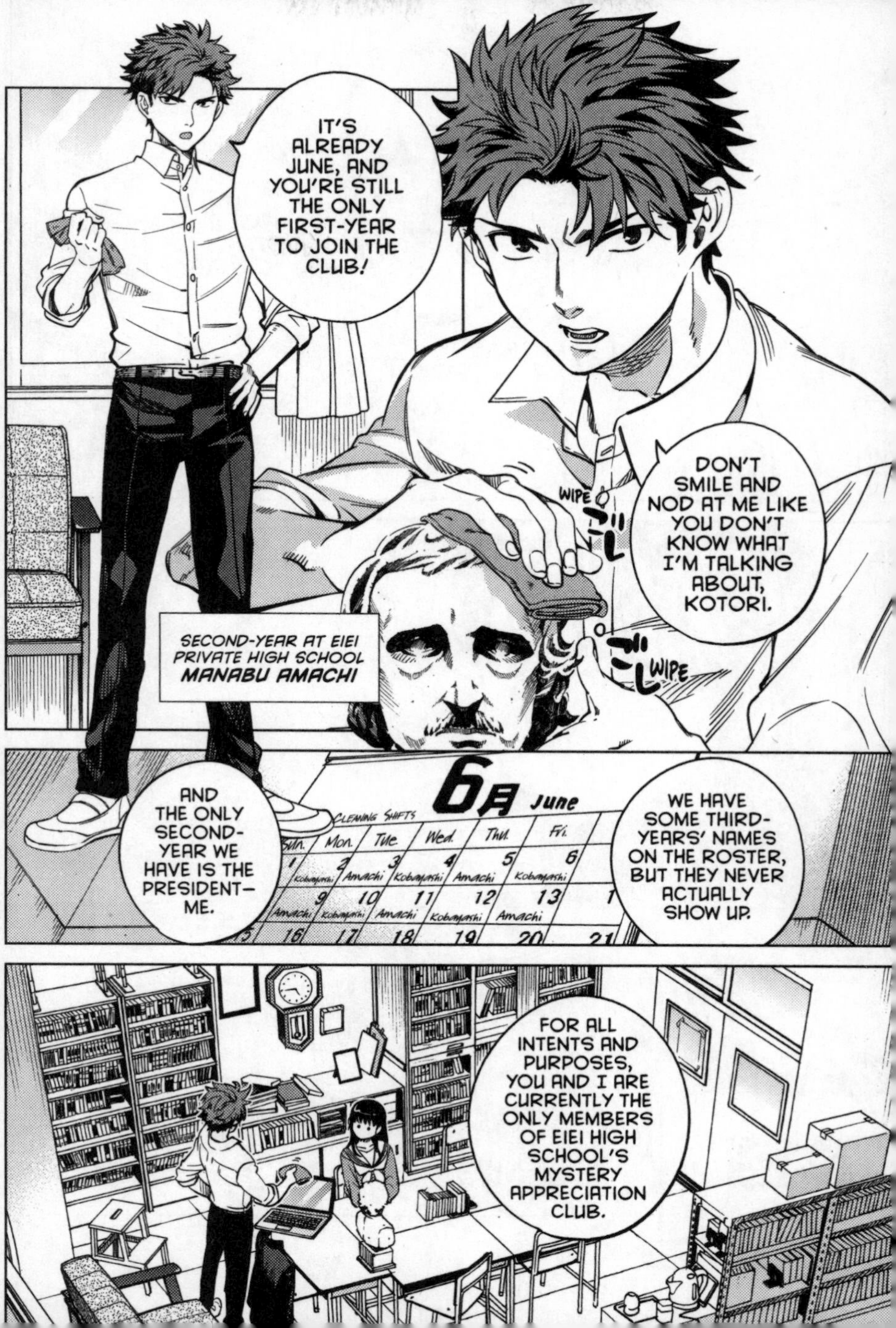
IT'S ALREADY JUNE, AND YOU'RE STILL THE ONLY FIRST-YEAR TO JOIN THE CLUB!
DON'T SMILE AND NOD AT ME LIKE YOU DON'T KNOW WHAT I'M TALKING ABOUT, KOTORI.
WIPE
WIPE
SECOND-YEAR AT EIEI PRIVATE HIGH SCHOOL
MANABU AMACHI
WE HAVE SOME THIRD-YEARS' NAMES ON THE ROSTER, BUT THEY NEVER ACTUALLY SHOW UP.
6月 June
CLEANING SHIFTS
Sun. Mon. Tue. Wed. Thu. Fri.
1 Kobayashi 2 Amachi 3 Kobayashi 4 Amachi 5 6 Kobayashi
9 Amachi 10 Kobayashi 11 Amachi 12 Kobayashi 13 Amachi
16 17 18 19 20 21
AND THE ONLY SECOND-YEAR WE HAVE IS THE PRESIDENT—ME.
FOR ALL INTENTS AND PURPOSES, YOU AND I ARE CURRENTLY THE ONLY MEMBERS OF EIEI HIGH SCHOOL'S MYSTERY APPRECIATION CLUB.

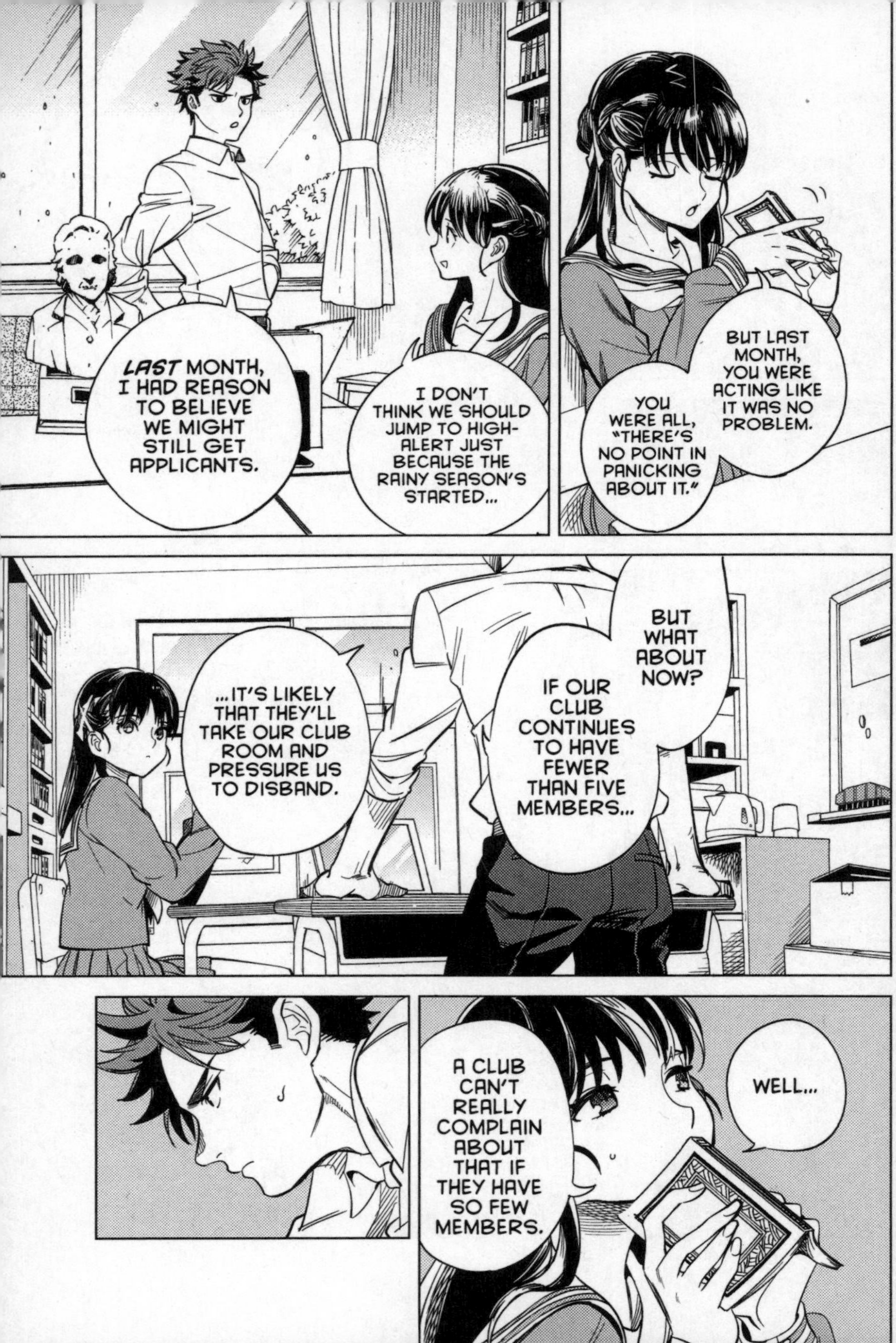
BUT LAST MONTH, YOU WERE ACTING LIKE IT WAS NO PROBLEM.
YOU WERE ALL, "THERE'S NO POINT IN PANICKING ABOUT IT."
I DON'T THINK WE SHOULD JUMP TO HIGH-ALERT JUST BECAUSE THE RAINY SEASON'S STARTED...
LAST MONTH, I HAD REASON TO BELIEVE WE MIGHT STILL GET APPLICANTS.
BUT WHAT ABOUT NOW?
IF OUR CLUB CONTINUES TO HAVE FEWER THAN FIVE MEMBERS...
...IT'S LIKELY THAT THEY'LL TAKE OUR CLUB ROOM AND PRESSURE US TO DISBAND.
WELL...
A CLUB CAN'T REALLY COMPLAIN ABOUT THAT IF THEY HAVE SO FEW MEMBERS.

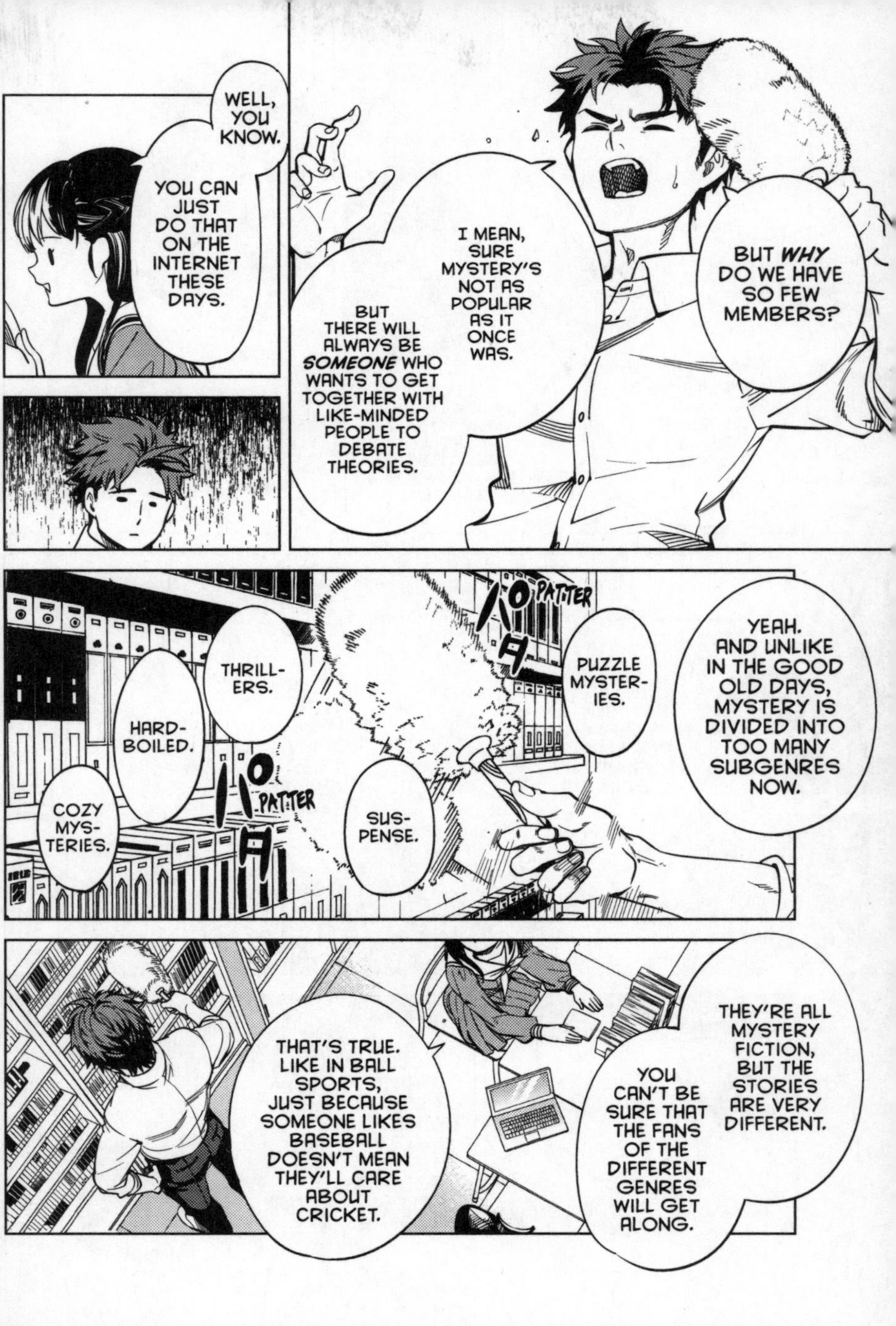
BUT *WHY* DO WE HAVE SO FEW MEMBERS?
I MEAN, SURE MYSTERY'S NOT AS POPULAR AS IT ONCE WAS.
BUT THERE WILL ALWAYS BE *SOMEONE* WHO WANTS TO GET TOGETHER WITH LIKE-MINDED PEOPLE TO DEBATE THEORIES.
WELL, YOU KNOW.
YOU CAN JUST DO THAT ON THE INTERNET THESE DAYS.
YEAH. AND UNLIKE IN THE GOOD OLD DAYS, MYSTERY IS DIVIDED INTO TOO MANY SUBGENRES NOW.
PATTER
PUZZLE MYSTER-IES.
SUS-PENSE.
THRILL-ERS.
HARD-BOILED.
PATTER
COZY MYS-TERIES.
THEY'RE ALL MYSTERY FICTION, BUT THE STORIES ARE VERY DIFFERENT.
YOU CAN'T BE SURE THAT THE FANS OF THE DIFFERENT GENRES WILL GET ALONG.
THAT'S TRUE. LIKE IN BALL SPORTS, JUST BECAUSE SOMEONE LIKES BASEBALL DOESN'T MEAN THEY'LL CARE ABOUT CRICKET.

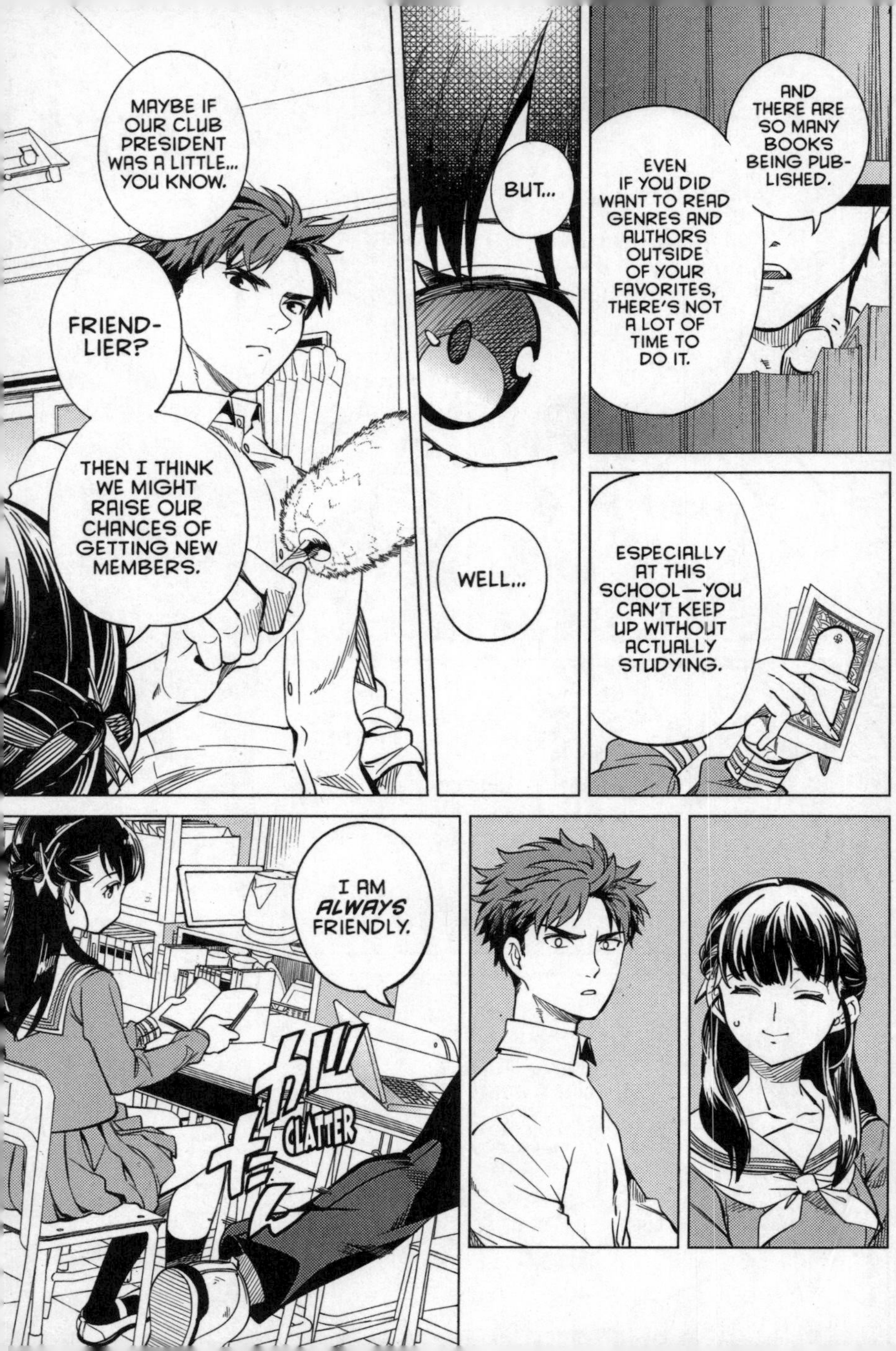
AND THERE ARE SO MANY BOOKS BEING PUB-LISHED.
EVEN IF YOU DID WANT TO READ GENRES AND AUTHORS OUTSIDE OF YOUR FAVORITES, THERE'S NOT A LOT OF TIME TO DO IT.
ESPECIALLY AT THIS SCHOOL—YOU CAN'T KEEP UP WITHOUT ACTUALLY STUDYING.
BUT...
WELL...
MAYBE IF OUR CLUB PRESIDENT WAS A LITTLE... YOU KNOW.
FRIEND-LIER?
THEN I THINK WE MIGHT RAISE OUR CHANCES OF GETTING NEW MEMBERS.
I AM *ALWAYS* FRIENDLY.
CLATTER

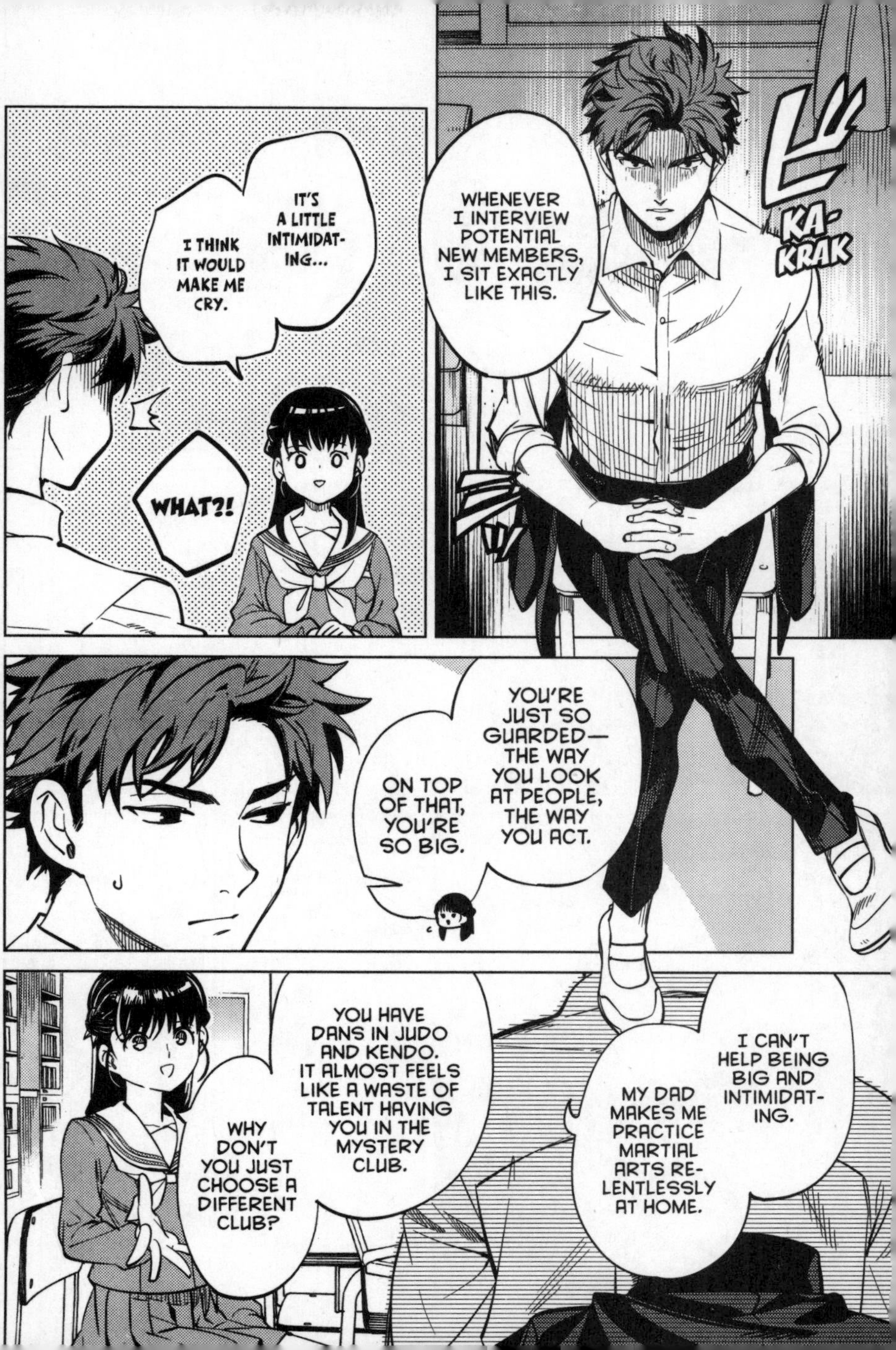
KA-KRAK
WHENEVER I INTERVIEW POTENTIAL NEW MEMBERS, I SIT EXACTLY LIKE THIS.
IT'S A LITTLE INTIMIDATING...
I THINK IT WOULD MAKE ME CRY.
WHAT?!
YOU'RE JUST SO GUARDED—THE WAY YOU LOOK AT PEOPLE, THE WAY YOU ACT.
ON TOP OF THAT, YOU'RE SO BIG.
I CAN'T HELP BEING BIG AND INTIMIDATING.
MY DAD MAKES ME PRACTICE MARTIAL ARTS RELENTLESSLY AT HOME.
YOU HAVE DANS IN JUDO AND KENDO. IT ALMOST FEELS LIKE A WASTE OF TALENT HAVING YOU IN THE MYSTERY CLUB.
WHY DON'T YOU JUST CHOOSE A DIFFERENT CLUB?

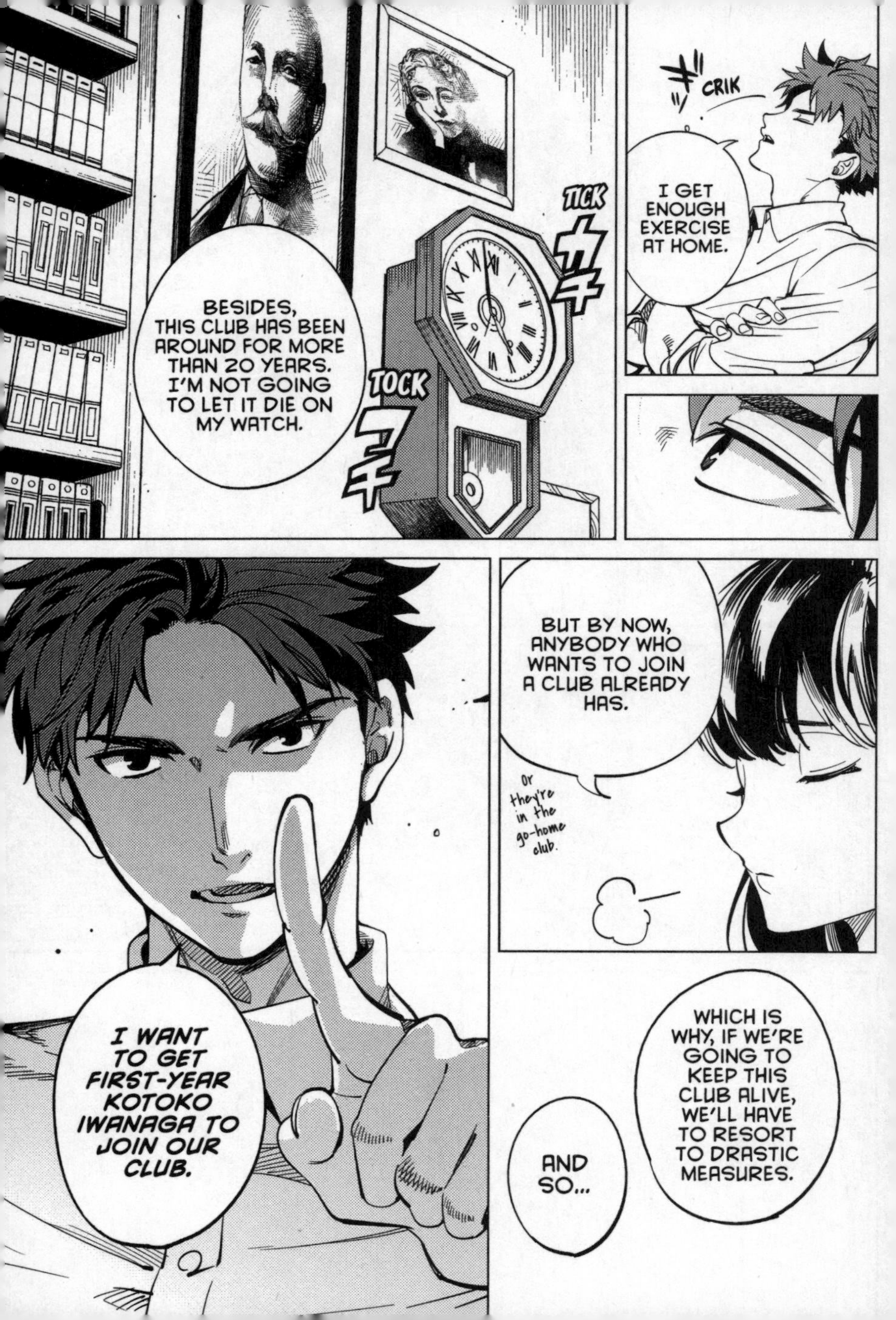
CRIK
I GET ENOUGH EXERCISE AT HOME.
TICK
BESIDES, THIS CLUB HAS BEEN AROUND FOR MORE THAN 20 YEARS. I'M NOT GOING TO LET IT DIE ON MY WATCH.
TOCK
BUT BY NOW, ANYBODY WHO WANTS TO JOIN A CLUB ALREADY HAS.
Or they're in the go-home club.
WHICH IS WHY, IF WE'RE GOING TO KEEP THIS CLUB ALIVE, WE'LL HAVE TO RESORT TO DRASTIC MEASURES.
AND SO...
I WANT TO GET FIRST-YEAR KOTOKO IWANAGA TO JOIN OUR CLUB.

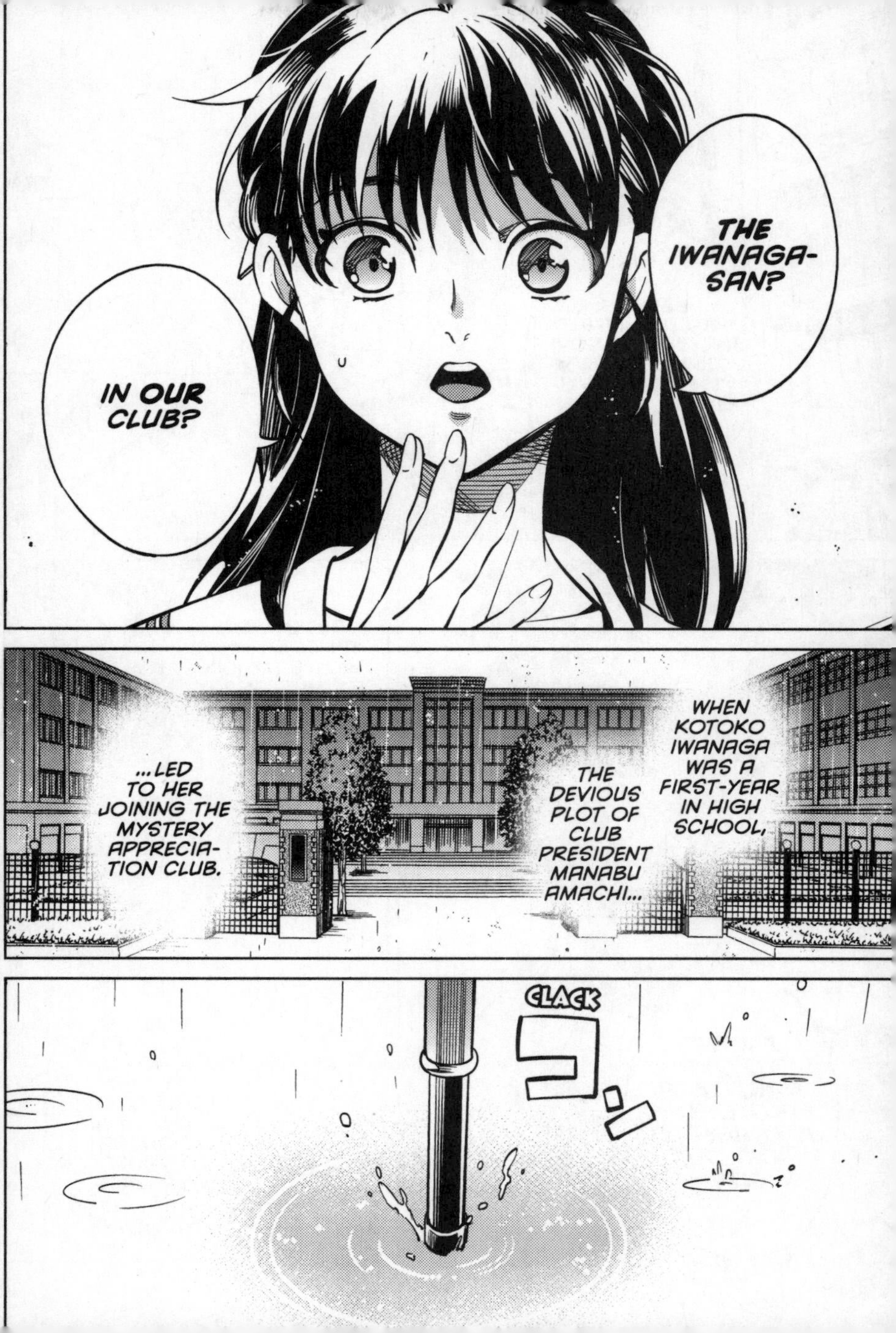
THE IWANAGA-SAN?
IN OUR CLUB?
WHEN KOTOKO IWANAGA WAS A FIRST-YEAR IN HIGH SCHOOL,
THE DEVIOUS PLOT OF CLUB PRESIDENT MANABU AMACHI...
...LED TO HER JOINING THE MYSTERY APPRECIATION CLUB.
CLACK

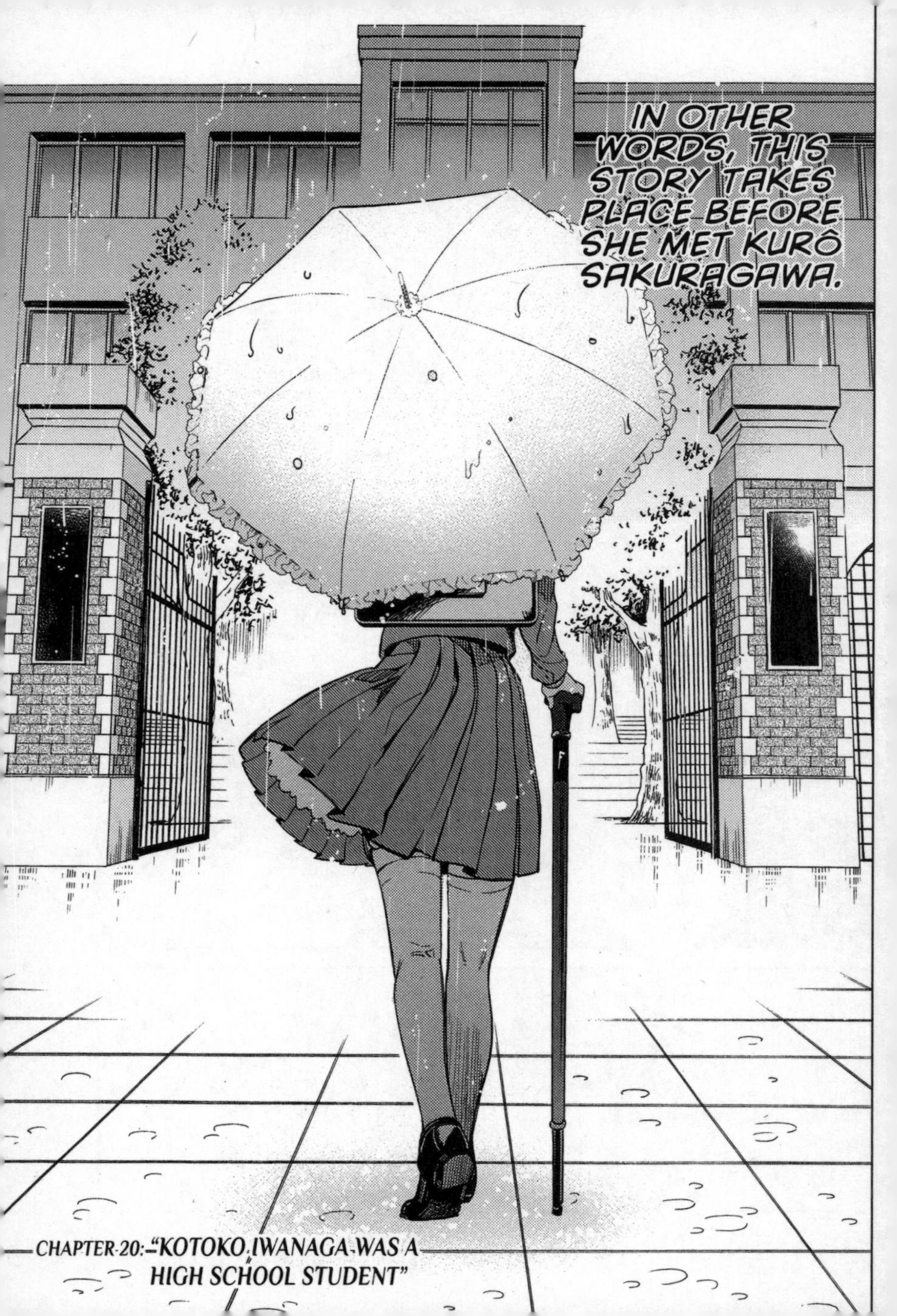
IN OTHER WORDS, THIS STORY TAKES PLACE BEFORE SHE MET KURÔ SAKURAGAWA.
CHAPTER 20: "KOTOKO IWANAGA WAS A HIGH SCHOOL STUDENT"

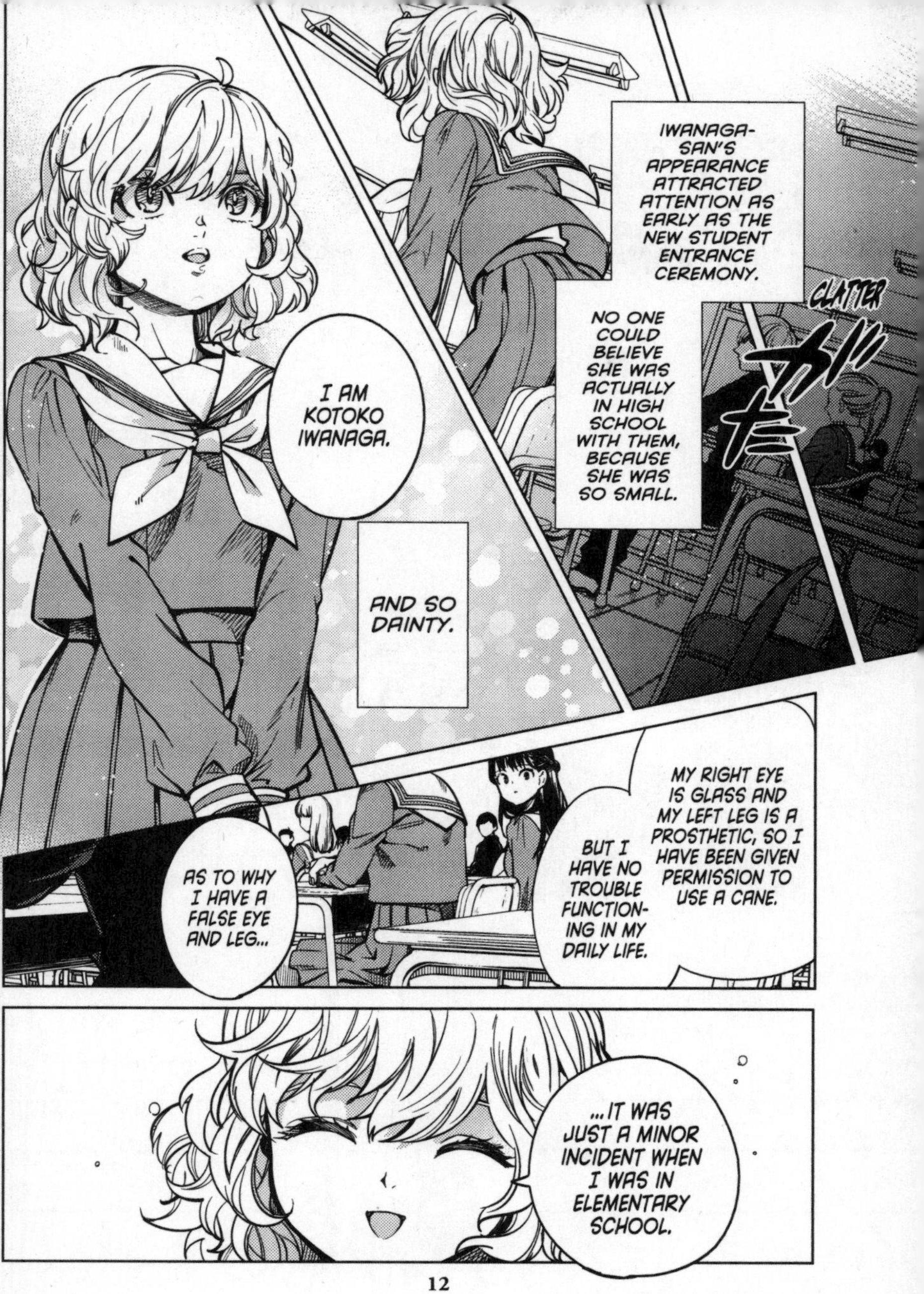
IWANAGA-SAN'S APPEARANCE ATTRACTED ATTENTION AS EARLY AS THE NEW STUDENT ENTRANCE CEREMONY.
NO ONE COULD BELIEVE SHE WAS ACTUALLY IN HIGH SCHOOL WITH THEM, BECAUSE SHE WAS SO SMALL.
CLATTER
I AM KOTOKO IWANAGA.
AND SO DAINTY.
MY RIGHT EYE IS GLASS AND MY LEFT LEG IS A PROSTHETIC, SO I HAVE BEEN GIVEN PERMISSION TO USE A CANE.
BUT I HAVE NO TROUBLE FUNCTION-ING IN MY DAILY LIFE.
AS TO WHY I HAVE A FALSE EYE AND LEG...
...IT WAS JUST A MINOR INCIDENT WHEN I WAS IN ELEMENTARY SCHOOL.

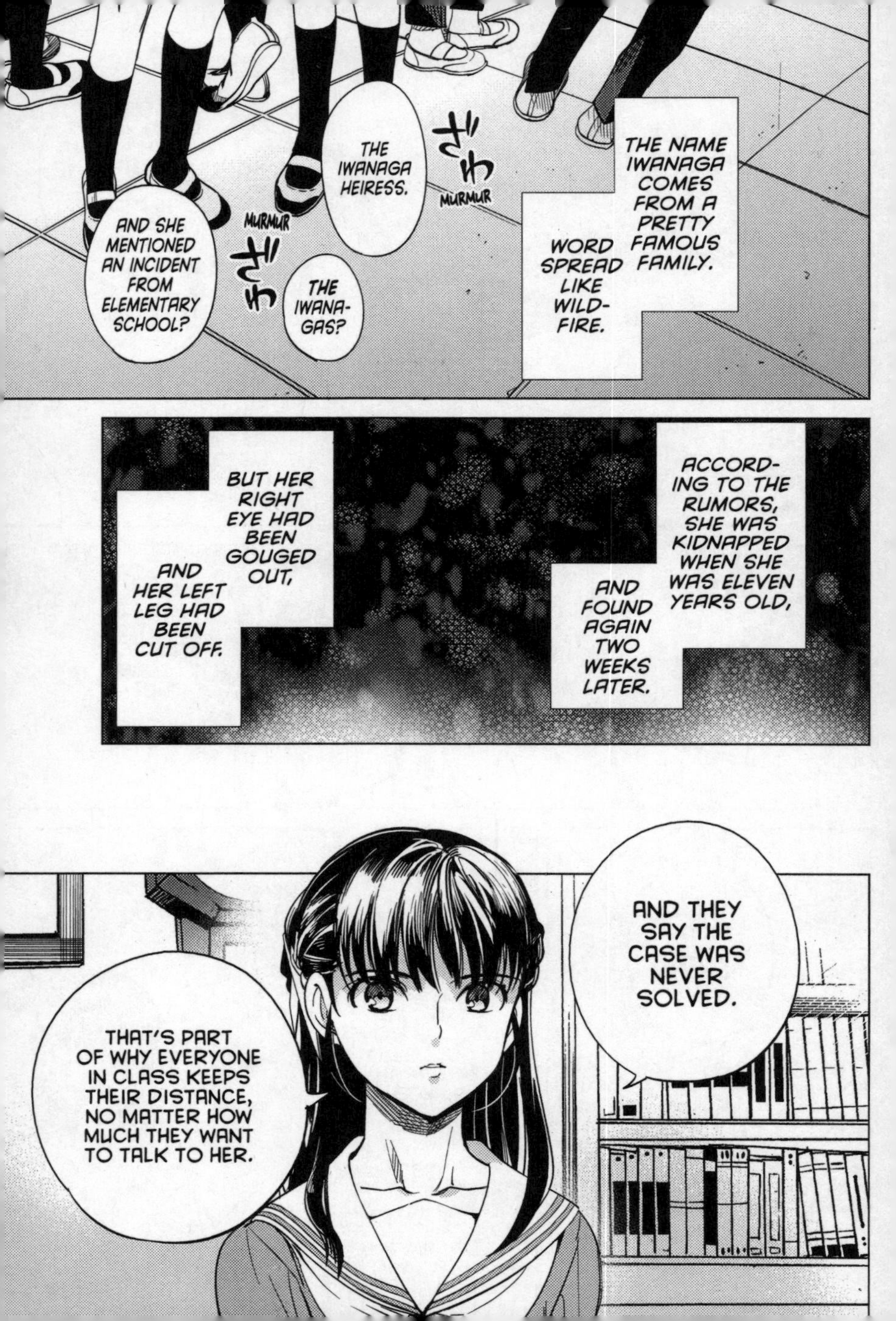
THE NAME IWANAGA COMES FROM A PRETTY FAMOUS FAMILY.
WORD SPREAD LIKE WILD-FIRE.
ざわ
MURMUR
THE IWANAGA HEIRESS.
ざわ
MURMUR
THE IWANA-GAS?
AND SHE MENTIONED AN INCIDENT FROM ELEMENTARY SCHOOL?
ACCORD-ING TO THE RUMORS, SHE WAS KIDNAPPED WHEN SHE WAS ELEVEN YEARS OLD,
AND FOUND AGAIN TWO WEEKS LATER.
BUT HER RIGHT EYE HAD BEEN GOUGED OUT,
AND HER LEFT LEG HAD BEEN CUT OFF.
AND THEY SAY THE CASE WAS NEVER SOLVED.
THAT'S PART OF WHY EVERYONE IN CLASS KEEPS THEIR DISTANCE, NO MATTER HOW MUCH THEY WANT TO TALK TO HER.

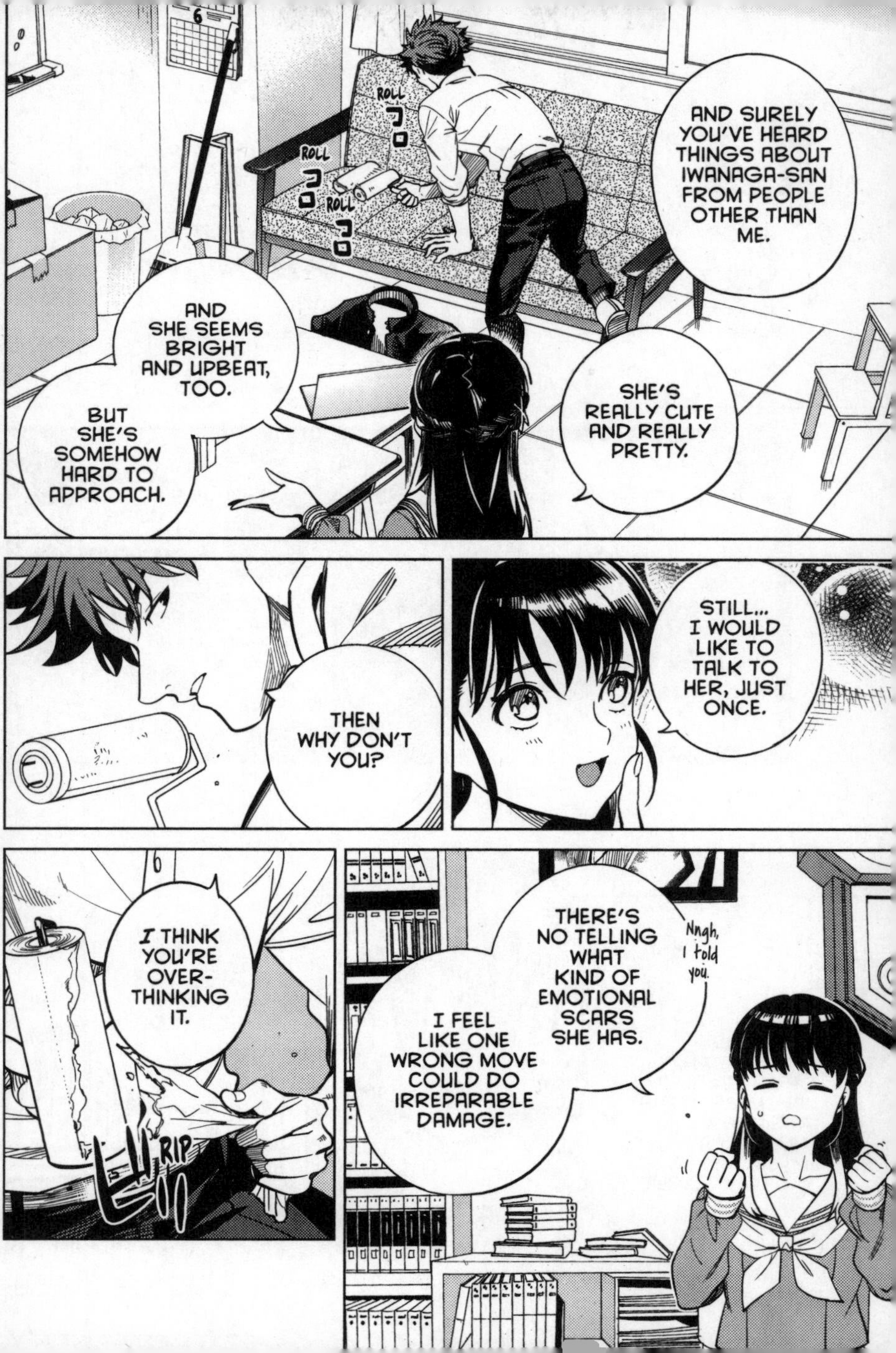
AND SURELY YOU'VE HEARD THINGS ABOUT IWANAGA-SAN FROM PEOPLE OTHER THAN ME.
ROLL
ROLL
ROLL
SHE'S REALLY CUTE AND REALLY PRETTY.
AND SHE SEEMS BRIGHT AND UPBEAT, TOO.
BUT SHE'S SOMEHOW HARD TO APPROACH.
STILL... I WOULD LIKE TO TALK TO HER, JUST ONCE.
THEN WHY DON'T YOU?
THERE'S NO TELLING WHAT KIND OF EMOTIONAL SCARS SHE HAS.
I FEEL LIKE ONE WRONG MOVE COULD DO IRREPARABLE DAMAGE.
Nngh, I told you.
I THINK YOU'RE OVER-THINKING IT.
RIP

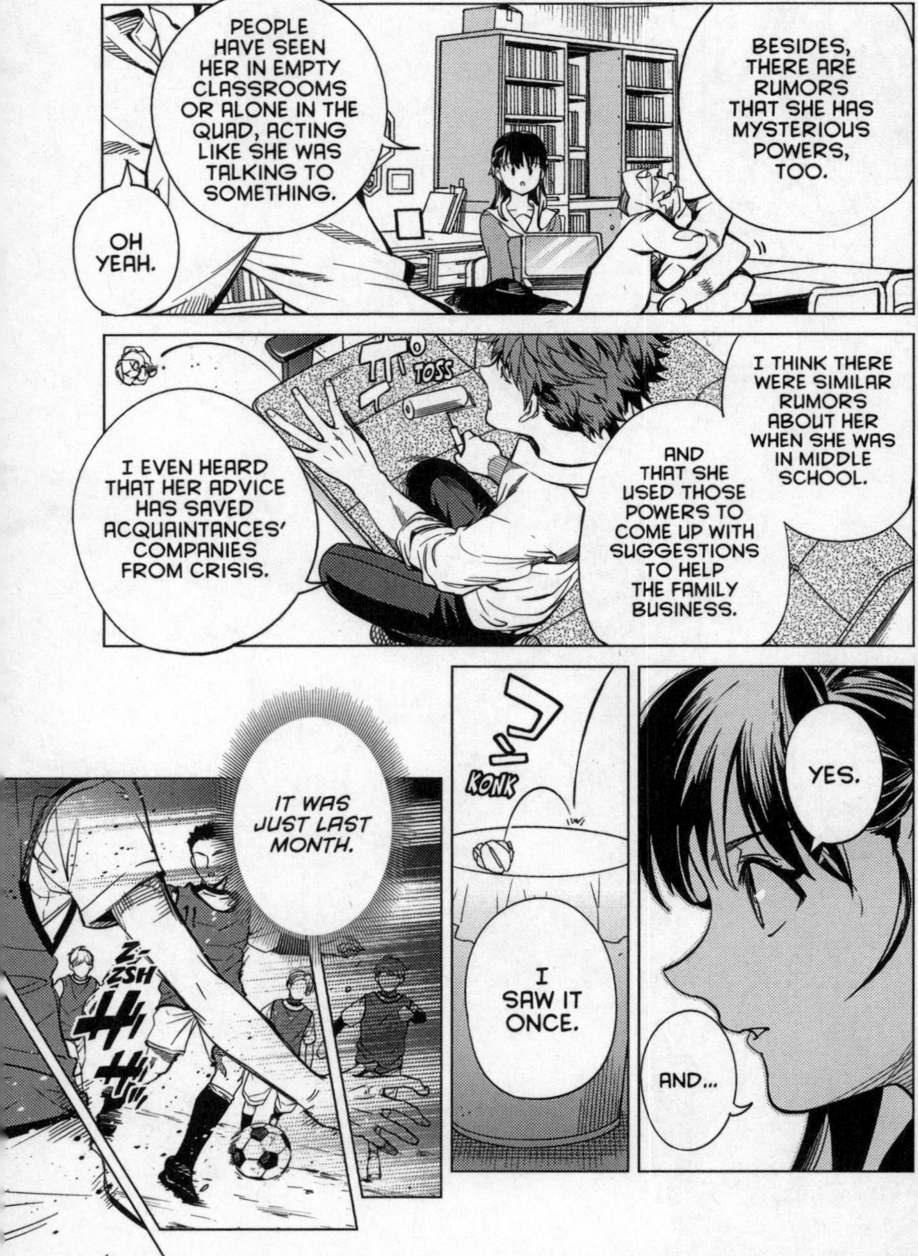
BESIDES, THERE ARE RUMORS THAT SHE HAS MYSTERIOUS POWERS, TOO.
PEOPLE HAVE SEEN HER IN EMPTY CLASSROOMS OR ALONE IN THE QUAD, ACTING LIKE SHE WAS TALKING TO SOMETHING.
OH YEAH.
I THINK THERE WERE SIMILAR RUMORS ABOUT HER WHEN SHE WAS IN MIDDLE SCHOOL.
AND THAT SHE USED THOSE POWERS TO COME UP WITH SUGGESTIONS TO HELP THE FAMILY BUSINESS.
TOSS
I EVEN HEARD THAT HER ADVICE HAS SAVED ACQUAINTANCES' COMPANIES FROM CRISIS.
YES.
AND...
KONK
I SAW IT ONCE.
IT WAS JUST LAST MONTH.
Z-ZSH

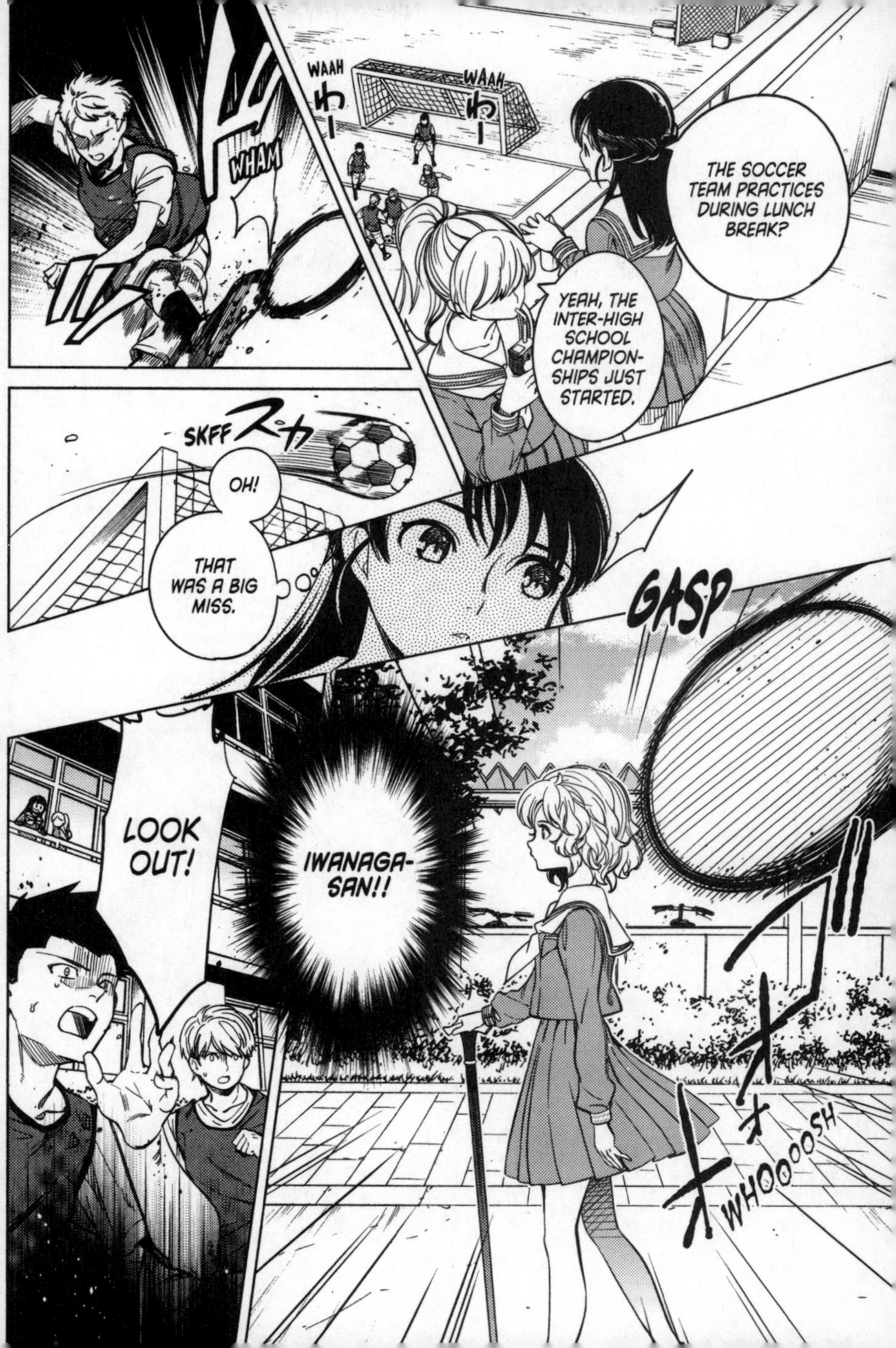
WAAH
わー
WAAH
わー
THE SOCCER TEAM PRACTICES DURING LUNCH BREAK?
YEAH, THE INTER-HIGH SCHOOL CHAMPION-SHIPS JUST STARTED.
WHAM
SKFF
スカ
OH!
THAT WAS A BIG MISS.
GASP
WHOOOOSH
IWANAGA-SAN!!
LOOK OUT!

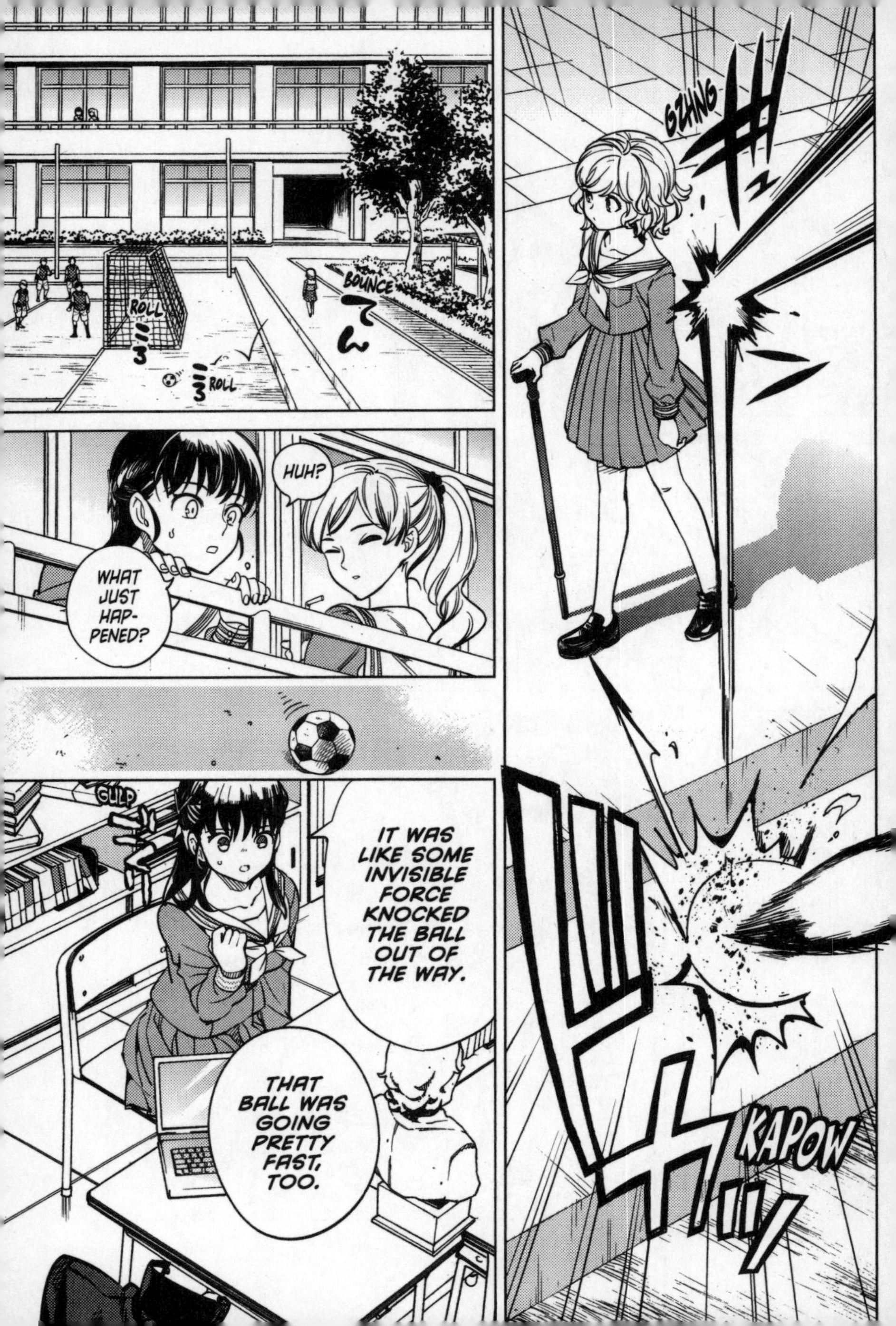
GZHNG
KAPOW
BOUNCE
てん
ROLL
ROLL
HUH?
WHAT JUST HAP-PENED?
GULP
IT WAS LIKE SOME INVISIBLE FORCE KNOCKED THE BALL OUT OF THE WAY.
THAT BALL WAS GOING PRETTY FAST, TOO.

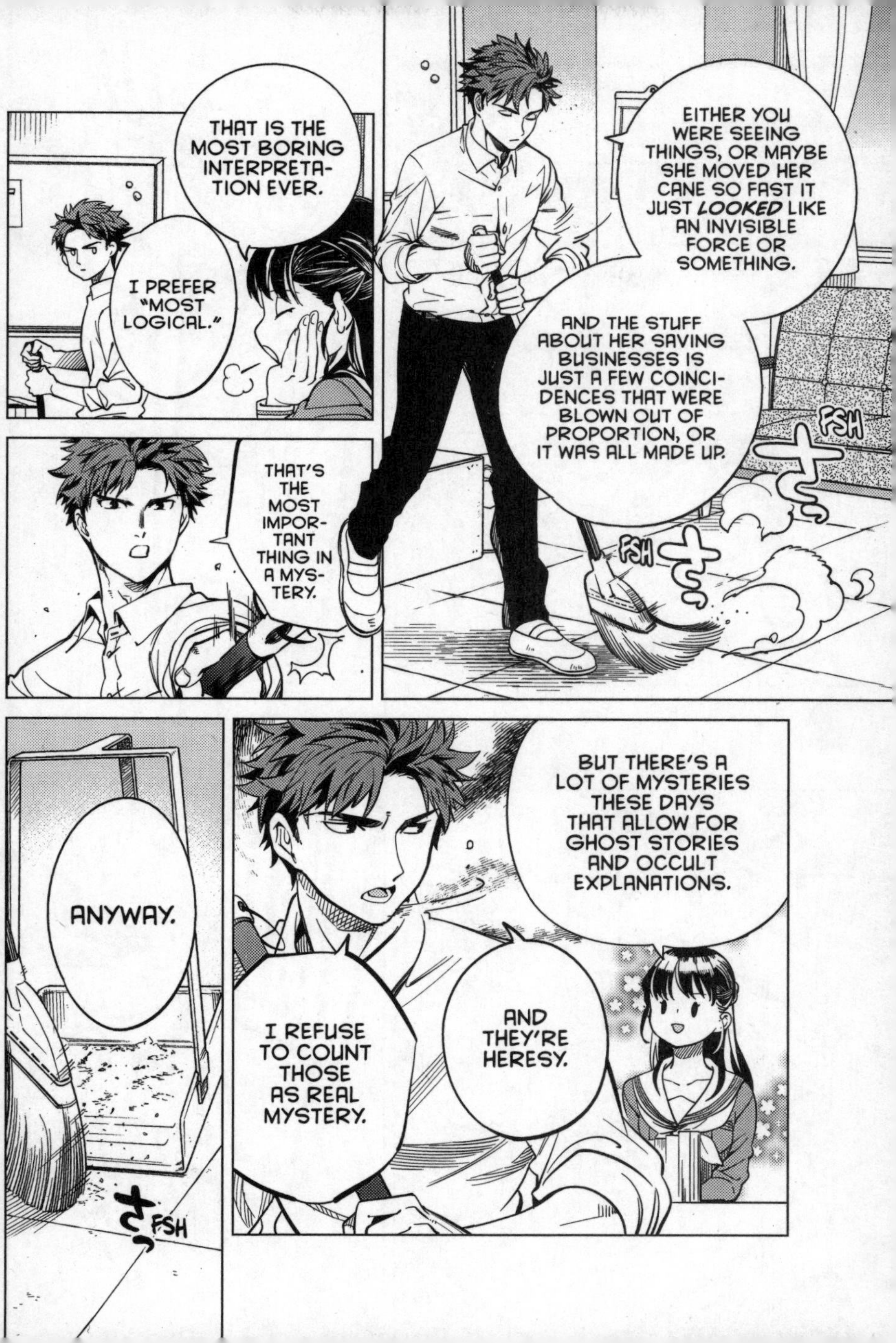
EITHER YOU WERE SEEING THINGS, OR MAYBE SHE MOVED HER CANE SO FAST IT JUST LOOKED LIKE AN INVISIBLE FORCE OR SOMETHING.
AND THE STUFF ABOUT HER SAVING BUSINESSES IS JUST A FEW COINCIDENCES THAT WERE BLOWN OUT OF PROPORTION, OR IT WAS ALL MADE UP.
FSH
FSH
THAT IS THE MOST BORING INTERPRETATION EVER.
I PREFER "MOST LOGICAL."
THAT'S THE MOST IMPORTANT THING IN A MYSTERY.
BUT THERE'S A LOT OF MYSTERIES THESE DAYS THAT ALLOW FOR GHOST STORIES AND OCCULT EXPLANATIONS.
AND THEY'RE HERESY.
I REFUSE TO COUNT THOSE AS REAL MYSTERY.
ANYWAY.
FSH

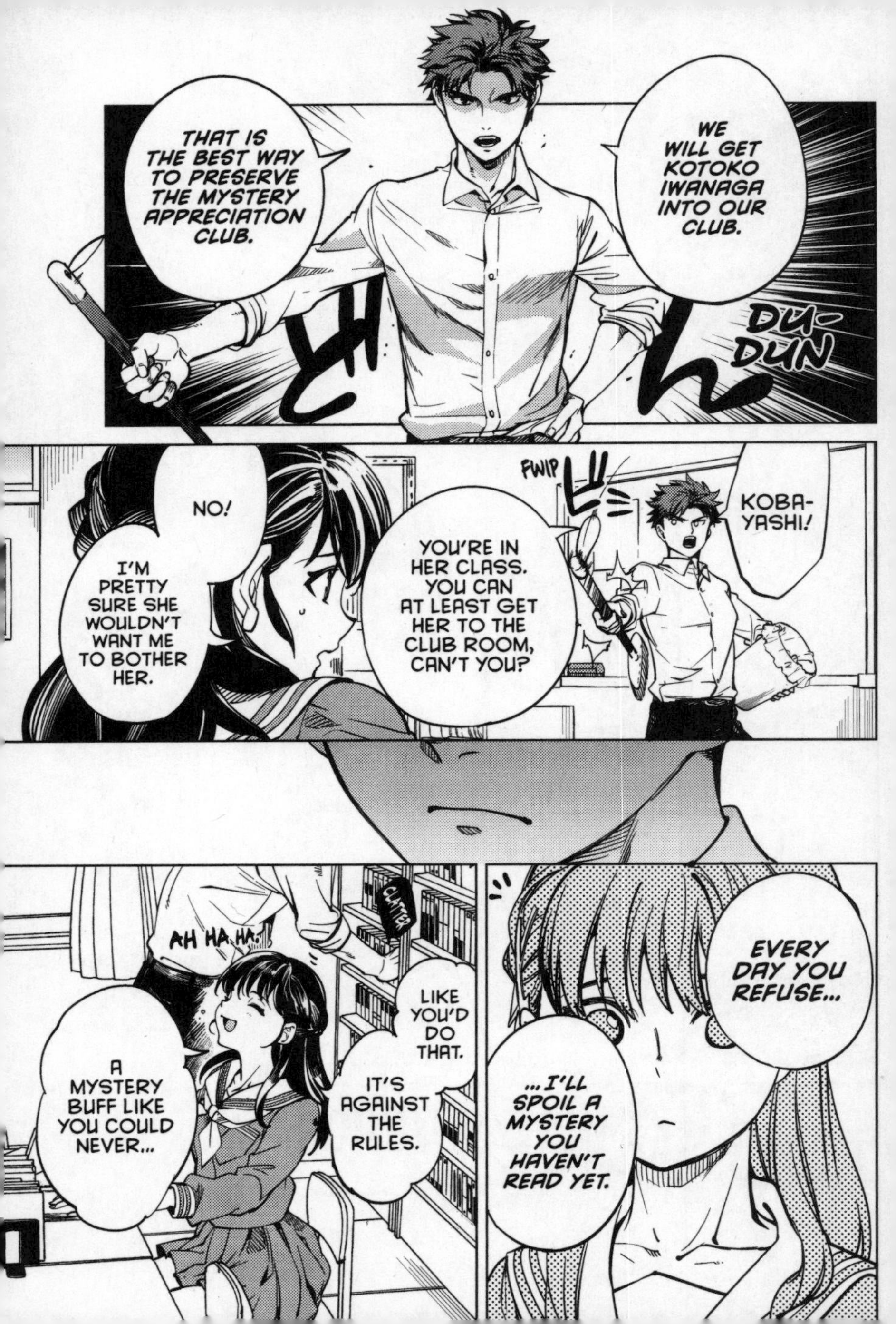
WE WILL GET KOTOKO IWANAGA INTO OUR CLUB.
DU-DUN
THAT IS THE BEST WAY TO PRESERVE THE MYSTERY APPRECIATION CLUB.
KOBA-YASHI!
FWIP
YOU'RE IN HER CLASS. YOU CAN AT LEAST GET HER TO THE CLUB ROOM, CAN'T YOU?
NO!
I'M PRETTY SURE SHE WOULDN'T WANT ME TO BOTHER HER.
EVERY DAY YOU REFUSE...
...I'LL SPOIL A MYSTERY YOU HAVEN'T READ YET.
LIKE YOU'D DO THAT.
IT'S AGAINST THE RULES.
CLATTER
AH HA HA.
A MYSTERY BUFF LIKE YOU COULD NEVER...

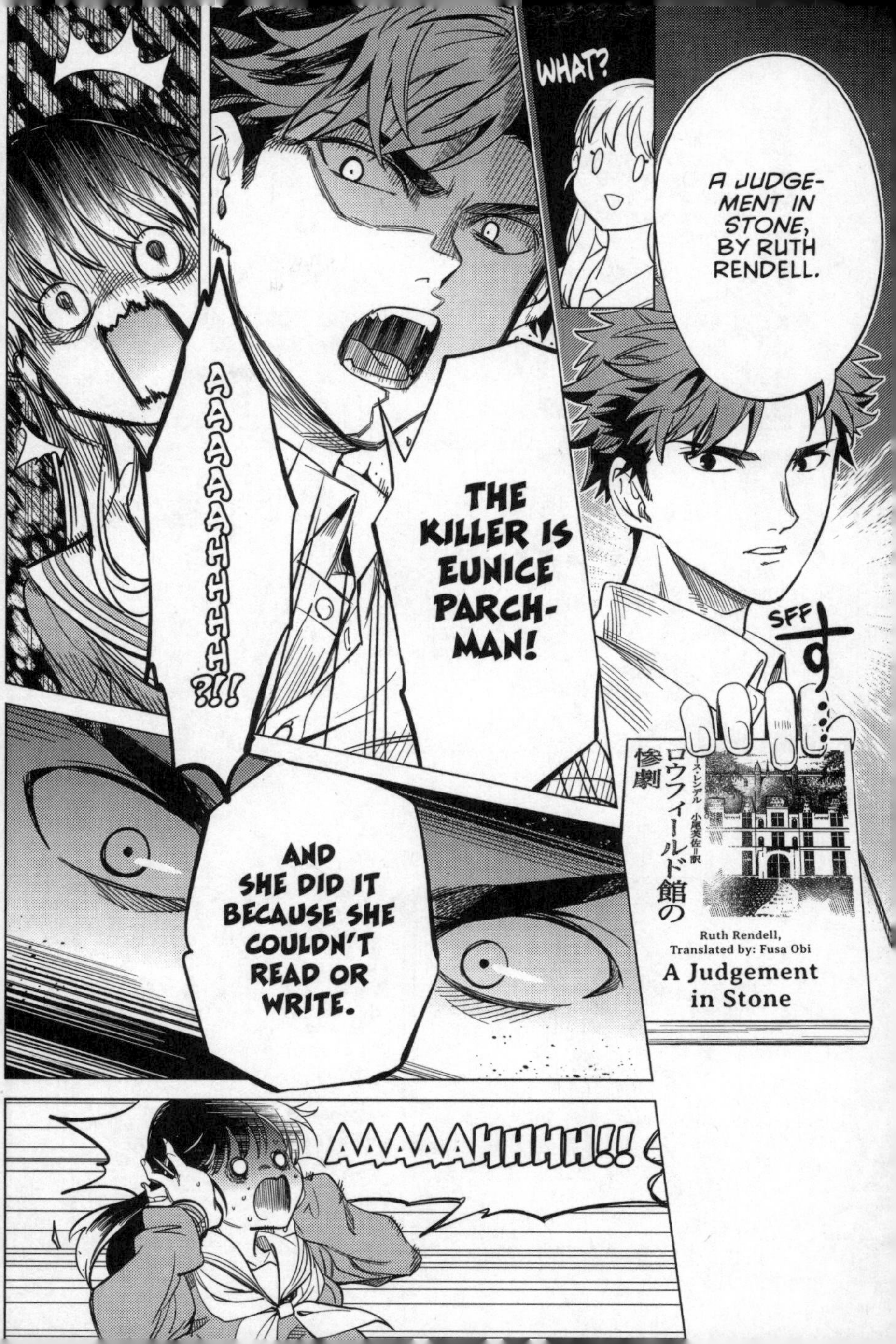
A JUDGEMENT IN STONE, BY RUTH RENDELL.
WHAT?
SFF
す
ース・レンデル 小尾芙佐＝訳
ロウフィールド館の惨劇
Ruth Rendell,
Translated by: Fusa Obi
A Judgement in Stone
THE KILLER IS EUNICE PARCH-MAN!
AAAAAAAHHHHH?!!
AND SHE DID IT BECAUSE SHE COULDN'T READ OR WRITE.
AAAAAHHHH!!

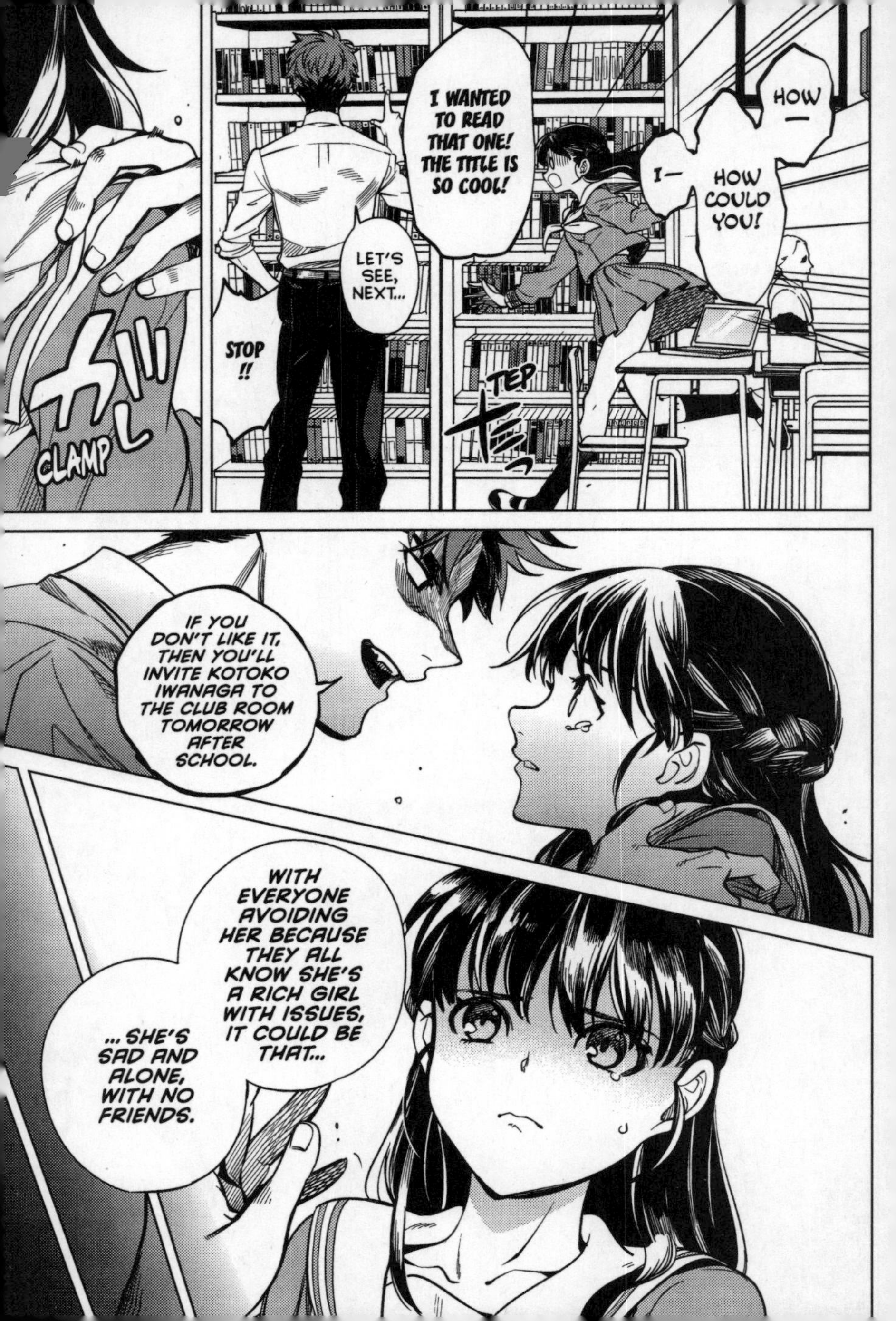
HOW—
HOW COULD YOU!
I—
TEP
I WANTED TO READ THAT ONE! THE TITLE IS SO COOL!
LET'S SEE, NEXT...
STOP!!
CLAMP
IF YOU DON'T LIKE IT, THEN YOU'LL INVITE KOTOKO IWANAGA TO THE CLUB ROOM TOMORROW AFTER SCHOOL.
WITH EVERYONE AVOIDING HER BECAUSE THEY ALL KNOW SHE'S A RICH GIRL WITH ISSUES, IT COULD BE THAT...
...SHE'S SAD AND ALONE, WITH NO FRIENDS.

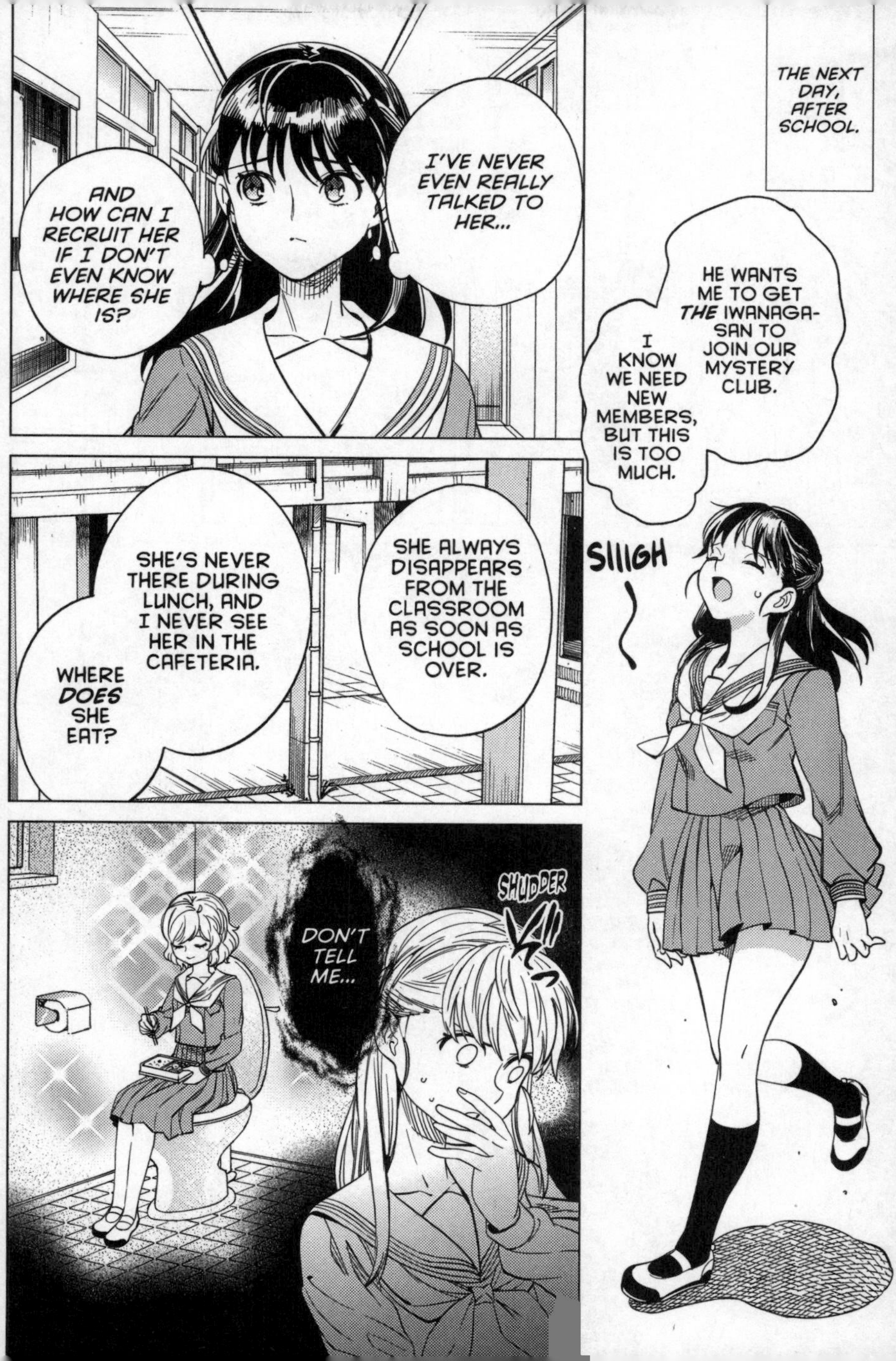
THE NEXT DAY, AFTER SCHOOL.
HE WANTS ME TO GET THE IWANAGA-SAN TO JOIN OUR MYSTERY CLUB.
I KNOW WE NEED NEW MEMBERS, BUT THIS IS TOO MUCH.
SIIIGH
I'VE NEVER EVEN REALLY TALKED TO HER...
AND HOW CAN I RECRUIT HER IF I DON'T EVEN KNOW WHERE SHE IS?
SHE ALWAYS DISAPPEARS FROM THE CLASSROOM AS SOON AS SCHOOL IS OVER.
SHE'S NEVER THERE DURING LUNCH, AND I NEVER SEE HER IN THE CAFETERIA.
WHERE DOES SHE EAT?
SHUDDER
DON'T TELL ME...

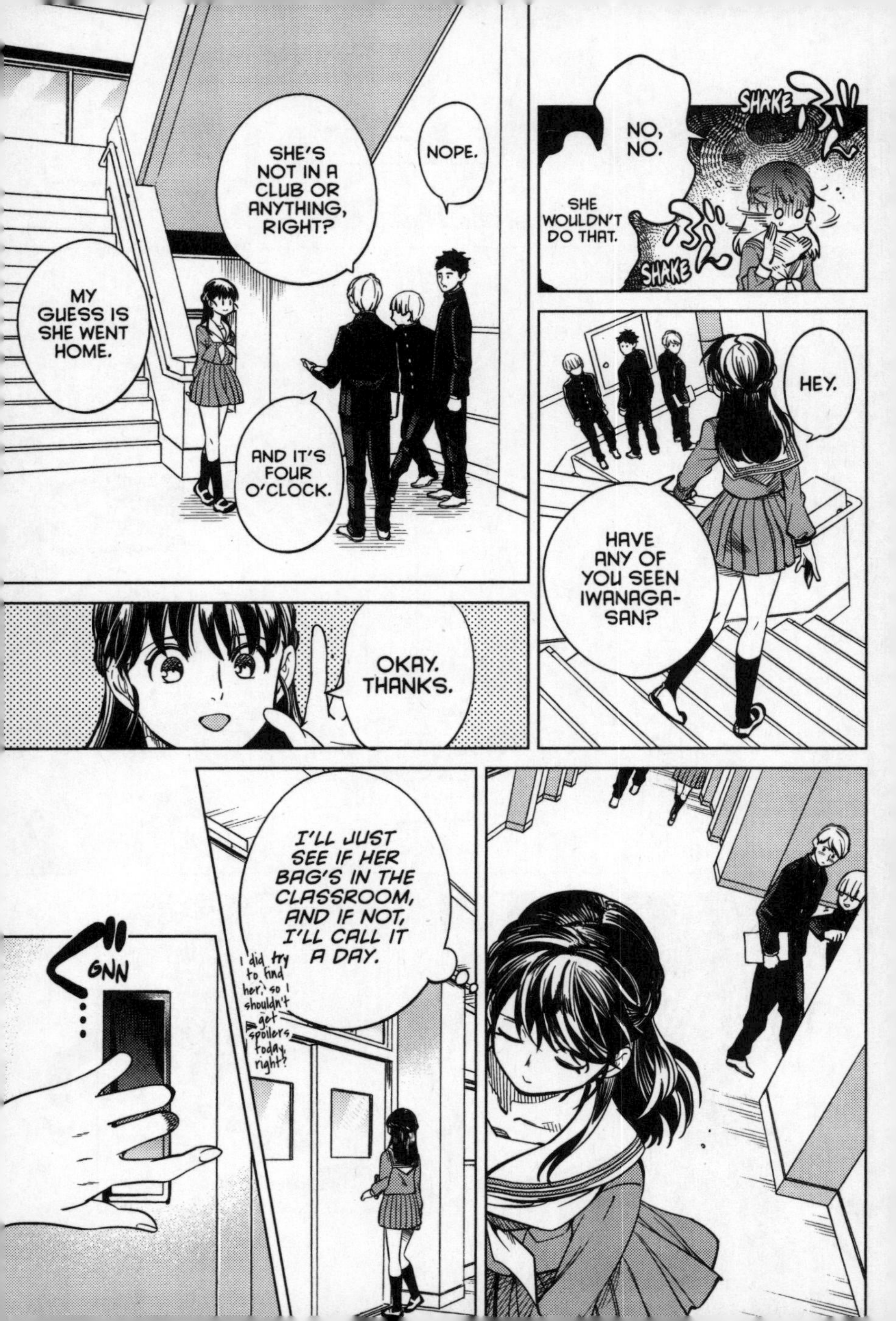
SHAKE
NO, NO.
SHE WOULDN'T DO THAT.
SHAKE
HEY.
HAVE ANY OF YOU SEEN IWANAGA-SAN?
NOPE.
SHE'S NOT IN A CLUB OR ANYTHING, RIGHT?
MY GUESS IS SHE WENT HOME.
AND IT'S FOUR O'CLOCK.
OKAY. THANKS.
I'LL JUST SEE IF HER BAG'S IN THE CLASSROOM, AND IF NOT, I'LL CALL IT A DAY.
I did try to find her, so I shouldn't get spoilers today, right?
GNN
...

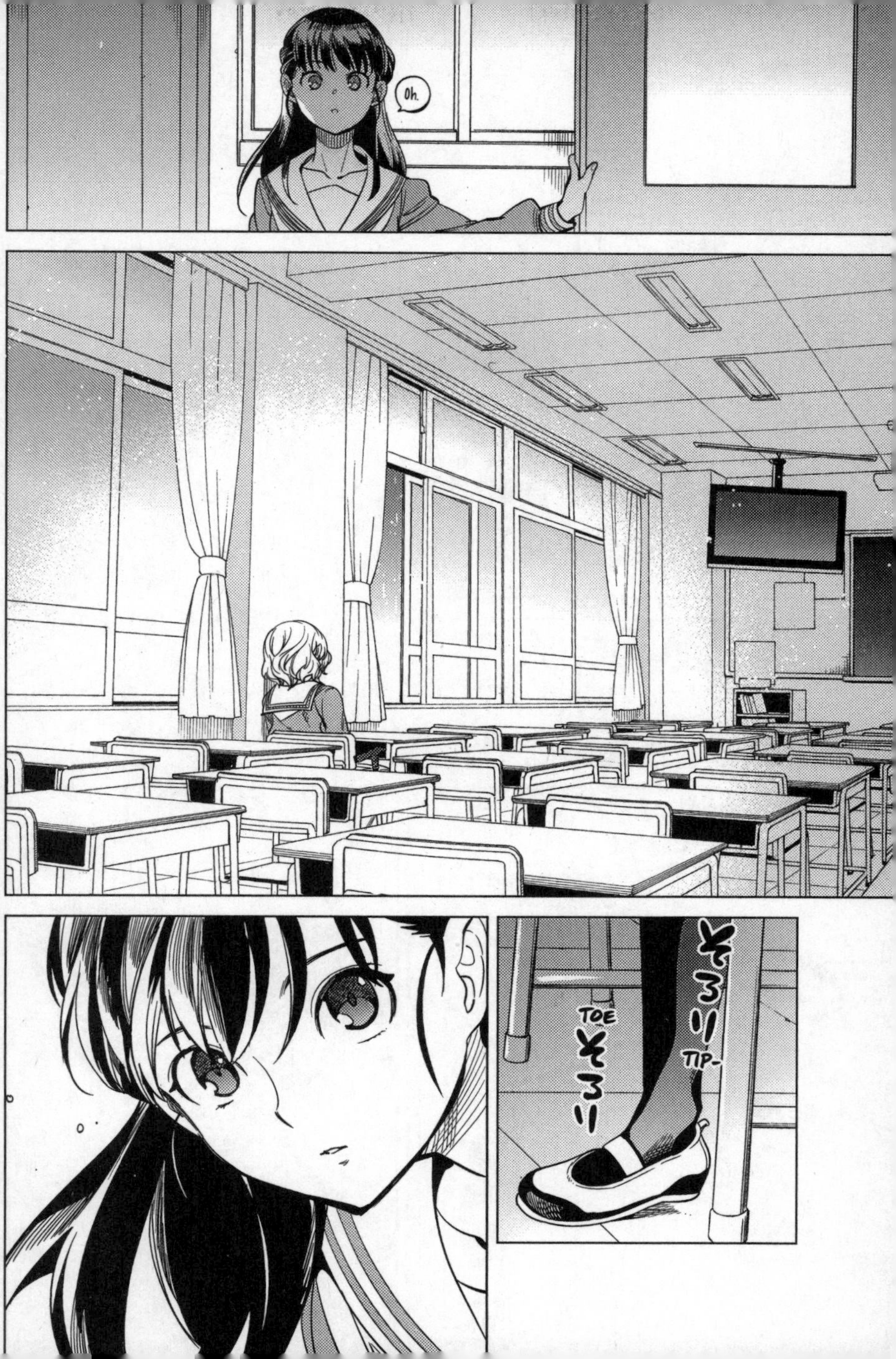
Oh.
そろり
TIP-
そろり
TOE

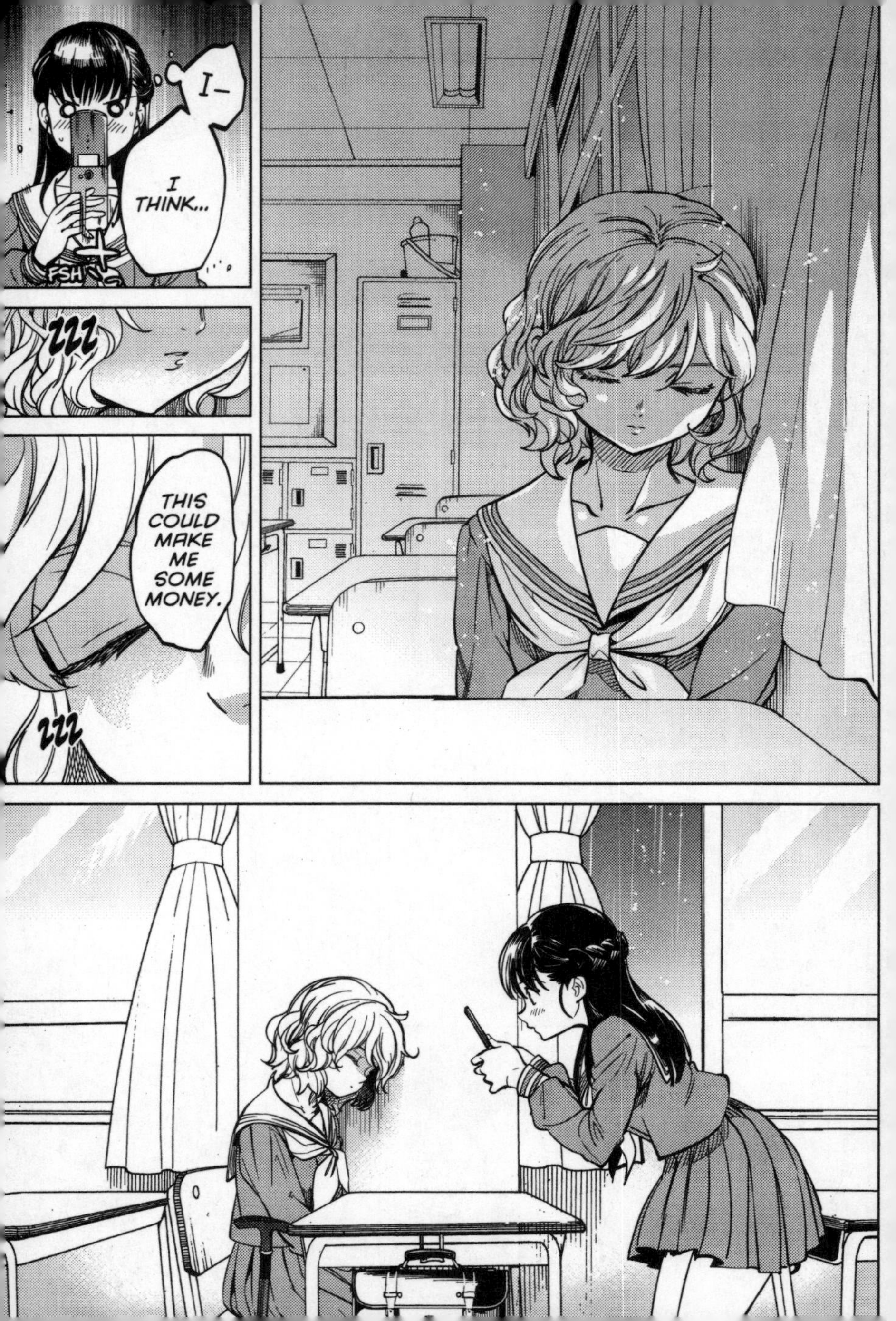
I—
I THINK...
FSH
ZZZ
THIS COULD MAKE ME SOME MONEY.
ZZZ

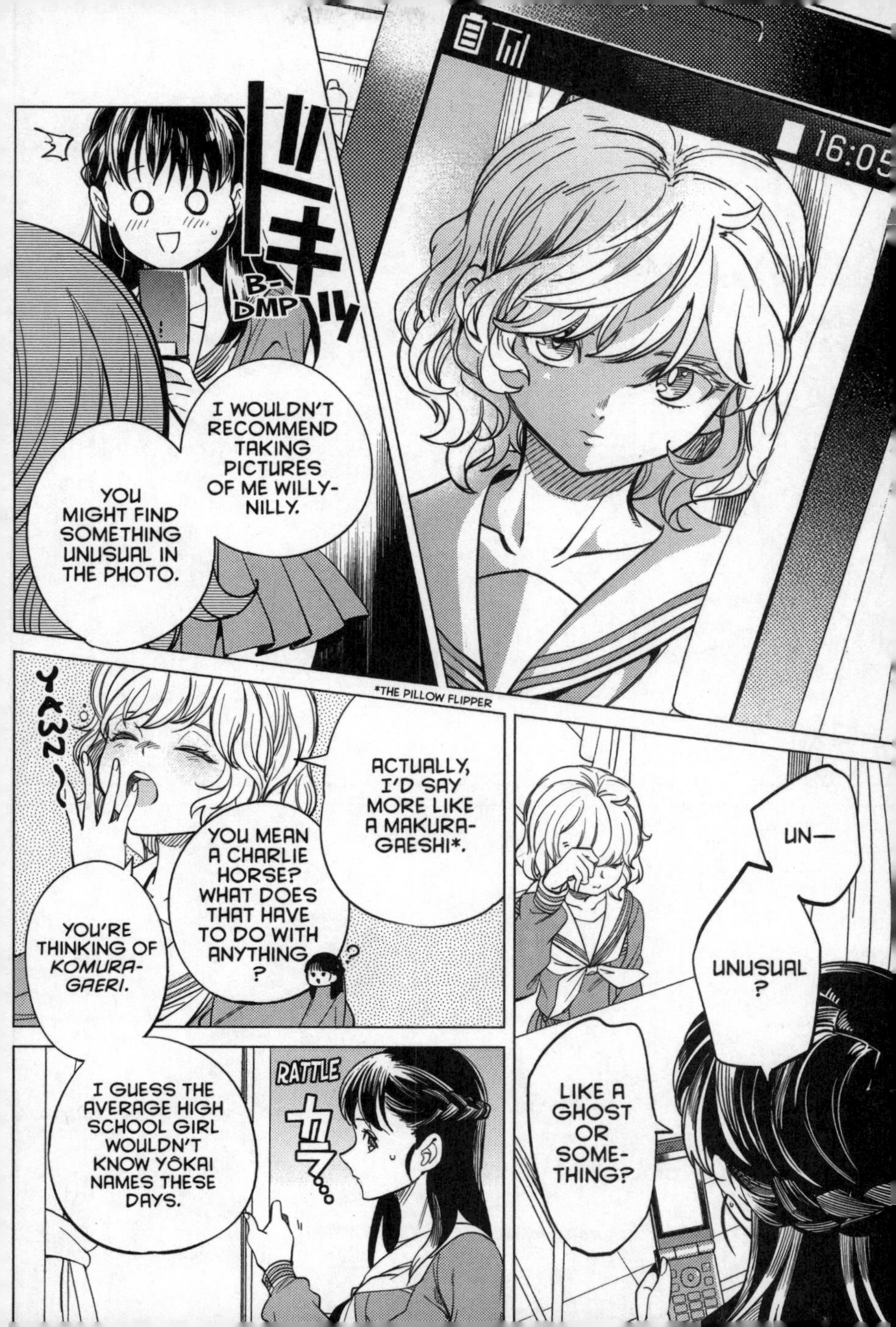
16:05
ドキッ
B-DMP
I WOULDN'T RECOMMEND TAKING PICTURES OF ME WILLY-NILLY.
YOU MIGHT FIND SOMETHING UNUSUAL IN THE PHOTO.
UN—
UNUSUAL?
LIKE A GHOST OR SOMETHING?
ACTUALLY, I'D SAY MORE LIKE A MAKURA-GAESHI*.
YOU MEAN A CHARLIE HORSE? WHAT DOES THAT HAVE TO DO WITH ANYTHING?
YOU'RE THINKING OF *KOMURA-GAERI*.
*THE PILLOW FLIPPER
RATTLE
I GUESS THE AVERAGE HIGH SCHOOL GIRL WOULDN'T KNOW YÔKAI NAMES THESE DAYS.

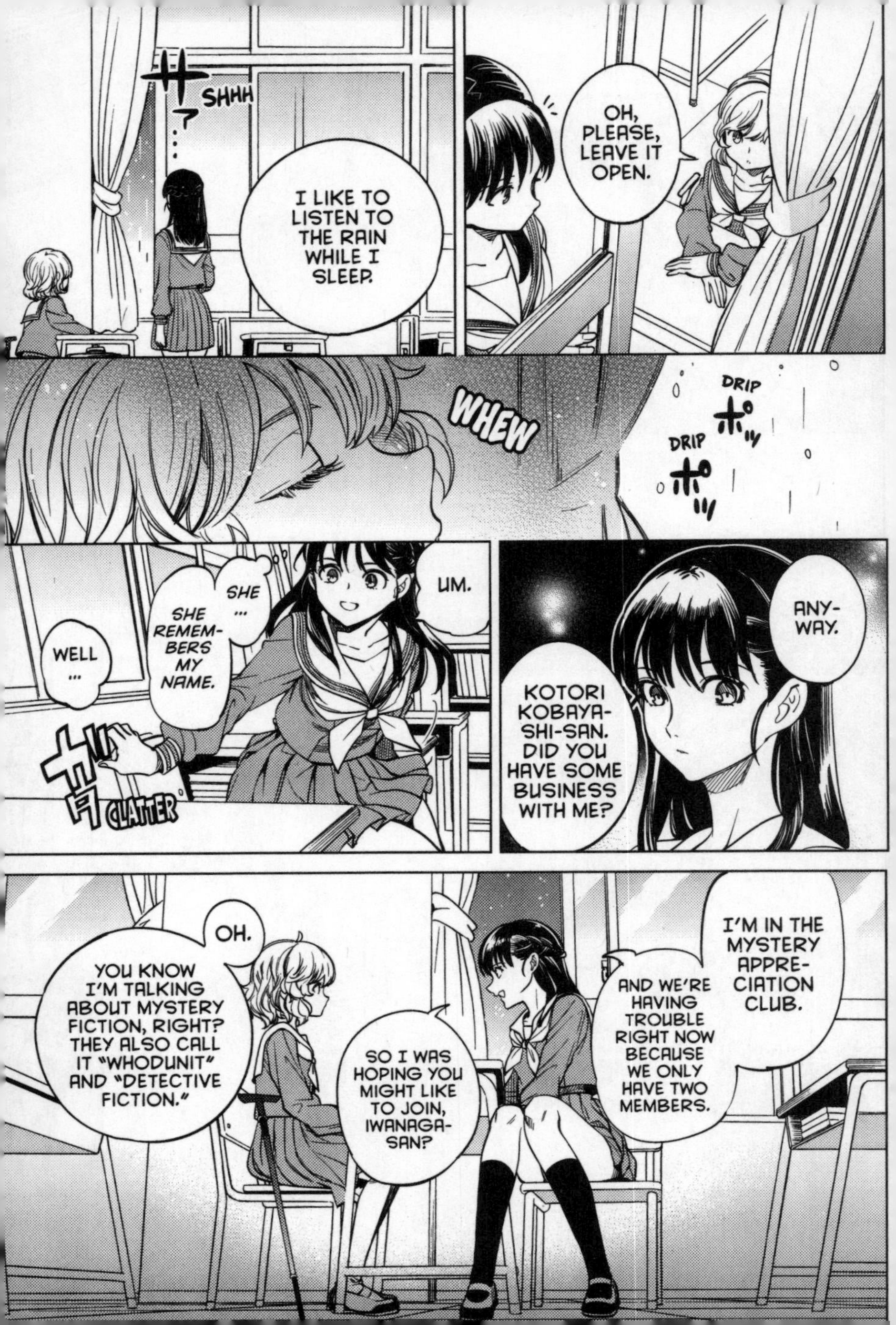
OH, PLEASE, LEAVE IT OPEN.
SHHH
...
I LIKE TO LISTEN TO THE RAIN WHILE I SLEEP.
DRIP
DRIP
WHEW
ANY-WAY.
KOTORI KOBAYA-SHI-SAN. DID YOU HAVE SOME BUSINESS WITH ME?
UM.
SHE ...
SHE REMEM-BERS MY NAME.
WELL ...
CLATTER
I'M IN THE MYSTERY APPRE-CIATION CLUB.
AND WE'RE HAVING TROUBLE RIGHT NOW BECAUSE WE ONLY HAVE TWO MEMBERS.
SO I WAS HOPING YOU MIGHT LIKE TO JOIN, IWANAGA-SAN?
OH.
YOU KNOW I'M TALKING ABOUT MYSTERY FICTION, RIGHT? THEY ALSO CALL IT "WHODUNIT" AND "DETECTIVE FICTION."

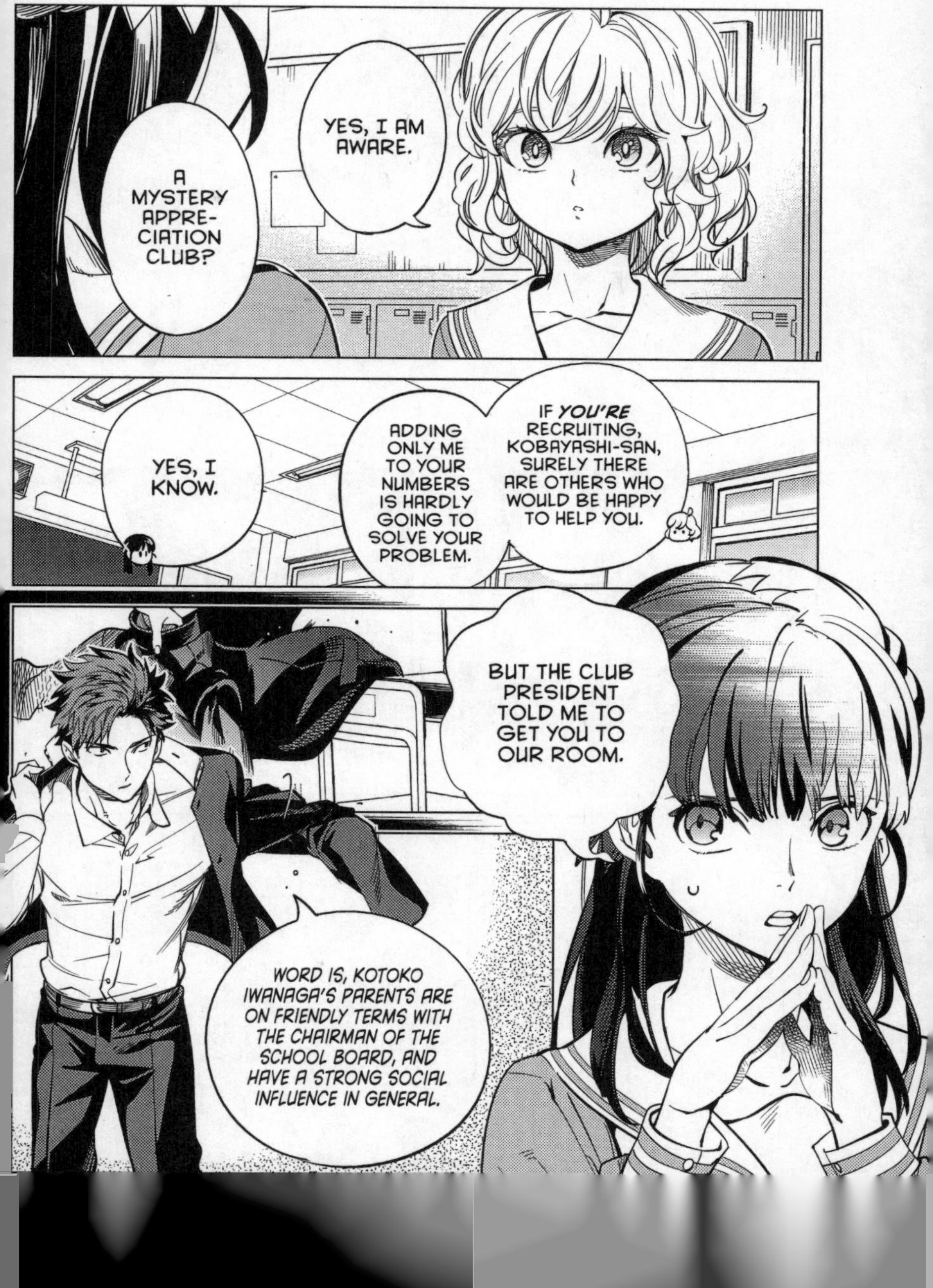
YES, I AM AWARE.
A MYSTERY APPRECIATION CLUB?
IF *YOU'RE* RECRUITING, KOBAYASHI-SAN, SURELY THERE ARE OTHERS WHO WOULD BE HAPPY TO HELP YOU.
ADDING ONLY ME TO YOUR NUMBERS IS HARDLY GOING TO SOLVE YOUR PROBLEM.
YES, I KNOW.
BUT THE CLUB PRESIDENT TOLD ME TO GET YOU TO OUR ROOM.
WORD IS, KOTOKO IWANAGA'S PARENTS ARE ON FRIENDLY TERMS WITH THE CHAIRMAN OF THE SCHOOL BOARD, AND HAVE A STRONG SOCIAL INFLUENCE IN GENERAL.

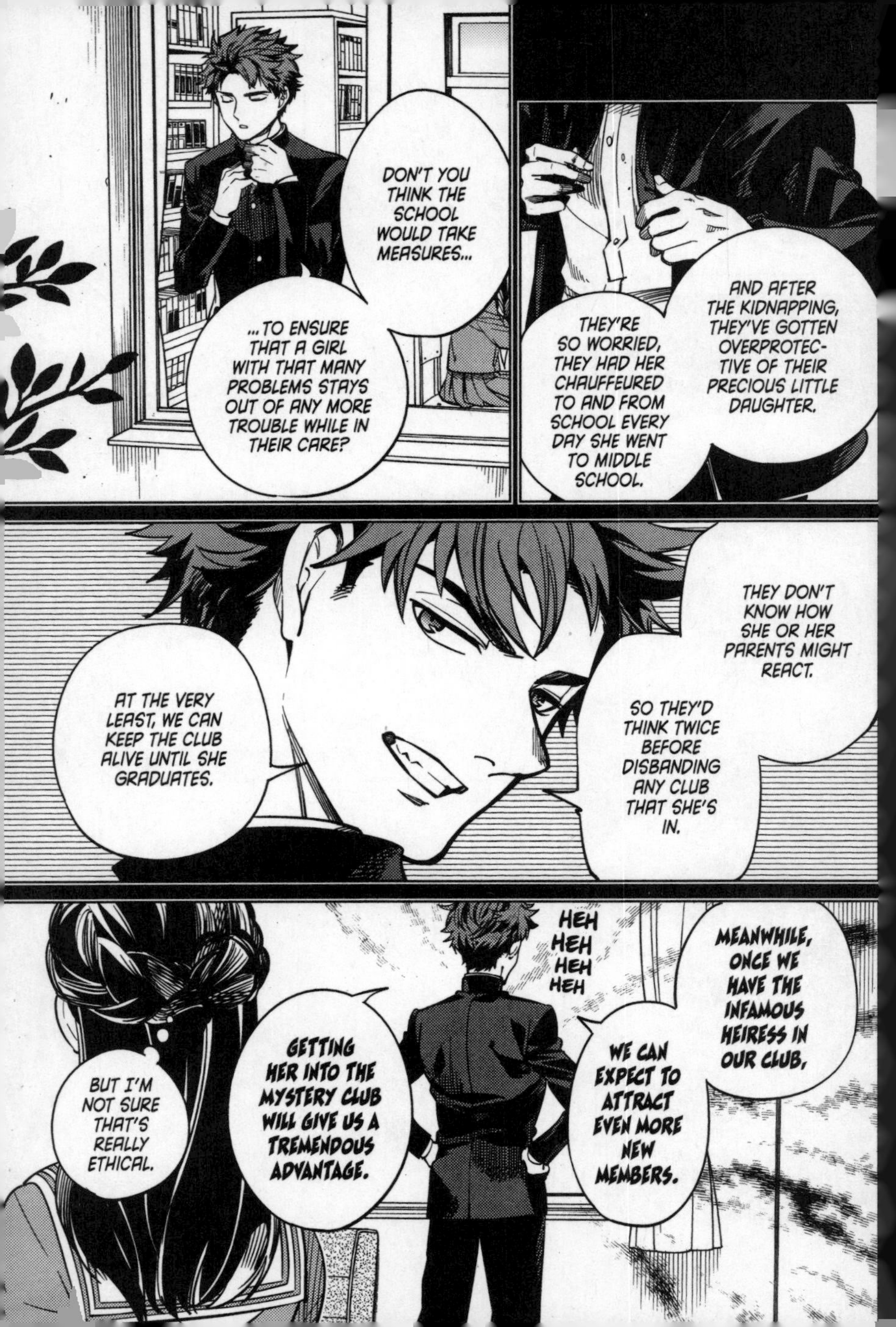
AND AFTER THE KIDNAPPING, THEY'VE GOTTEN OVERPROTECTIVE OF THEIR PRECIOUS LITTLE DAUGHTER.
THEY'RE SO WORRIED, THEY HAD HER CHAUFFEURED TO AND FROM SCHOOL EVERY DAY SHE WENT TO MIDDLE SCHOOL.
DON'T YOU THINK THE SCHOOL WOULD TAKE MEASURES...
...TO ENSURE THAT A GIRL WITH THAT MANY PROBLEMS STAYS OUT OF ANY MORE TROUBLE WHILE IN THEIR CARE?
THEY DON'T KNOW HOW SHE OR HER PARENTS MIGHT REACT.
SO THEY'D THINK TWICE BEFORE DISBANDING ANY CLUB THAT SHE'S IN.
AT THE VERY LEAST, WE CAN KEEP THE CLUB ALIVE UNTIL SHE GRADUATES.
MEANWHILE, ONCE WE HAVE THE INFAMOUS HEIRESS IN OUR CLUB,
HEH HEH HEH HEH
WE CAN EXPECT TO ATTRACT EVEN MORE NEW MEMBERS.
GETTING HER INTO THE MYSTERY CLUB WILL GIVE US A TREMENDOUS ADVANTAGE.
BUT I'M NOT SURE THAT'S REALLY ETHICAL.

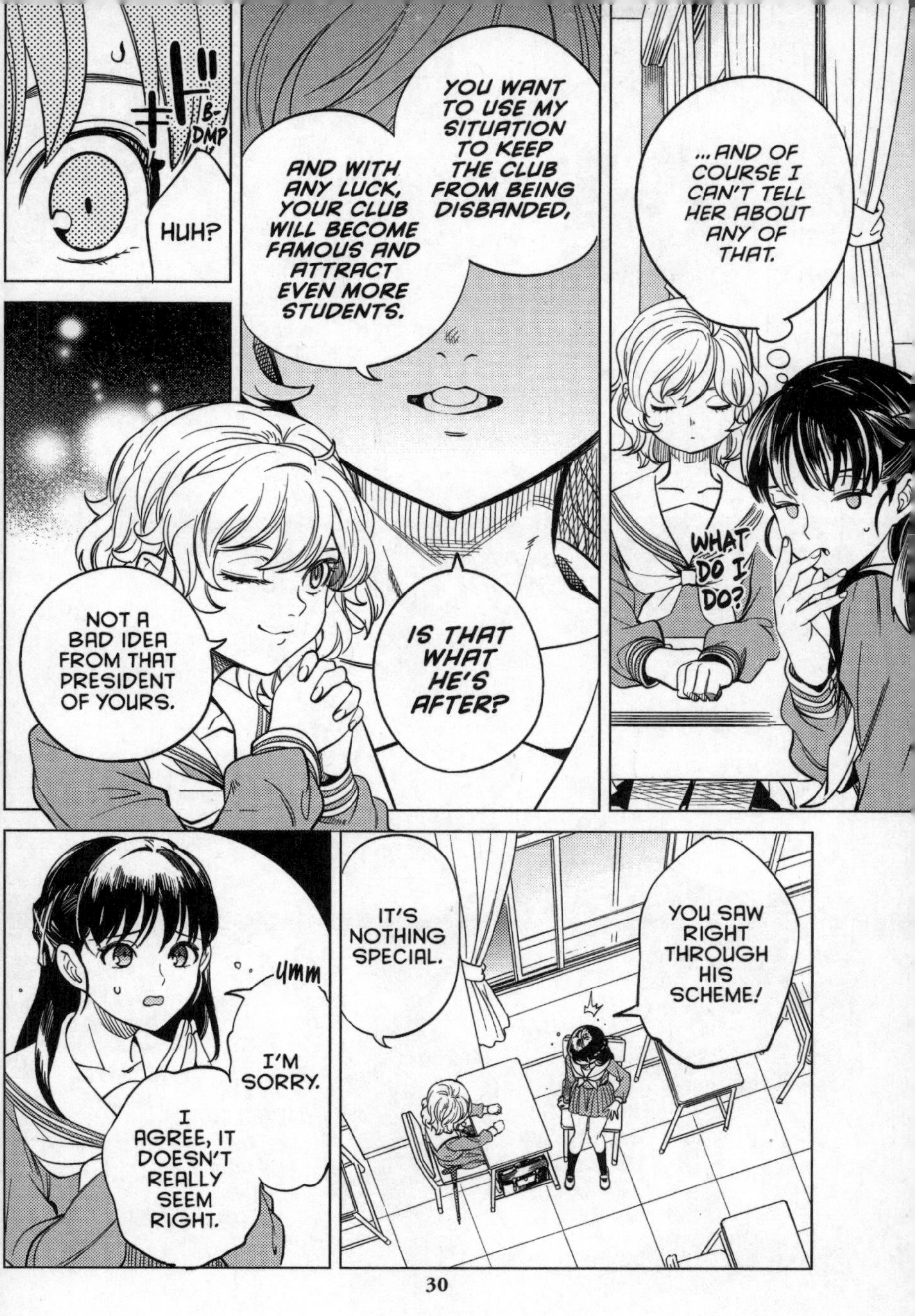
...AND OF COURSE I CAN'T TELL HER ABOUT ANY OF THAT.
WHAT DO I DO?
YOU WANT TO USE MY SITUATION TO KEEP THE CLUB FROM BEING DISBANDED,
AND WITH ANY LUCK, YOUR CLUB WILL BECOME FAMOUS AND ATTRACT EVEN MORE STUDENTS.
B-DMP
HUH?
IS THAT WHAT HE'S AFTER?
NOT A BAD IDEA FROM THAT PRESIDENT OF YOURS.
YOU SAW RIGHT THROUGH HIS SCHEME!
IT'S NOTHING SPECIAL.
UMM
I'M SORRY.
I AGREE, IT DOESN'T REALLY SEEM RIGHT.

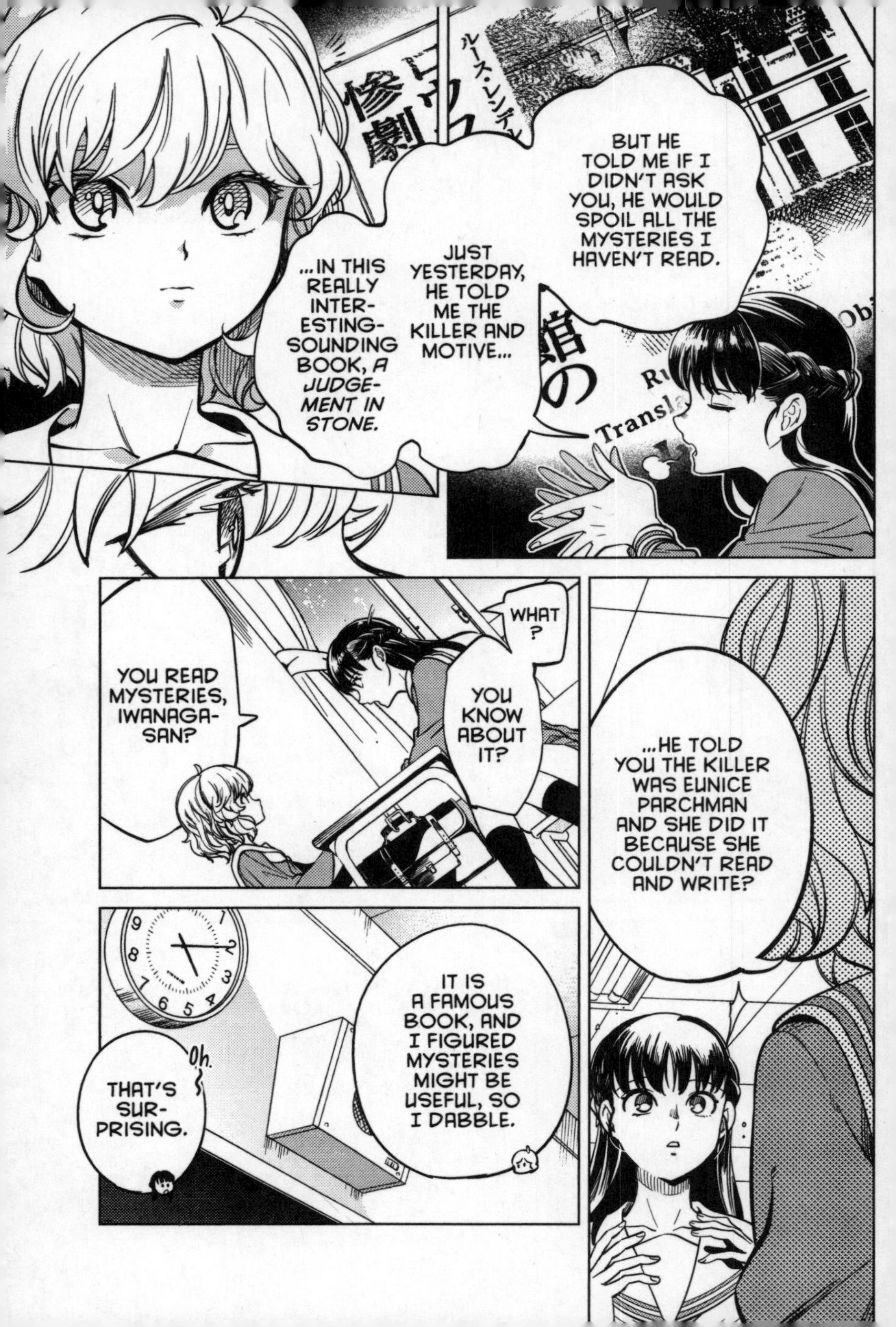
BUT HE TOLD ME IF I DIDN'T ASK YOU, HE WOULD SPOIL ALL THE MYSTERIES I HAVEN'T READ.
JUST YESTERDAY, HE TOLD ME THE KILLER AND MOTIVE...
...IN THIS REALLY INTERESTING-SOUNDING BOOK, *A JUDGEMENT IN STONE*.
...HE TOLD YOU THE KILLER WAS EUNICE PARCHMAN AND SHE DID IT BECAUSE SHE COULDN'T READ AND WRITE?
WHAT?
YOU KNOW ABOUT IT?
YOU READ MYSTERIES, IWANAGA-SAN?
IT IS A FAMOUS BOOK, AND I FIGURED MYSTERIES MIGHT BE USEFUL, SO I DABBLE.
Oh.
THAT'S SURPRISING.

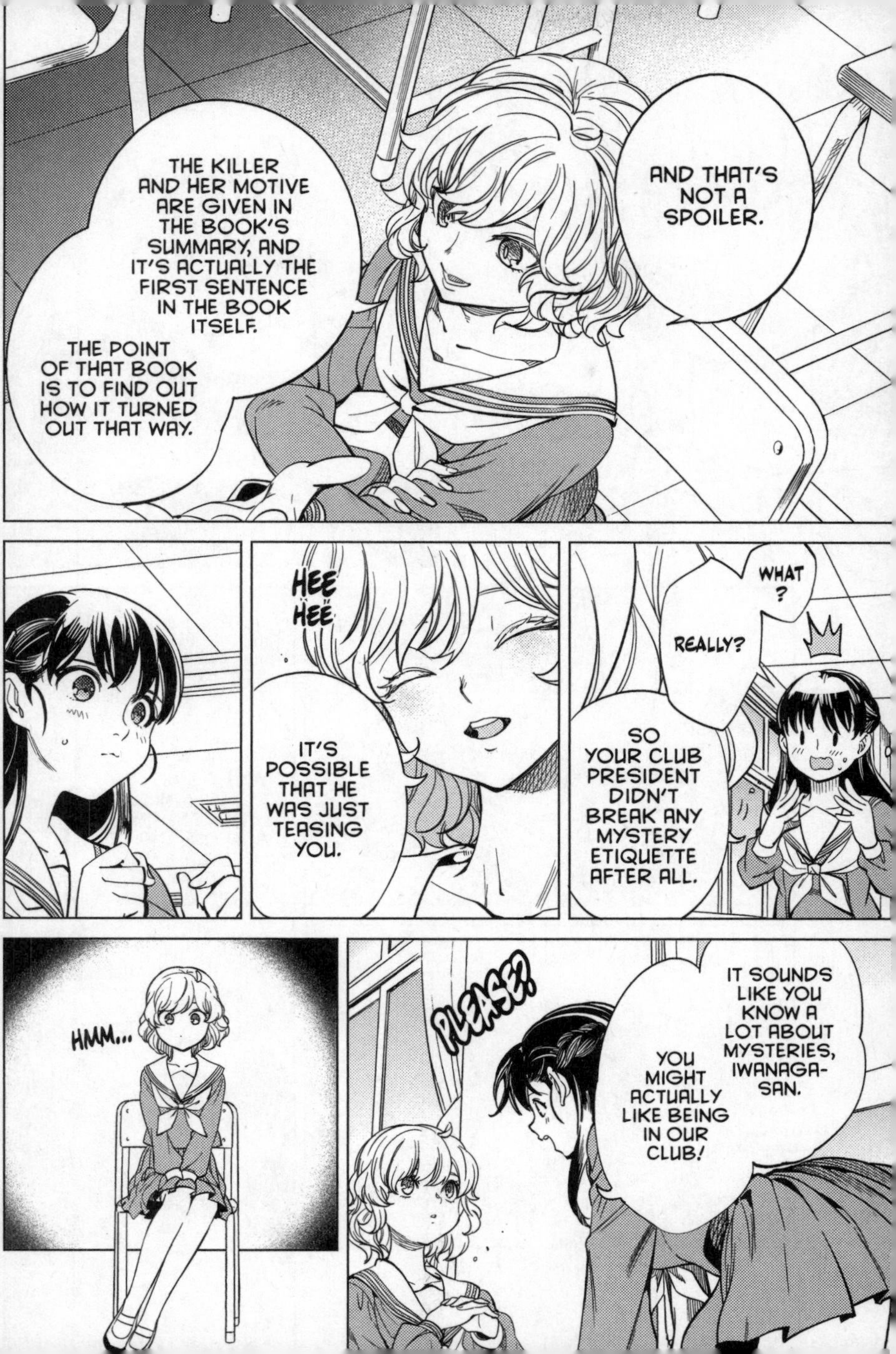
AND THAT'S NOT A SPOILER.
THE KILLER AND HER MOTIVE ARE GIVEN IN THE BOOK'S SUMMARY, AND IT'S ACTUALLY THE FIRST SENTENCE IN THE BOOK ITSELF.
THE POINT OF THAT BOOK IS TO FIND OUT HOW IT TURNED OUT THAT WAY.
WHAT?
REALLY?
SO YOUR CLUB PRESIDENT DIDN'T BREAK ANY MYSTERY ETIQUETTE AFTER ALL.
HEE HEE
IT'S POSSIBLE THAT HE WAS JUST TEASING YOU.
IT SOUNDS LIKE YOU KNOW A LOT ABOUT MYSTERIES, IWANAGA-SAN.
PLEASE?
YOU MIGHT ACTUALLY LIKE BEING IN OUR CLUB!
HMM...

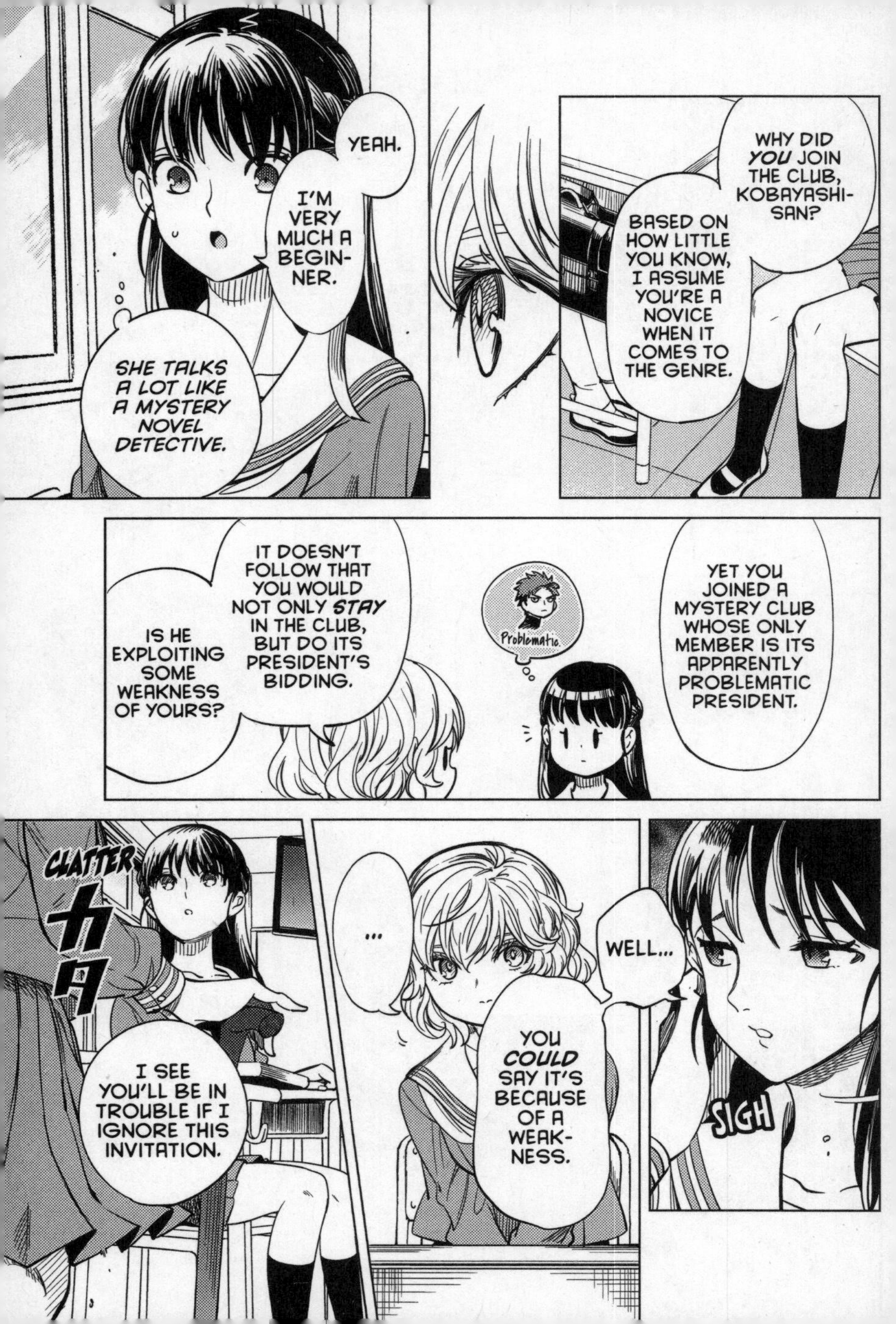
WHY DID *YOU* JOIN THE CLUB, KOBAYASHI-SAN?
BASED ON HOW LITTLE YOU KNOW, I ASSUME YOU'RE A NOVICE WHEN IT COMES TO THE GENRE.
YEAH.
I'M VERY MUCH A BEGIN-NER.
SHE TALKS A LOT LIKE A MYSTERY NOVEL DETECTIVE.
YET YOU JOINED A MYSTERY CLUB WHOSE ONLY MEMBER IS ITS APPARENTLY PROBLEMATIC PRESIDENT.
Problematic.
IT DOESN'T FOLLOW THAT YOU WOULD NOT ONLY *STAY* IN THE CLUB, BUT DO ITS PRESIDENT'S BIDDING.
IS HE EXPLOITING SOME WEAKNESS OF YOURS?
WELL...
SIGH
...
YOU *COULD* SAY IT'S BECAUSE OF A WEAK-NESS.
CLATTER
カタ
I SEE YOU'LL BE IN TROUBLE IF I IGNORE THIS INVITATION.

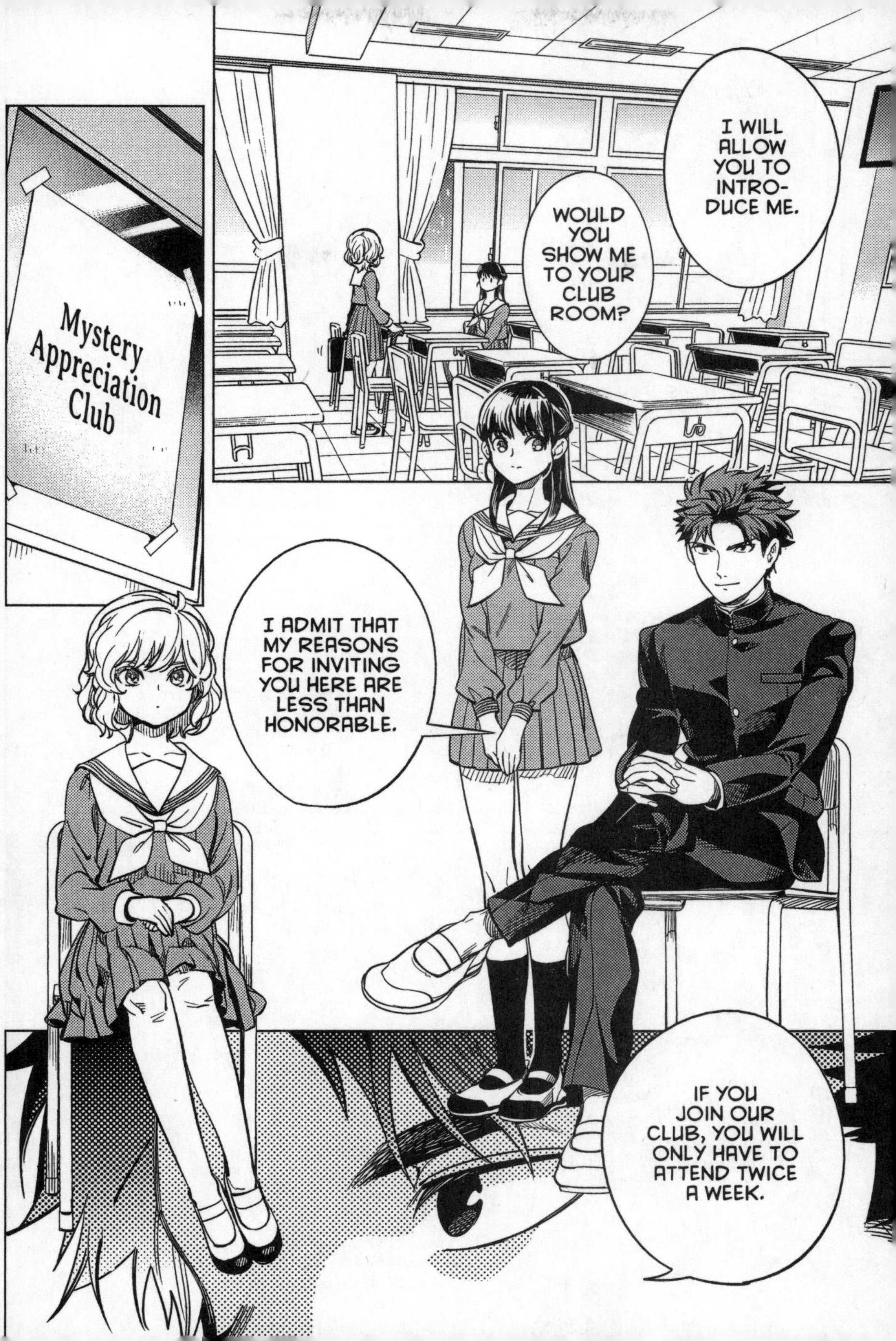
I WILL ALLOW YOU TO INTRO-DUCE ME.
WOULD YOU SHOW ME TO YOUR CLUB ROOM?
Mystery Appreciation Club
I ADMIT THAT MY REASONS FOR INVITING YOU HERE ARE LESS THAN HONORABLE.
IF YOU JOIN OUR CLUB, YOU WILL ONLY HAVE TO ATTEND TWICE A WEEK.

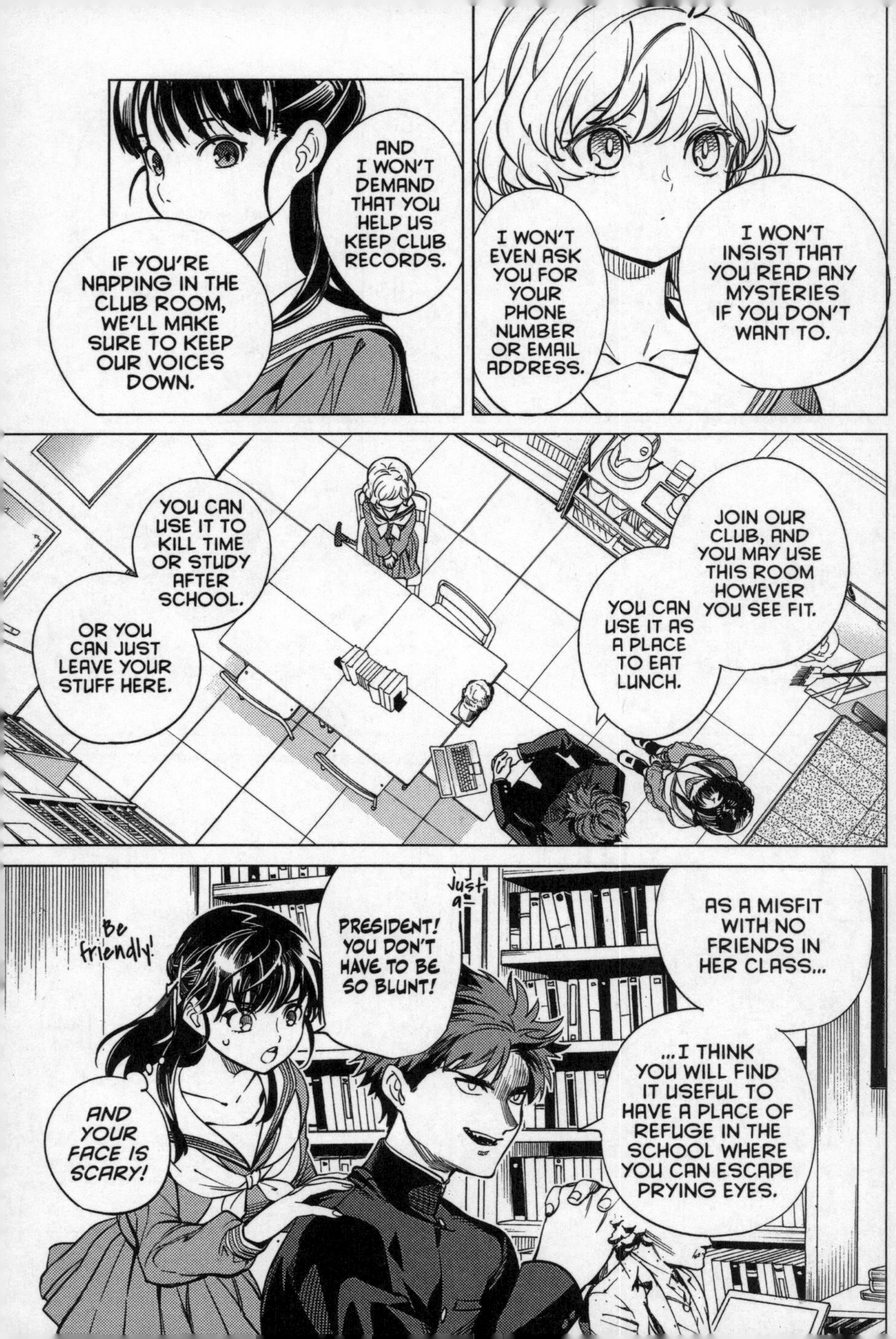
I WON'T INSIST THAT YOU READ ANY MYSTERIES IF YOU DON'T WANT TO.
I WON'T EVEN ASK YOU FOR YOUR PHONE NUMBER OR EMAIL ADDRESS.
AND I WON'T DEMAND THAT YOU HELP US KEEP CLUB RECORDS.
IF YOU'RE NAPPING IN THE CLUB ROOM, WE'LL MAKE SURE TO KEEP OUR VOICES DOWN.
JOIN OUR CLUB, AND YOU MAY USE THIS ROOM HOWEVER YOU SEE FIT.
YOU CAN USE IT AS A PLACE TO EAT LUNCH.
YOU CAN USE IT TO KILL TIME OR STUDY AFTER SCHOOL.
OR YOU CAN JUST LEAVE YOUR STUFF HERE.
AS A MISFIT WITH NO FRIENDS IN HER CLASS...
...I THINK YOU WILL FIND IT USEFUL TO HAVE A PLACE OF REFUGE IN THE SCHOOL WHERE YOU CAN ESCAPE PRYING EYES.
Just a—
PRESIDENT! YOU DON'T HAVE TO BE SO BLUNT!
Be friendly!
AND YOUR FACE IS SCARY!

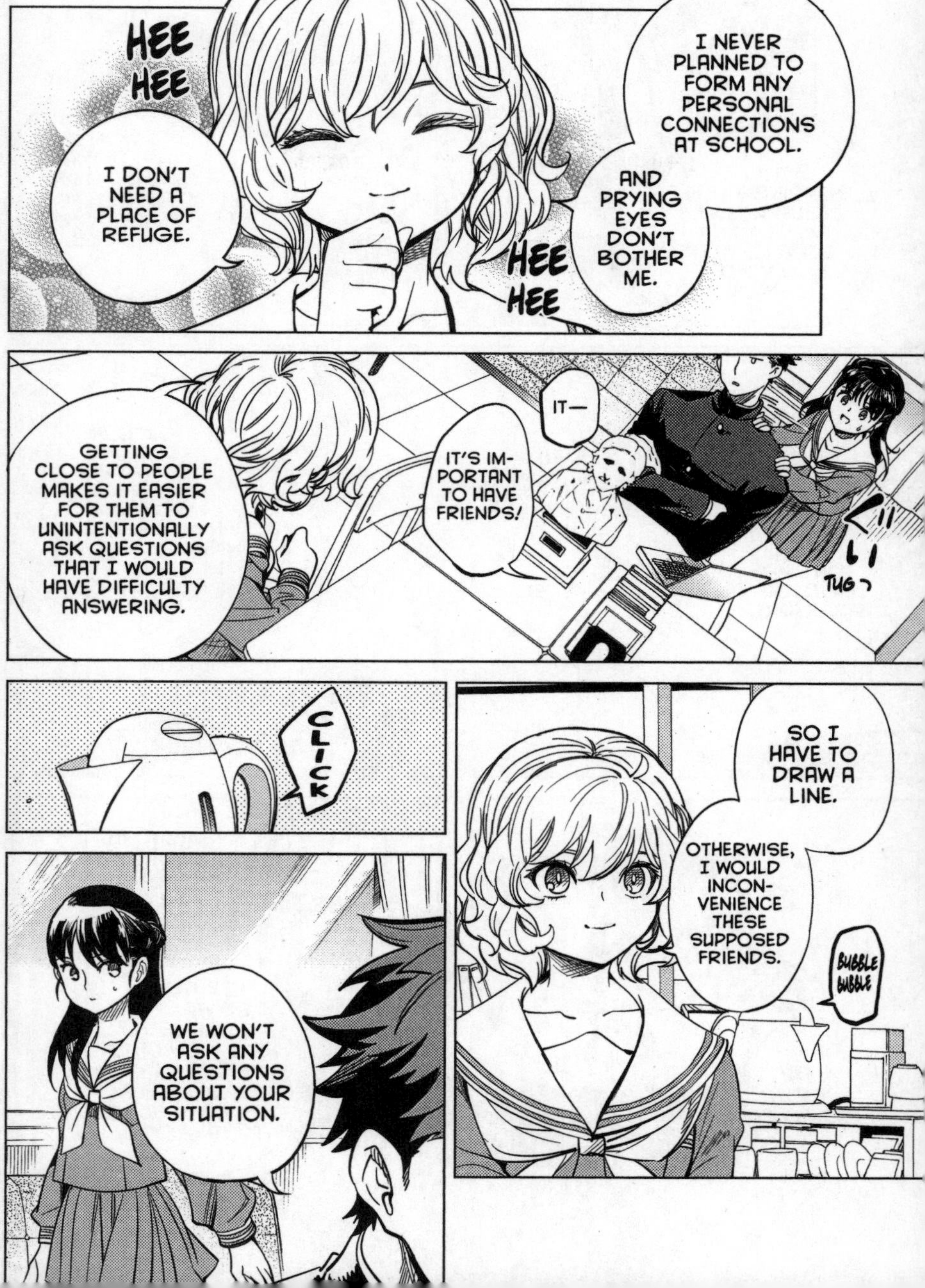
I NEVER PLANNED TO FORM ANY PERSONAL CONNECTIONS AT SCHOOL.
AND PRYING EYES DON'T BOTHER ME.
HEE HEE
HEE HEE
I DON'T NEED A PLACE OF REFUGE.
IT—
IT'S IMPORTANT TO HAVE FRIENDS!
TUG
GETTING CLOSE TO PEOPLE MAKES IT EASIER FOR THEM TO UNINTENTIONALLY ASK QUESTIONS THAT I WOULD HAVE DIFFICULTY ANSWERING.
SO I HAVE TO DRAW A LINE.
OTHERWISE, I WOULD INCONVENIENCE THESE SUPPOSED FRIENDS.
BUBBLE BUBBLE
CLICK
WE WON'T ASK ANY QUESTIONS ABOUT YOUR SITUATION.

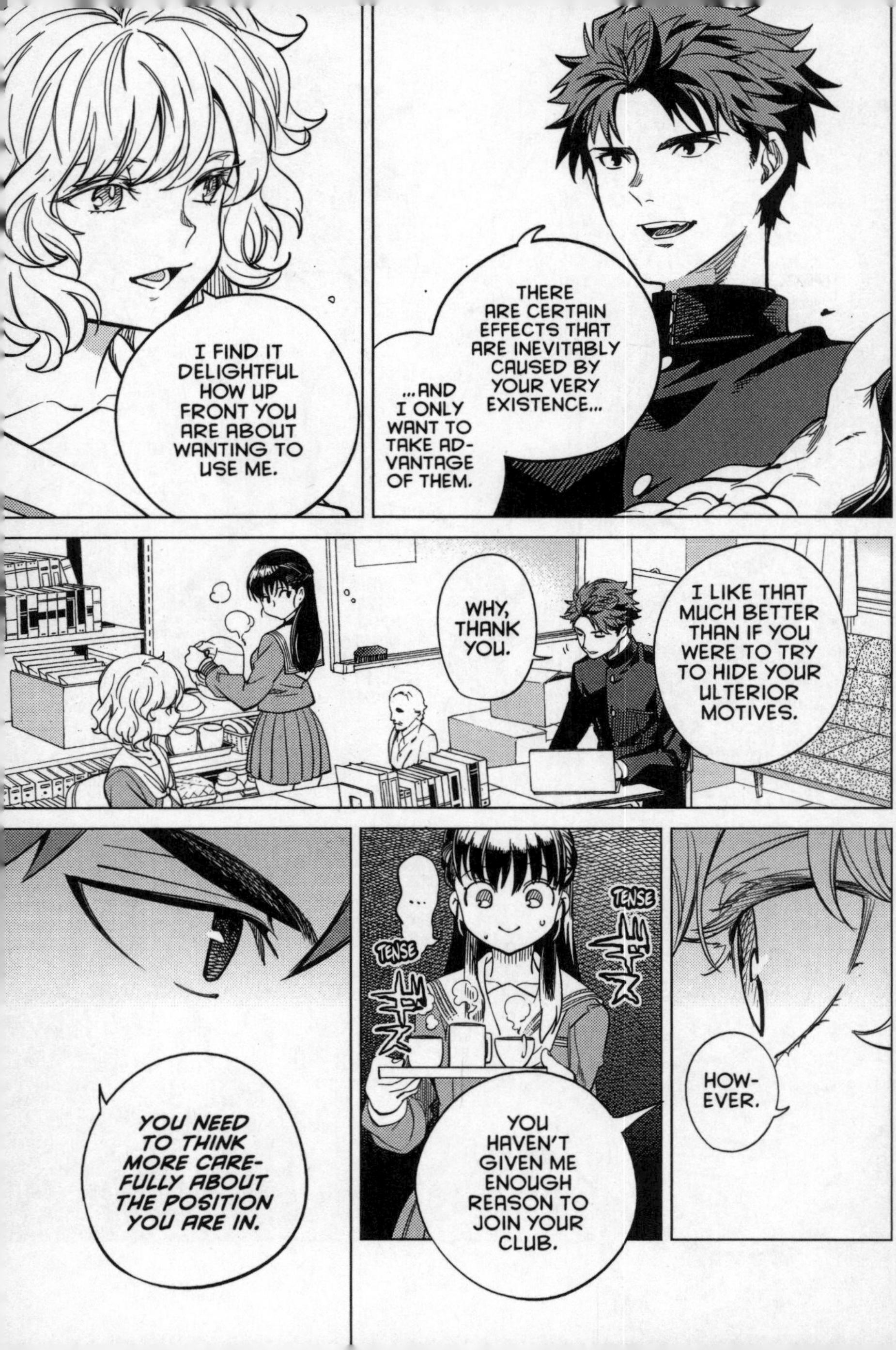
THERE ARE CERTAIN EFFECTS THAT ARE INEVITABLY CAUSED BY YOUR VERY EXISTENCE...
...AND I ONLY WANT TO TAKE ADVANTAGE OF THEM.
I FIND IT DELIGHTFUL HOW UP FRONT YOU ARE ABOUT WANTING TO USE ME.
I LIKE THAT MUCH BETTER THAN IF YOU WERE TO TRY TO HIDE YOUR ULTERIOR MOTIVES.
WHY, THANK YOU.
HOWEVER.
TENSE
...
TENSE
YOU HAVEN'T GIVEN ME ENOUGH REASON TO JOIN YOUR CLUB.
YOU NEED TO THINK MORE CAREFULLY ABOUT THE POSITION YOU ARE IN.

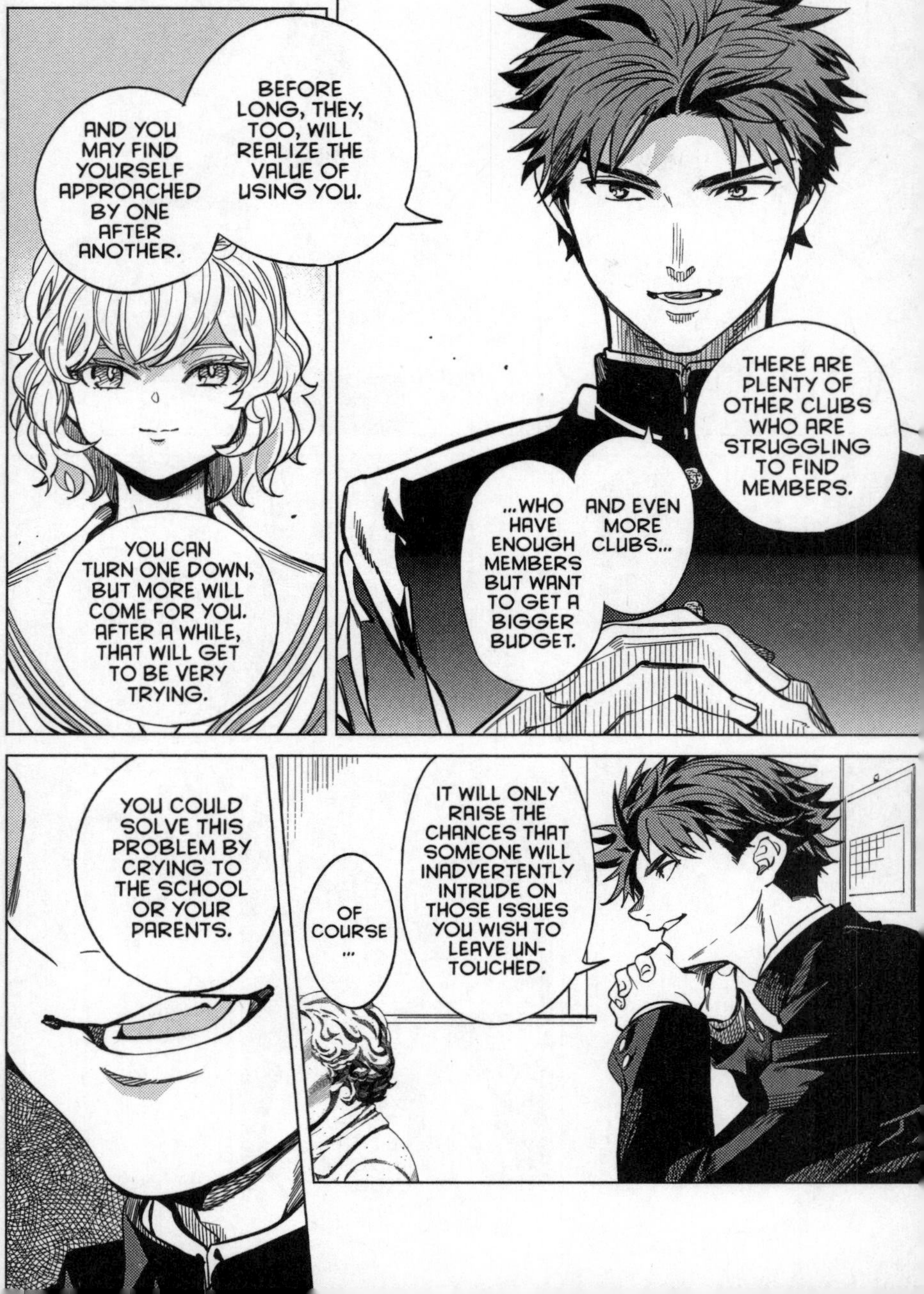
THERE ARE PLENTY OF OTHER CLUBS WHO ARE STRUGGLING TO FIND MEMBERS.
AND EVEN MORE CLUBS...
...WHO HAVE ENOUGH MEMBERS BUT WANT TO GET A BIGGER BUDGET.
BEFORE LONG, THEY, TOO, WILL REALIZE THE VALUE OF USING YOU.
AND YOU MAY FIND YOURSELF APPROACHED BY ONE AFTER ANOTHER.
YOU CAN TURN ONE DOWN, BUT MORE WILL COME FOR YOU. AFTER A WHILE, THAT WILL GET TO BE VERY TRYING.
IT WILL ONLY RAISE THE CHANCES THAT SOMEONE WILL INADVERTENTLY INTRUDE ON THOSE ISSUES YOU WISH TO LEAVE UN-TOUCHED.
OF COURSE...
YOU COULD SOLVE THIS PROBLEM BY CRYING TO THE SCHOOL OR YOUR PARENTS.

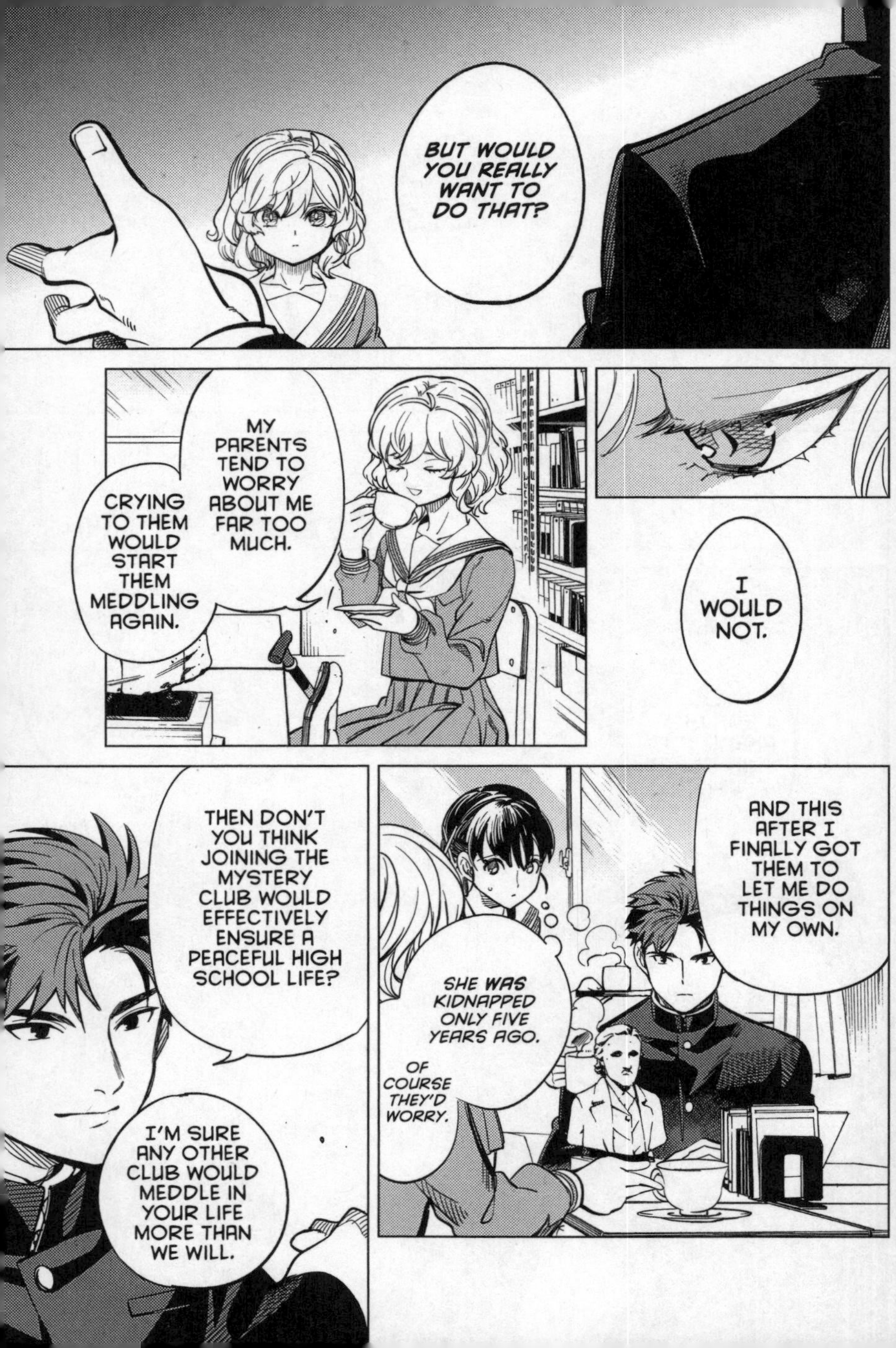
BUT WOULD YOU REALLY WANT TO DO THAT?
I WOULD NOT.
MY PARENTS TEND TO WORRY ABOUT ME FAR TOO MUCH.
CRYING TO THEM WOULD START THEM MEDDLING AGAIN.
AND THIS AFTER I FINALLY GOT THEM TO LET ME DO THINGS ON MY OWN.
SHE WAS KIDNAPPED ONLY FIVE YEARS AGO.
OF COURSE THEY'D WORRY.
THEN DON'T YOU THINK JOINING THE MYSTERY CLUB WOULD EFFECTIVELY ENSURE A PEACEFUL HIGH SCHOOL LIFE?
I'M SURE ANY OTHER CLUB WOULD MEDDLE IN YOUR LIFE MORE THAN WE WILL.

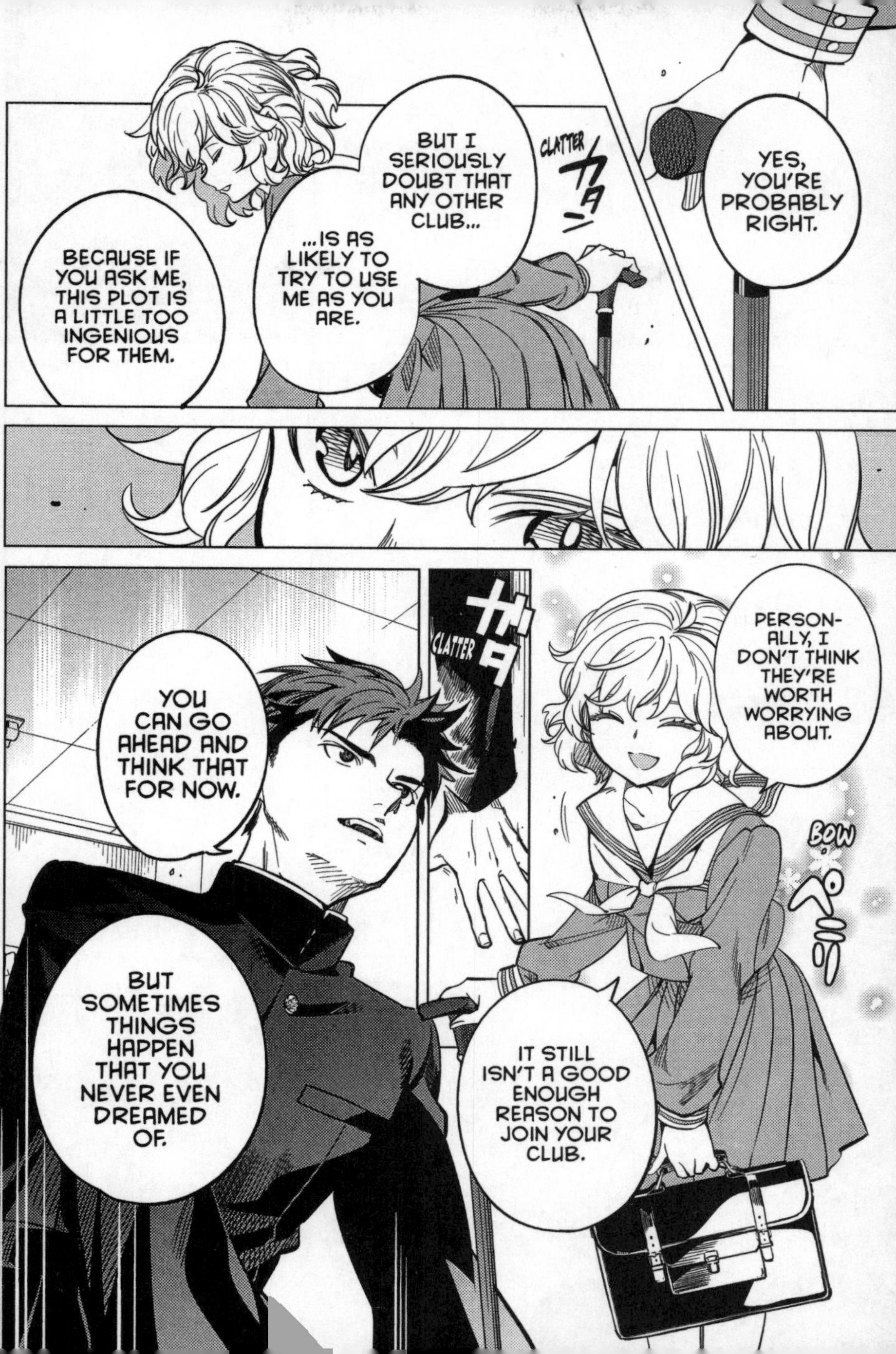
YES, YOU'RE PROBABLY RIGHT.
CLATTER
BUT I SERIOUSLY DOUBT THAT ANY OTHER CLUB...
...IS AS LIKELY TO TRY TO USE ME AS YOU ARE.
BECAUSE IF YOU ASK ME, THIS PLOT IS A LITTLE TOO INGENIOUS FOR THEM.
PERSON-ALLY, I DON'T THINK THEY'RE WORTH WORRYING ABOUT.
BOW
IT STILL ISN'T A GOOD ENOUGH REASON TO JOIN YOUR CLUB.
CLATTER
YOU CAN GO AHEAD AND THINK THAT FOR NOW.
BUT SOMETIMES THINGS HAPPEN THAT YOU NEVER EVEN DREAMED OF.

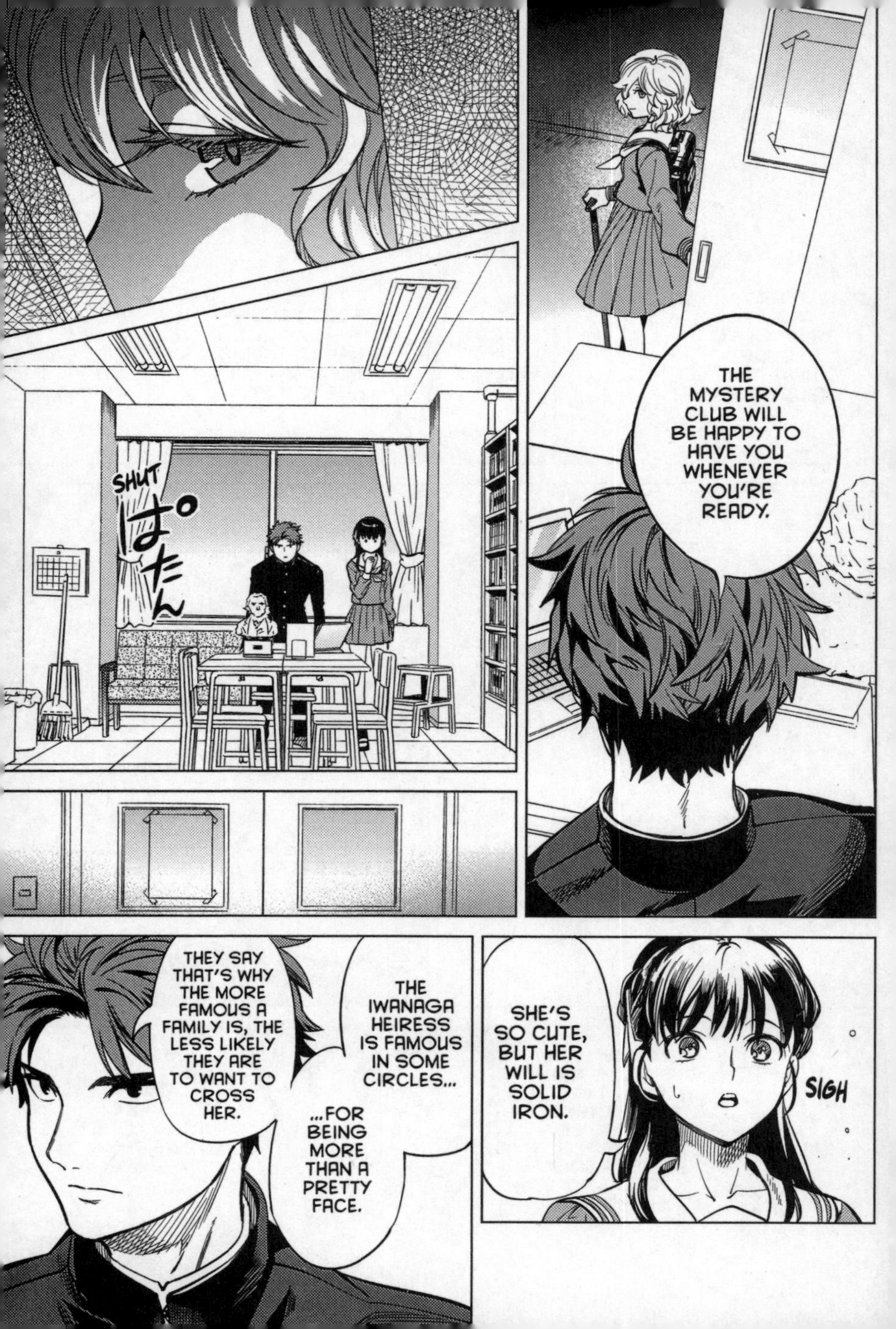
THE MYSTERY CLUB WILL BE HAPPY TO HAVE YOU WHENEVER YOU'RE READY.
SHUT
ぱたん
SHE'S SO CUTE, BUT HER WILL IS SOLID IRON.
SIGH
THE IWANAGA HEIRESS IS FAMOUS IN SOME CIRCLES...
...FOR BEING MORE THAN A PRETTY FACE.
THEY SAY THAT'S WHY THE MORE FAMOUS A FAMILY IS, THE LESS LIKELY THEY ARE TO WANT TO CROSS HER.

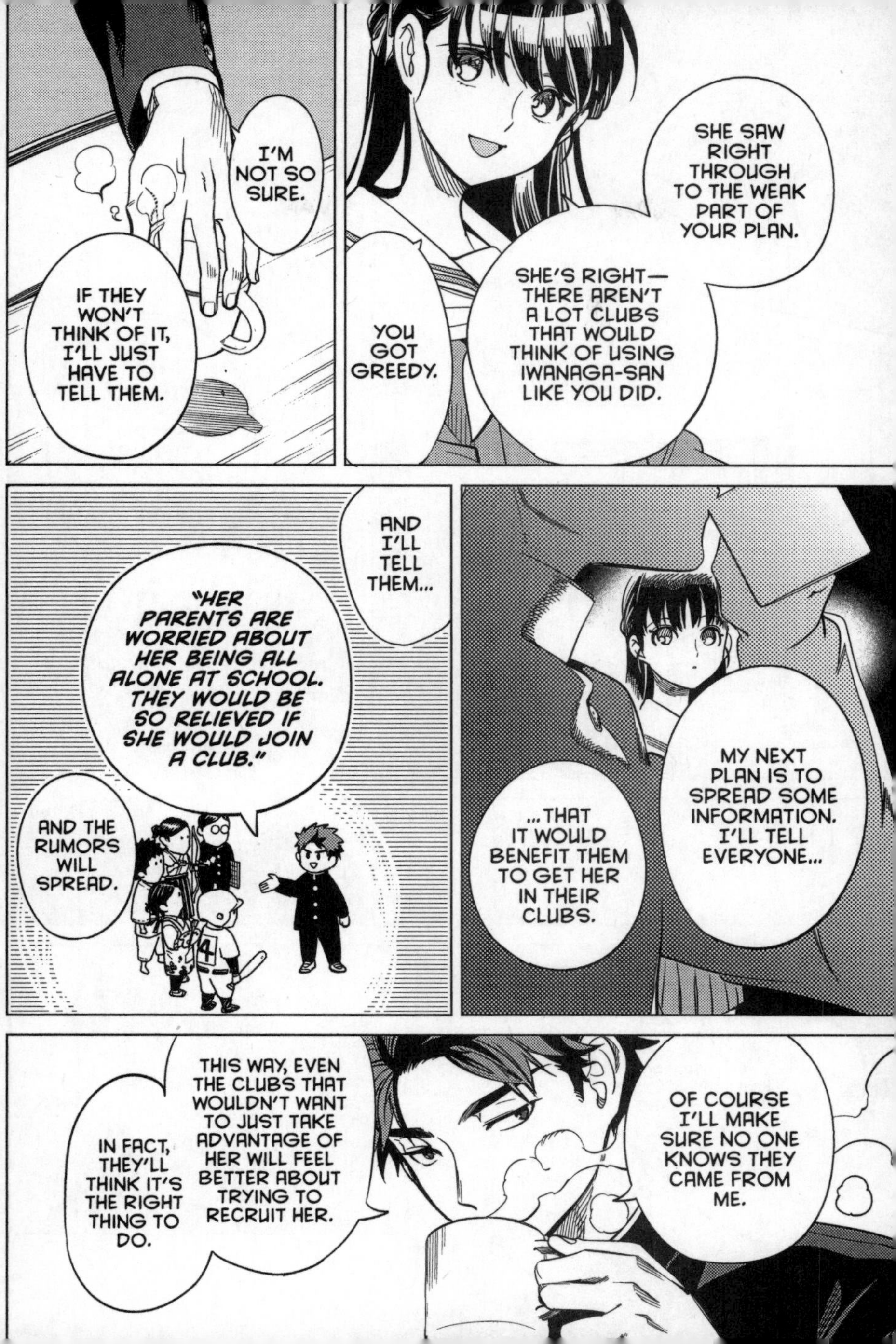

SHE SAW RIGHT THROUGH TO THE WEAK PART OF YOUR PLAN.
SHE'S RIGHT— THERE AREN'T A LOT CLUBS THAT WOULD THINK OF USING IWANAGA-SAN LIKE YOU DID.
YOU GOT GREEDY.
I'M NOT SO SURE.
IF THEY WON'T THINK OF IT, I'LL JUST HAVE TO TELL THEM.
MY NEXT PLAN IS TO SPREAD SOME INFORMATION. I'LL TELL EVERYONE...
...THAT IT WOULD BENEFIT THEM TO GET HER IN THEIR CLUBS.
AND I'LL TELL THEM...
"HER PARENTS ARE WORRIED ABOUT HER BEING ALL ALONE AT SCHOOL. THEY WOULD BE SO RELIEVED IF SHE WOULD JOIN A CLUB."
AND THE RUMORS WILL SPREAD.
OF COURSE I'LL MAKE SURE NO ONE KNOWS THEY CAME FROM ME.
THIS WAY, EVEN THE CLUBS THAT WOULDN'T WANT TO JUST TAKE ADVANTAGE OF HER WILL FEEL BETTER ABOUT TRYING TO RECRUIT HER.
IN FACT, THEY'LL THINK IT'S THE RIGHT THING TO DO.

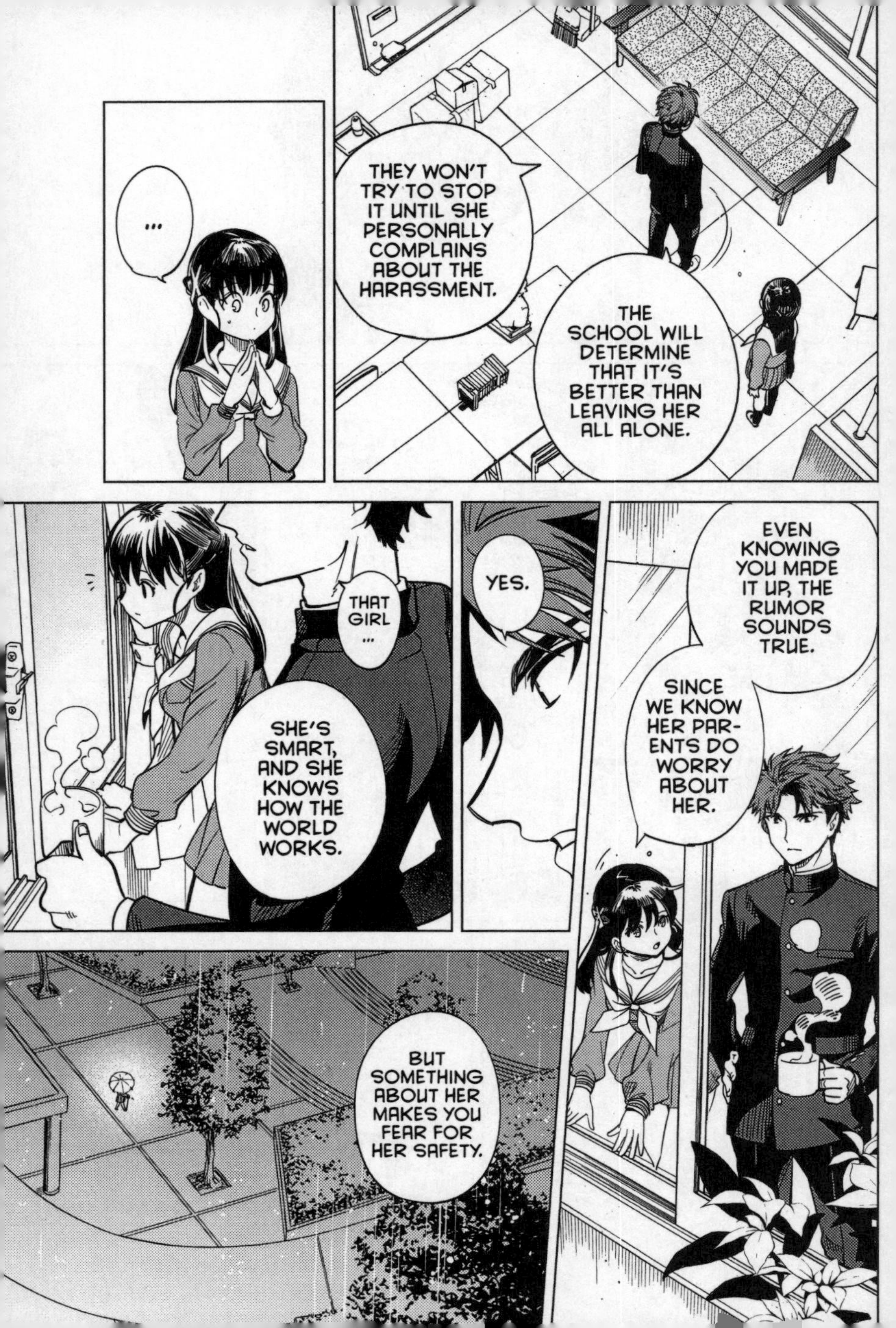
THEY WON'T TRY TO STOP IT UNTIL SHE PERSONALLY COMPLAINS ABOUT THE HARASSMENT.
THE SCHOOL WILL DETERMINE THAT IT'S BETTER THAN LEAVING HER ALL ALONE.
...
EVEN KNOWING YOU MADE IT UP, THE RUMOR SOUNDS TRUE.
SINCE WE KNOW HER PAR-ENTS DO WORRY ABOUT HER.
YES.
THAT GIRL...
SHE'S SMART, AND SHE KNOWS HOW THE WORLD WORKS.
BUT SOMETHING ABOUT HER MAKES YOU FEAR FOR HER SAFETY.

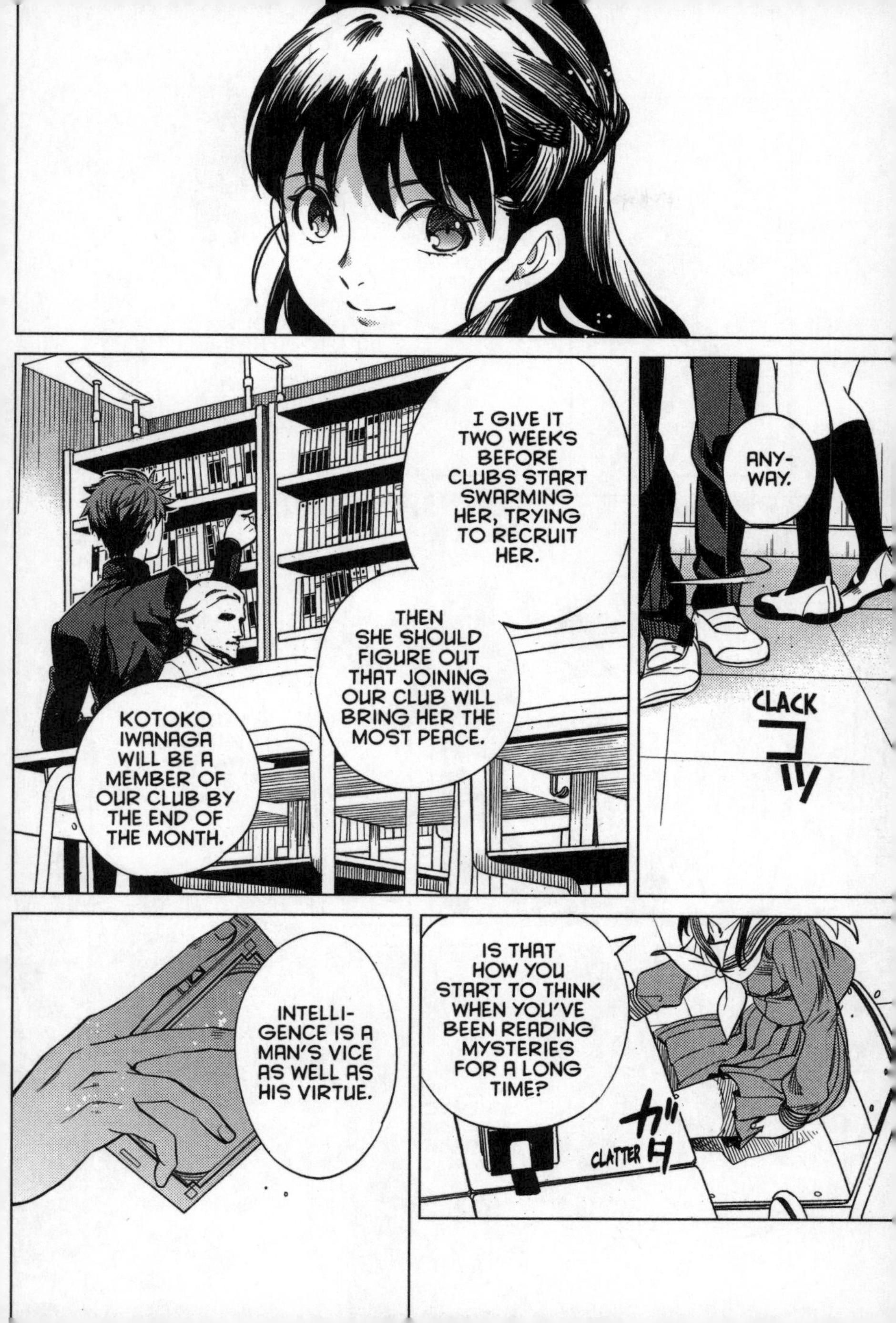
ANY-WAY.
CLACK
I GIVE IT TWO WEEKS BEFORE CLUBS START SWARMING HER, TRYING TO RECRUIT HER.
THEN SHE SHOULD FIGURE OUT THAT JOINING OUR CLUB WILL BRING HER THE MOST PEACE.
KOTOKO IWANAGA WILL BE A MEMBER OF OUR CLUB BY THE END OF THE MONTH.
IS THAT HOW YOU START TO THINK WHEN YOU'VE BEEN READING MYSTERIES FOR A LONG TIME?
CLATTER
INTELLI-GENCE IS A MAN'S VICE AS WELL AS HIS VIRTUE.

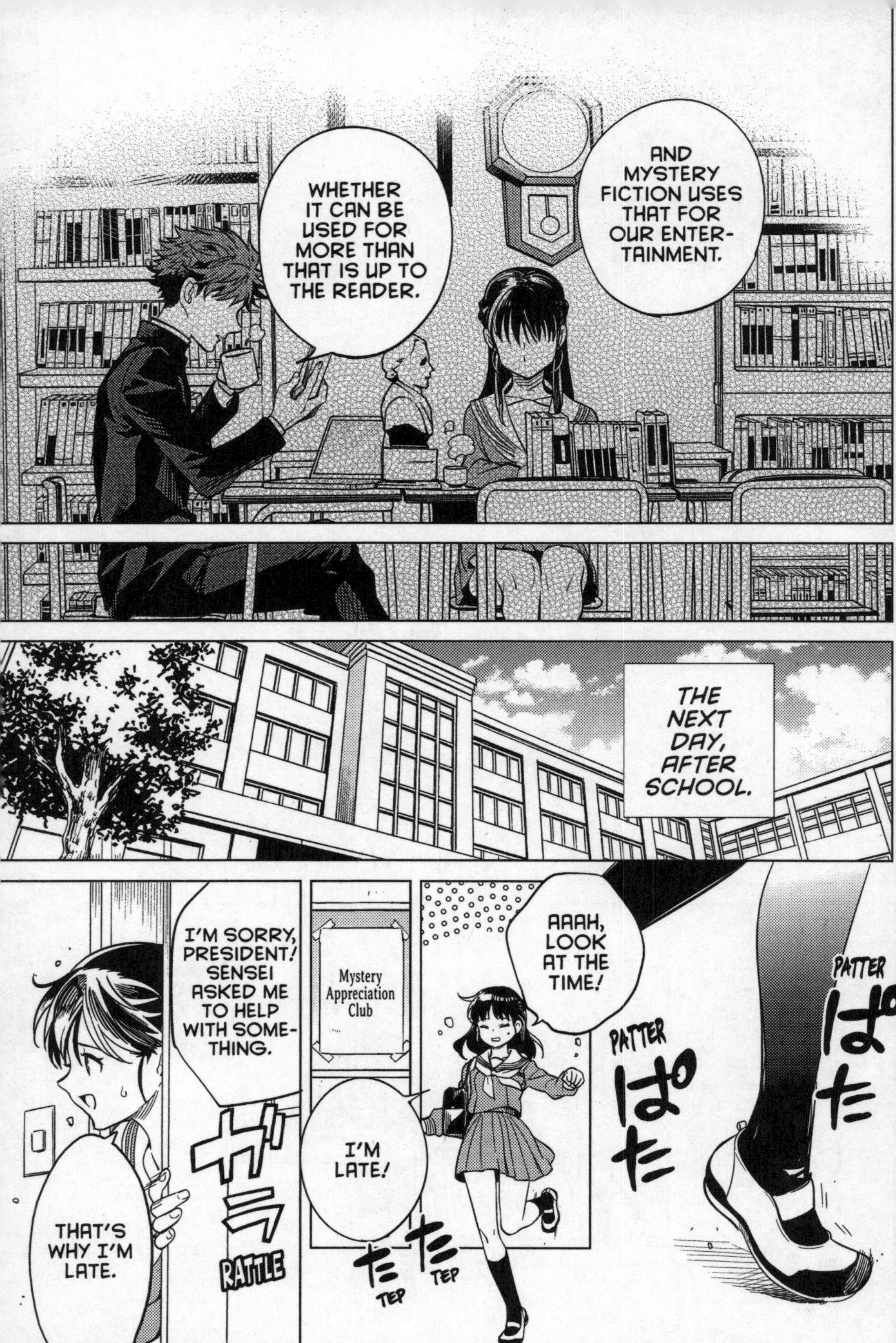
AND MYSTERY FICTION USES THAT FOR OUR ENTER-TAINMENT.
WHETHER IT CAN BE USED FOR MORE THAN THAT IS UP TO THE READER.
THE NEXT DAY, AFTER SCHOOL.
PATTER
ぱた
PATTER
ぱた
AAAH, LOOK AT THE TIME!
I'M LATE!
たた
TEP TEP
Mystery Appreciation Club
ガラ
RATTLE
I'M SORRY, PRESIDENT! SENSEI ASKED ME TO HELP WITH SOME-THING.
THAT'S WHY I'M LATE.

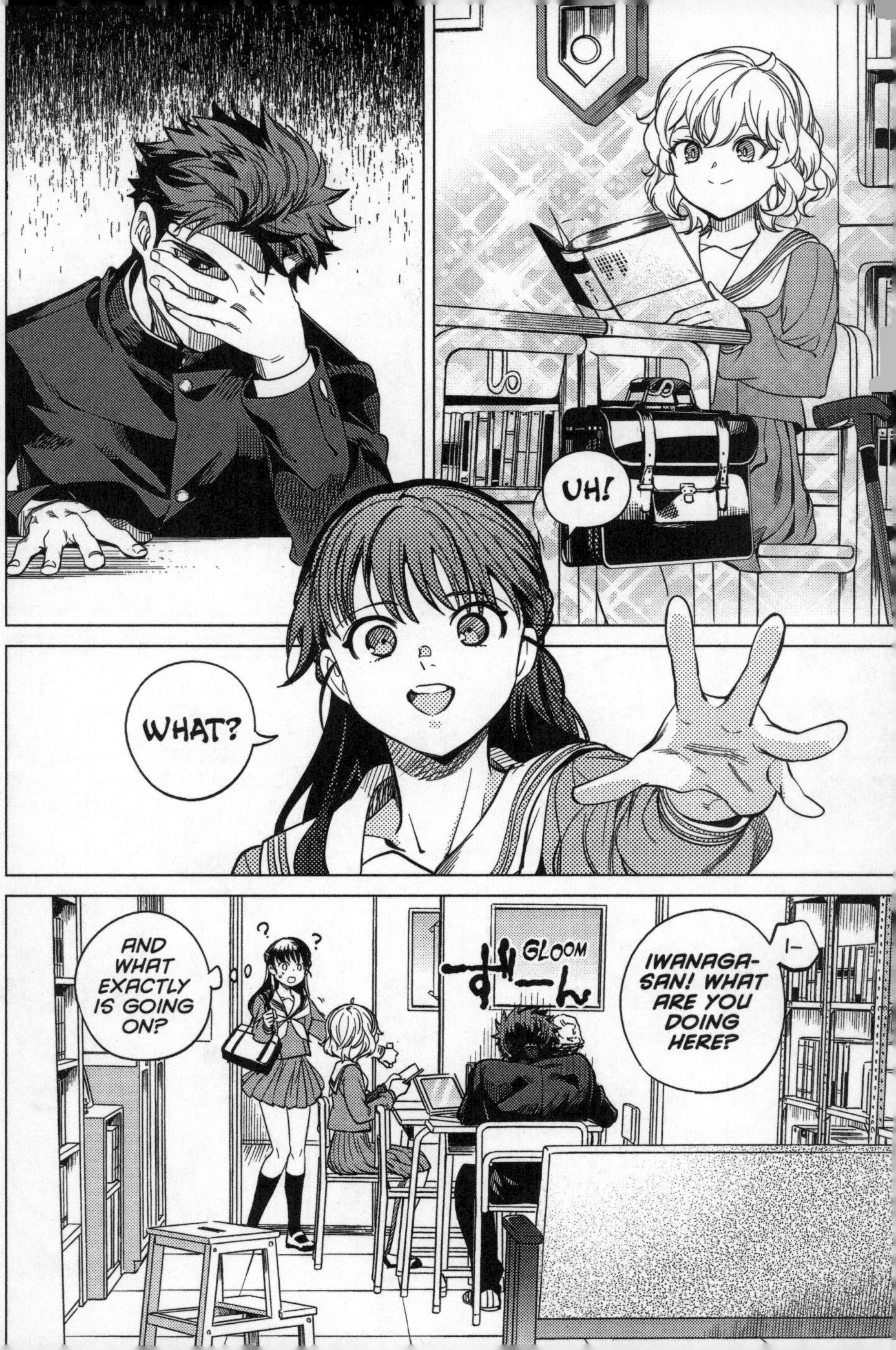
UH!
WHAT?
I-
IWANAGA-SAN! WHAT ARE YOU DOING HERE?
GLOOM
AND WHAT EXACTLY IS GOING ON?

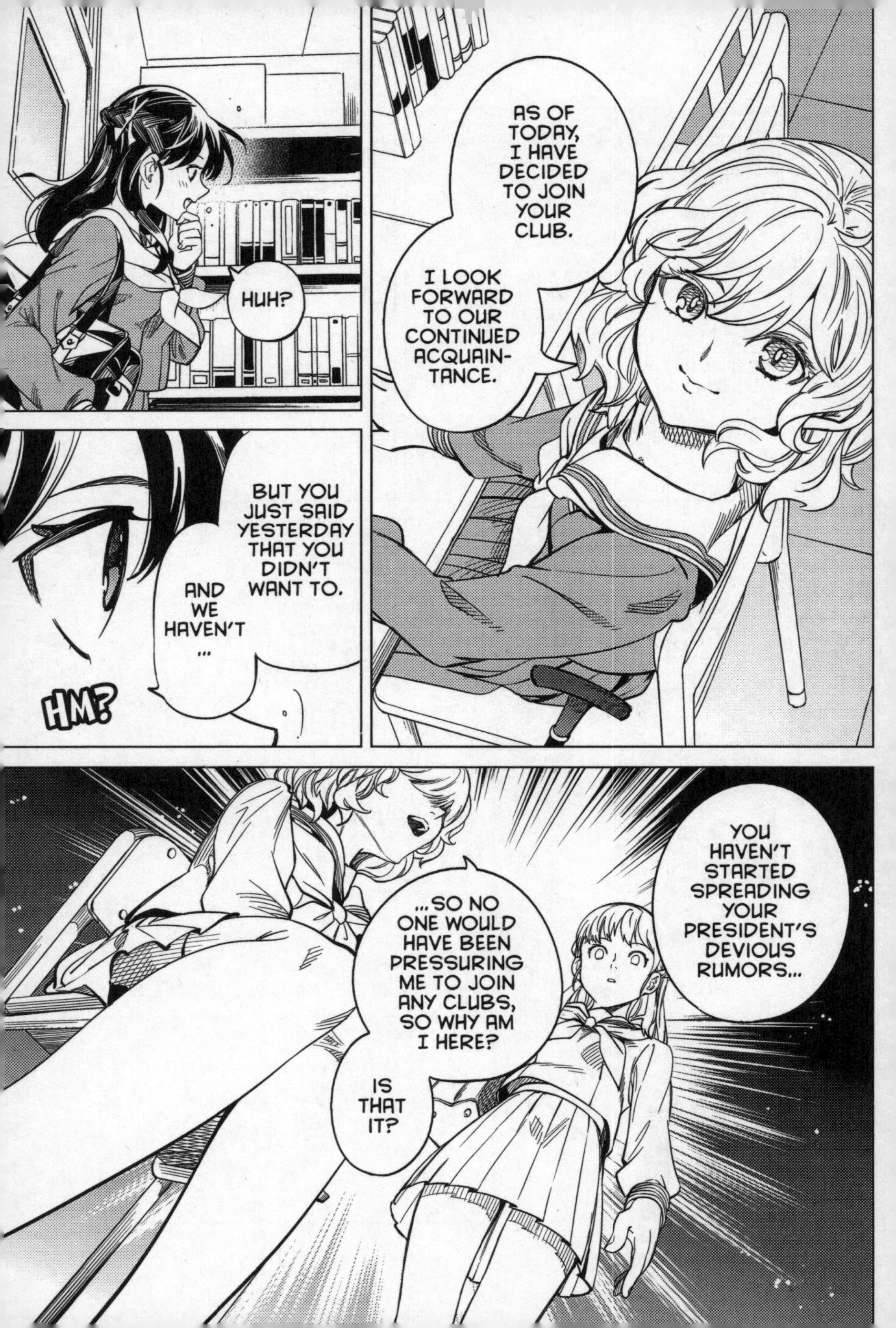
AS OF TODAY, I HAVE DECIDED TO JOIN YOUR CLUB.
I LOOK FORWARD TO OUR CONTINUED ACQUAINTANCE.
HUH?
BUT YOU JUST SAID YESTERDAY THAT YOU DIDN'T WANT TO.
AND WE HAVEN'T ...
HM?
YOU HAVEN'T STARTED SPREADING YOUR PRESIDENT'S DEVIOUS RUMORS...
...SO NO ONE WOULD HAVE BEEN PRESSURING ME TO JOIN ANY CLUBS, SO WHY AM I HERE?
IS THAT IT?

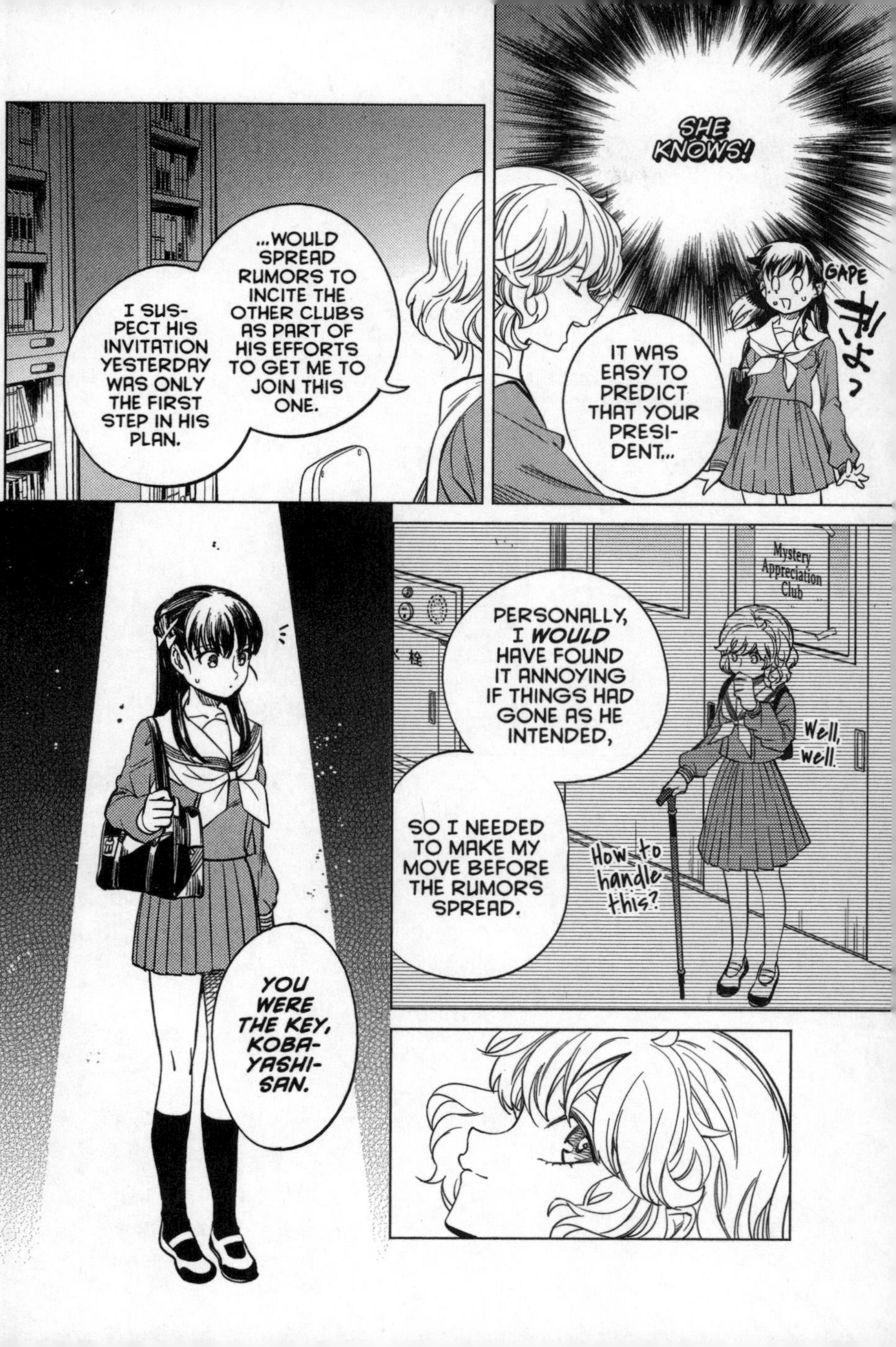
SHE KNOWS!
GAPE
IT WAS EASY TO PREDICT THAT YOUR PRESIDENT...
...WOULD SPREAD RUMORS TO INCITE THE OTHER CLUBS AS PART OF HIS EFFORTS TO GET ME TO JOIN THIS ONE.
I SUSPECT HIS INVITATION YESTERDAY WAS ONLY THE FIRST STEP IN HIS PLAN.
Mystery Appreciation Club
Well, well.
PERSONALLY, I ***WOULD*** HAVE FOUND IT ANNOYING IF THINGS HAD GONE AS HE INTENDED,
How to handle this?
SO I NEEDED TO MAKE MY MOVE BEFORE THE RUMORS SPREAD.
YOU WERE THE KEY, KOBAYASHI-SAN.

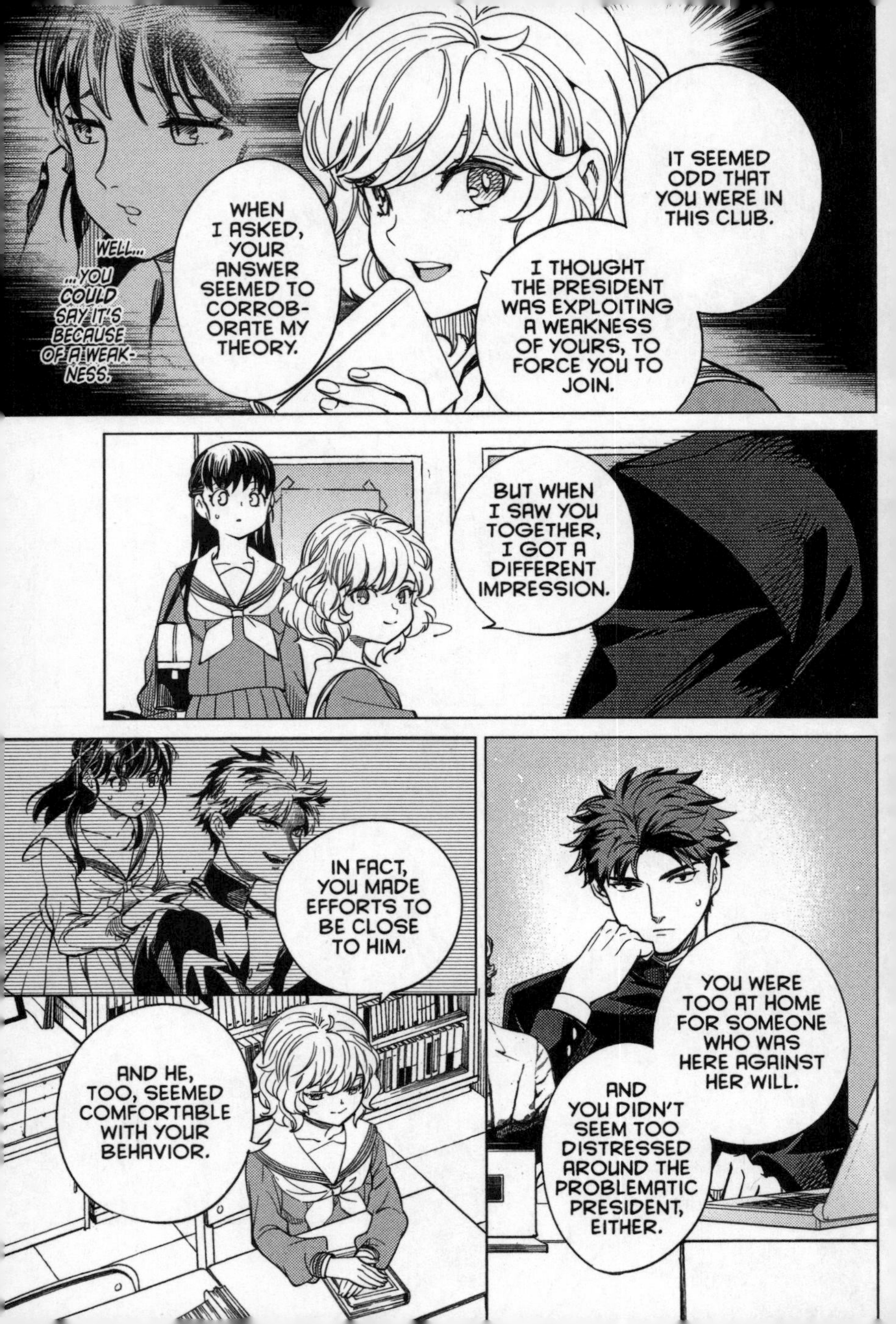
IT SEEMED ODD THAT YOU WERE IN THIS CLUB.
I THOUGHT THE PRESIDENT WAS EXPLOITING A WEAKNESS OF YOURS, TO FORCE YOU TO JOIN.
WHEN I ASKED, YOUR ANSWER SEEMED TO CORROBORATE MY THEORY.
WELL...
...YOU COULD SAY IT'S BECAUSE OF A WEAKNESS.
BUT WHEN I SAW YOU TOGETHER, I GOT A DIFFERENT IMPRESSION.
YOU WERE TOO AT HOME FOR SOMEONE WHO WAS HERE AGAINST HER WILL.
AND YOU DIDN'T SEEM TOO DISTRESSED AROUND THE PROBLEMATIC PRESIDENT, EITHER.
IN FACT, YOU MADE EFFORTS TO BE CLOSE TO HIM.
AND HE, TOO, SEEMED COMFORTABLE WITH YOUR BEHAVIOR.

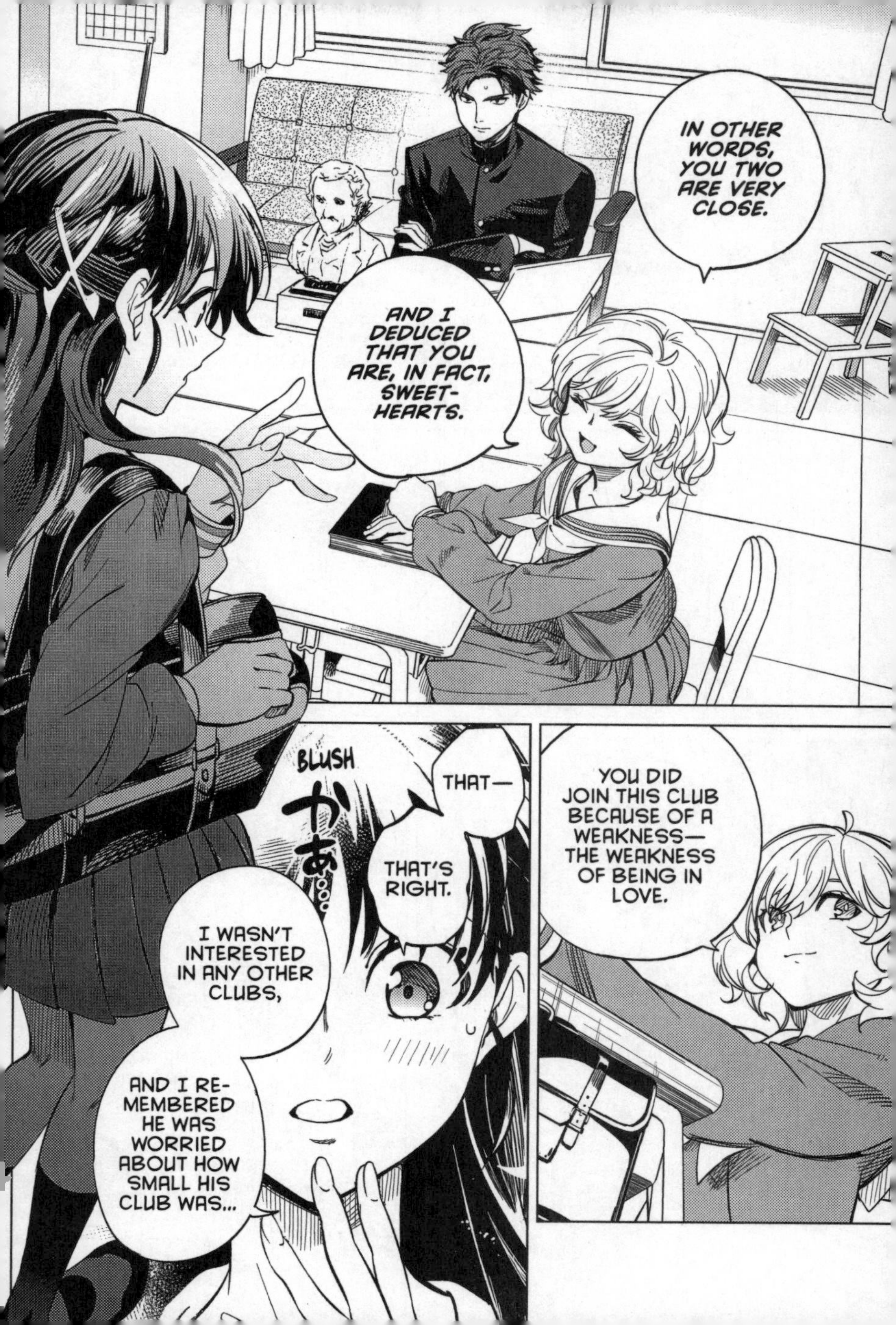
IN OTHER WORDS, YOU TWO ARE VERY CLOSE.
AND I DEDUCED THAT YOU ARE, IN FACT, SWEET-HEARTS.
YOU DID JOIN THIS CLUB BECAUSE OF A WEAKNESS—THE WEAKNESS OF BEING IN LOVE.
BLUSH
THAT—
THAT'S RIGHT.
I WASN'T INTERESTED IN ANY OTHER CLUBS,
AND I RE-MEMBERED HE WAS WORRIED ABOUT HOW SMALL HIS CLUB WAS...

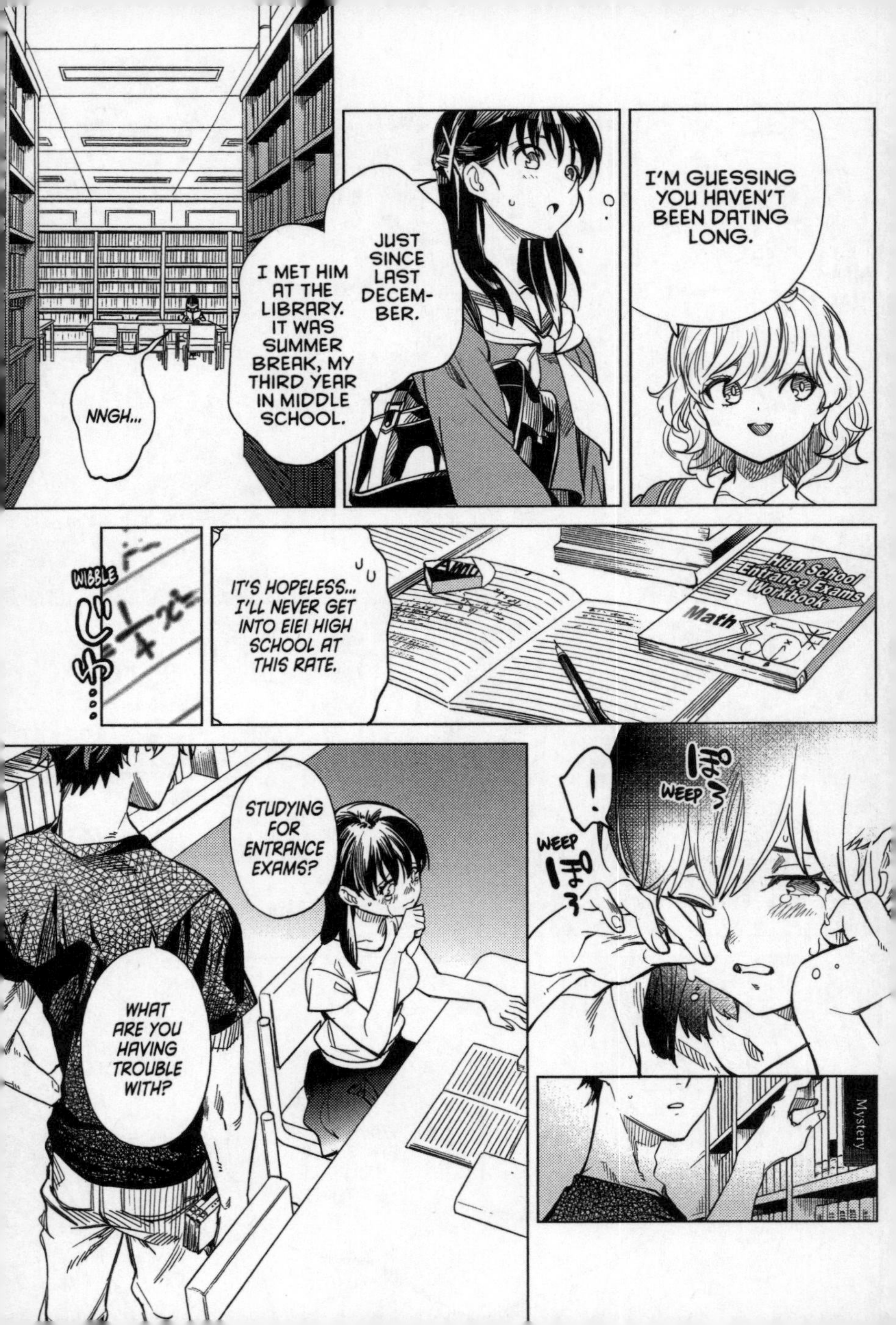
I'M GUESSING YOU HAVEN'T BEEN DATING LONG.
JUST SINCE LAST DECEMBER.
I MET HIM AT THE LIBRARY. IT WAS SUMMER BREAK, MY THIRD YEAR IN MIDDLE SCHOOL.
NNGH...
High School Entrance Exams Workbook
Math
IT'S HOPELESS... I'LL NEVER GET INTO EIEI HIGH SCHOOL AT THIS RATE.
WIBBLE
!
WEEP
ぽろ
WEEP
ぽろ
Mystery
STUDYING FOR ENTRANCE EXAMS?
WHAT ARE YOU HAVING TROUBLE WITH?

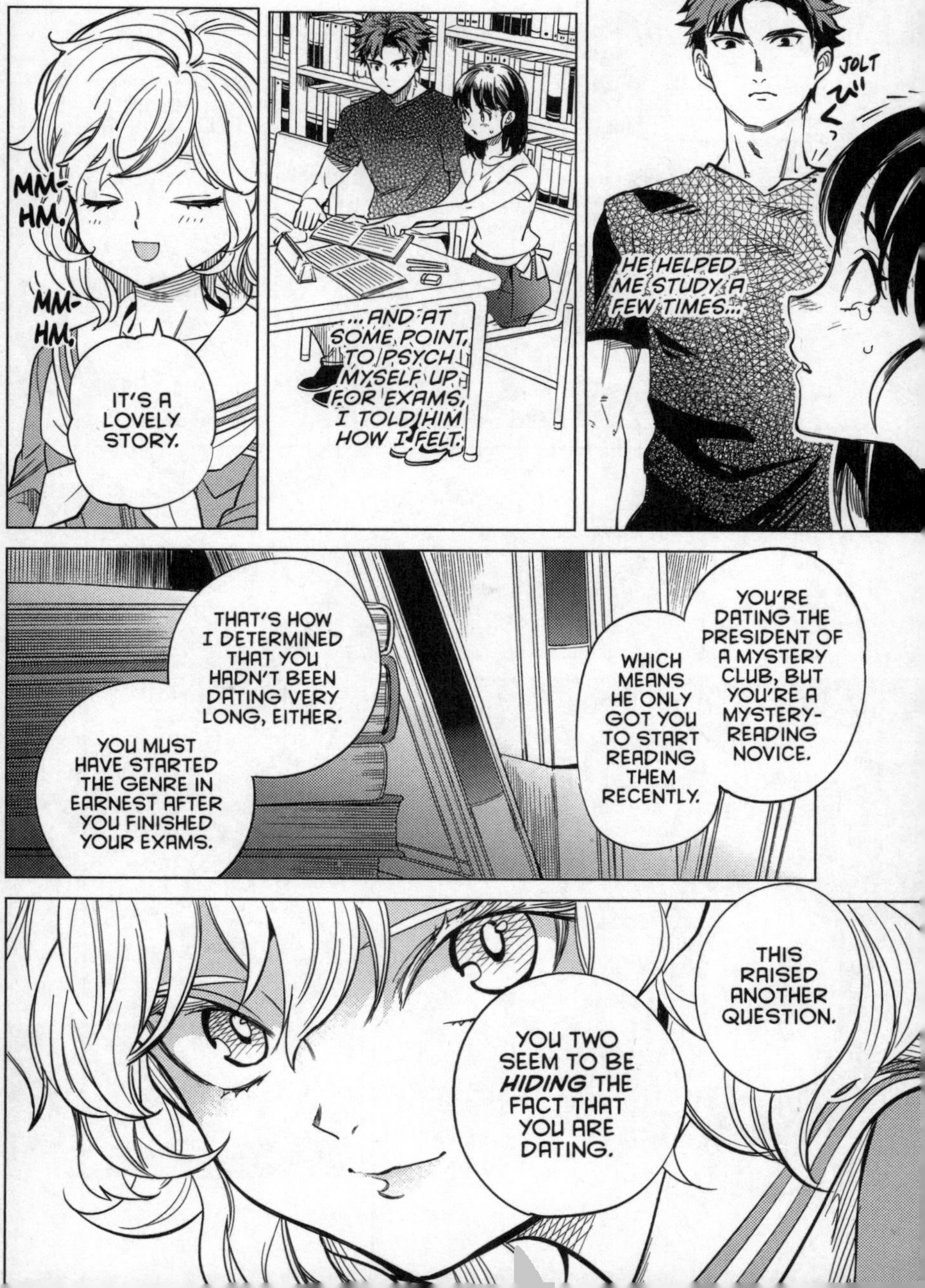
JOLT
HE HELPED ME STUDY A FEW TIMES...
...AND AT SOME POINT, TO PSYCH MYSELF UP FOR EXAMS, I TOLD HIM HOW I FELT.
MM-HM.
MM-HM.
IT'S A LOVELY STORY.
YOU'RE DATING THE PRESIDENT OF A MYSTERY CLUB, BUT YOU'RE A MYSTERY-READING NOVICE.
WHICH MEANS HE ONLY GOT YOU TO START READING THEM RECENTLY.
THAT'S HOW I DETERMINED THAT YOU HADN'T BEEN DATING VERY LONG, EITHER.
YOU MUST HAVE STARTED THE GENRE IN EARNEST AFTER YOU FINISHED YOUR EXAMS.
THIS RAISED ANOTHER QUESTION.
YOU TWO SEEM TO BE *HIDING* THE FACT THAT YOU ARE DATING.

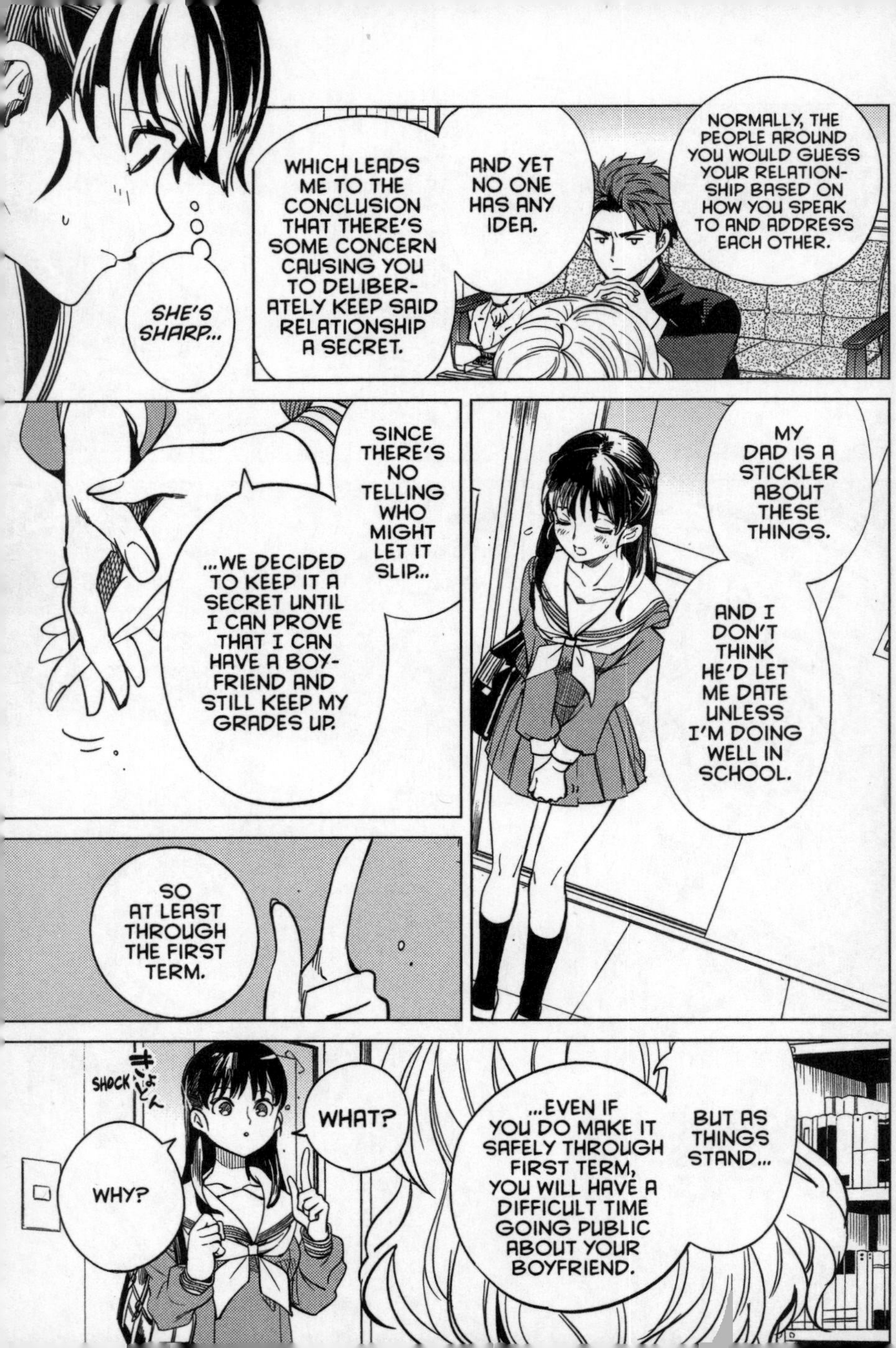
NORMALLY, THE PEOPLE AROUND YOU WOULD GUESS YOUR RELATIONSHIP BASED ON HOW YOU SPEAK TO AND ADDRESS EACH OTHER.
AND YET NO ONE HAS ANY IDEA.
WHICH LEADS ME TO THE CONCLUSION THAT THERE'S SOME CONCERN CAUSING YOU TO DELIBERATELY KEEP SAID RELATIONSHIP A SECRET.
SHE'S SHARP...
MY DAD IS A STICKLER ABOUT THESE THINGS.
AND I DON'T THINK HE'D LET ME DATE UNLESS I'M DOING WELL IN SCHOOL.
SINCE THERE'S NO TELLING WHO MIGHT LET IT SLIP...
...WE DECIDED TO KEEP IT A SECRET UNTIL I CAN PROVE THAT I CAN HAVE A BOYFRIEND AND STILL KEEP MY GRADES UP.
SO AT LEAST THROUGH THE FIRST TERM.
BUT AS THINGS STAND...
...EVEN IF YOU DO MAKE IT SAFELY THROUGH FIRST TERM, YOU WILL HAVE A DIFFICULT TIME GOING PUBLIC ABOUT YOUR BOYFRIEND.
WHAT?
きょとん
SHOCK
WHY?

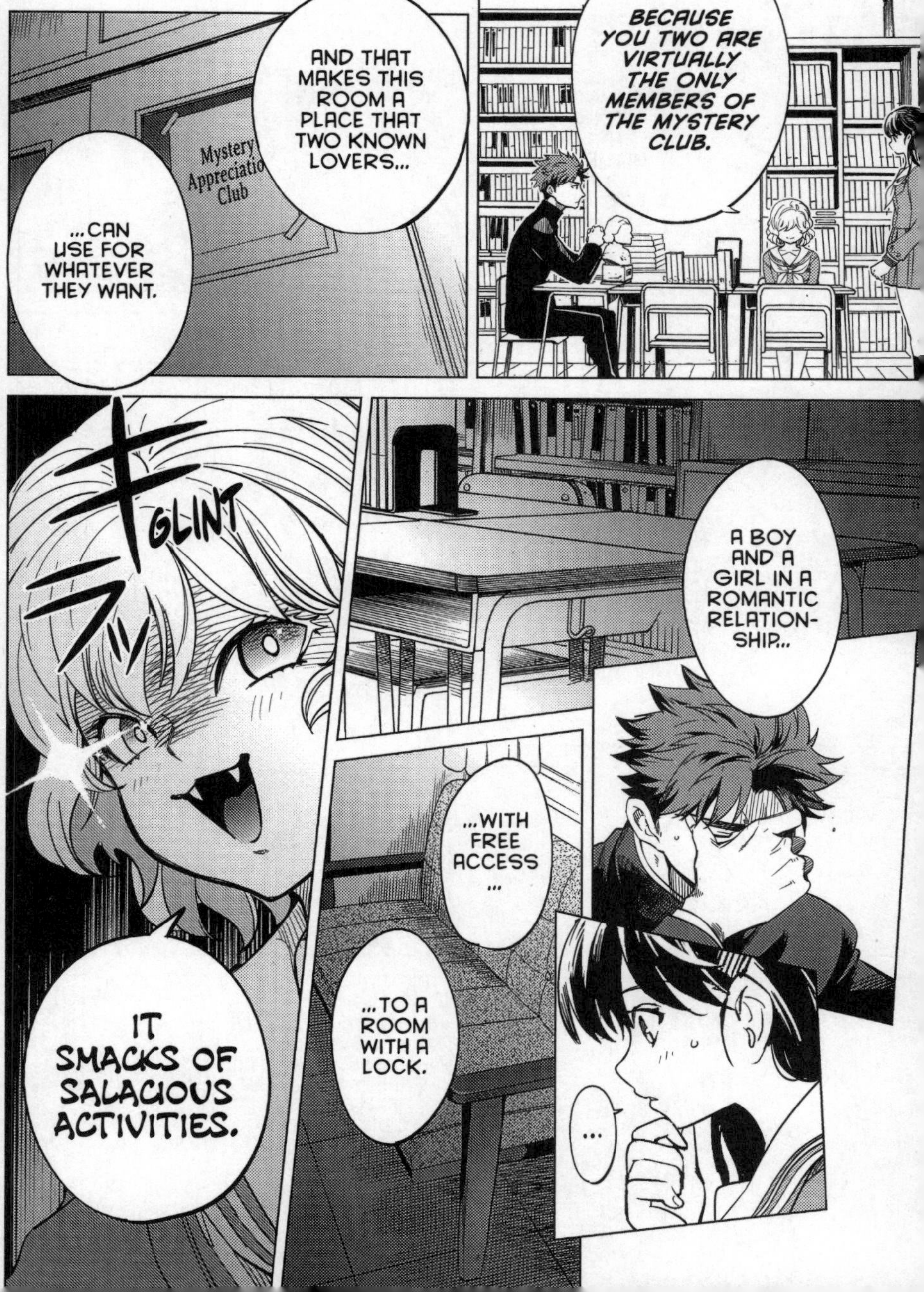
BECAUSE YOU TWO ARE VIRTUALLY THE ONLY MEMBERS OF THE MYSTERY CLUB.
AND THAT MAKES THIS ROOM A PLACE THAT TWO KNOWN LOVERS...
...CAN USE FOR WHATEVER THEY WANT.
A BOY AND A GIRL IN A ROMANTIC RELATION-SHIP...
...WITH FREE ACCESS ...
...TO A ROOM WITH A LOCK.
...
GLINT
IT SMACKS OF SALACIOUS ACTIVITIES.

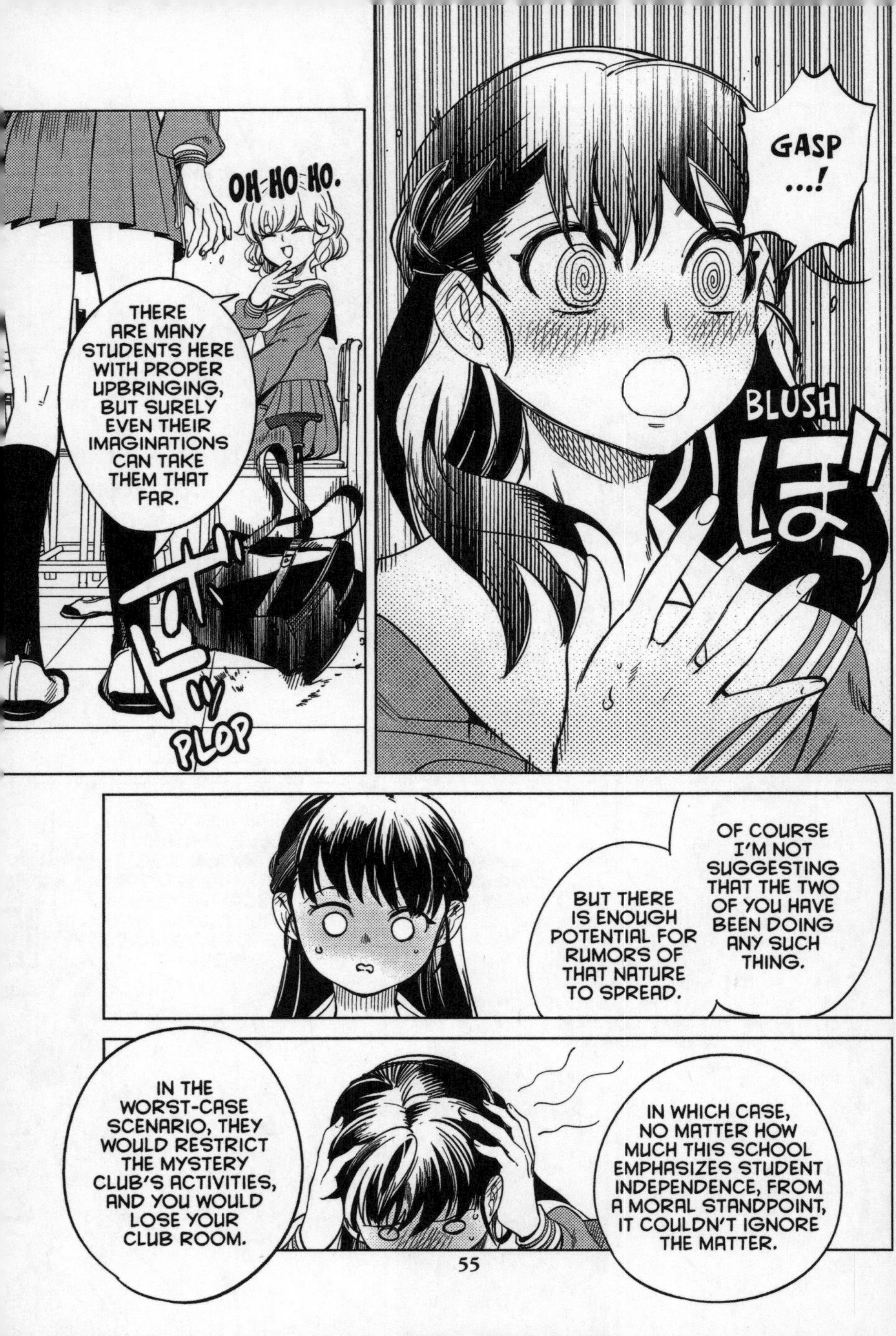
GASP ...!
BLUSH
ぼっ
OH-HO-HO.
THERE ARE MANY STUDENTS HERE WITH PROPER UPBRINGING, BUT SURELY EVEN THEIR IMAGINATIONS CAN TAKE THEM THAT FAR.
PLOP
OF COURSE I'M NOT SUGGESTING THAT THE TWO OF YOU HAVE BEEN DOING ANY SUCH THING.
BUT THERE IS ENOUGH POTENTIAL FOR RUMORS OF THAT NATURE TO SPREAD.
IN WHICH CASE, NO MATTER HOW MUCH THIS SCHOOL EMPHASIZES STUDENT INDEPENDENCE, FROM A MORAL STANDPOINT, IT COULDN'T IGNORE THE MATTER.
IN THE WORST-CASE SCENARIO, THEY WOULD RESTRICT THE MYSTERY CLUB'S ACTIVITIES, AND YOU WOULD LOSE YOUR CLUB ROOM.

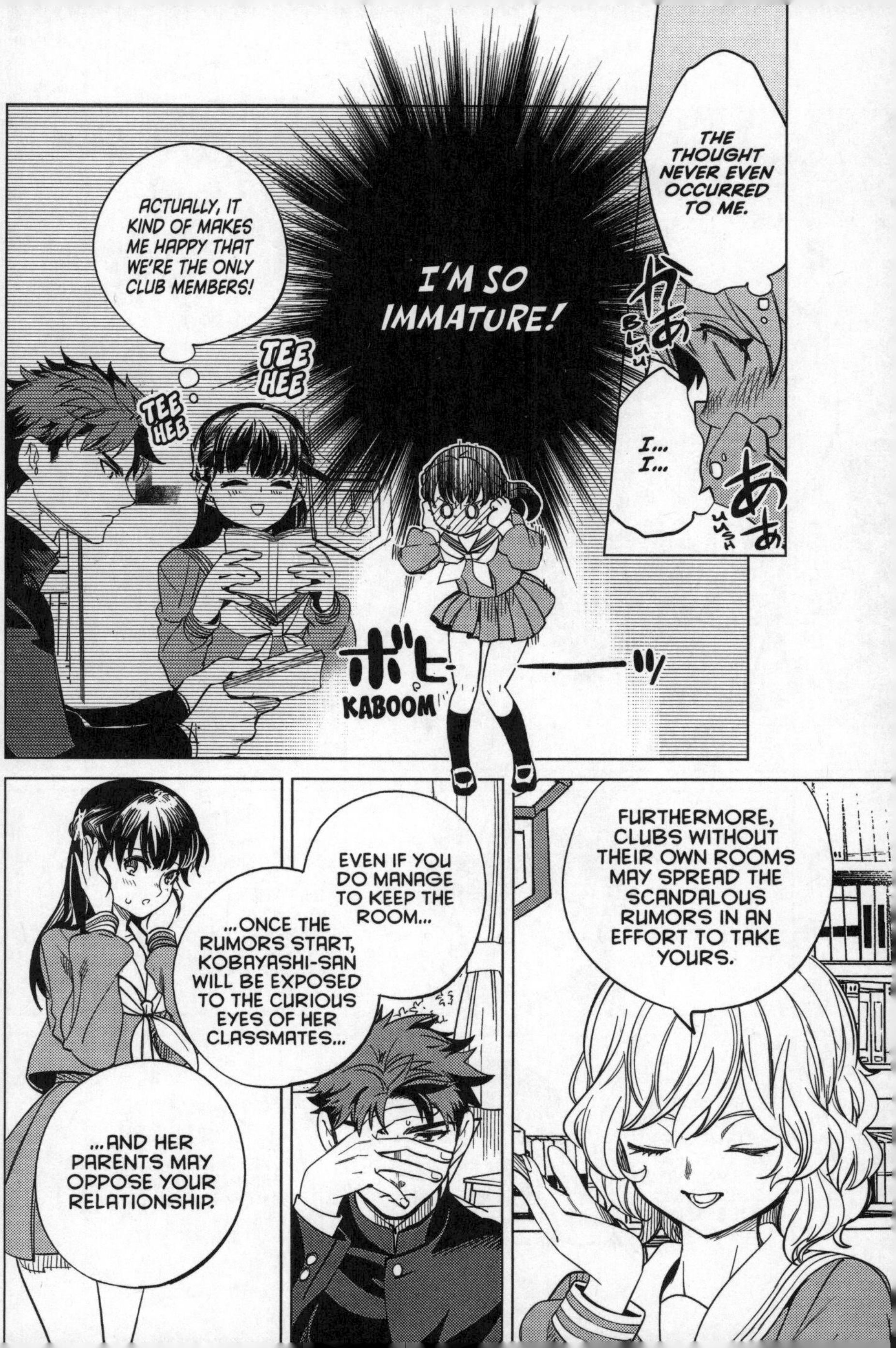
THE THOUGHT NEVER EVEN OCCURRED TO ME.
かあ
BLUSH
I... I...
ああ
ACTUALLY, IT KIND OF MAKES ME HAPPY THAT WE'RE THE ONLY CLUB MEMBERS!
TEE HEE
TEE HEE
I'M SO IMMATURE!
ボヒーーッ
KABOOM
FURTHERMORE, CLUBS WITHOUT THEIR OWN ROOMS MAY SPREAD THE SCANDALOUS RUMORS IN AN EFFORT TO TAKE YOURS.
EVEN IF YOU DO MANAGE TO KEEP THE ROOM...
...ONCE THE RUMORS START, KOBAYASHI-SAN WILL BE EXPOSED TO THE CURIOUS EYES OF HER CLASSMATES...
...AND HER PARENTS MAY OPPOSE YOUR RELATIONSHIP.

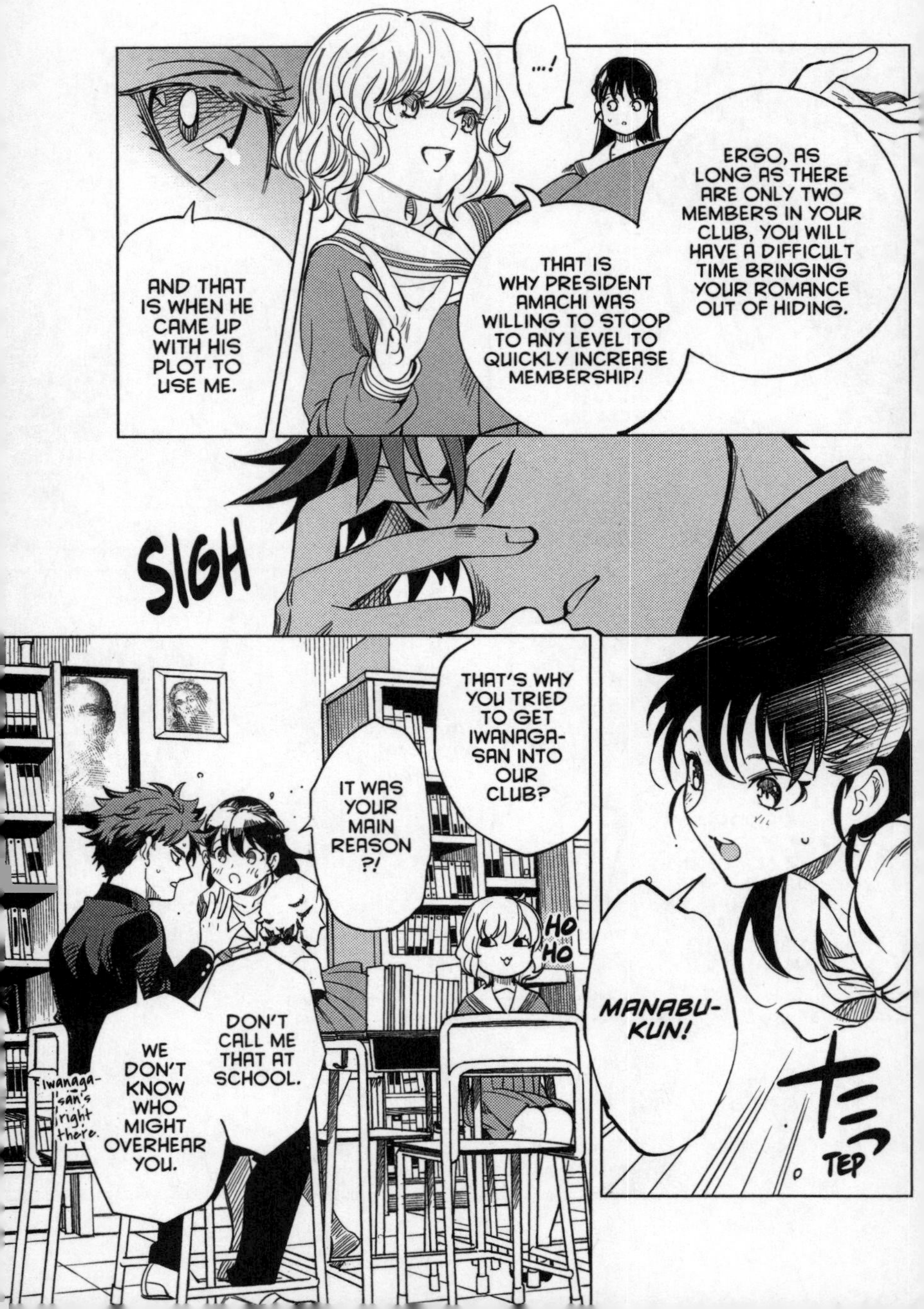
...!
ERGO, AS LONG AS THERE ARE ONLY TWO MEMBERS IN YOUR CLUB, YOU WILL HAVE A DIFFICULT TIME BRINGING YOUR ROMANCE OUT OF HIDING.
THAT IS WHY PRESIDENT AMACHI WAS WILLING TO STOOP TO ANY LEVEL TO QUICKLY INCREASE MEMBERSHIP!
AND THAT IS WHEN HE CAME UP WITH HIS PLOT TO USE ME.
SIGH
MANABU-KUN!
TEP
THAT'S WHY YOU TRIED TO GET IWANAGA-SAN INTO OUR CLUB?
IT WAS YOUR MAIN REASON?!
HO HO
DON'T CALL ME THAT AT SCHOOL.
WE DON'T KNOW WHO MIGHT OVERHEAR YOU.
Iwanaga-san's right there.

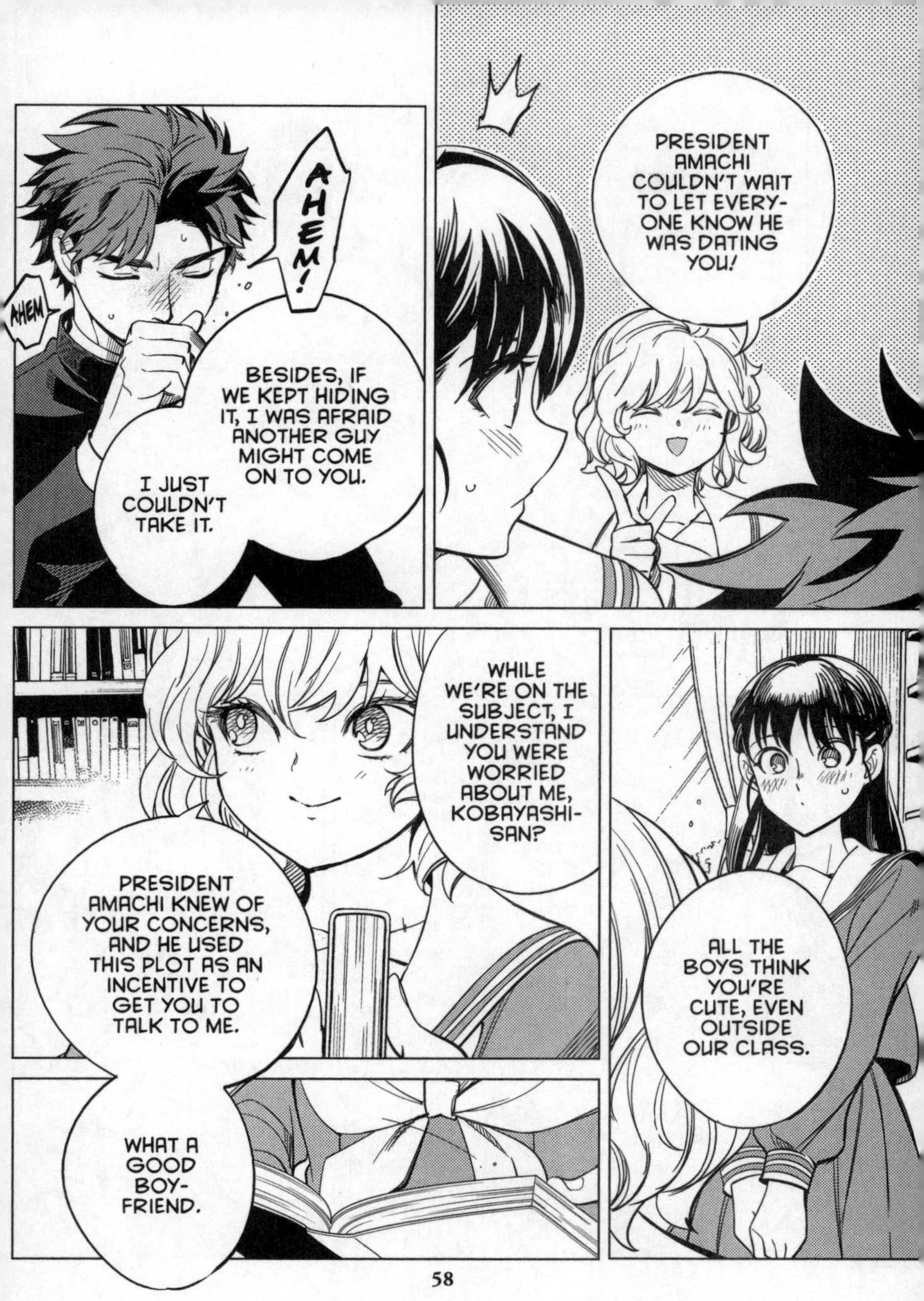
PRESIDENT AMACHI COULDN'T WAIT TO LET EVERY-ONE KNOW HE WAS DATING YOU!
AHEM!
AHEM
BESIDES, IF WE KEPT HIDING IT, I WAS AFRAID ANOTHER GUY MIGHT COME ON TO YOU.
I JUST COULDN'T TAKE IT.
ALL THE BOYS THINK YOU'RE CUTE, EVEN OUTSIDE OUR CLASS.
WHILE WE'RE ON THE SUBJECT, I UNDERSTAND YOU WERE WORRIED ABOUT ME, KOBAYASHI-SAN?
PRESIDENT AMACHI KNEW OF YOUR CONCERNS, AND HE USED THIS PLOT AS AN INCENTIVE TO GET YOU TO TALK TO ME.
WHAT A GOOD BOY-FRIEND.

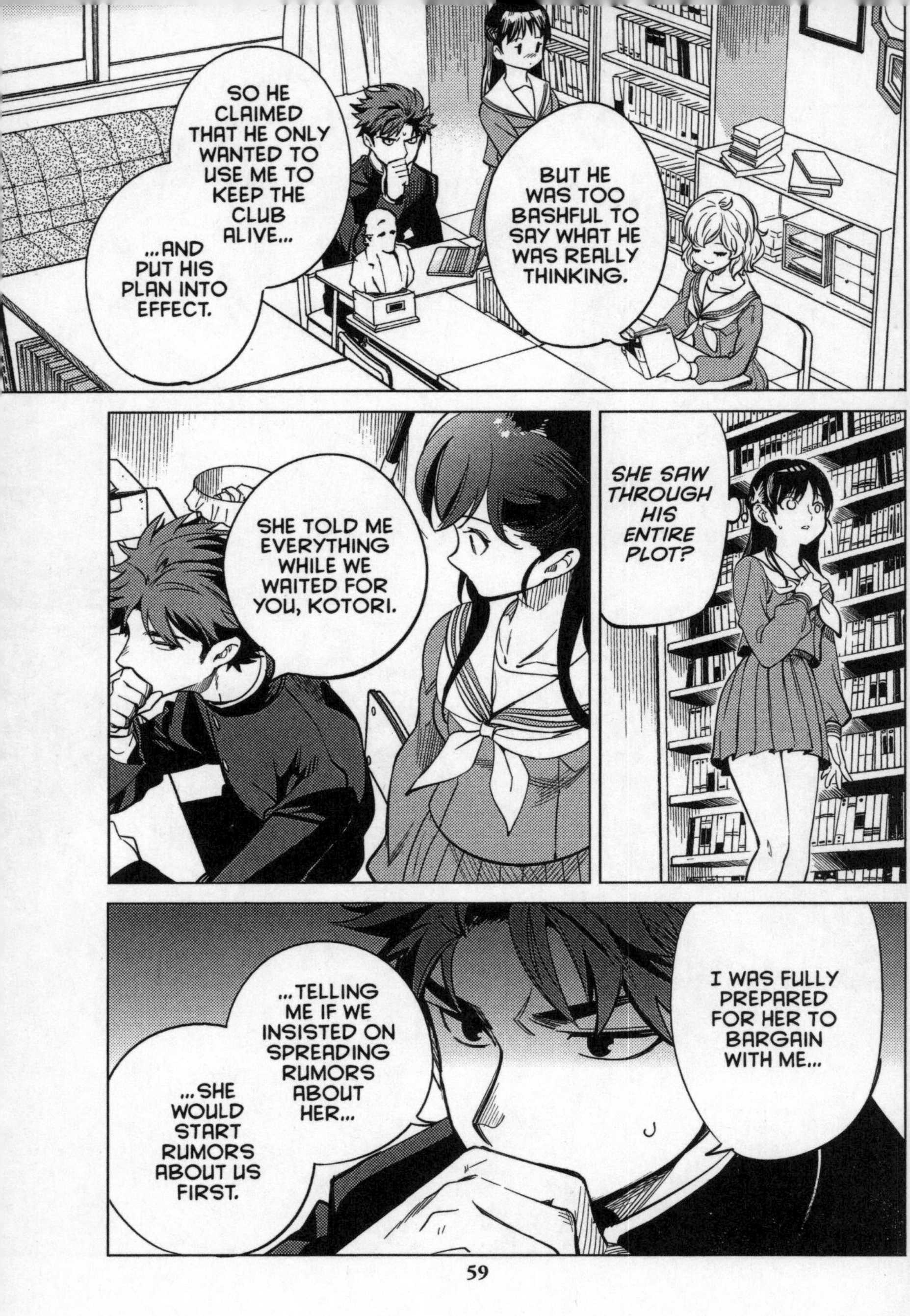
BUT HE WAS TOO BASHFUL TO SAY WHAT HE WAS REALLY THINKING.
SO HE CLAIMED THAT HE ONLY WANTED TO USE ME TO KEEP THE CLUB ALIVE...
...AND PUT HIS PLAN INTO EFFECT.
SHE SAW THROUGH HIS ENTIRE PLOT?
SHE TOLD ME EVERYTHING WHILE WE WAITED FOR YOU, KOTORI.
I WAS FULLY PREPARED FOR HER TO BARGAIN WITH ME...
...TELLING ME IF WE INSISTED ON SPREADING RUMORS ABOUT HER...
...SHE WOULD START RUMORS ABOUT US FIRST.

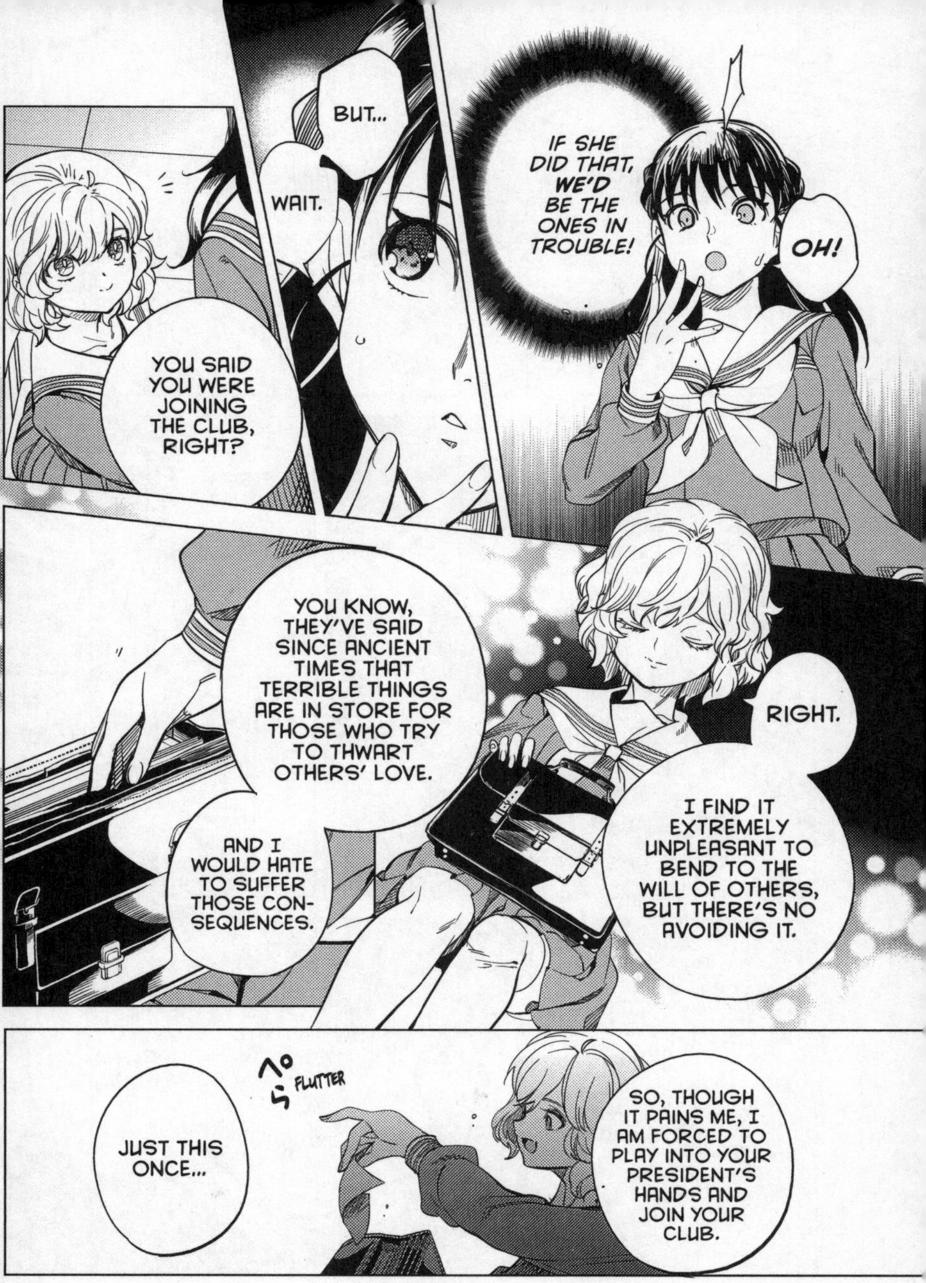
OH!
IF SHE DID THAT, WE'D BE THE ONES IN TROUBLE!
BUT...
WAIT.
YOU SAID YOU WERE JOINING THE CLUB, RIGHT?
RIGHT.
I FIND IT EXTREMELY UNPLEASANT TO BEND TO THE WILL OF OTHERS, BUT THERE'S NO AVOIDING IT.
YOU KNOW, THEY'VE SAID SINCE ANCIENT TIMES THAT TERRIBLE THINGS ARE IN STORE FOR THOSE WHO TRY TO THWART OTHERS' LOVE.
AND I WOULD HATE TO SUFFER THOSE CON-SEQUENCES.
SO, THOUGH IT PAINS ME, I AM FORCED TO PLAY INTO YOUR PRESIDENT'S HANDS AND JOIN YOUR CLUB.
FLUTTER
JUST THIS ONCE...

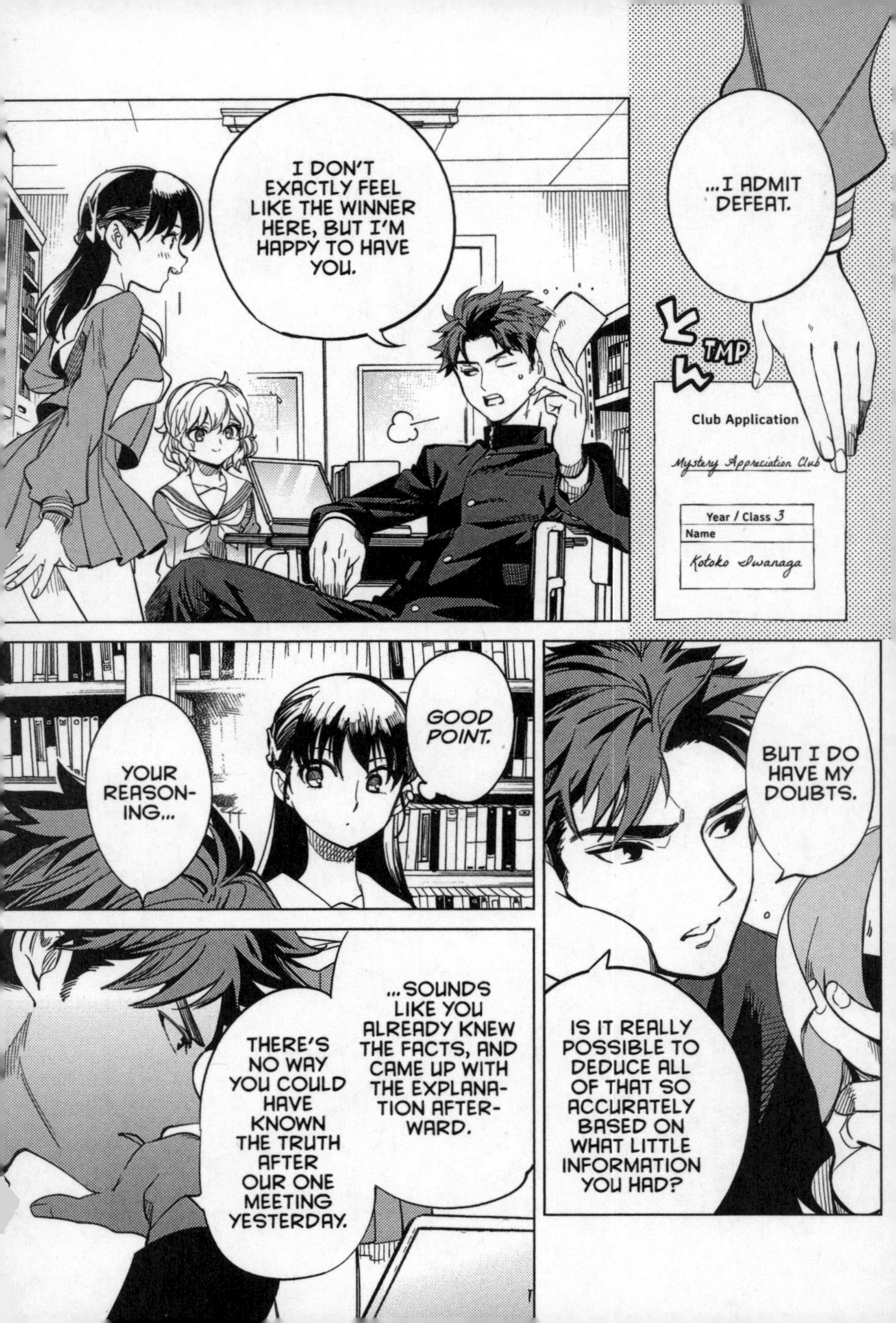
...I ADMIT DEFEAT.
TMP
Club Application
Mystery Appreciation Club
Year / Class 3
Name
Kotoko Iwanaga
I DON'T EXACTLY FEEL LIKE THE WINNER HERE, BUT I'M HAPPY TO HAVE YOU.
BUT I DO HAVE MY DOUBTS.
IS IT REALLY POSSIBLE TO DEDUCE ALL OF THAT SO ACCURATELY BASED ON WHAT LITTLE INFORMATION YOU HAD?
GOOD POINT.
YOUR REASONING...
...SOUNDS LIKE YOU ALREADY KNEW THE FACTS, AND CAME UP WITH THE EXPLANATION AFTERWARD.
THERE'S NO WAY YOU COULD HAVE KNOWN THE TRUTH AFTER OUR ONE MEETING YESTERDAY.

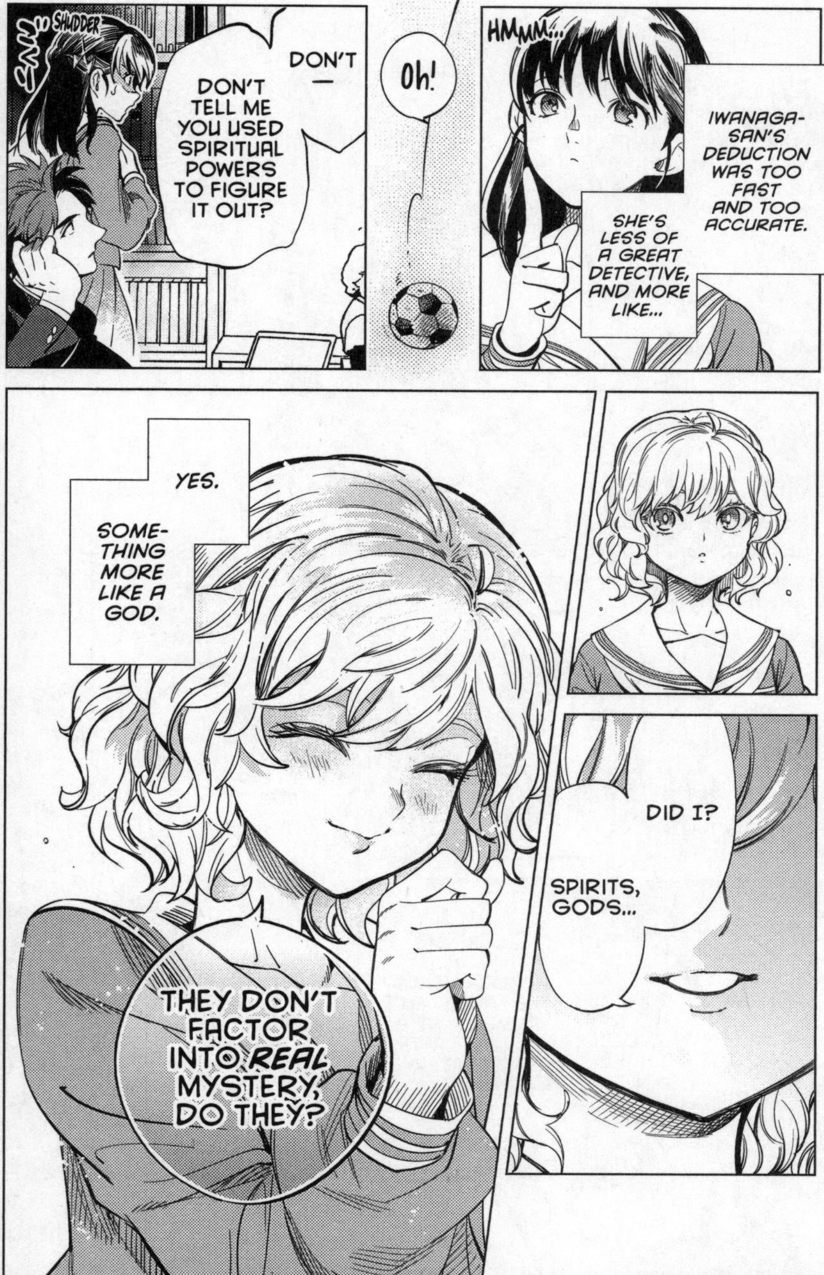
HMMM...
IWANAGA-SAN'S DEDUCTION WAS TOO FAST AND TOO ACCURATE.
SHE'S LESS OF A GREAT DETECTIVE, AND MORE LIKE...
Oh!
SHUDDER
DON'T —
DON'T TELL ME YOU USED SPIRITUAL POWERS TO FIGURE IT OUT?
DID I?
SPIRITS, GODS...
YES.
SOME-THING MORE LIKE A GOD.
THEY DON'T FACTOR INTO *REAL* MYSTERY, DO THEY?

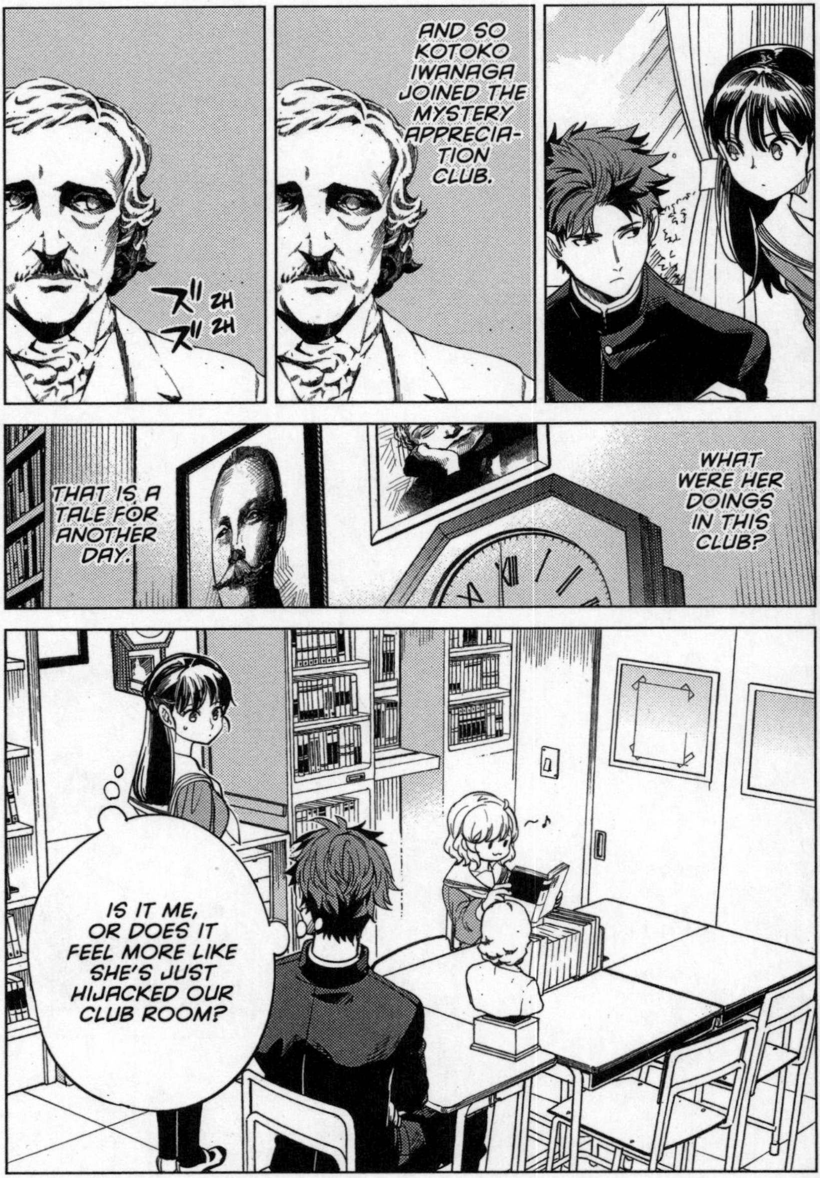
AND SO KOTOKO IWANAGA JOINED THE MYSTERY APPRECIATION CLUB.
ズ ZH
ズ ZH
WHAT WERE HER DOINGS IN THIS CLUB?
THAT IS A TALE FOR ANOTHER DAY.
IS IT ME, OR DOES IT FEEL MORE LIKE SHE'S JUST HIJACKED OUR CLUB ROOM?

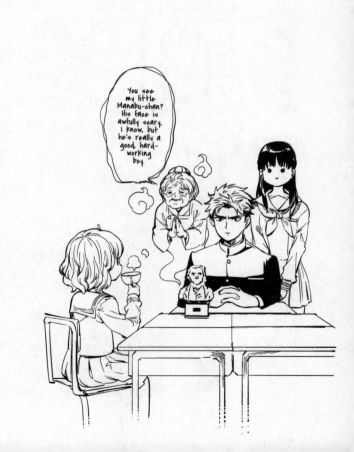

You see my little Manabu-chan? His face is awfully scary, I know, but he's really a good, hard-working boy.

An illustration of the thought: "I wonder if the president's ancestors were there or something."

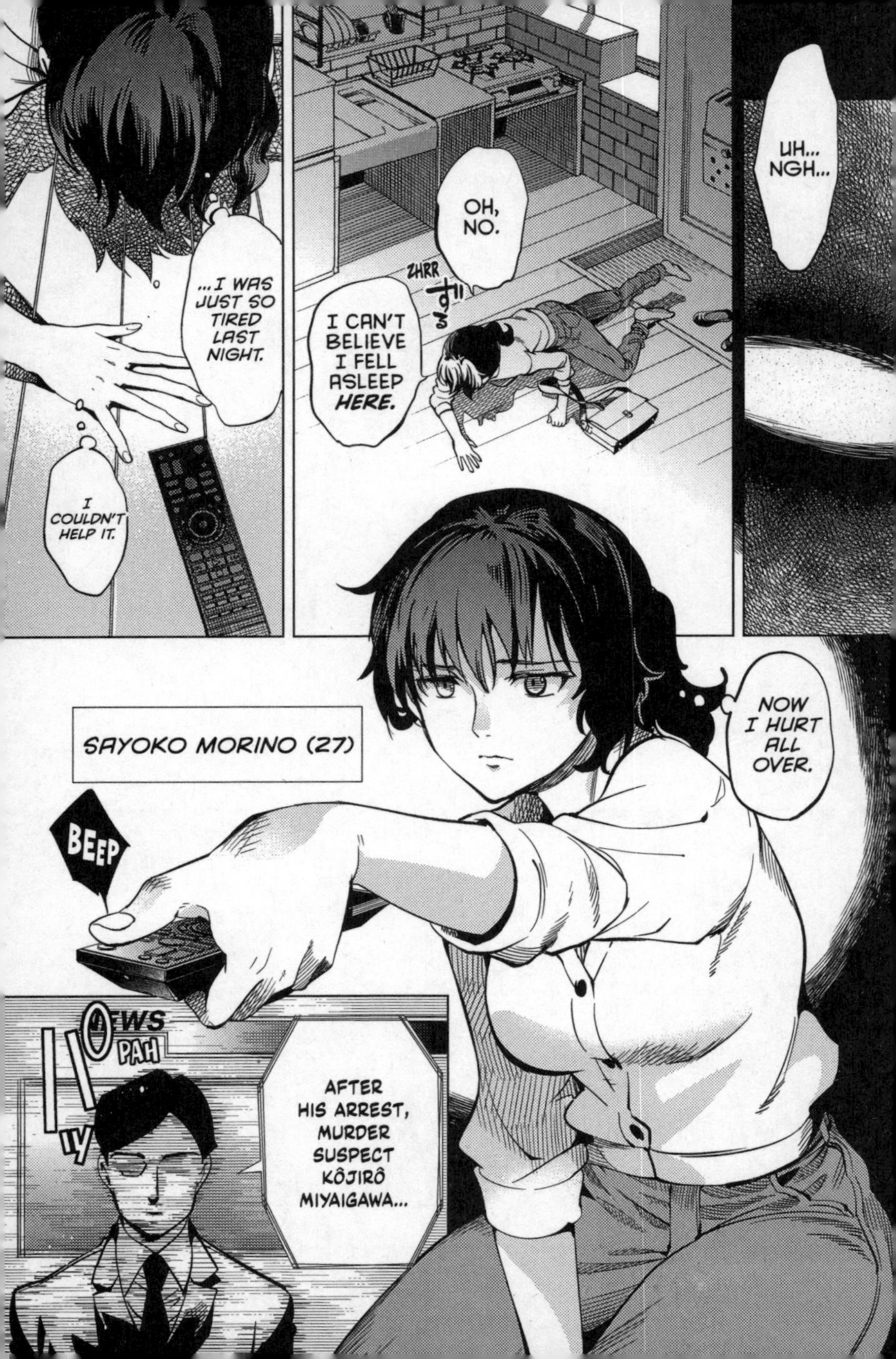
UH... NGH...
OH, NO.
ZHRR
I CAN'T BELIEVE I FELL ASLEEP HERE.
...I WAS JUST SO TIRED LAST NIGHT.
I COULDN'T HELP IT.
NOW I HURT ALL OVER.
SAYOKO MORINO (27)
BEEP
NEWS
PAH
AFTER HIS ARREST, MURDER SUSPECT KÔJIRÔ MIYAIGAWA...

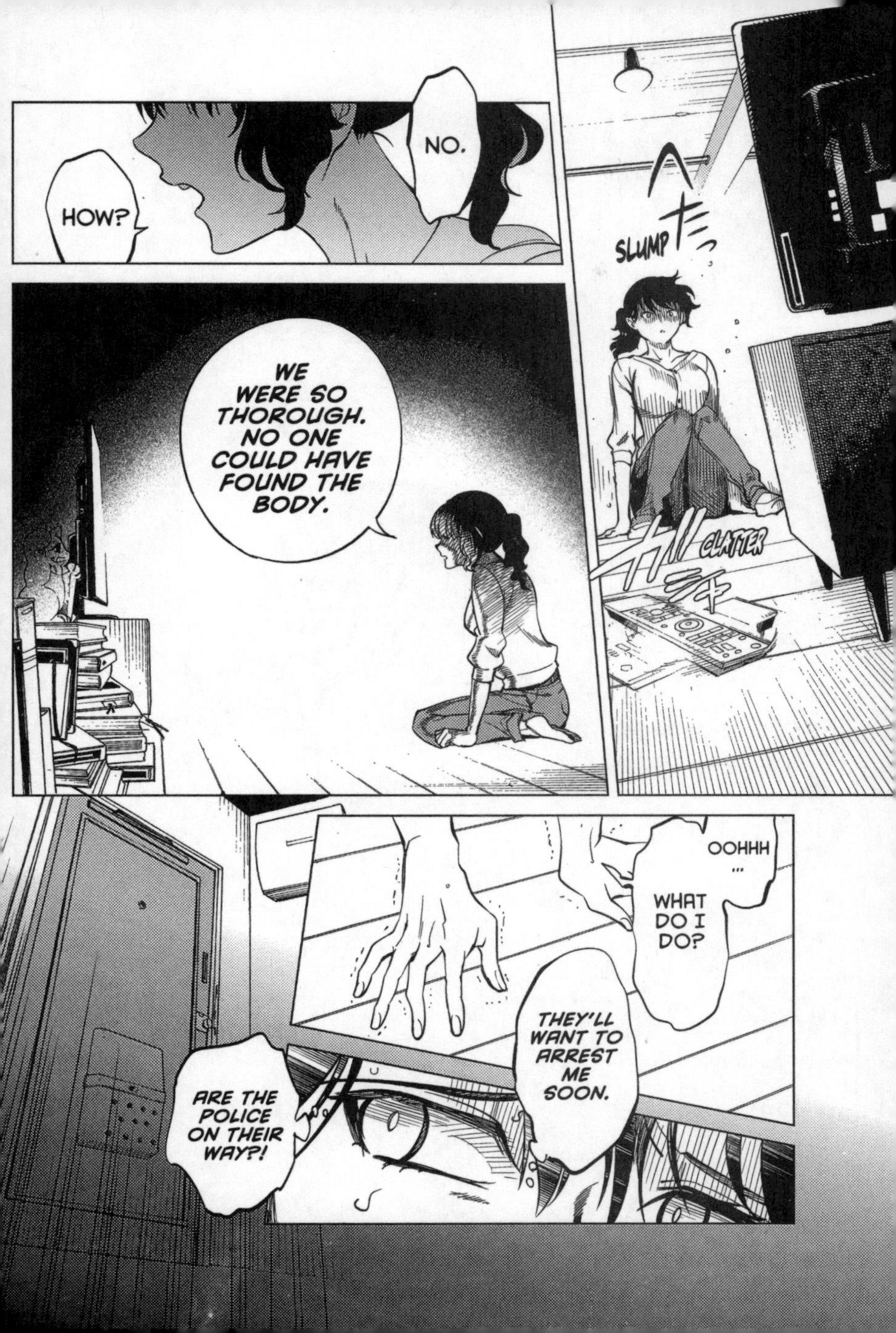
SLUMP
CLATTER
NO.
HOW?
WE WERE SO THOROUGH. NO ONE COULD HAVE FOUND THE BODY.
OOHHH ... WHAT DO I DO?
THEY'LL WANT TO ARREST ME SOON.
ARE THE POLICE ON THEIR WAY?!

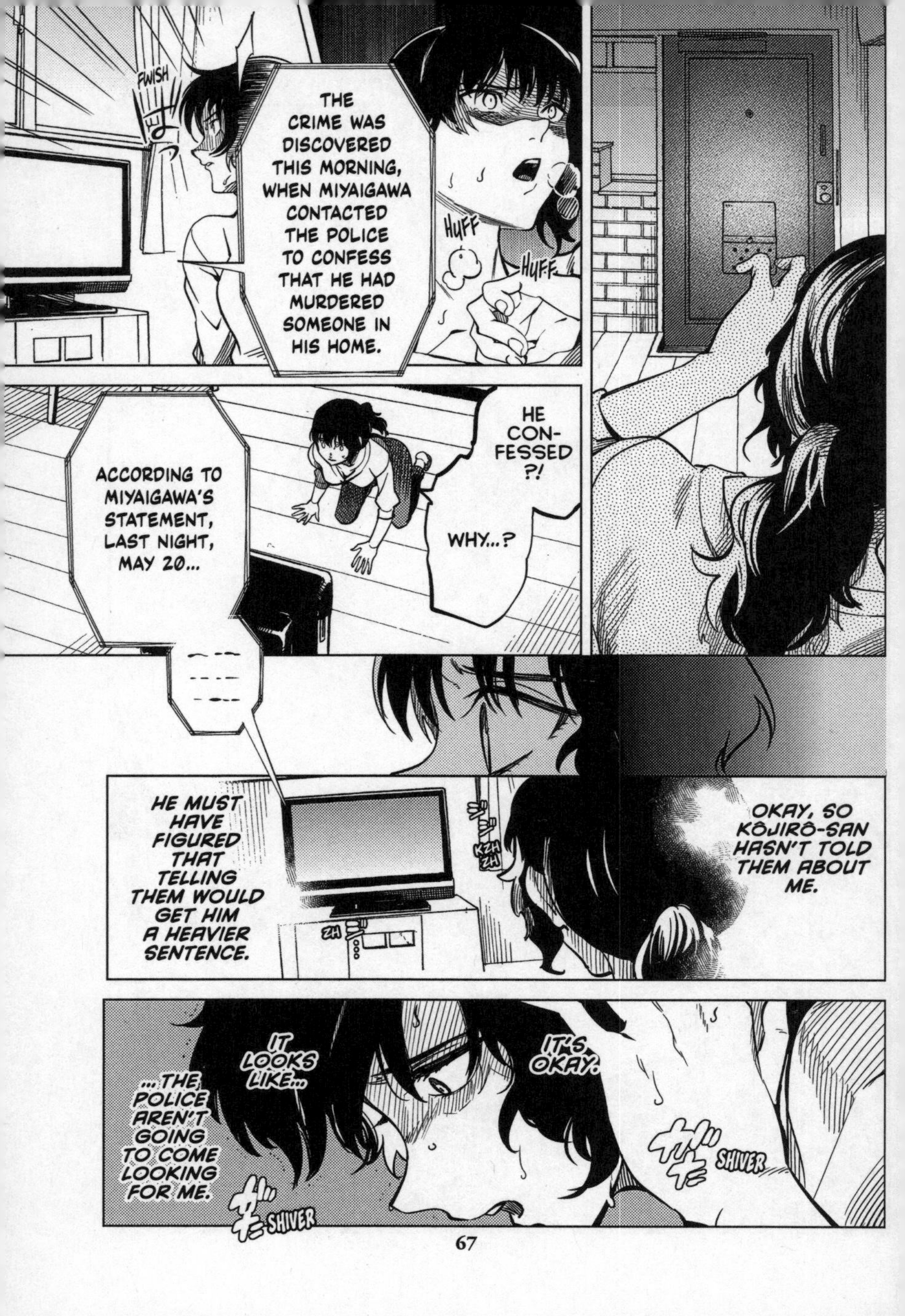
THE CRIME WAS DISCOVERED THIS MORNING, WHEN MIYAIGAWA CONTACTED THE POLICE TO CONFESS THAT HE HAD MURDERED SOMEONE IN HIS HOME.
HUFF
HUFF
FWISH
HE CON-FESSED ?!
WHY...?
ACCORDING TO MIYAIGAWA'S STATEMENT, LAST NIGHT, MAY 20...
OKAY, SO KÔJIRÔ-SAN HASN'T TOLD THEM ABOUT ME.
KZH ZH
HE MUST HAVE FIGURED THAT TELLING THEM WOULD GET HIM A HEAVIER SENTENCE.
ZH
IT'S OKAY.
IT LOOKS LIKE...
...THE POLICE AREN'T GOING TO COME LOOKING FOR ME.
SHIVER
SHIVER

CHAPTER 21: "GUILLOTINE SANSHIRÔ PART ONE"

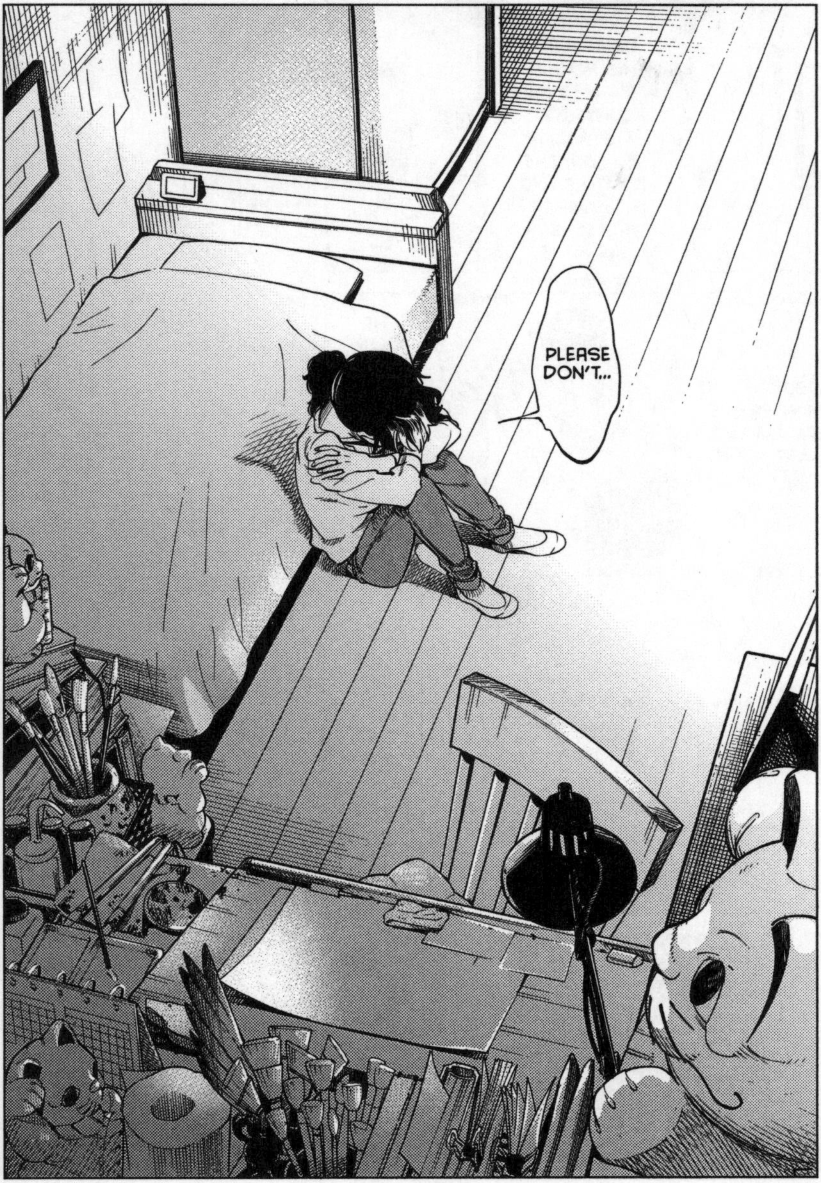
PLEASE DON'T...

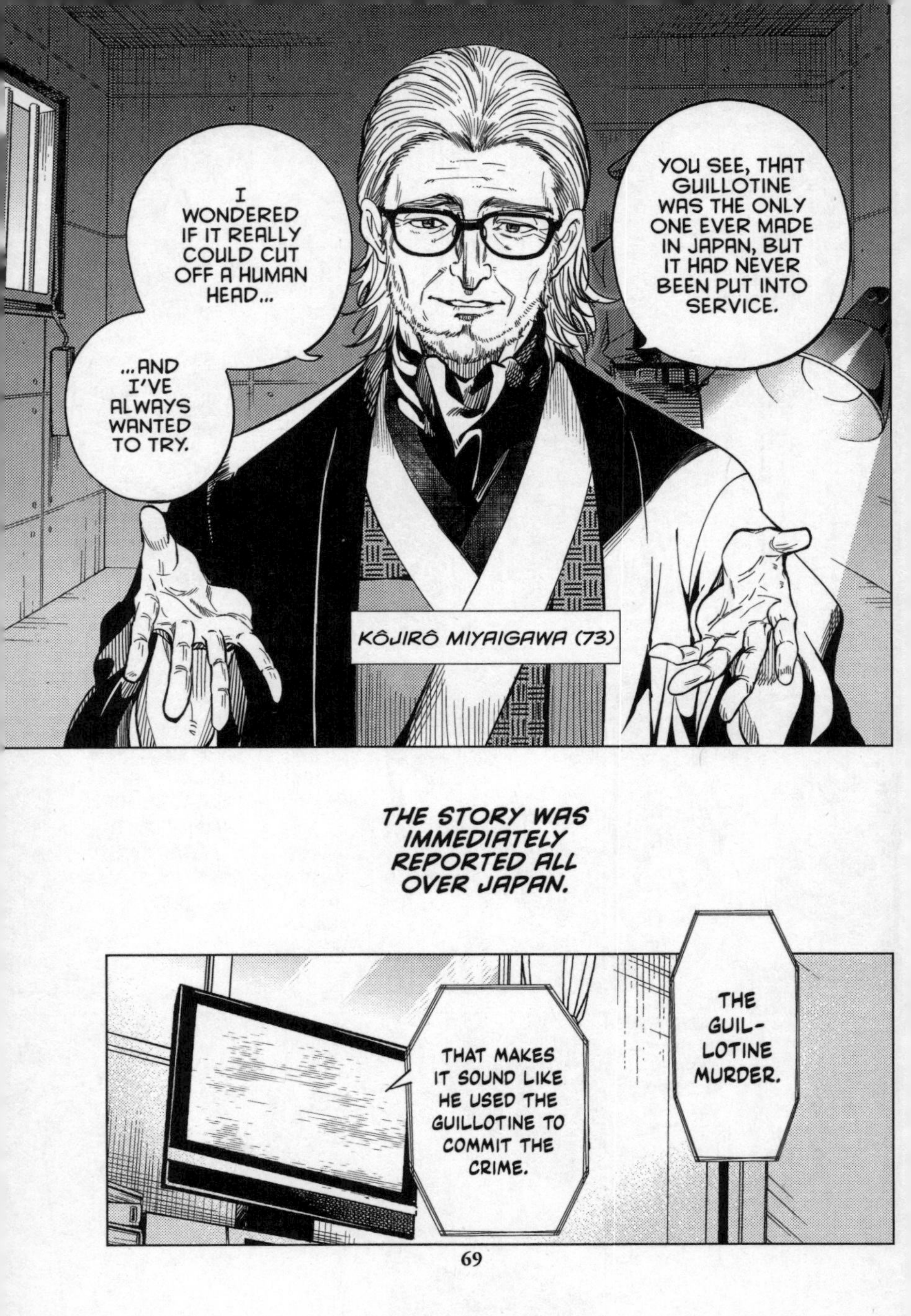
YOU SEE, THAT GUILLOTINE WAS THE ONLY ONE EVER MADE IN JAPAN, BUT IT HAD NEVER BEEN PUT INTO SERVICE.
I WONDERED IF IT REALLY COULD CUT OFF A HUMAN HEAD...
...AND I'VE ALWAYS WANTED TO TRY.
KÔJIRÔ MIYAIGAWA (73)
THE STORY WAS IMMEDIATELY REPORTED ALL OVER JAPAN.
THE GUIL-LOTINE MURDER.
THAT MAKES IT SOUND LIKE HE USED THE GUILLOTINE TO COMMIT THE CRIME.

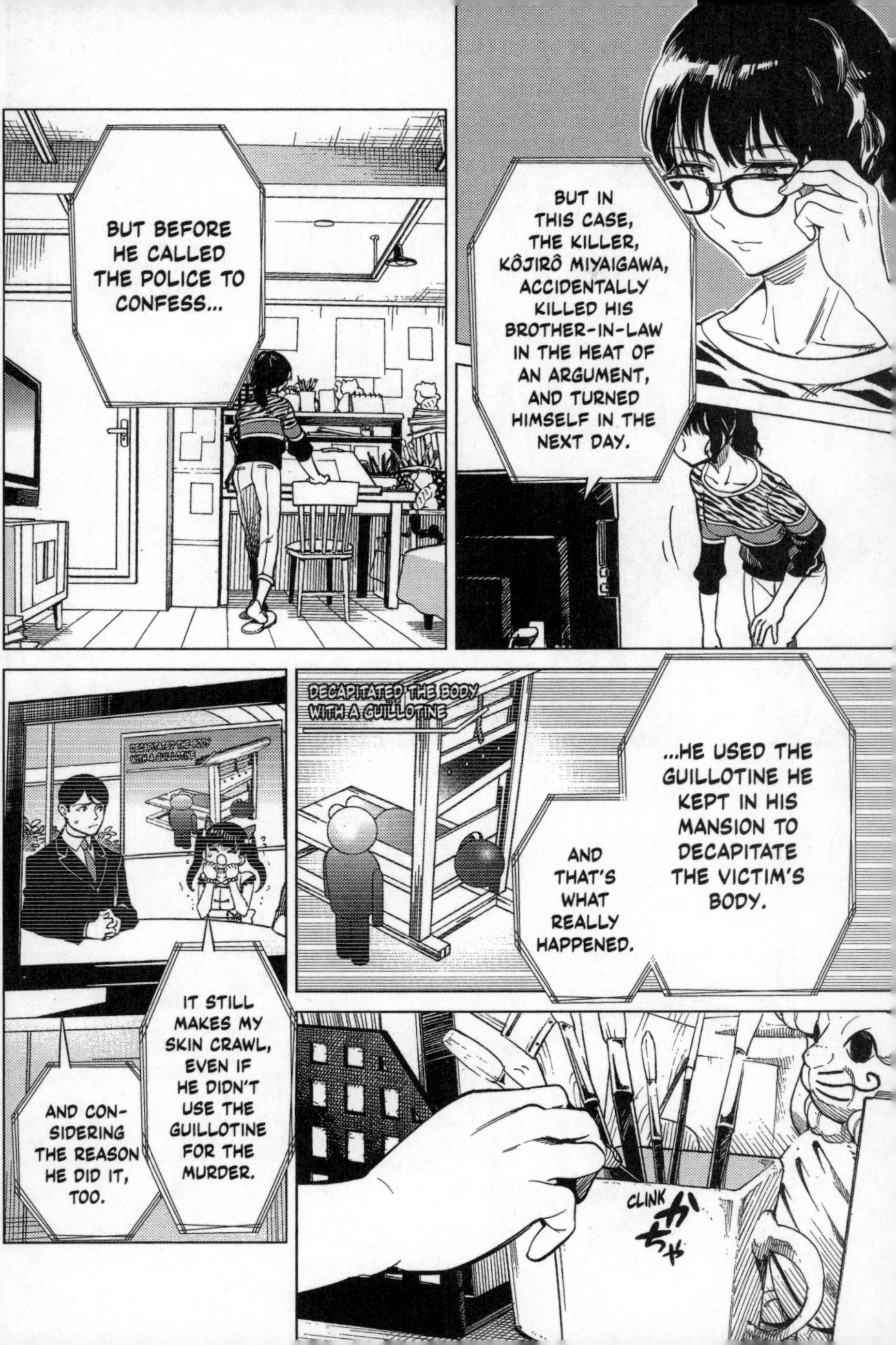
BUT IN THIS CASE, THE KILLER, KÔJIRÔ MIYAIGAWA, ACCIDENTALLY KILLED HIS BROTHER-IN-LAW IN THE HEAT OF AN ARGUMENT, AND TURNED HIMSELF IN THE NEXT DAY.
BUT BEFORE HE CALLED THE POLICE TO CONFESS...
...HE USED THE GUILLOTINE HE KEPT IN HIS MANSION TO DECAPITATE THE VICTIM'S BODY.
AND THAT'S WHAT REALLY HAPPENED.
DECAPITATED THE BODY WITH A GUILLOTINE
DECAPITATED THE BODY WITH A GUILLOTINE
CLINK
かちゃ
IT STILL MAKES MY SKIN CRAWL, EVEN IF HE DIDN'T USE THE GUILLOTINE FOR THE MURDER.
AND CON-SIDERING THE REASON HE DID IT, TOO.

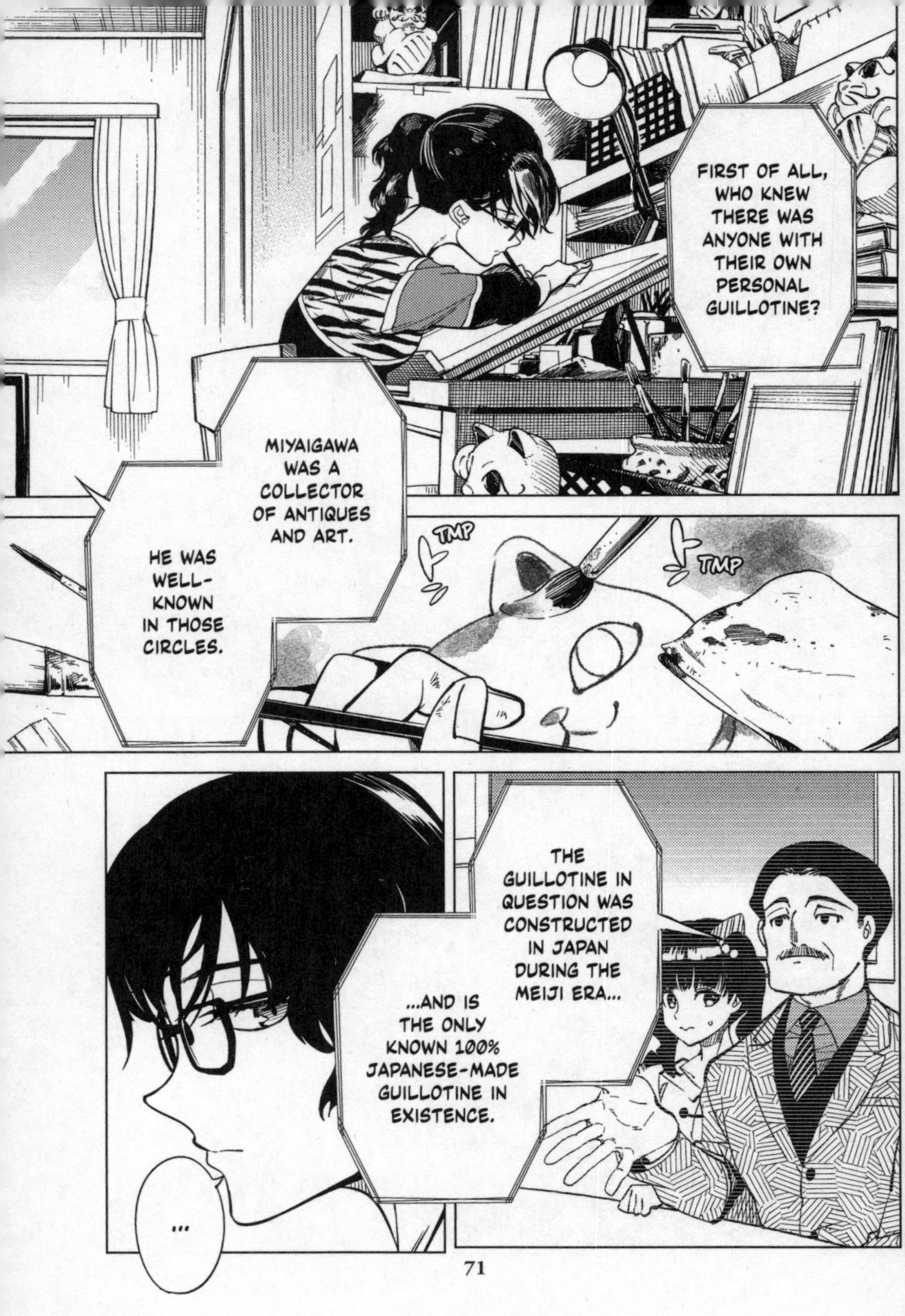
FIRST OF ALL, WHO KNEW THERE WAS ANYONE WITH THEIR OWN PERSONAL GUILLOTINE?
MIYAIGAWA WAS A COLLECTOR OF ANTIQUES AND ART.
HE WAS WELL-KNOWN IN THOSE CIRCLES.
TMP
TMP
THE GUILLOTINE IN QUESTION WAS CONSTRUCTED IN JAPAN DURING THE MEIJI ERA...
...AND IS THE ONLY KNOWN 100% JAPANESE-MADE GUILLOTINE IN EXISTENCE.
...

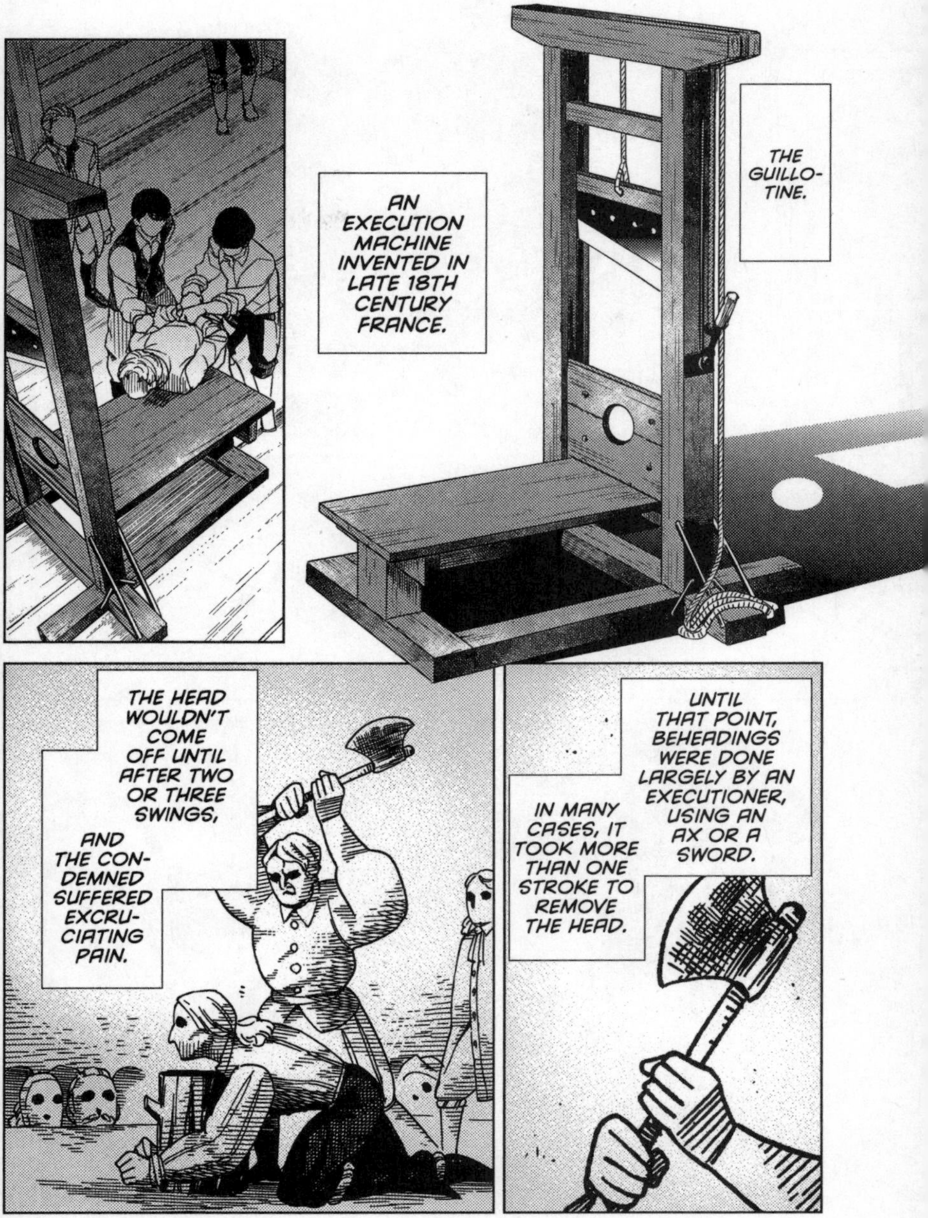
THE GUILLOTINE.
AN EXECUTION MACHINE INVENTED IN LATE 18TH CENTURY FRANCE.
UNTIL THAT POINT, BEHEADINGS WERE DONE LARGELY BY AN EXECUTIONER, USING AN AX OR A SWORD.
IN MANY CASES, IT TOOK MORE THAN ONE STROKE TO REMOVE THE HEAD.
THE HEAD WOULDN'T COME OFF UNTIL AFTER TWO OR THREE SWINGS,
AND THE CONDEMNED SUFFERED EXCRUCIATING PAIN.

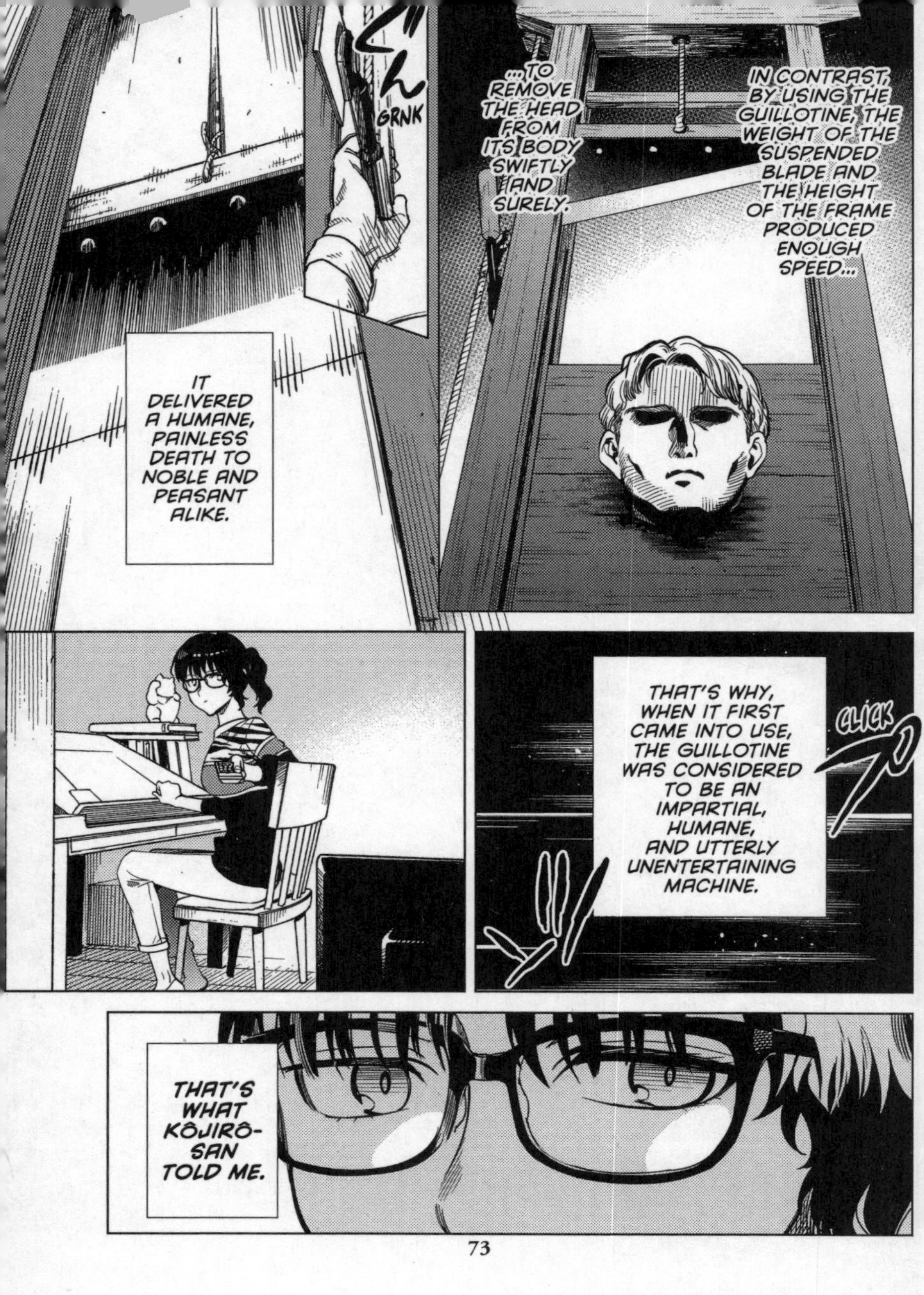
IN CONTRAST, BY USING THE GUILLOTINE, THE WEIGHT OF THE SUSPENDED BLADE AND THE HEIGHT OF THE FRAME PRODUCED ENOUGH SPEED...
...TO REMOVE THE HEAD FROM ITS BODY SWIFTLY AND SURELY.
ぐん
GRNK
IT DELIVERED A HUMANE, PAINLESS DEATH TO NOBLE AND PEASANT ALIKE.
CLICK
THAT'S WHY, WHEN IT FIRST CAME INTO USE, THE GUILLOTINE WAS CONSIDERED TO BE AN IMPARTIAL, HUMANE, AND UTTERLY UNENTERTAINING MACHINE.
THAT'S WHAT KÔJIRÔ-SAN TOLD ME.

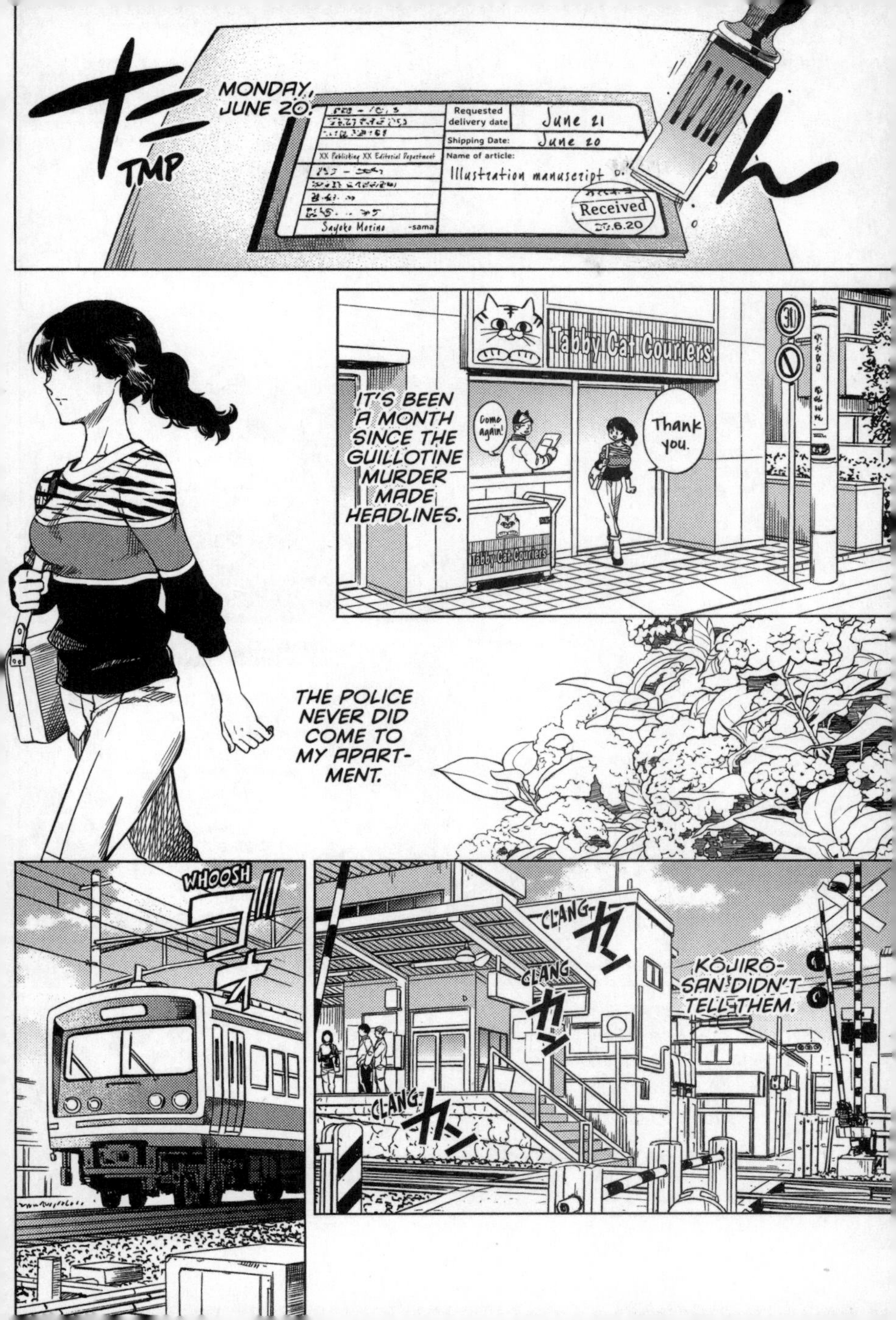
TMP
MONDAY, JUNE 20.
Requested delivery date
June 21
Shipping Date:
June 20
Name of article:
Illustration manuscript
XX Publishing XX Editorial Department
Sayoko Morino -sama
Received
20.6.20
Tabby Cat Couriers
Thank you.
Come again!
IT'S BEEN A MONTH SINCE THE GUILLOTINE MURDER MADE HEADLINES.
Tabby Cat Couriers
THE POLICE NEVER DID COME TO MY APART-MENT.
KÔJIRÔ-SAN DIDN'T TELL THEM.
CLANG
CLANG
CLANG
WHOOSH

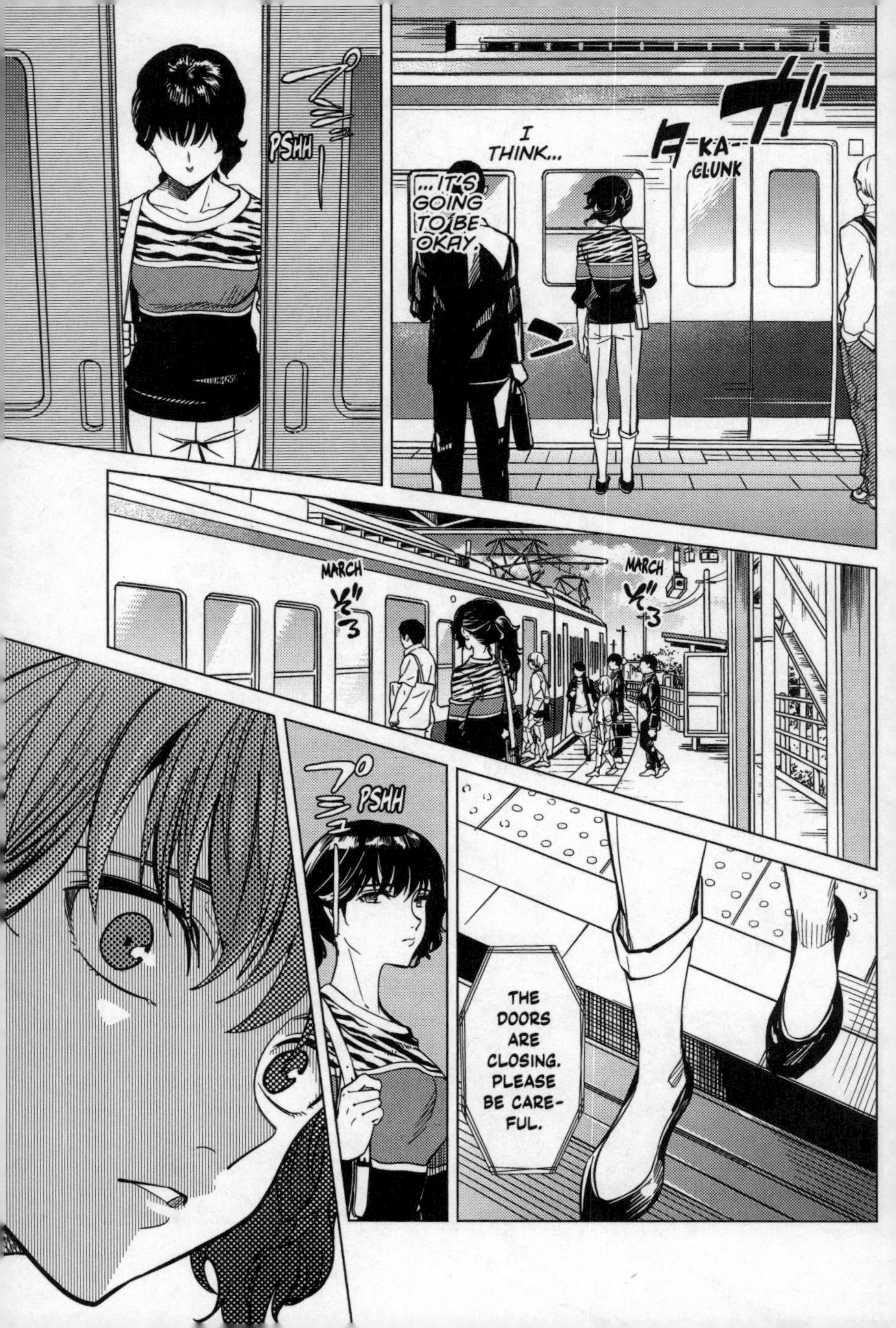
KA-CLUNK
I THINK...
...IT'S GOING TO BE OKAY.
PSHH
MARCH
MARCH
THE DOORS ARE CLOSING. PLEASE BE CARE-FUL.
PSHH

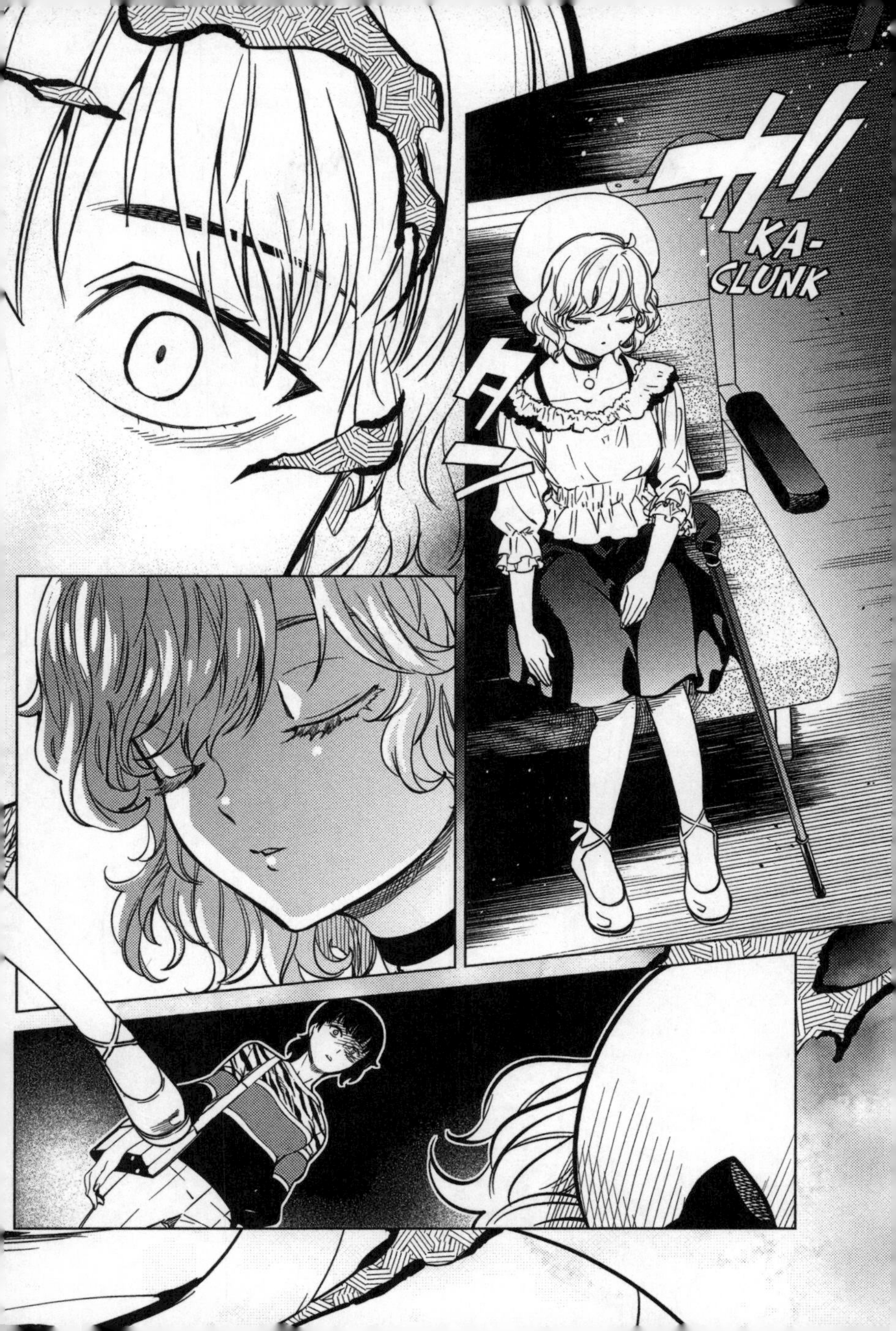
KA-
CLUNK

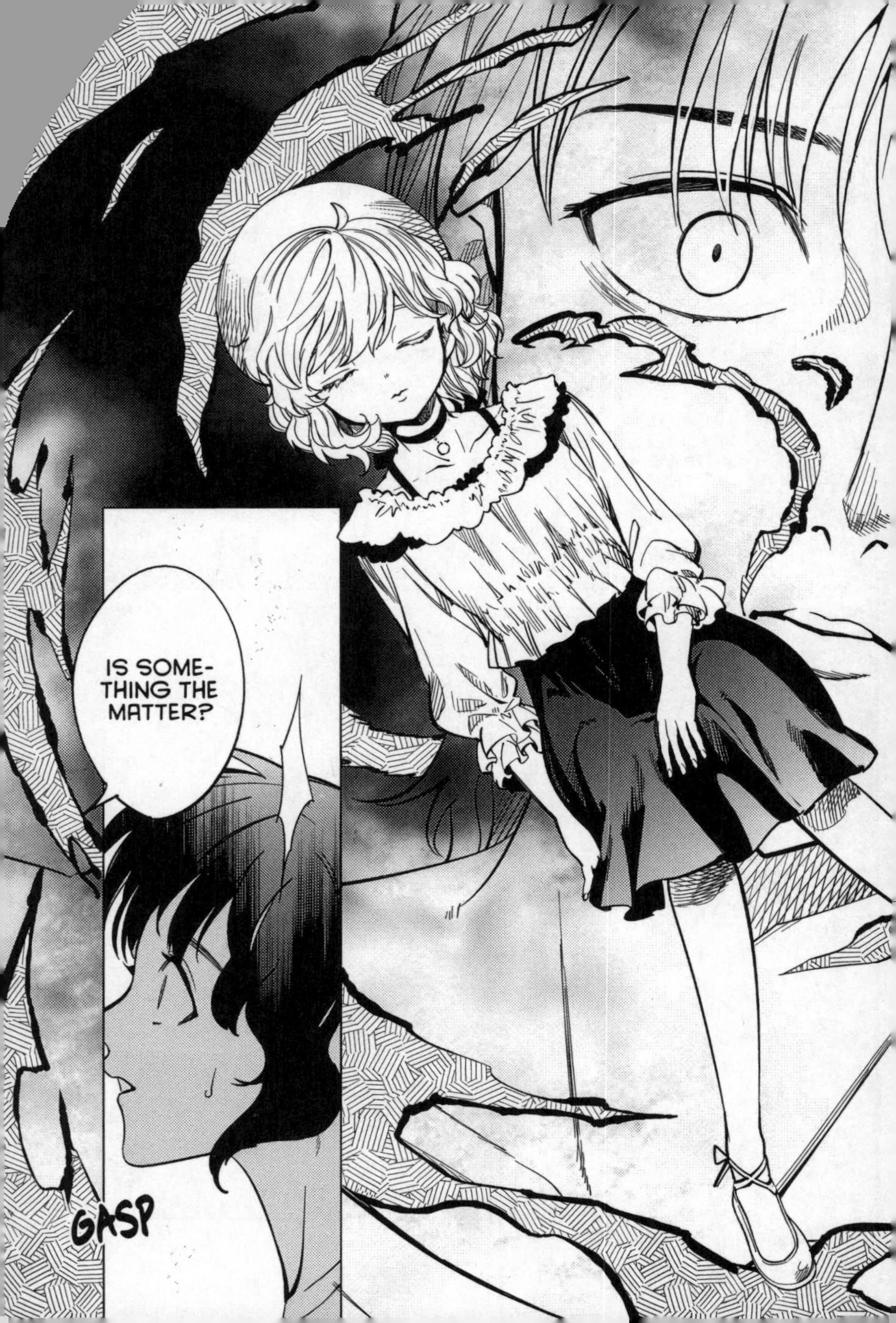
IS SOME-THING THE MATTER?
GASP

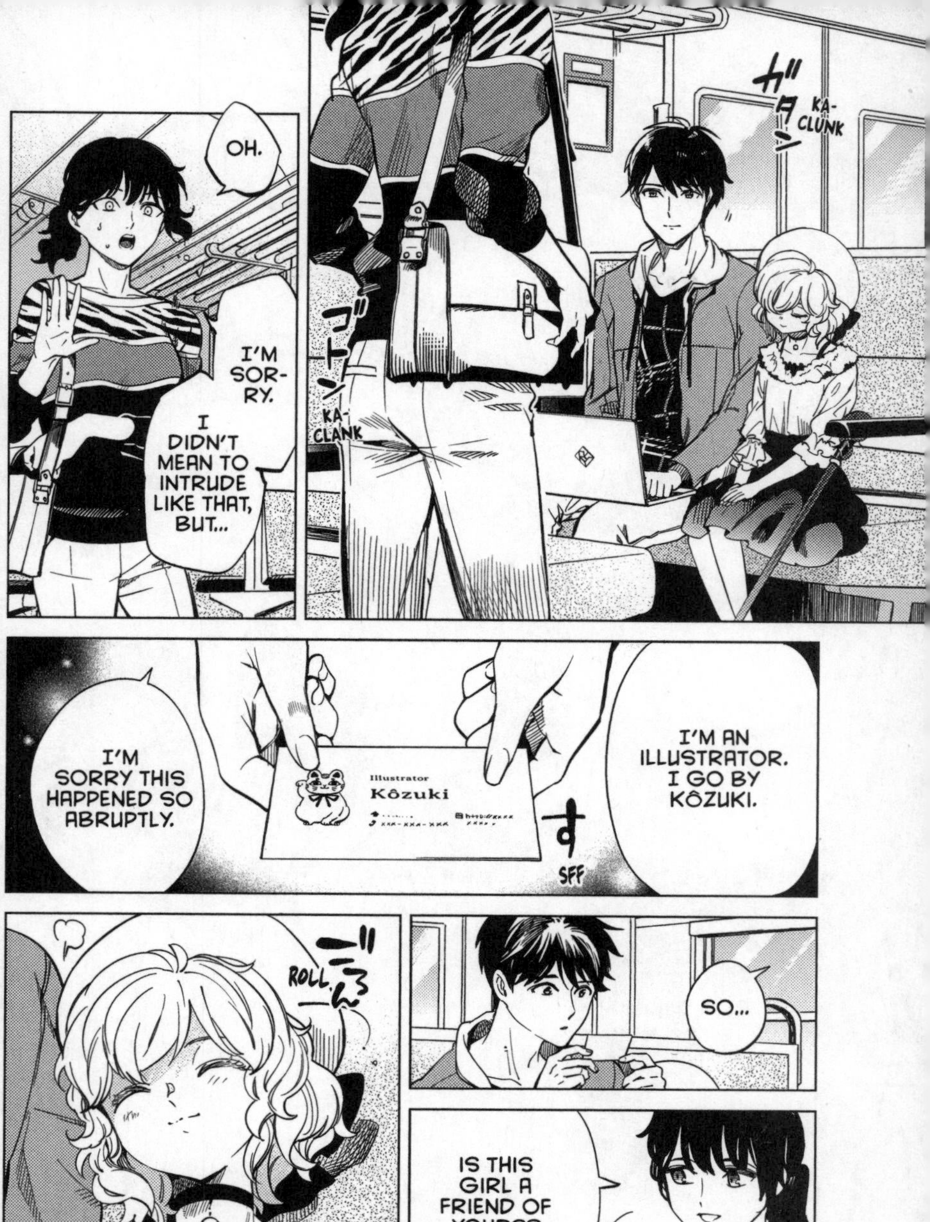
ガタン
KA-CLUNK
ゴトン
KA-CLANK
OH.
I'M SORRY.
I DIDN'T MEAN TO INTRUDE LIKE THAT, BUT...
I'M AN ILLUSTRATOR. I GO BY KÔZUKI.
す
SFF
Illustrator
Kôzuki
I'M SORRY THIS HAPPENED SO ABRUPTLY.
SO...
IS THIS GIRL A FRIEND OF YOURS?
ごろん
ROLL

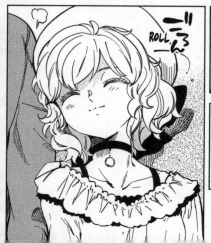

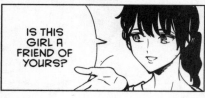

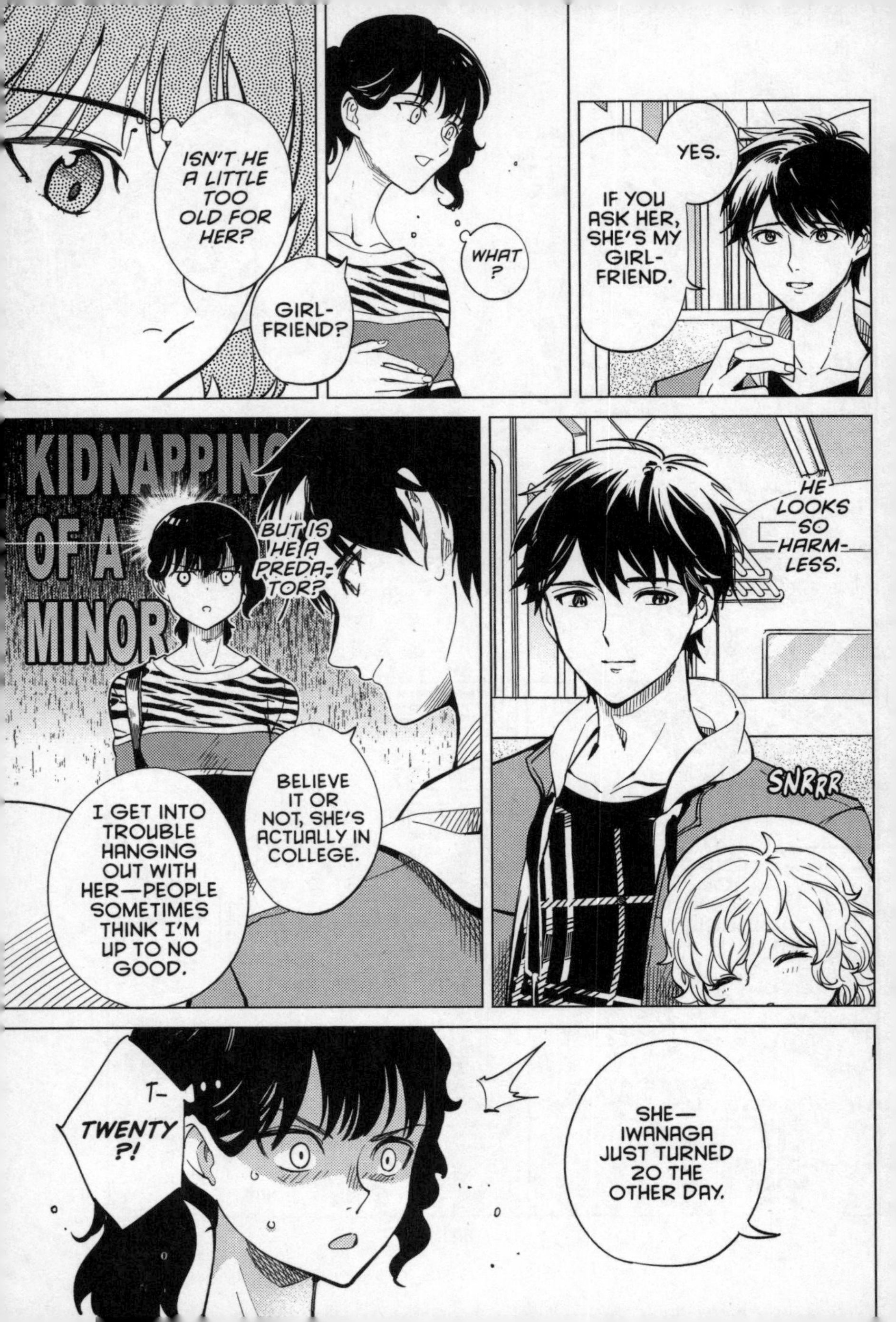
YES.
IF YOU ASK HER, SHE'S MY GIRL-FRIEND.
WHAT?
GIRL-FRIEND?
ISN'T HE A LITTLE TOO OLD FOR HER?
HE LOOKS SO HARM-LESS.
SNRRR
KIDNAPPING OF A MINOR
BUT IS HE A PREDA-TOR?
BELIEVE IT OR NOT, SHE'S ACTUALLY IN COLLEGE.
I GET INTO TROUBLE HANGING OUT WITH HER—PEOPLE SOMETIMES THINK I'M UP TO NO GOOD.
SHE—IWANAGA JUST TURNED 20 THE OTHER DAY.
T-TWENTY?!

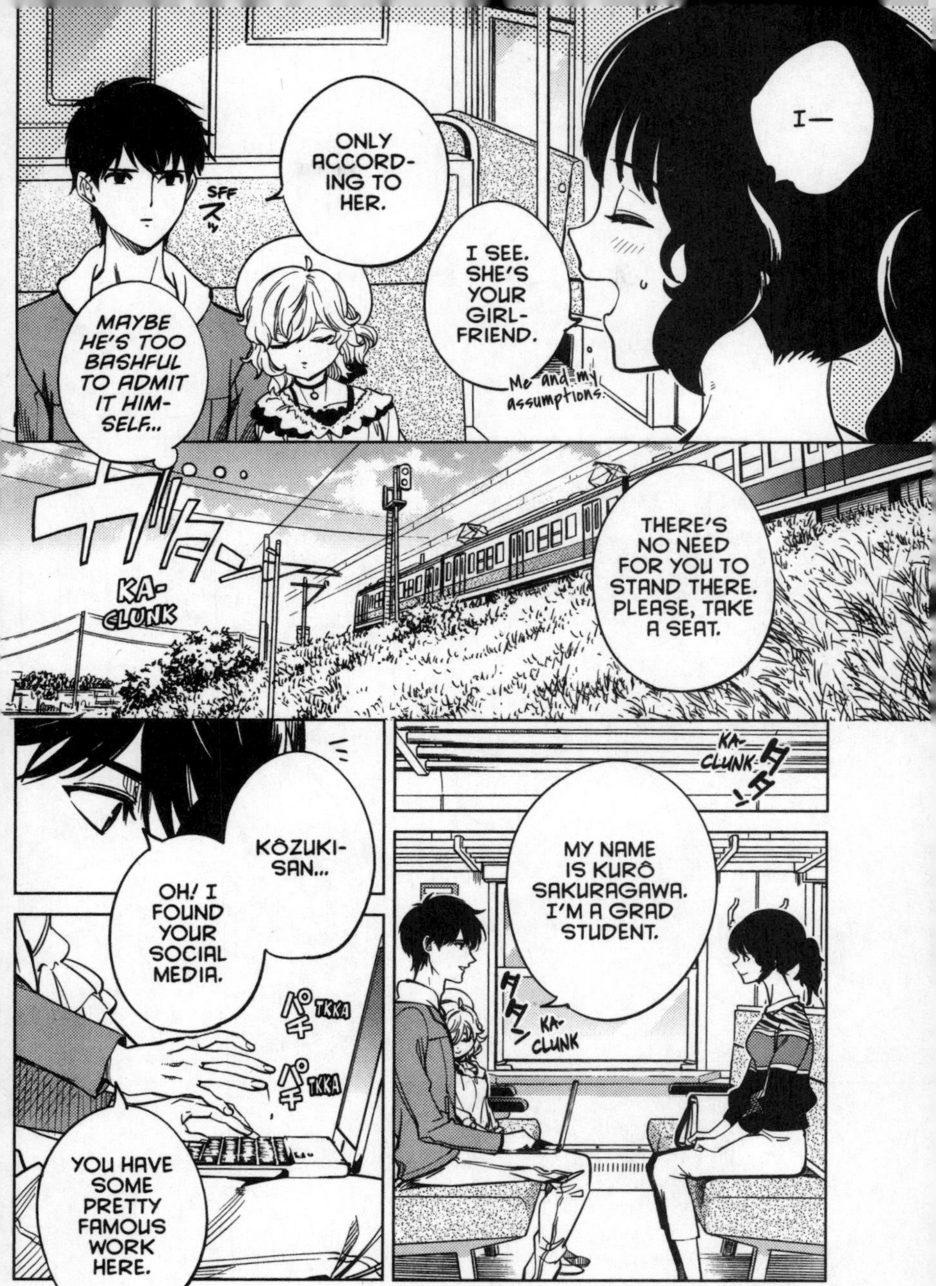
I—
I SEE. SHE'S YOUR GIRLFRIEND.
ONLY ACCORDING TO HER.
SFF
Me and my assumptions.
MAYBE HE'S TOO BASHFUL TO ADMIT IT HIMSELF...
THERE'S NO NEED FOR YOU TO STAND THERE. PLEASE, TAKE A SEAT.
KA-CLUNK
KA-CLUNK
MY NAME IS KURÔ SAKURAGAWA. I'M A GRAD STUDENT.
KA-CLUNK
KÔZUKI-SAN...
OH! I FOUND YOUR SOCIAL MEDIA.
TKKA
TKKA
YOU HAVE SOME PRETTY FAMOUS WORK HERE.

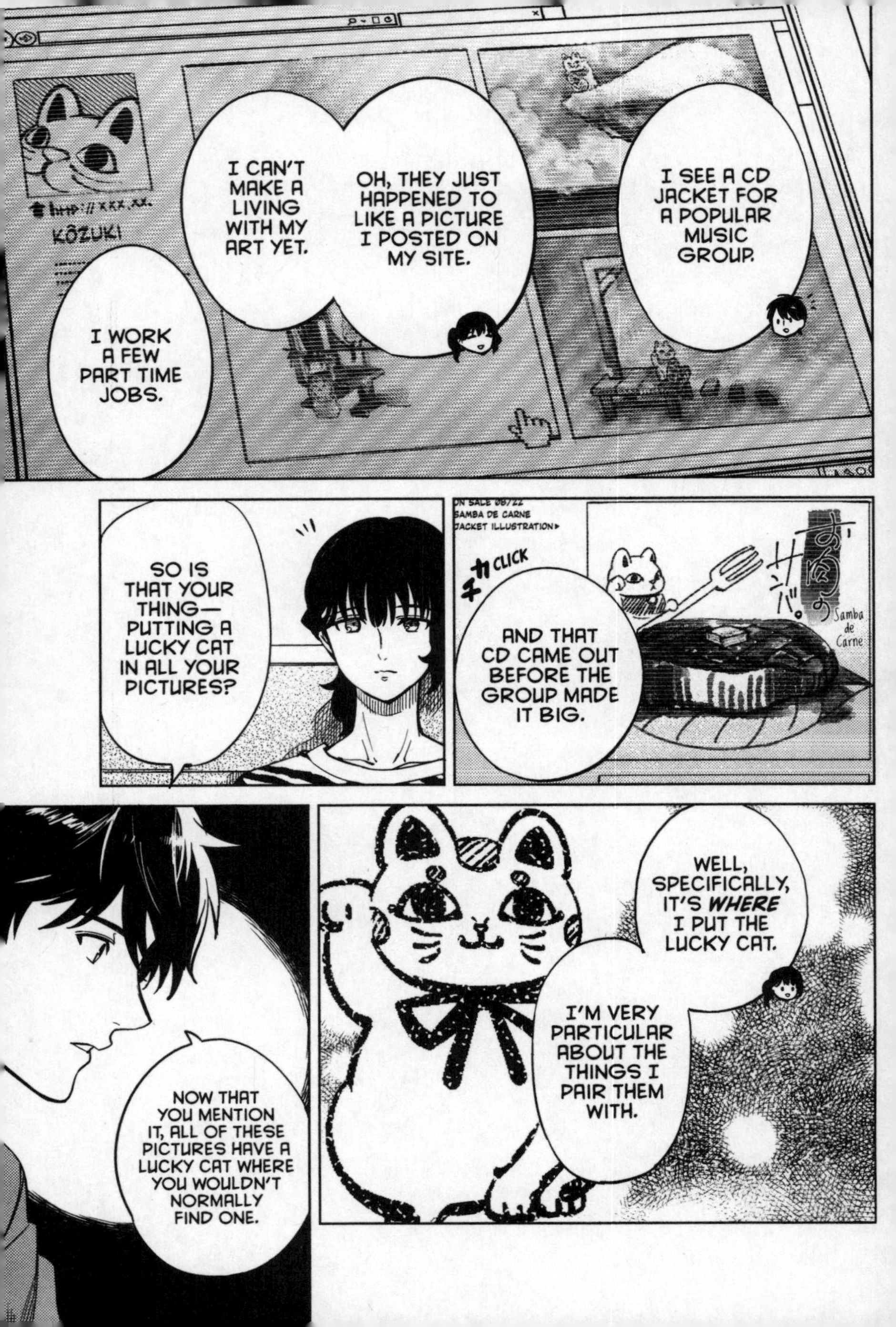
KŌZUKI
I SEE A CD JACKET FOR A POPULAR MUSIC GROUP.
OH, THEY JUST HAPPENED TO LIKE A PICTURE I POSTED ON MY SITE.
I CAN'T MAKE A LIVING WITH MY ART YET.
I WORK A FEW PART TIME JOBS.
ON SALE 08/22
SAMBA DE CARNE
JACKET ILLUSTRATION▸
CLICK
AND THAT CD CAME OUT BEFORE THE GROUP MADE IT BIG.
Samba de Carne
SO IS THAT YOUR THING—PUTTING A LUCKY CAT IN ALL YOUR PICTURES?
WELL, SPECIFICALLY, IT'S *WHERE* I PUT THE LUCKY CAT.
I'M VERY PARTICULAR ABOUT THE THINGS I PAIR THEM WITH.
NOW THAT YOU MENTION IT, ALL OF THESE PICTURES HAVE A LUCKY CAT WHERE YOU WOULDN'T NORMALLY FIND ONE.

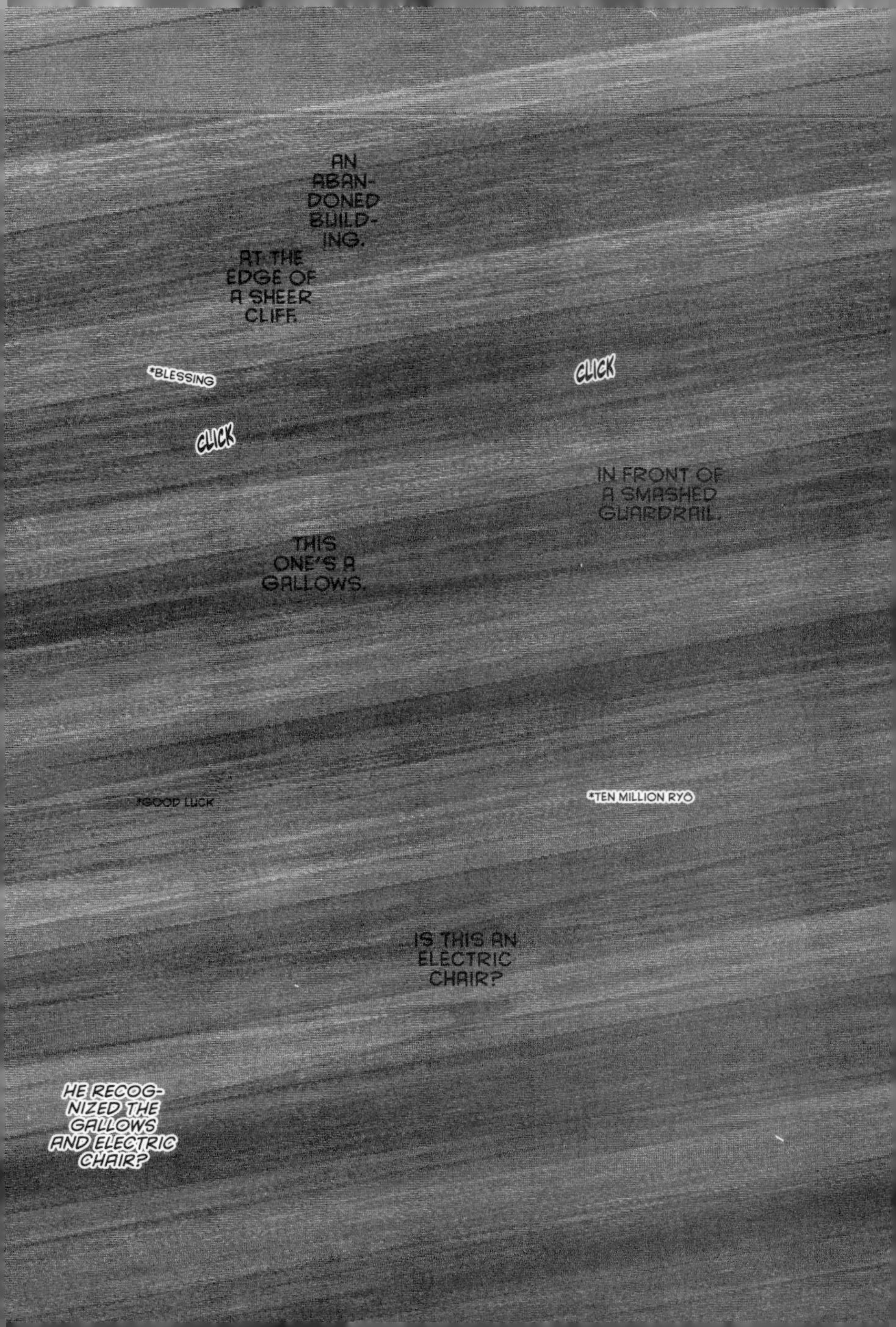
AN ABANDONED BUILDING.
AT THE EDGE OF A SHEER CLIFF.
CLICK
*BLESSING
IN FRONT OF A SMASHED GUARDRAIL.
CLICK
THIS ONE'S A GALLOWS.
*TEN MILLION RYŌ
*GOOD LUCK
IS THIS AN ELECTRIC CHAIR?
HE RECOGNIZED THE GALLOWS AND ELECTRIC CHAIR?

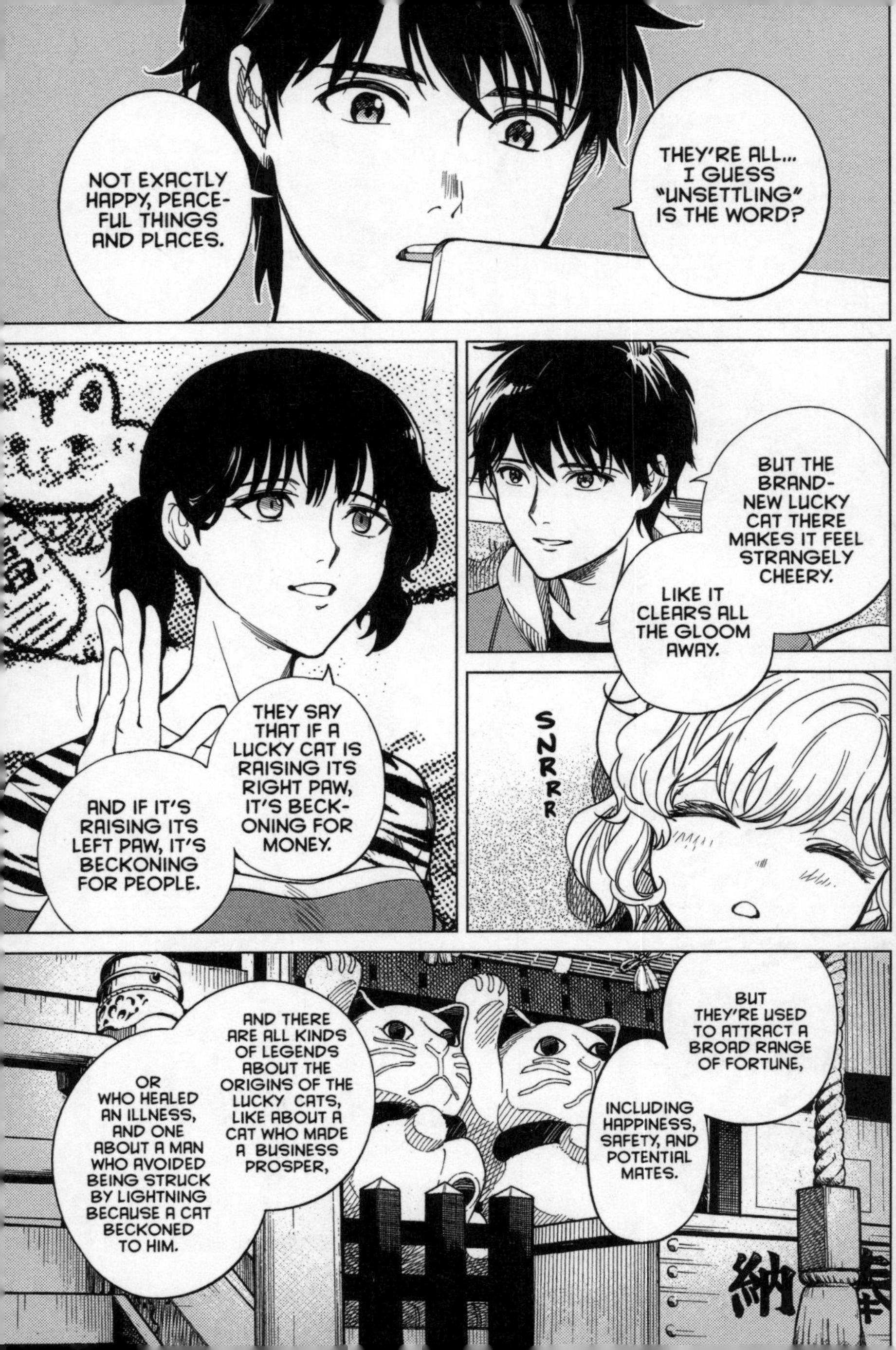
THEY'RE ALL... I GUESS "UNSETTLING" IS THE WORD?
NOT EXACTLY HAPPY, PEACE-FUL THINGS AND PLACES.
BUT THE BRAND-NEW LUCKY CAT THERE MAKES IT FEEL STRANGELY CHEERY.
LIKE IT CLEARS ALL THE GLOOM AWAY.
SNRRR
THEY SAY THAT IF A LUCKY CAT IS RAISING ITS RIGHT PAW, IT'S BECK-ONING FOR MONEY.
AND IF IT'S RAISING ITS LEFT PAW, IT'S BECKONING FOR PEOPLE.
BUT THEY'RE USED TO ATTRACT A BROAD RANGE OF FORTUNE,
INCLUDING HAPPINESS, SAFETY, AND POTENTIAL MATES.
AND THERE ARE ALL KINDS OF LEGENDS ABOUT THE ORIGINS OF THE LUCKY CATS, LIKE ABOUT A CAT WHO MADE A BUSINESS PROSPER,
OR WHO HEALED AN ILLNESS, AND ONE ABOUT A MAN WHO AVOIDED BEING STRUCK BY LIGHTNING BECAUSE A CAT BECKONED TO HIM.
納
*OFFERINGS

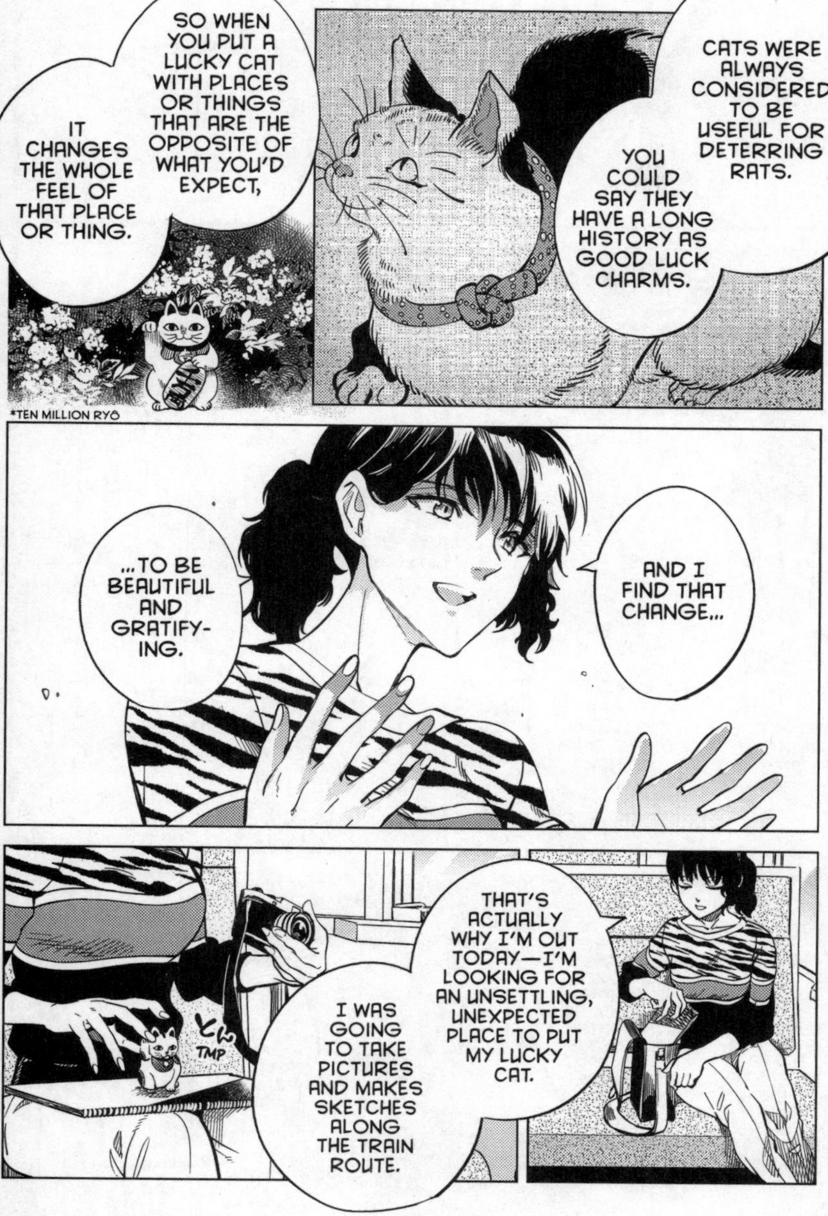
CATS WERE ALWAYS CONSIDERED TO BE USEFUL FOR DETERRING RATS.
YOU COULD SAY THEY HAVE A LONG HISTORY AS GOOD LUCK CHARMS.
SO WHEN YOU PUT A LUCKY CAT WITH PLACES OR THINGS THAT ARE THE OPPOSITE OF WHAT YOU'D EXPECT,
IT CHANGES THE WHOLE FEEL OF THAT PLACE OR THING.
*TEN MILLION RYŌ
AND I FIND THAT CHANGE...
...TO BE BEAUTIFUL AND GRATIFY-ING.
THAT'S ACTUALLY WHY I'M OUT TODAY—I'M LOOKING FOR AN UNSETTLING, UNEXPECTED PLACE TO PUT MY LUCKY CAT.
I WAS GOING TO TAKE PICTURES AND MAKES SKETCHES ALONG THE TRAIN ROUTE.
とん
TMP

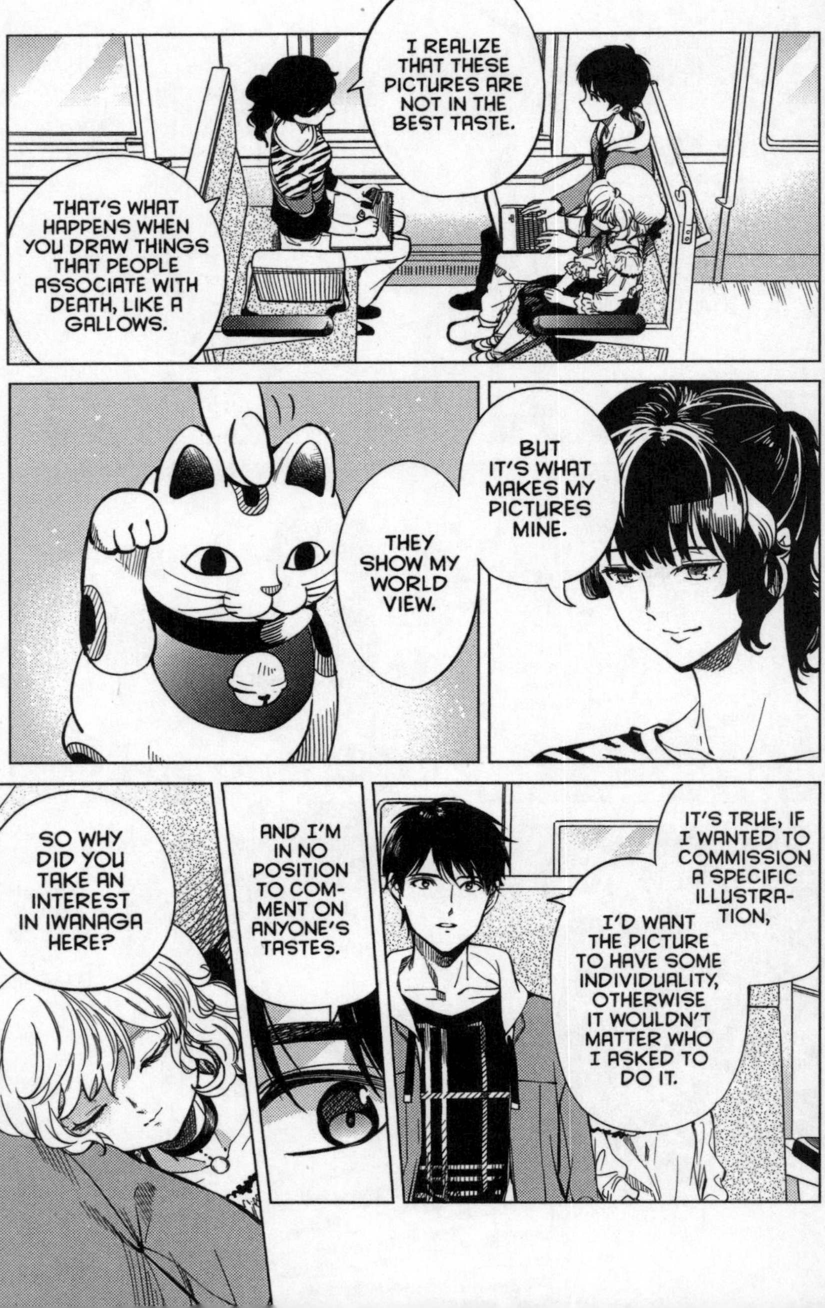
I REALIZE THAT THESE PICTURES ARE NOT IN THE BEST TASTE.
THAT'S WHAT HAPPENS WHEN YOU DRAW THINGS THAT PEOPLE ASSOCIATE WITH DEATH, LIKE A GALLOWS.
BUT IT'S WHAT MAKES MY PICTURES MINE.
THEY SHOW MY WORLD VIEW.
IT'S TRUE, IF I WANTED TO COMMISSION A SPECIFIC ILLUSTRA-TION,
I'D WANT THE PICTURE TO HAVE SOME INDIVIDUALITY, OTHERWISE IT WOULDN'T MATTER WHO I ASKED TO DO IT.
AND I'M IN NO POSITION TO COM-MENT ON ANYONE'S TASTES.
SO WHY DID YOU TAKE AN INTEREST IN IWANAGA HERE?

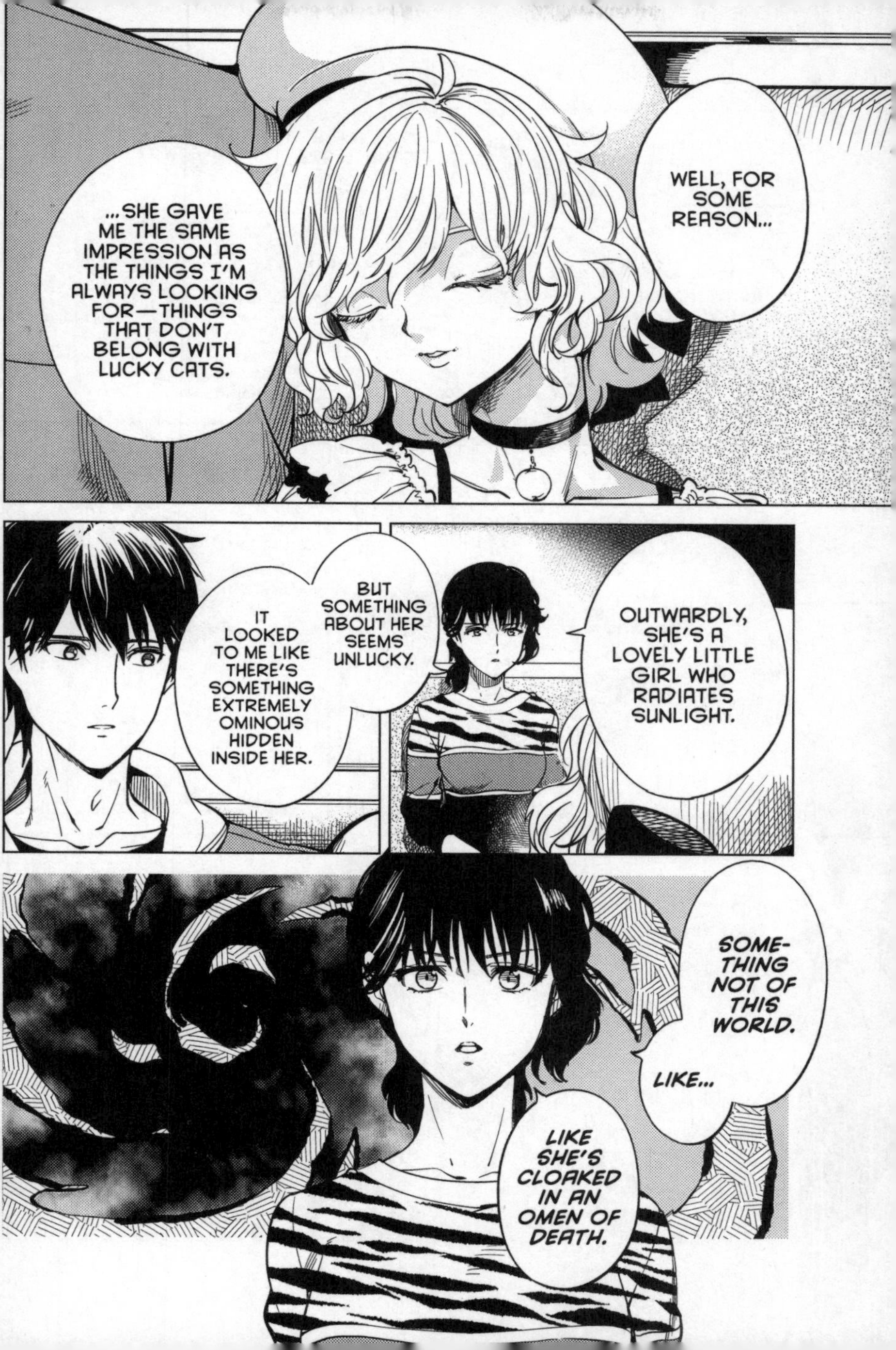
WELL, FOR SOME REASON...
...SHE GAVE ME THE SAME IMPRESSION AS THE THINGS I'M ALWAYS LOOKING FOR—THINGS THAT DON'T BELONG WITH LUCKY CATS.
OUTWARDLY, SHE'S A LOVELY LITTLE GIRL WHO RADIATES SUNLIGHT.
BUT SOMETHING ABOUT HER SEEMS UNLUCKY.
IT LOOKED TO ME LIKE THERE'S SOMETHING EXTREMELY OMINOUS HIDDEN INSIDE HER.
SOME-THING NOT OF THIS WORLD.
LIKE...
LIKE SHE'S CLOAKED IN AN OMEN OF DEATH.

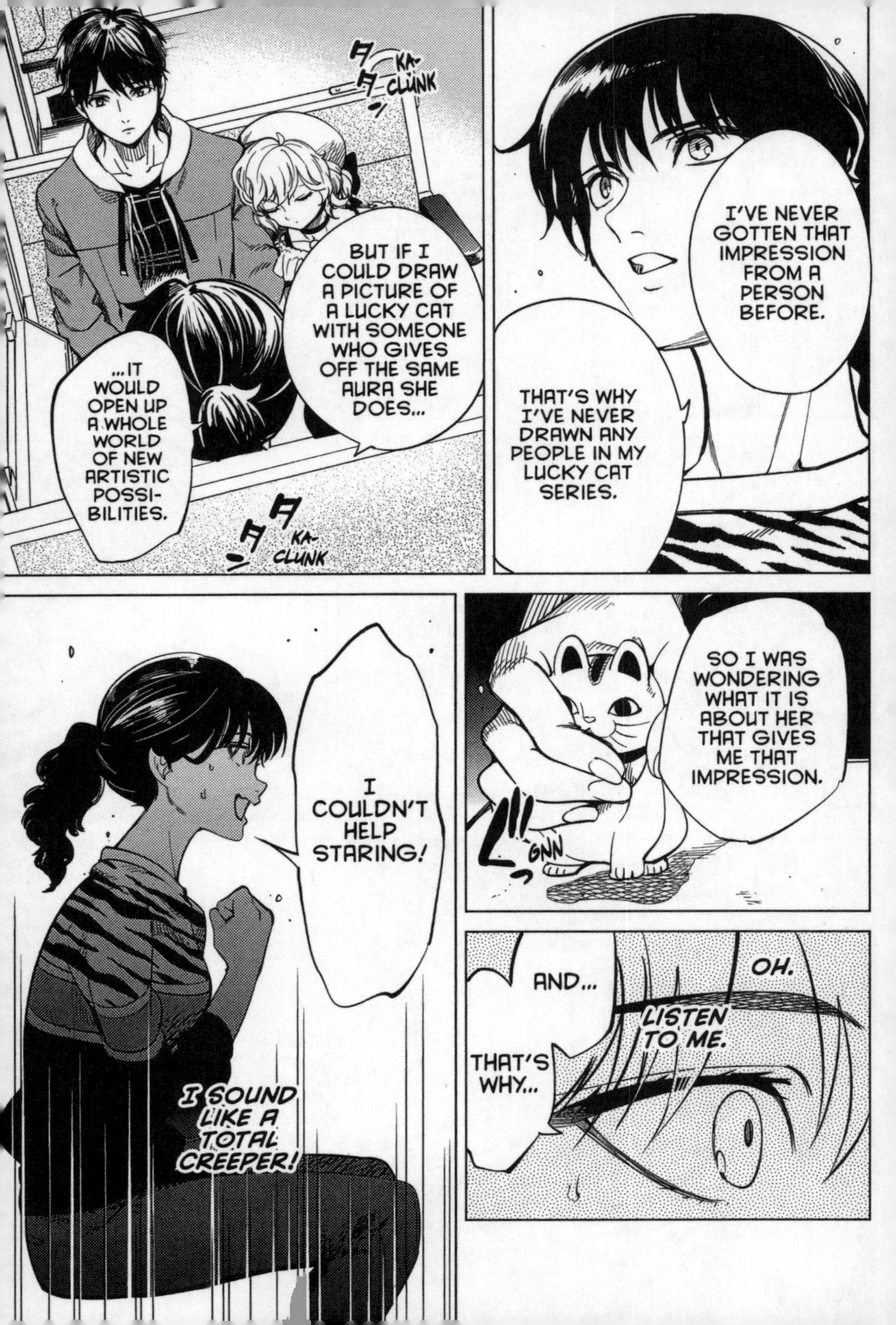
I'VE NEVER GOTTEN THAT IMPRESSION FROM A PERSON BEFORE.
THAT'S WHY I'VE NEVER DRAWN ANY PEOPLE IN MY LUCKY CAT SERIES.
KA-CLUNK
BUT IF I COULD DRAW A PICTURE OF A LUCKY CAT WITH SOMEONE WHO GIVES OFF THE SAME AURA SHE DOES...
...IT WOULD OPEN UP A WHOLE WORLD OF NEW ARTISTIC POSSI-BILITIES.
KA-CLUNK
SO I WAS WONDERING WHAT IT IS ABOUT HER THAT GIVES ME THAT IMPRESSION.
GNN
AND...
THAT'S WHY...
OH.
LISTEN TO ME.
I COULDN'T HELP STARING!
I SOUND LIKE A TOTAL CREEPER!

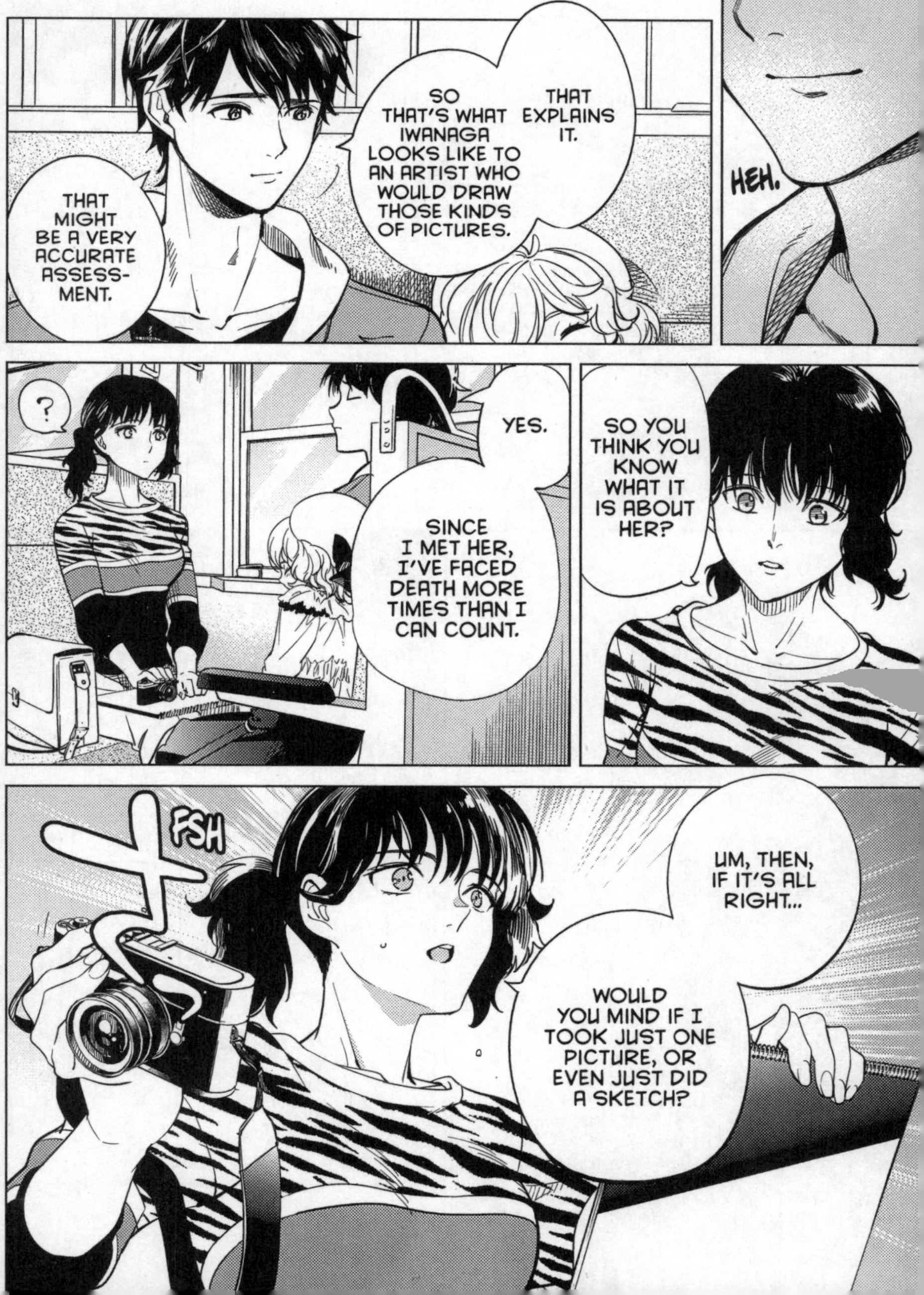
HEH.
SO THAT'S WHAT IWANAGA LOOKS LIKE TO AN ARTIST WHO WOULD DRAW THOSE KINDS OF PICTURES.
THAT EXPLAINS IT.
THAT MIGHT BE A VERY ACCURATE ASSESS-MENT.
SO YOU THINK YOU KNOW WHAT IT IS ABOUT HER?
YES.
SINCE I MET HER, I'VE FACED DEATH MORE TIMES THAN I CAN COUNT.
?
UM, THEN, IF IT'S ALL RIGHT...
WOULD YOU MIND IF I TOOK JUST ONE PICTURE, OR EVEN JUST DID A SKETCH?
FSH

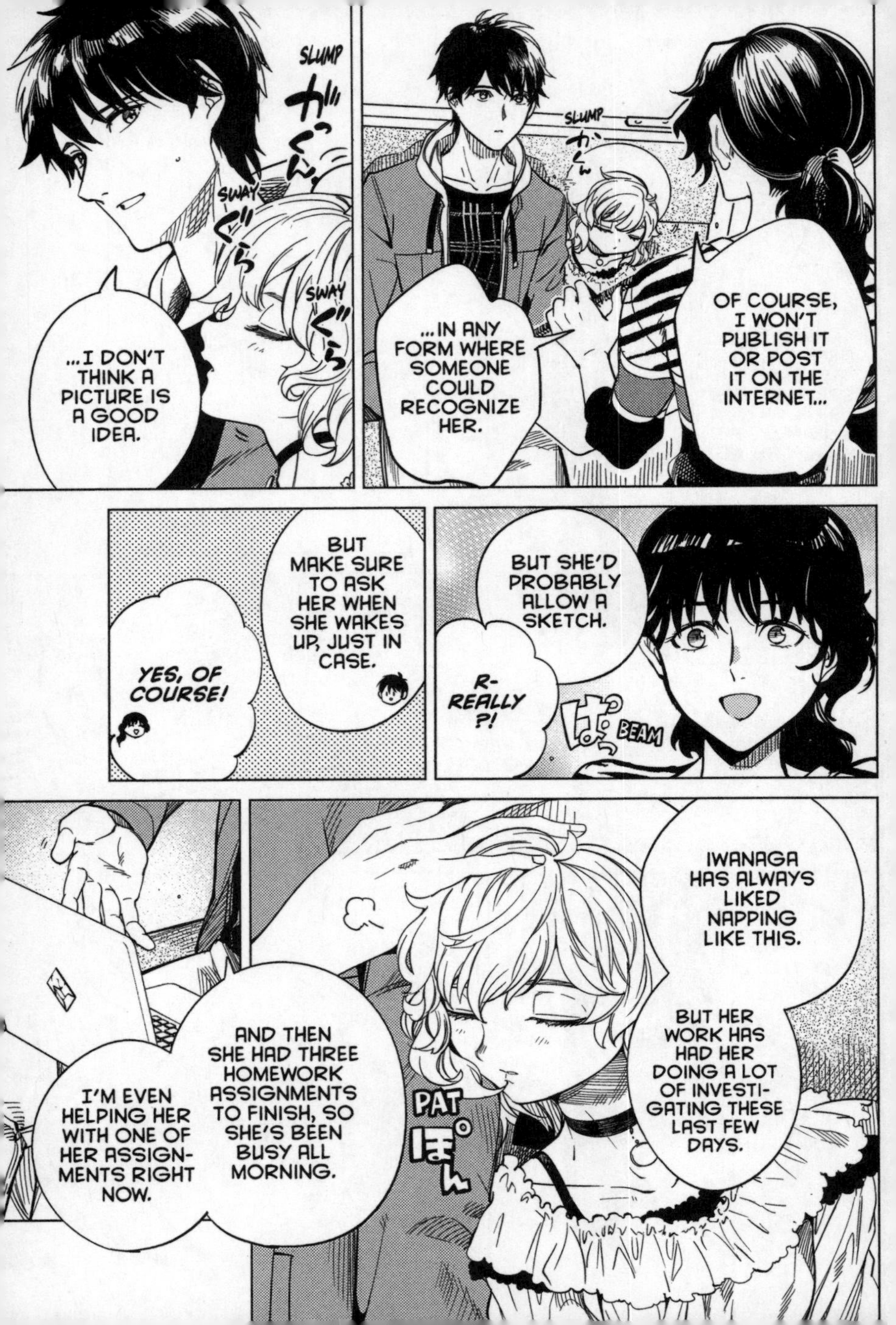
OF COURSE, I WON'T PUBLISH IT OR POST IT ON THE INTERNET...
SLUMP がくん
...IN ANY FORM WHERE SOMEONE COULD RECOGNIZE HER.
SLUMP がっくん
SWAY ぐら
SWAY ぐら
...I DON'T THINK A PICTURE IS A GOOD IDEA.
BUT SHE'D PROBABLY ALLOW A SKETCH.
ぱっ BEAM
R-REALLY?!
BUT MAKE SURE TO ASK HER WHEN SHE WAKES UP, JUST IN CASE.
YES, OF COURSE!
IWANAGA HAS ALWAYS LIKED NAPPING LIKE THIS.
BUT HER WORK HAS HAD HER DOING A LOT OF INVESTIGATING THESE LAST FEW DAYS.
PAT ぽん
AND THEN SHE HAD THREE HOMEWORK ASSIGNMENTS TO FINISH, SO SHE'S BEEN BUSY ALL MORNING.
I'M EVEN HELPING HER WITH ONE OF HER ASSIGNMENTS RIGHT NOW.

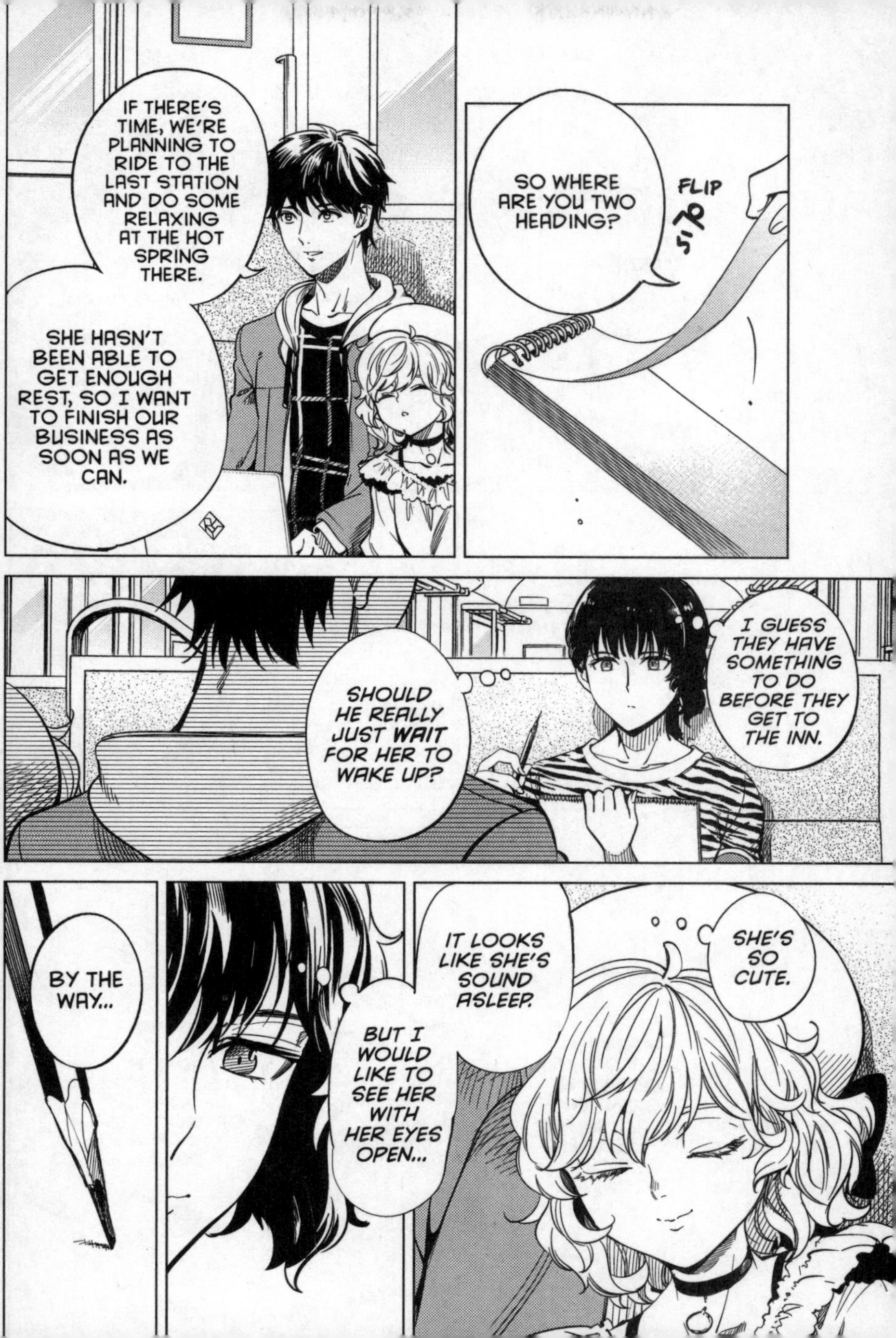
SO WHERE ARE YOU TWO HEADING?
FLIP
IF THERE'S TIME, WE'RE PLANNING TO RIDE TO THE LAST STATION AND DO SOME RELAXING AT THE HOT SPRING THERE.
SHE HASN'T BEEN ABLE TO GET ENOUGH REST, SO I WANT TO FINISH OUR BUSINESS AS SOON AS WE CAN.
I GUESS THEY HAVE SOMETHING TO DO BEFORE THEY GET TO THE INN.
SHOULD HE REALLY JUST WAIT FOR HER TO WAKE UP?
SHE'S SO CUTE.
IT LOOKS LIKE SHE'S SOUND ASLEEP.
BUT I WOULD LIKE TO SEE HER WITH HER EYES OPEN...
BY THE WAY...

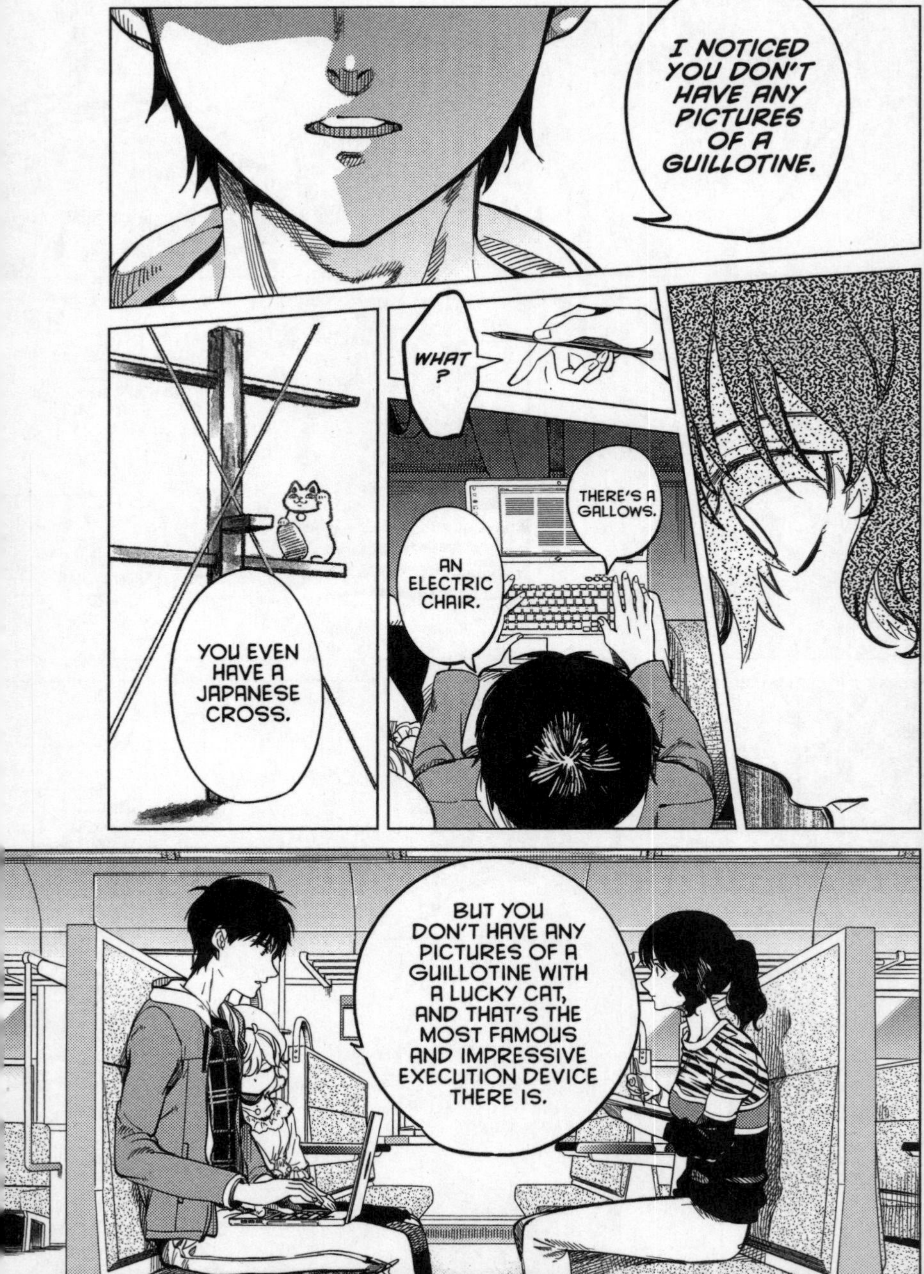
I NOTICED YOU DON'T HAVE ANY PICTURES OF A GUILLOTINE.
WHAT?
THERE'S A GALLOWS.
AN ELECTRIC CHAIR.
YOU EVEN HAVE A JAPANESE CROSS.
BUT YOU DON'T HAVE ANY PICTURES OF A GUILLOTINE WITH A LUCKY CAT, AND THAT'S THE MOST FAMOUS AND IMPRESSIVE EXECUTION DEVICE THERE IS.

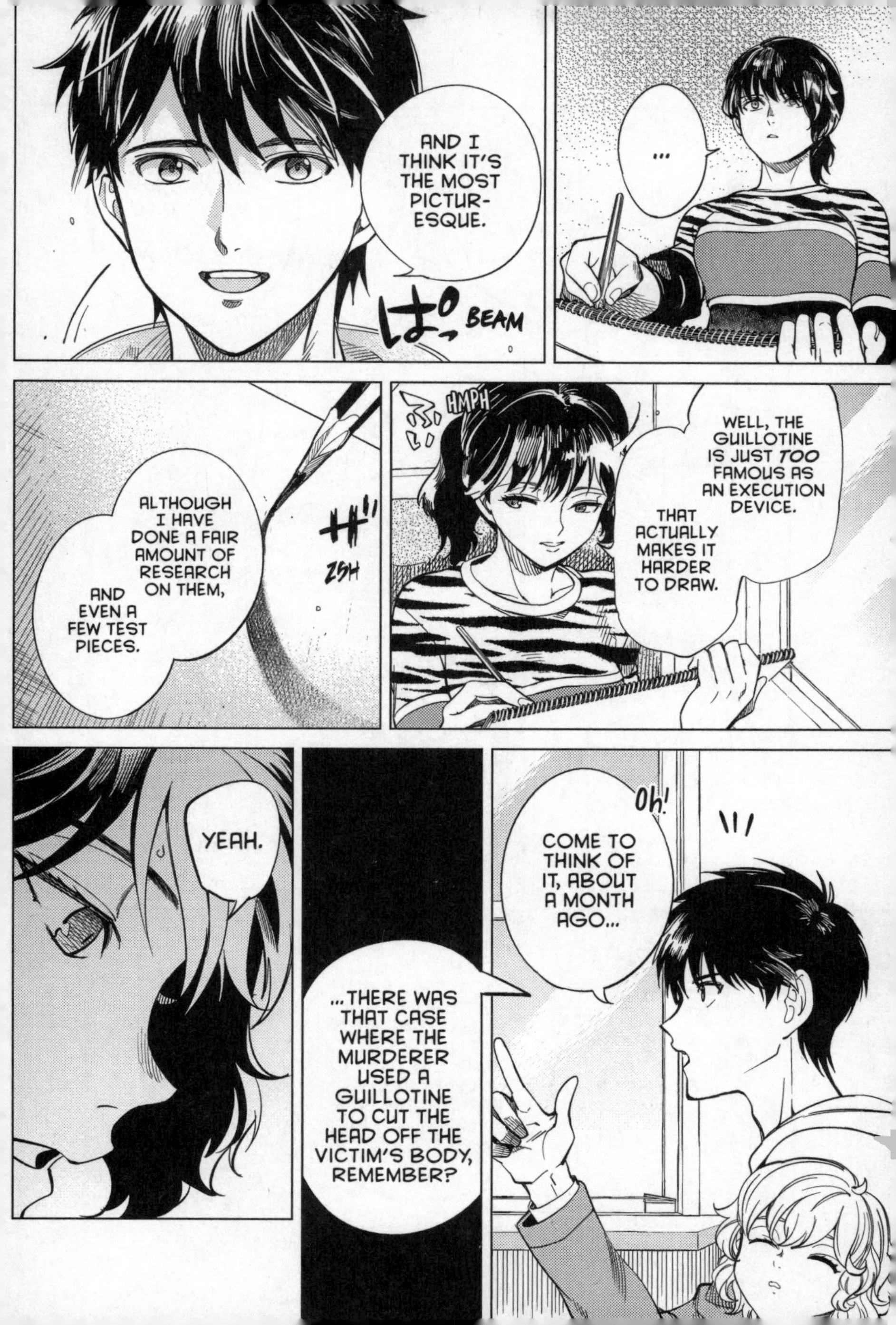
...
AND I THINK IT'S THE MOST PICTURE-ESQUE.
BEAM
HMPH
WELL, THE GUILLOTINE IS JUST TOO FAMOUS AS AN EXECUTION DEVICE.
THAT ACTUALLY MAKES IT HARDER TO DRAW.
ZSH
ALTHOUGH I HAVE DONE A FAIR AMOUNT OF RESEARCH ON THEM,
AND EVEN A FEW TEST PIECES.
Oh!
COME TO THINK OF IT, ABOUT A MONTH AGO...
...THERE WAS THAT CASE WHERE THE MURDERER USED A GUILLOTINE TO CUT THE HEAD OFF THE VICTIM'S BODY, REMEMBER?
YEAH.

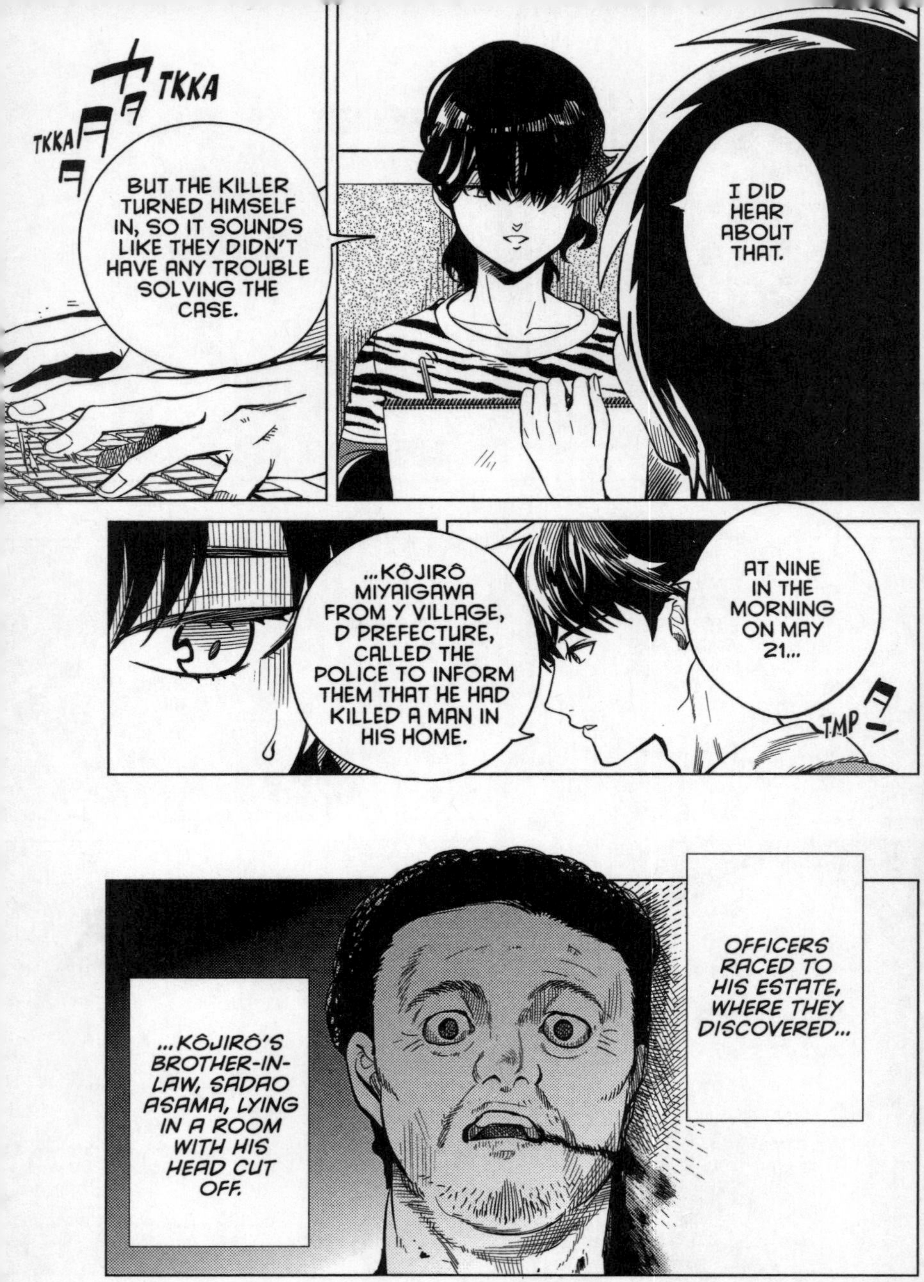
I DID HEAR ABOUT THAT.
BUT THE KILLER TURNED HIMSELF IN, SO IT SOUNDS LIKE THEY DIDN'T HAVE ANY TROUBLE SOLVING THE CASE.
TKKA
TKKA
AT NINE IN THE MORNING ON MAY 21...
TMP
...KÔJIRÔ MIYAIGAWA FROM Y VILLAGE, D PREFECTURE, CALLED THE POLICE TO INFORM THEM THAT HE HAD KILLED A MAN IN HIS HOME.
OFFICERS RACED TO HIS ESTATE, WHERE THEY DISCOVERED...
...KÔJIRÔ'S BROTHER-IN-LAW, SADAO ASAMA, LYING IN A ROOM WITH HIS HEAD CUT OFF.

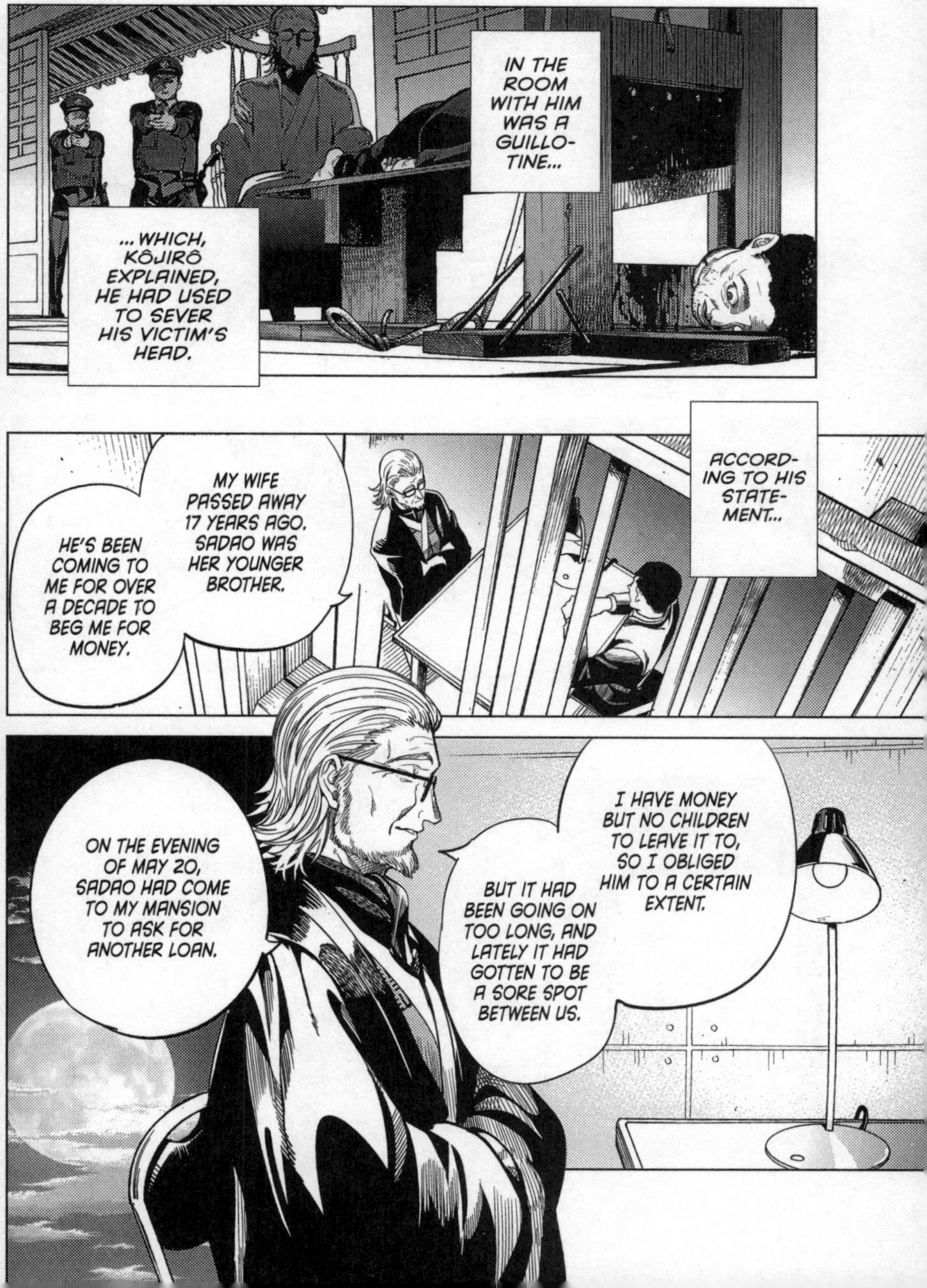
IN THE ROOM WITH HIM WAS A GUILLO-TINE...
...WHICH, KÔJIRÔ EXPLAINED, HE HAD USED TO SEVER HIS VICTIM'S HEAD.
ACCORD-ING TO HIS STATE-MENT...
MY WIFE PASSED AWAY 17 YEARS AGO. SADAO WAS HER YOUNGER BROTHER.
HE'S BEEN COMING TO ME FOR OVER A DECADE TO BEG ME FOR MONEY.
I HAVE MONEY BUT NO CHILDREN TO LEAVE IT TO, SO I OBLIGED HIM TO A CERTAIN EXTENT.
BUT IT HAD BEEN GOING ON TOO LONG, AND LATELY IT HAD GOTTEN TO BE A SORE SPOT BETWEEN US.
ON THE EVENING OF MAY 20, SADAO HAD COME TO MY MANSION TO ASK FOR ANOTHER LOAN.

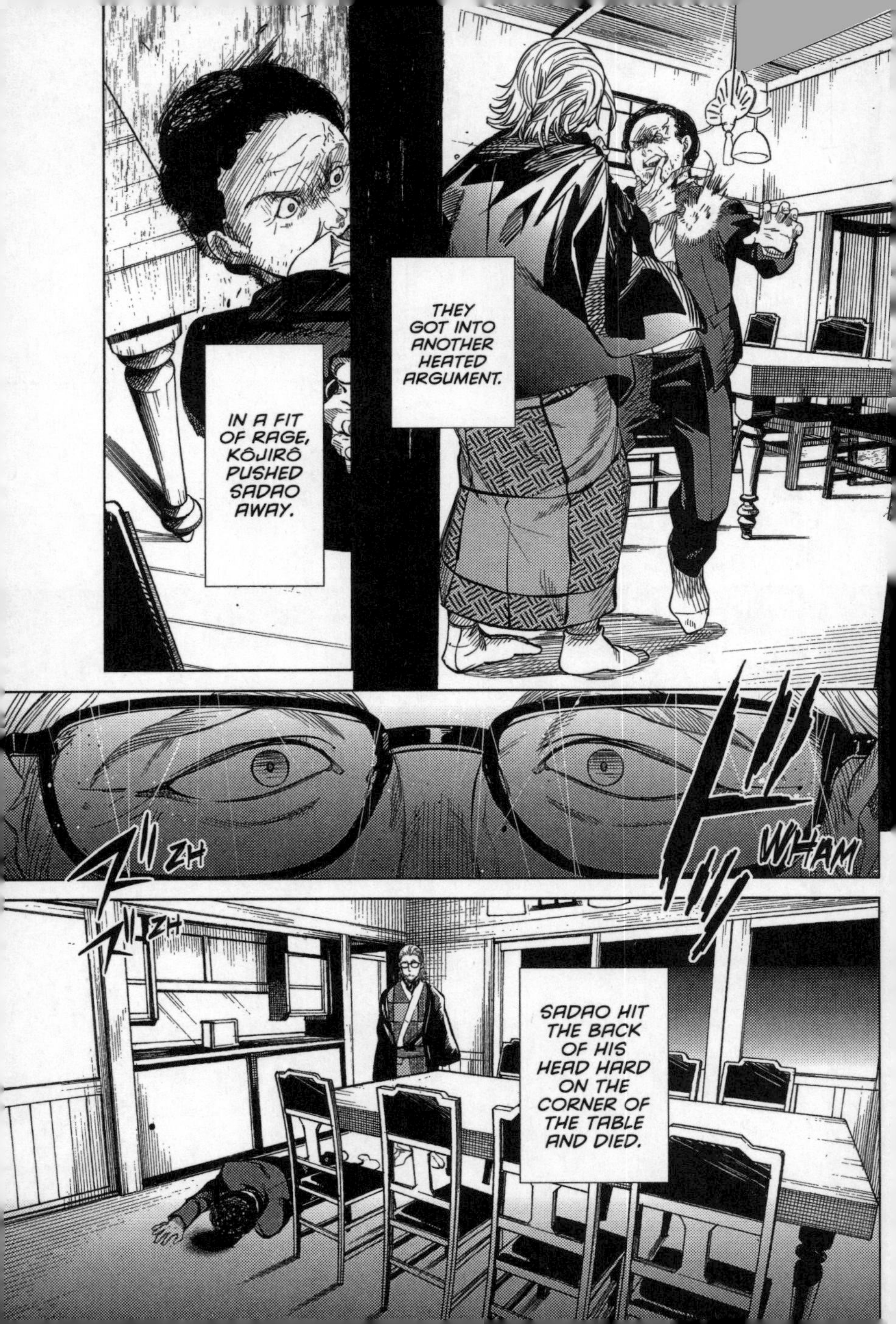
THEY GOT INTO ANOTHER HEATED ARGUMENT.
IN A FIT OF RAGE, KÔJIRÔ PUSHED SADAO AWAY.
WHAM
ZZH
ZZH
SADAO HIT THE BACK OF HIS HEAD HARD ON THE CORNER OF THE TABLE AND DIED.

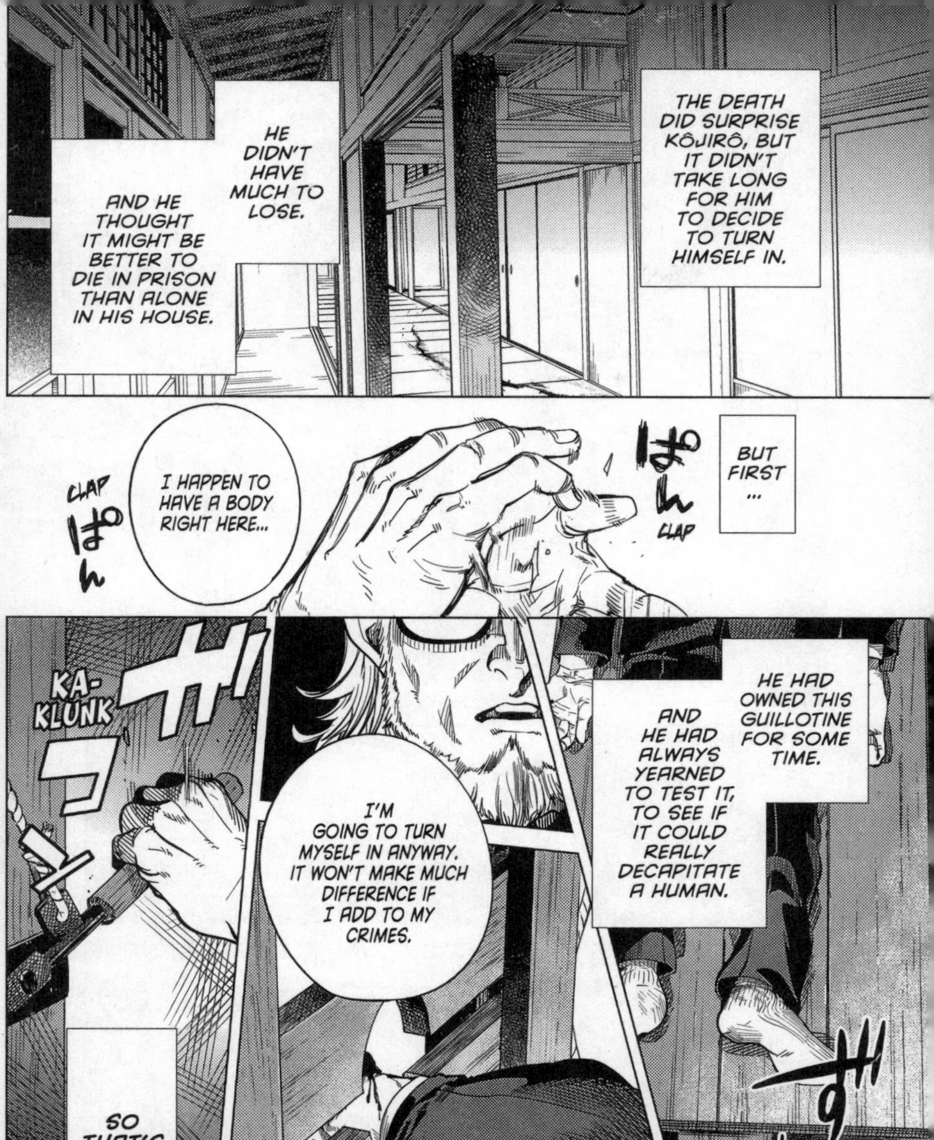
THE DEATH DID SURPRISE KÔJIRÔ, BUT IT DIDN'T TAKE LONG FOR HIM TO DECIDE TO TURN HIMSELF IN.
HE DIDN'T HAVE MUCH TO LOSE.
AND HE THOUGHT IT MIGHT BE BETTER TO DIE IN PRISON THAN ALONE IN HIS HOUSE.
BUT FIRST ...
ぱん
CLAP
I HAPPEN TO HAVE A BODY RIGHT HERE...
CLAP
ぱん
HE HAD OWNED THIS GUILLOTINE FOR SOME TIME.
AND HE HAD ALWAYS YEARNED TO TEST IT, TO SEE IF IT COULD REALLY DECAPITATE A HUMAN.
ずし
ZOOSH
I'M GOING TO TURN MYSELF IN ANYWAY. IT WON'T MAKE MUCH DIFFERENCE IF I ADD TO MY CRIMES.
ガコ
KA-KLUNK
SO THAT'S WHAT HE DID.

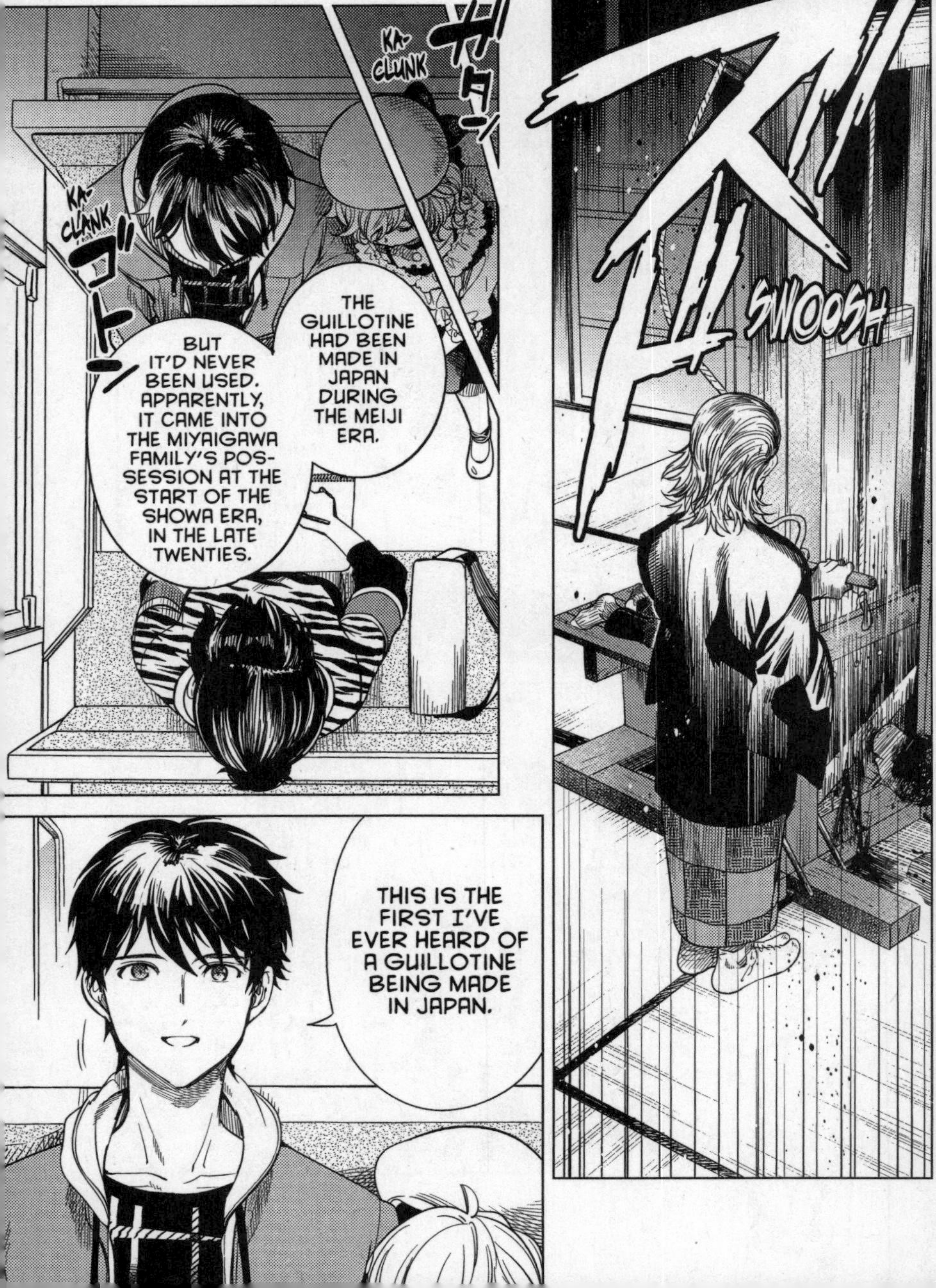
SWOOSH
KA-CLUNK
KA-CLANK
THE GUILLOTINE HAD BEEN MADE IN JAPAN DURING THE MEIJI ERA.
BUT IT'D NEVER BEEN USED. APPARENTLY, IT CAME INTO THE MIYAIGAWA FAMILY'S POSSESSION AT THE START OF THE SHOWA ERA, IN THE LATE TWENTIES.
THIS IS THE FIRST I'VE EVER HEARD OF A GUILLOTINE BEING MADE IN JAPAN.

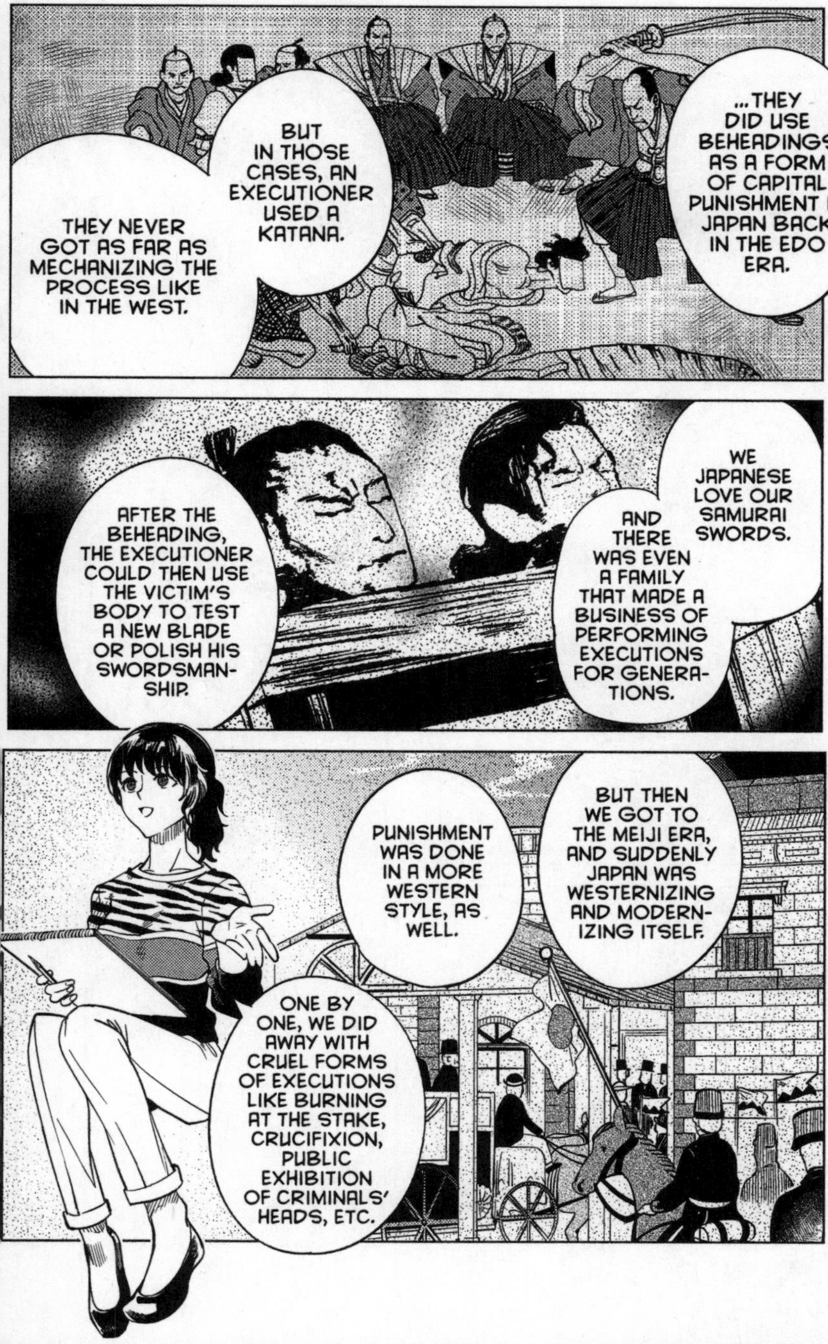
...THEY DID USE BEHEADINGS AS A FORM OF CAPITAL PUNISHMENT IN JAPAN BACK IN THE EDO ERA.
BUT IN THOSE CASES, AN EXECUTIONER USED A KATANA.
THEY NEVER GOT AS FAR AS MECHANIZING THE PROCESS LIKE IN THE WEST.
WE JAPANESE LOVE OUR SAMURAI SWORDS.
AND THERE WAS EVEN A FAMILY THAT MADE A BUSINESS OF PERFORMING EXECUTIONS FOR GENERATIONS.
AFTER THE BEHEADING, THE EXECUTIONER COULD THEN USE THE VICTIM'S BODY TO TEST A NEW BLADE OR POLISH HIS SWORDSMANSHIP.
BUT THEN WE GOT TO THE MEIJI ERA, AND SUDDENLY JAPAN WAS WESTERNIZING AND MODERNIZING ITSELF.
PUNISHMENT WAS DONE IN A MORE WESTERN STYLE, AS WELL.
ONE BY ONE, WE DID AWAY WITH CRUEL FORMS OF EXECUTIONS LIKE BURNING AT THE STAKE, CRUCIFIXION, PUBLIC EXHIBITION OF CRIMINALS' HEADS, ETC.

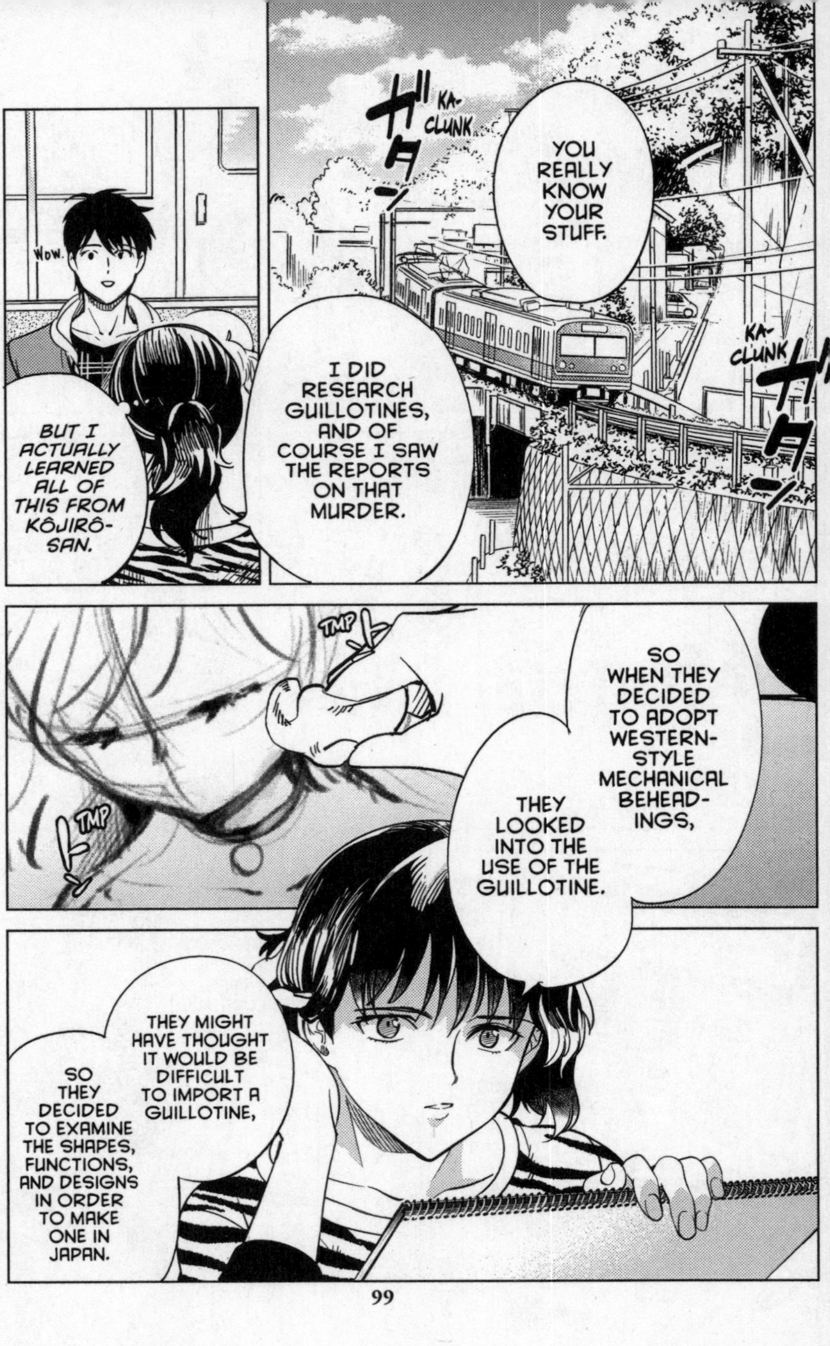
KA-CLUNK
KA-CLUNK
YOU REALLY KNOW YOUR STUFF.
WOW.
I DID RESEARCH GUILLOTINES, AND OF COURSE I SAW THE REPORTS ON THAT MURDER.
BUT I ACTUALLY LEARNED ALL OF THIS FROM KÔJIRÔ-SAN.
TMP
TMP
SO WHEN THEY DECIDED TO ADOPT WESTERN-STYLE MECHANICAL BEHEAD-INGS,
THEY LOOKED INTO THE USE OF THE GUILLOTINE.
THEY MIGHT HAVE THOUGHT IT WOULD BE DIFFICULT TO IMPORT A GUILLOTINE,
SO THEY DECIDED TO EXAMINE THE SHAPES, FUNCTIONS, AND DESIGNS IN ORDER TO MAKE ONE IN JAPAN.

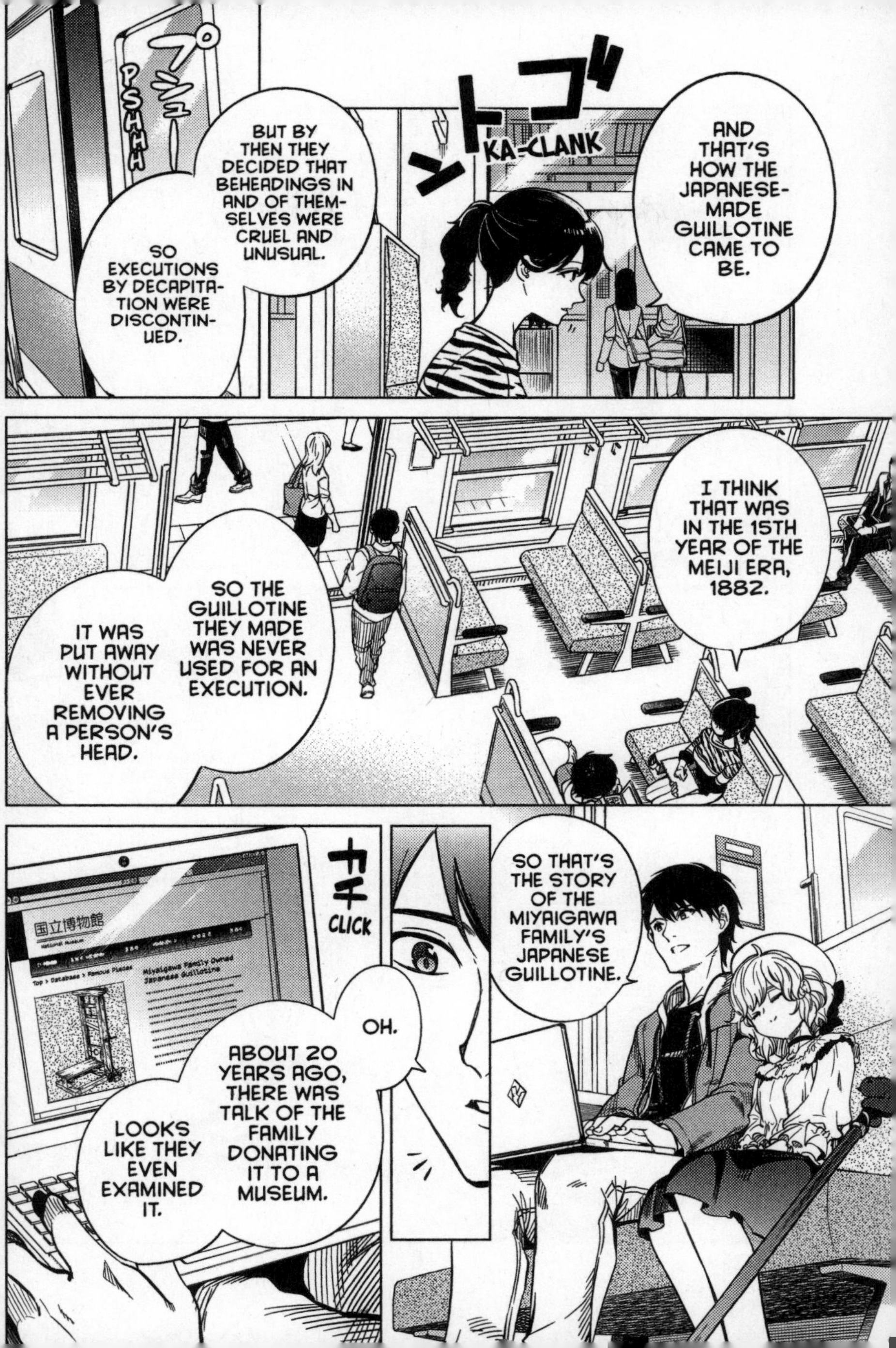
ゴトン
KA-CLANK
AND THAT'S HOW THE JAPANESE-MADE GUILLOTINE CAME TO BE.
プシュ
PSHHH
BUT BY THEN THEY DECIDED THAT BEHEADINGS IN AND OF THEMSELVES WERE CRUEL AND UNUSUAL.
SO EXECUTIONS BY DECAPITATION WERE DISCONTINUED.
I THINK THAT WAS IN THE 15TH YEAR OF THE MEIJI ERA, 1882.
SO THE GUILLOTINE THEY MADE WAS NEVER USED FOR AN EXECUTION.
IT WAS PUT AWAY WITHOUT EVER REMOVING A PERSON'S HEAD.
SO THAT'S THE STORY OF THE MIYAIGAWA FAMILY'S JAPANESE GUILLOTINE.
カチ
CLICK
国立博物館
National Museum
Miyaigawa Family Owned Japanese Guillotine
OH.
ABOUT 20 YEARS AGO, THERE WAS TALK OF THE FAMILY DONATING IT TO A MUSEUM.
LOOKS LIKE THEY EVEN EXAMINED IT.

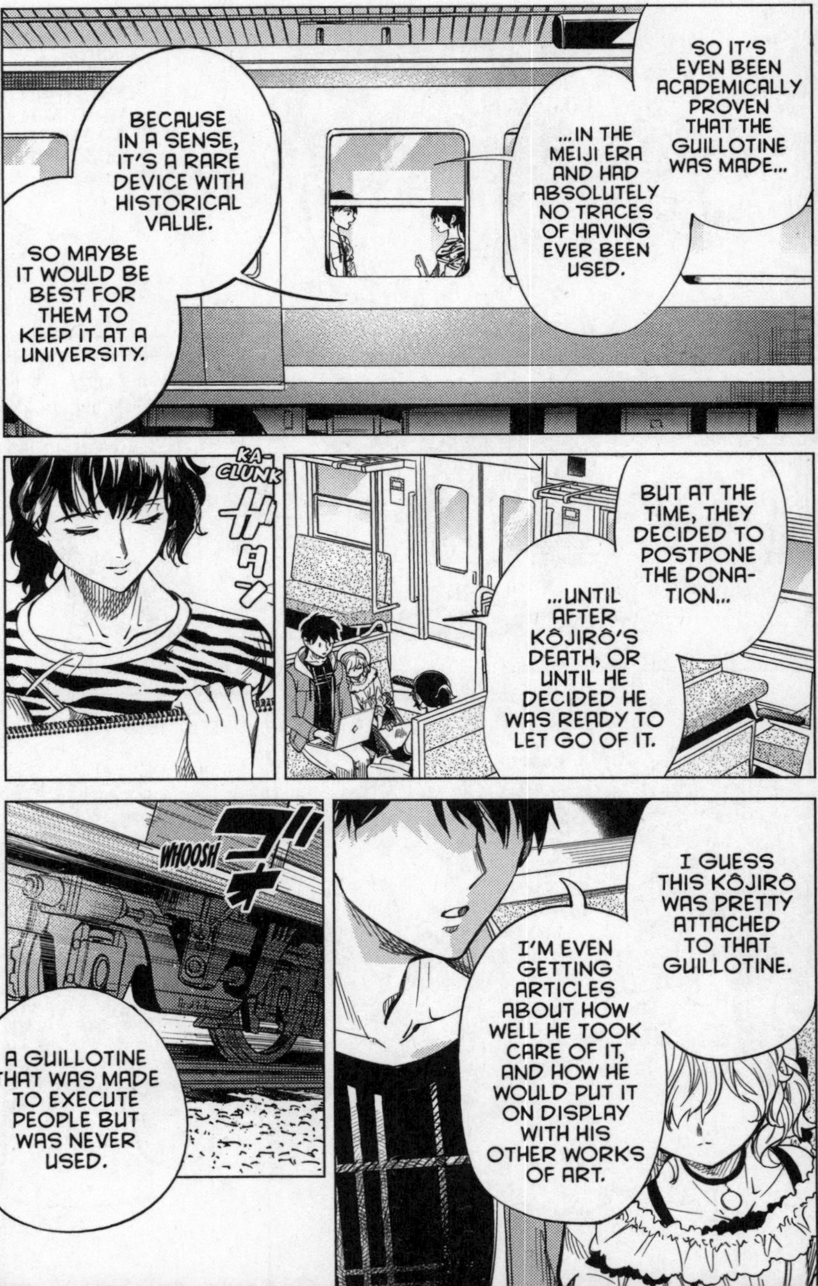
SO IT'S EVEN BEEN ACADEMICALLY PROVEN THAT THE GUILLOTINE WAS MADE...
...IN THE MEIJI ERA AND HAD ABSOLUTELY NO TRACES OF HAVING EVER BEEN USED.
BECAUSE IN A SENSE, IT'S A RARE DEVICE WITH HISTORICAL VALUE.
SO MAYBE IT WOULD BE BEST FOR THEM TO KEEP IT AT A UNIVERSITY.
BUT AT THE TIME, THEY DECIDED TO POSTPONE THE DONATION...
...UNTIL AFTER KÔJIRÔ'S DEATH, OR UNTIL HE DECIDED HE WAS READY TO LET GO OF IT.
KA-CLUNK
I GUESS THIS KÔJIRÔ WAS PRETTY ATTACHED TO THAT GUILLOTINE.
I'M EVEN GETTING ARTICLES ABOUT HOW WELL HE TOOK CARE OF IT, AND HOW HE WOULD PUT IT ON DISPLAY WITH HIS OTHER WORKS OF ART.
WHOOSH
A GUILLOTINE THAT WAS MADE TO EXECUTE PEOPLE BUT WAS NEVER USED.

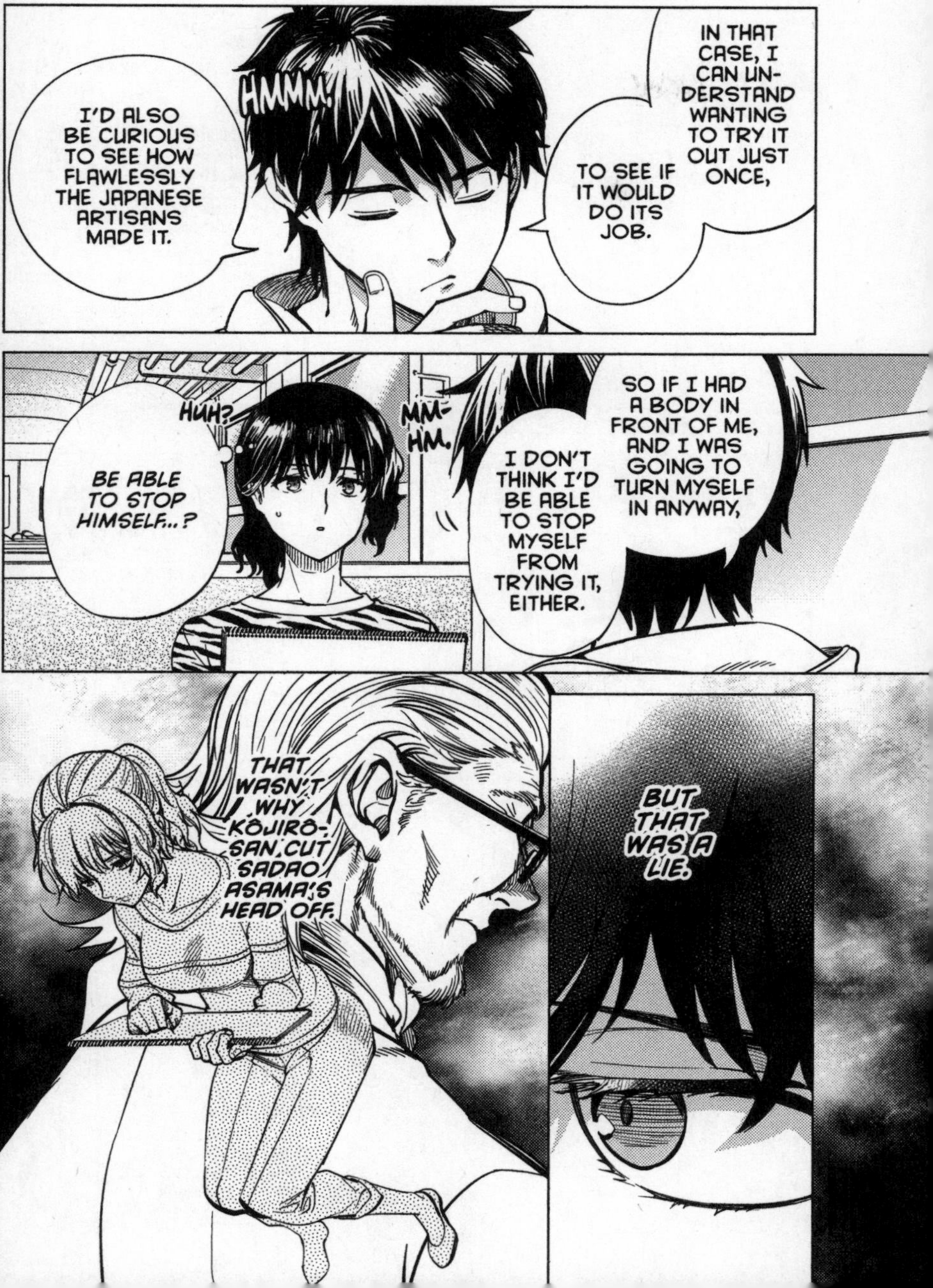
IN THAT CASE, I CAN UNDERSTAND WANTING TO TRY IT OUT JUST ONCE,
TO SEE IF IT WOULD DO ITS JOB.
HMMM.
I'D ALSO BE CURIOUS TO SEE HOW FLAWLESSLY THE JAPANESE ARTISANS MADE IT.
SO IF I HAD A BODY IN FRONT OF ME, AND I WAS GOING TO TURN MYSELF IN ANYWAY,
I DON'T THINK I'D BE ABLE TO STOP MYSELF FROM TRYING IT, EITHER.
MM-HM.
HUH?
BE ABLE TO STOP HIMSELF...?
BUT THAT WAS A LIE.
THAT WASN'T WHY KÔJIRÔ-SAN CUT SADAO ASAMA'S HEAD OFF.

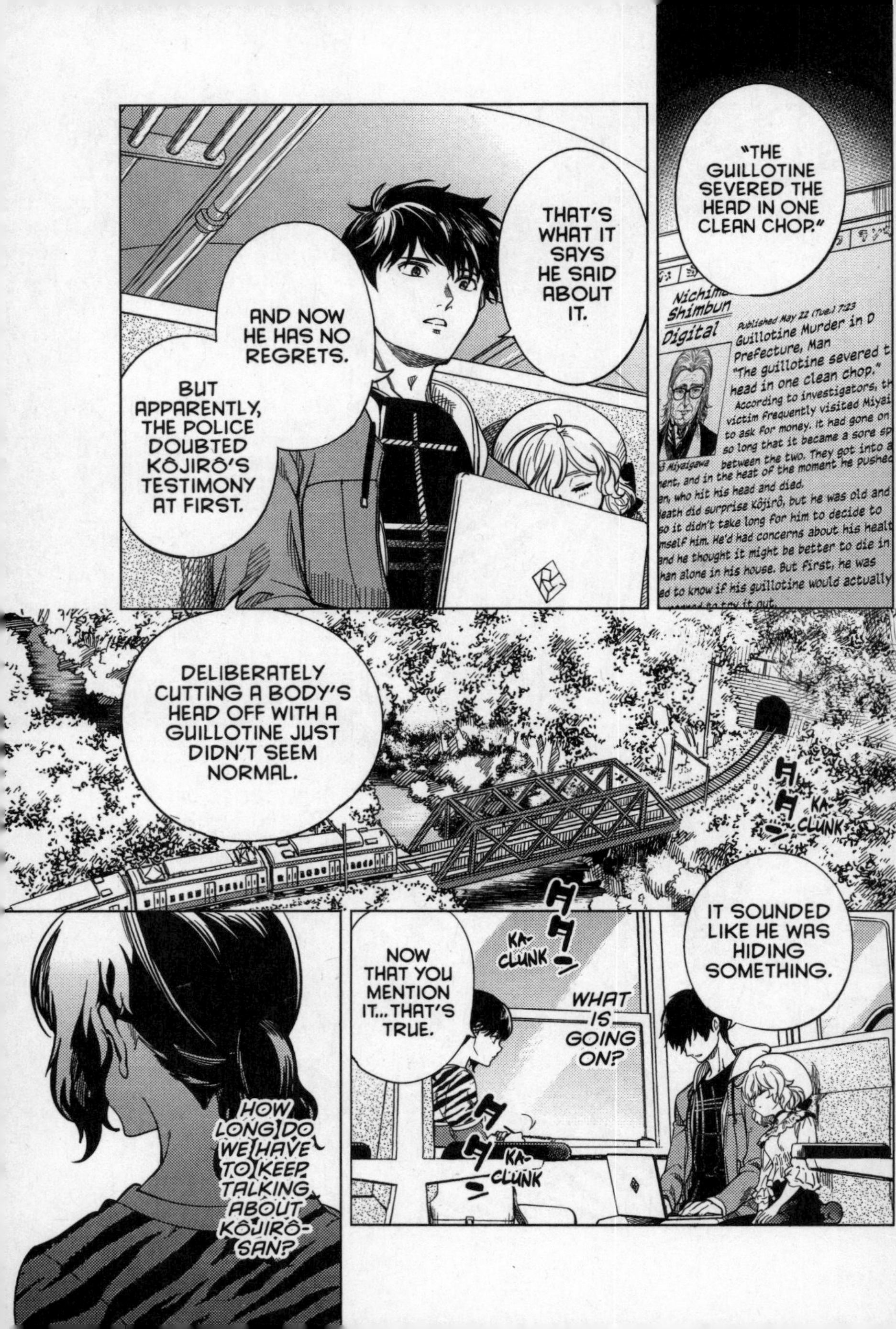
"THE GUILLOTINE SEVERED THE HEAD IN ONE CLEAN CHOP."
Nichima
Shimbun
Digital
Published May 22 (Tue.) 7:23
Guillotine Murder in D
Prefecture, Man
"The guillotine severed t
head in one clean chop."
According to investigators, th
victim frequently visited Miyai
to ask for money. It had gone on
so long that it became a sore sp
between the two. They got into a
Miyaigawa
between the two. They got into a
ment, and in the heat of the moment he pushed
an, who hit his head and died.
death did surprise Kôjirô, but he was old and
so it didn't take long for him to decide to
mself him. He'd had concerns about his healt
and he thought it might be better to die in
han alone in his house. But first, he was
ed to know if his guillotine would actually
THAT'S WHAT IT SAYS HE SAID ABOUT IT.
AND NOW HE HAS NO REGRETS.
BUT APPARENTLY, THE POLICE DOUBTED KÔJIRÔ'S TESTIMONY AT FIRST.
DELIBERATELY CUTTING A BODY'S HEAD OFF WITH A GUILLOTINE JUST DIDN'T SEEM NORMAL.
KA-CLUNK
IT SOUNDED LIKE HE WAS HIDING SOMETHING.
WHAT IS GOING ON?
KA-CLUNK
NOW THAT YOU MENTION IT... THAT'S TRUE.
KA-CLUNK
HOW LONG DO WE HAVE TO KEEP TALKING ABOUT KÔJIRÔ-SAN?

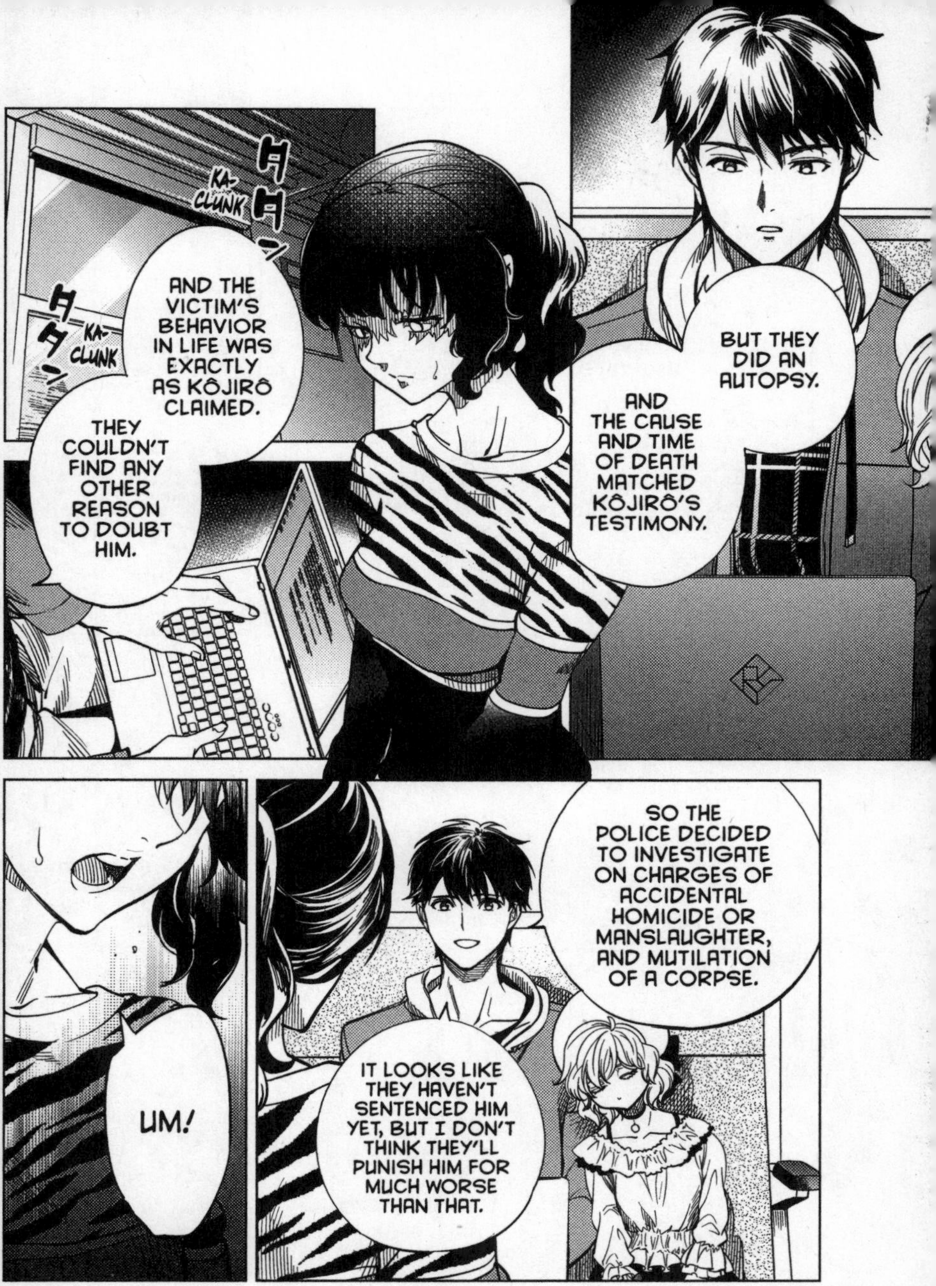
BUT THEY DID AN AUTOPSY.
AND THE CAUSE AND TIME OF DEATH MATCHED KÔJIRÔ'S TESTIMONY.
KA-CLUNK
AND THE VICTIM'S BEHAVIOR IN LIFE WAS EXACTLY AS KÔJIRÔ CLAIMED.
KA-CLUNK
THEY COULDN'T FIND ANY OTHER REASON TO DOUBT HIM.
SO THE POLICE DECIDED TO INVESTIGATE ON CHARGES OF ACCIDENTAL HOMICIDE OR MANSLAUGHTER, AND MUTILATION OF A CORPSE.
IT LOOKS LIKE THEY HAVEN'T SENTENCED HIM YET, BUT I DON'T THINK THEY'LL PUNISH HIM FOR MUCH WORSE THAN THAT.
UM!

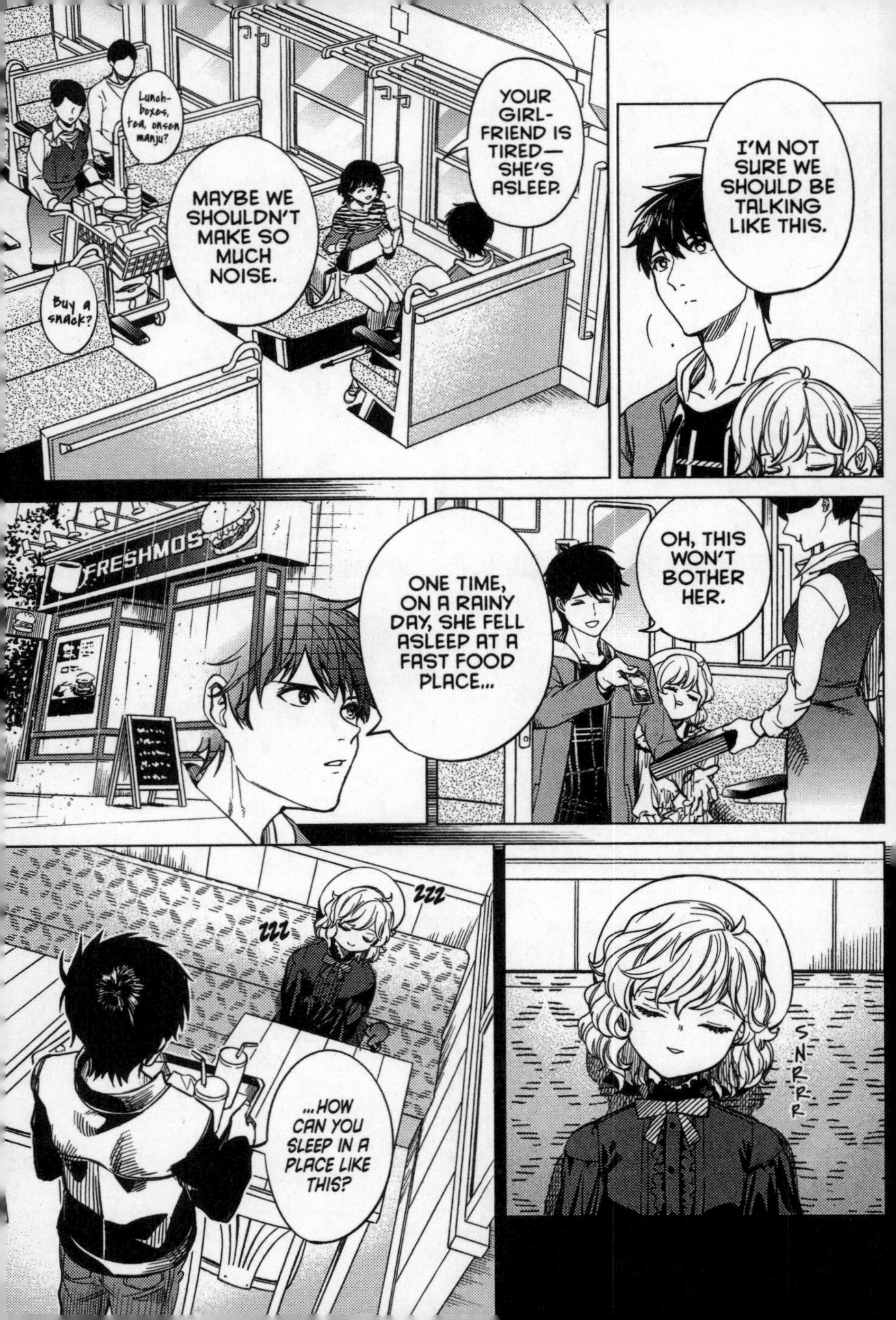
I'M NOT SURE WE SHOULD BE TALKING LIKE THIS.
YOUR GIRL-FRIEND IS TIRED—SHE'S ASLEEP.
MAYBE WE SHOULDN'T MAKE SO MUCH NOISE.
Lunch-boxes, tea, onsen manju?
Buy a snack?
OH, THIS WON'T BOTHER HER.
ONE TIME, ON A RAINY DAY, SHE FELL ASLEEP AT A FAST FOOD PLACE...
FRESHMOS
S-N-R-R-R
ZZZ
ZZZ
...HOW CAN YOU SLEEP IN A PLACE LIKE THIS?

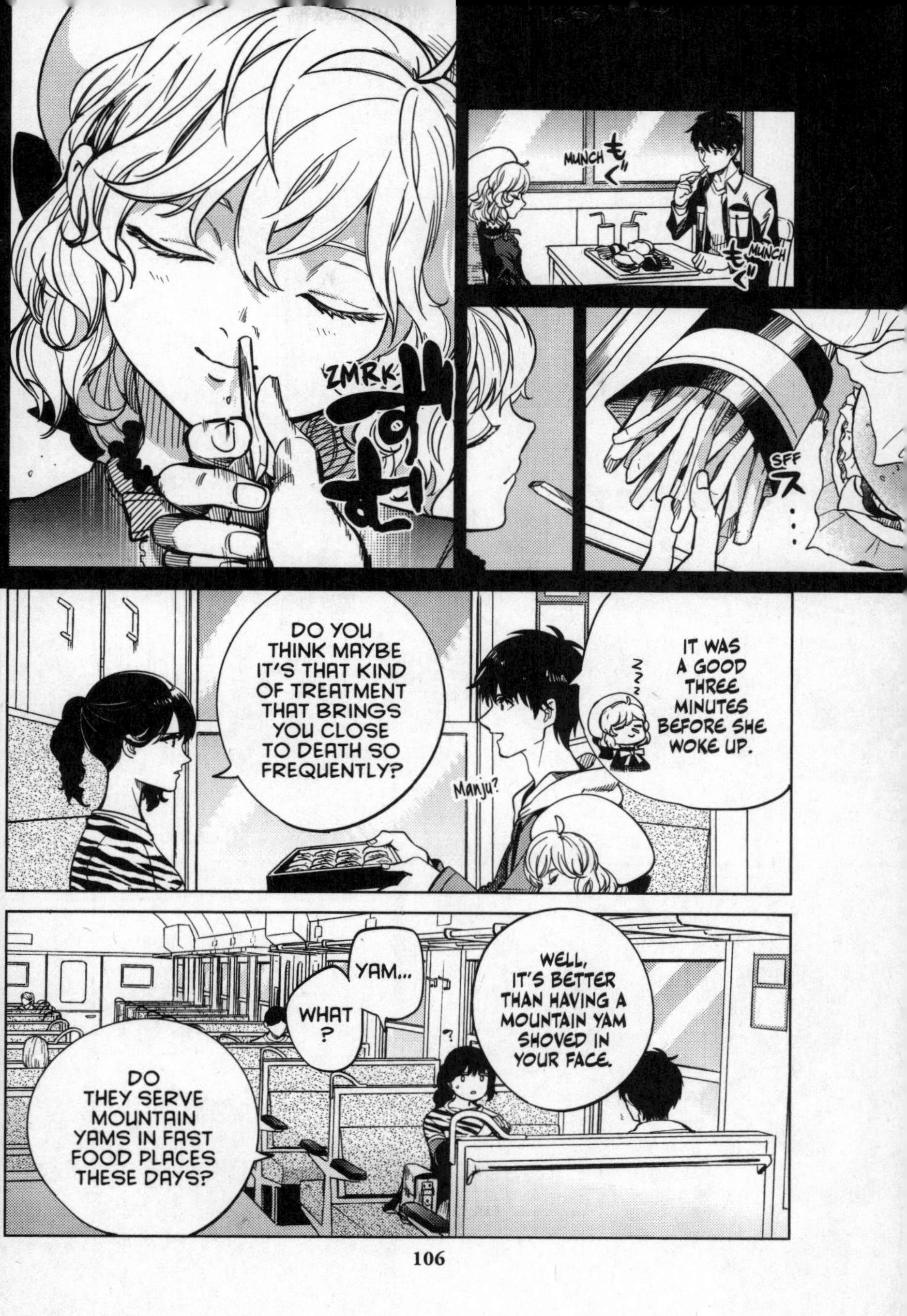

MUNCH もぐ
MUNCH もぐ
SFF ス
...
ZMRK
IT WAS A GOOD THREE MINUTES BEFORE SHE WOKE UP.
Z Z Z
Manju?
DO YOU THINK MAYBE IT'S THAT KIND OF TREATMENT THAT BRINGS YOU CLOSE TO DEATH SO FREQUENTLY?
WELL, IT'S BETTER THAN HAVING A MOUNTAIN YAM SHOVED IN YOUR FACE.
YAM...
WHAT ?
?
DO THEY SERVE MOUNTAIN YAMS IN FAST FOOD PLACES THESE DAYS?

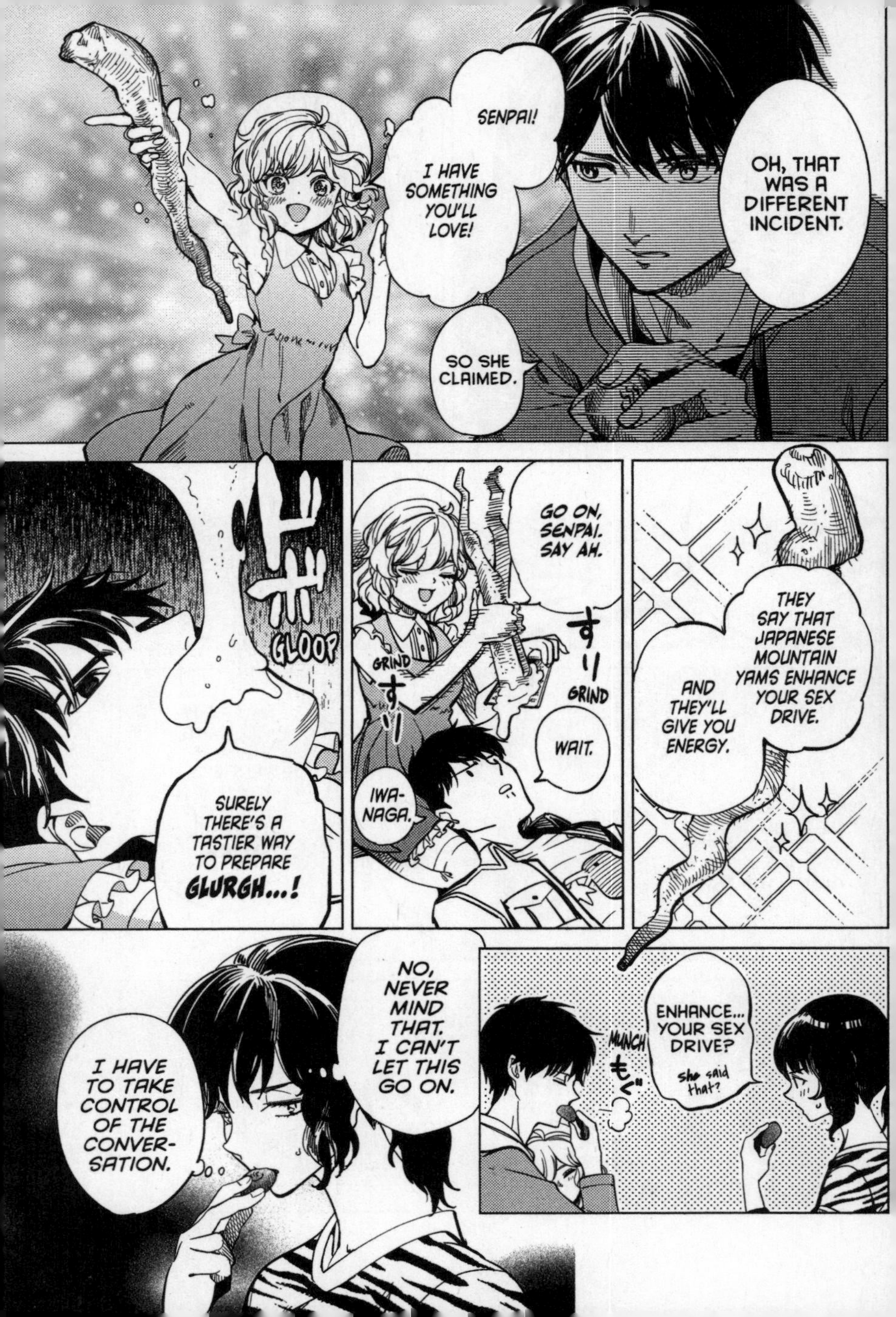
OH, THAT WAS A DIFFERENT INCIDENT.
SENPAI!
I HAVE SOMETHING YOU'LL LOVE!
SO SHE CLAIMED.
THEY SAY THAT JAPANESE MOUNTAIN YAMS ENHANCE YOUR SEX DRIVE.
AND THEY'LL GIVE YOU ENERGY.
GO ON, SENPAI. SAY AH.
すり
GRIND
GRIND
すり
WAIT.
IWANAGA.
GLOOP
SURELY THERE'S A TASTIER WAY TO PREPARE GLURGH...!
ENHANCE... YOUR SEX DRIVE?
she said that?
MUNCH
もぐ
NO, NEVER MIND THAT. I CAN'T LET THIS GO ON.
I HAVE TO TAKE CONTROL OF THE CONVERSATION.

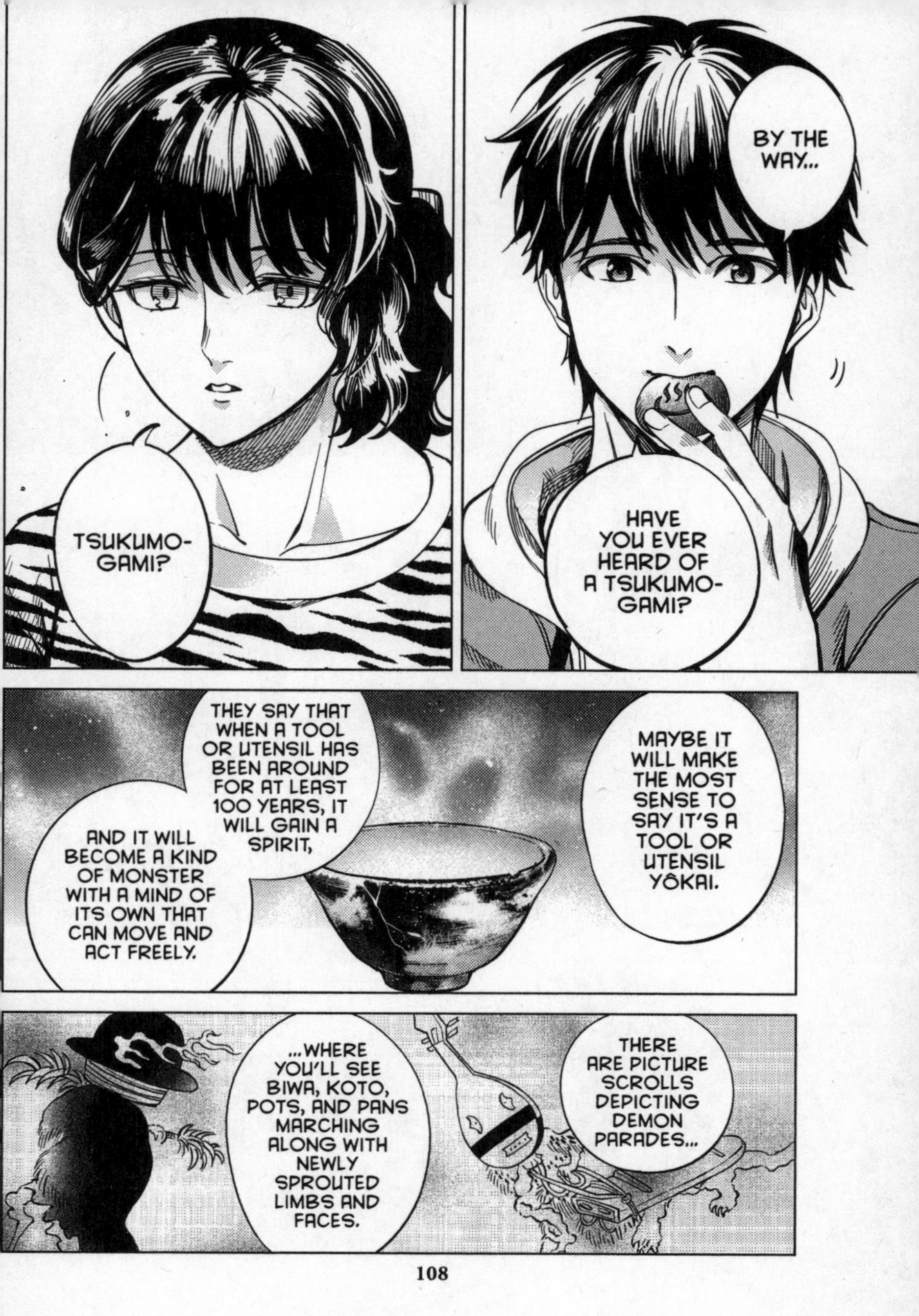
BY THE WAY...
HAVE YOU EVER HEARD OF A TSUKUMO-GAMI?
TSUKUMO-GAMI?
MAYBE IT WILL MAKE THE MOST SENSE TO SAY IT'S A TOOL OR UTENSIL YÔKAI.
THEY SAY THAT WHEN A TOOL OR UTENSIL HAS BEEN AROUND FOR AT LEAST 100 YEARS, IT WILL GAIN A SPIRIT,
AND IT WILL BECOME A KIND OF MONSTER WITH A MIND OF ITS OWN THAT CAN MOVE AND ACT FREELY.
THERE ARE PICTURE SCROLLS DEPICTING DEMON PARADES...
...WHERE YOU'LL SEE BIWA, KOTO, POTS, AND PANS MARCHING ALONG WITH NEWLY SPROUTED LIMBS AND FACES.

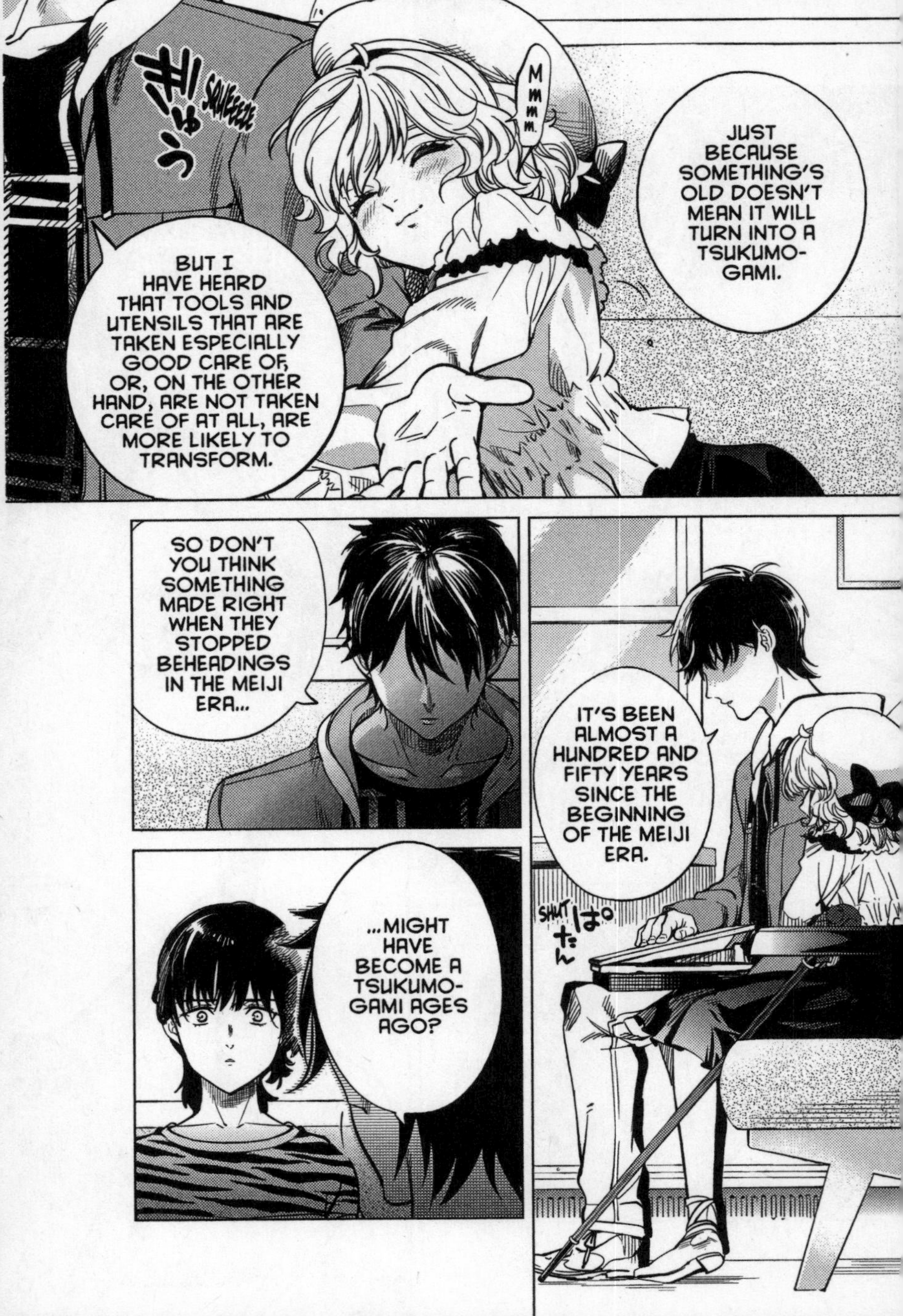
JUST BECAUSE SOMETHING'S OLD DOESN'T MEAN IT WILL TURN INTO A TSUKUMO-GAMI.
MMMM.
ぎゅう
SQUEEEEZE
BUT I HAVE HEARD THAT TOOLS AND UTENSILS THAT ARE TAKEN ESPECIALLY GOOD CARE OF, OR, ON THE OTHER HAND, ARE NOT TAKEN CARE OF AT ALL, ARE MORE LIKELY TO TRANSFORM.
IT'S BEEN ALMOST A HUNDRED AND FIFTY YEARS SINCE THE BEGINNING OF THE MEIJI ERA.
SHUT
ぱたん
SO DON'T YOU THINK SOMETHING MADE RIGHT WHEN THEY STOPPED BEHEADINGS IN THE MEIJI ERA...
...MIGHT HAVE BECOME A TSUKUMO-GAMI AGES AGO?

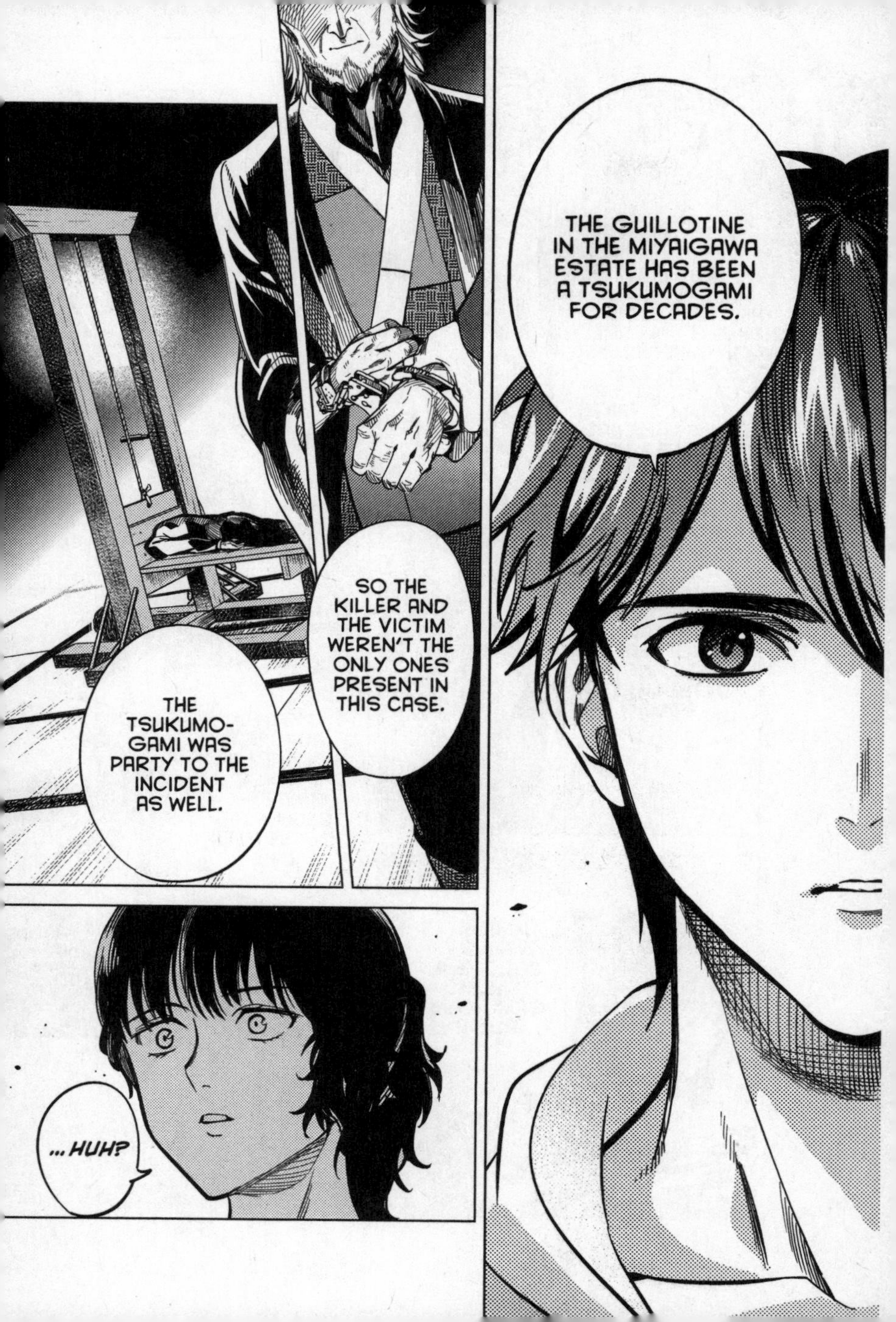
THE GUILLOTINE IN THE MIYAIGAWA ESTATE HAS BEEN A TSUKUMOGAMI FOR DECADES.
SO THE KILLER AND THE VICTIM WEREN'T THE ONLY ONES PRESENT IN THIS CASE.
THE TSUKUMO-GAMI WAS PARTY TO THE INCIDENT AS WELL.
...HUH?

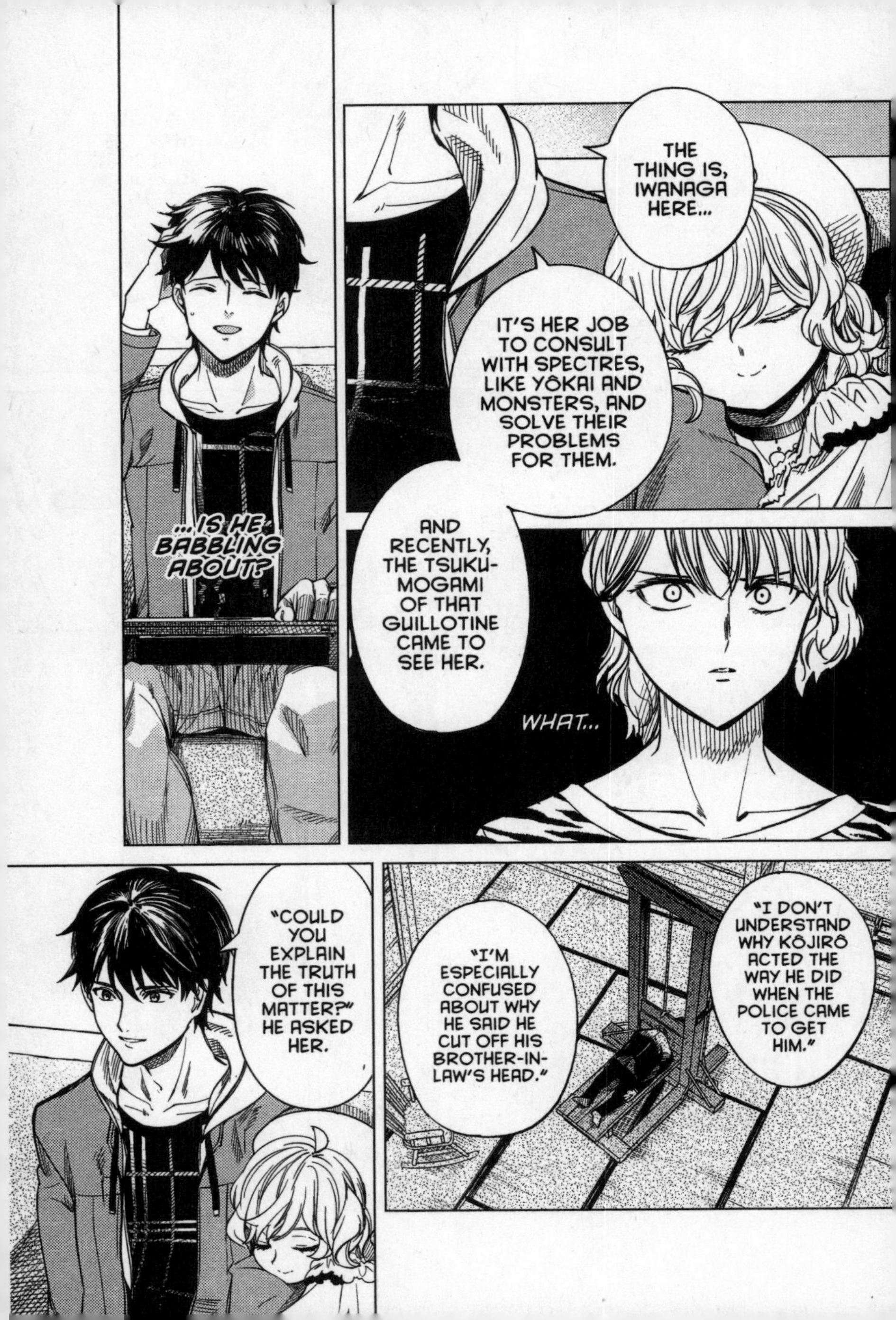
THE THING IS, IWANAGA HERE...
IT'S HER JOB TO CONSULT WITH SPECTRES, LIKE YÔKAI AND MONSTERS, AND SOLVE THEIR PROBLEMS FOR THEM.
AND RECENTLY, THE TSUKU-MOGAMI OF THAT GUILLOTINE CAME TO SEE HER.
WHAT...
...IS HE BABBLING ABOUT?
"I DON'T UNDERSTAND WHY KÔJIRÔ ACTED THE WAY HE DID WHEN THE POLICE CAME TO GET HIM."
"I'M ESPECIALLY CONFUSED ABOUT WHY HE SAID HE CUT OFF HIS BROTHER-IN-LAW'S HEAD."
"COULD YOU EXPLAIN THE TRUTH OF THIS MATTER?" HE ASKED HER.

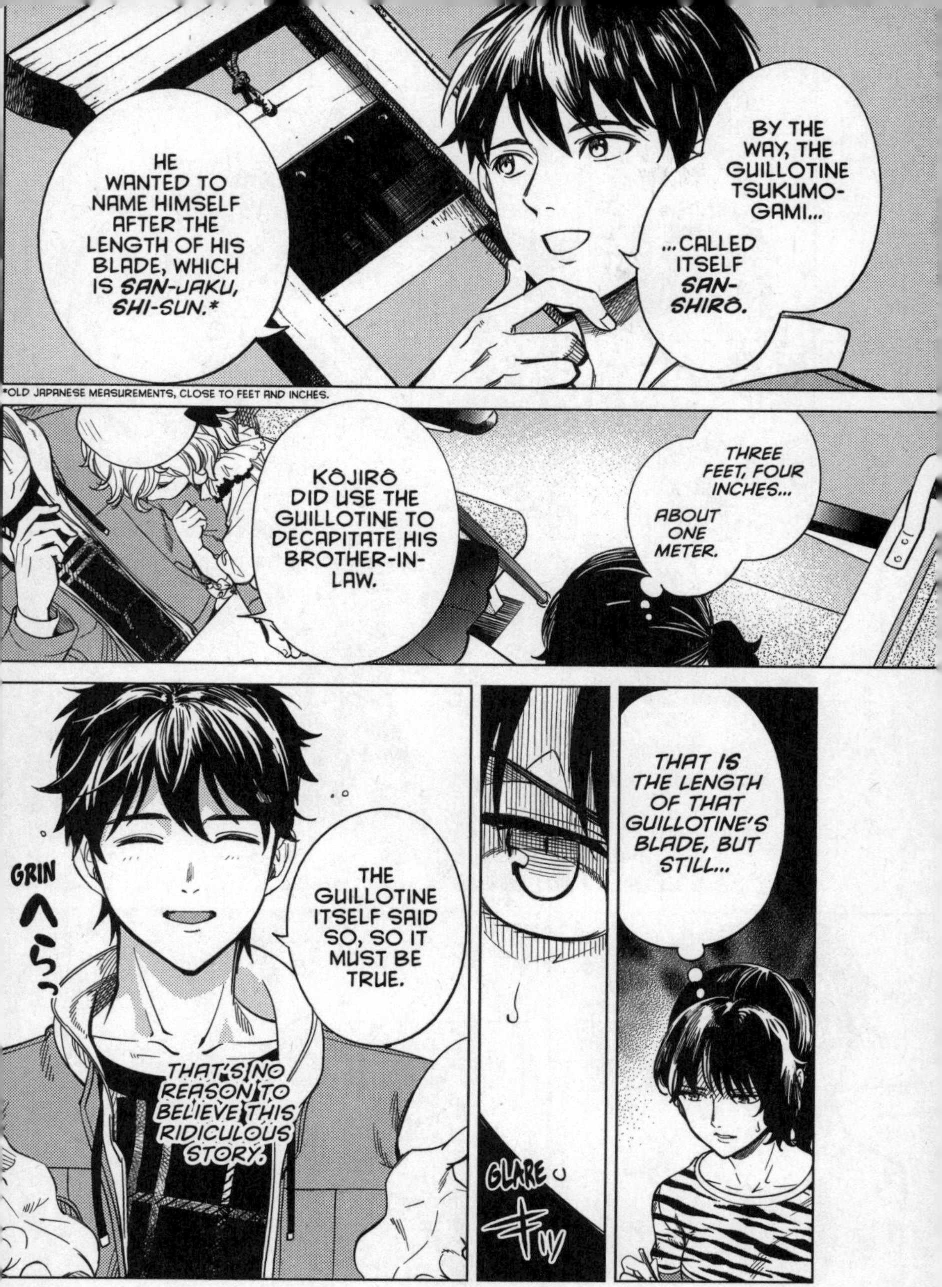
BY THE WAY, THE GUILLOTINE TSUKUMO-GAMI...
...CALLED ITSELF SAN-SHIRÔ.
HE WANTED TO NAME HIMSELF AFTER THE LENGTH OF HIS BLADE, WHICH IS SAN-JAKU, SHI-SUN.*
THREE FEET, FOUR INCHES...
ABOUT ONE METER.
KÔJIRÔ DID USE THE GUILLOTINE TO DECAPITATE HIS BROTHER-IN-LAW.
THAT IS THE LENGTH OF THAT GUILLOTINE'S BLADE, BUT STILL...
GLARE
キッ
THE GUILLOTINE ITSELF SAID SO, SO IT MUST BE TRUE.
GRIN
へらっ
THAT'S NO REASON TO BELIEVE THIS RIDICULOUS STORY.

*OLD JAPANESE MEASUREMENTS, CLOSE TO FEET AND INCHES.

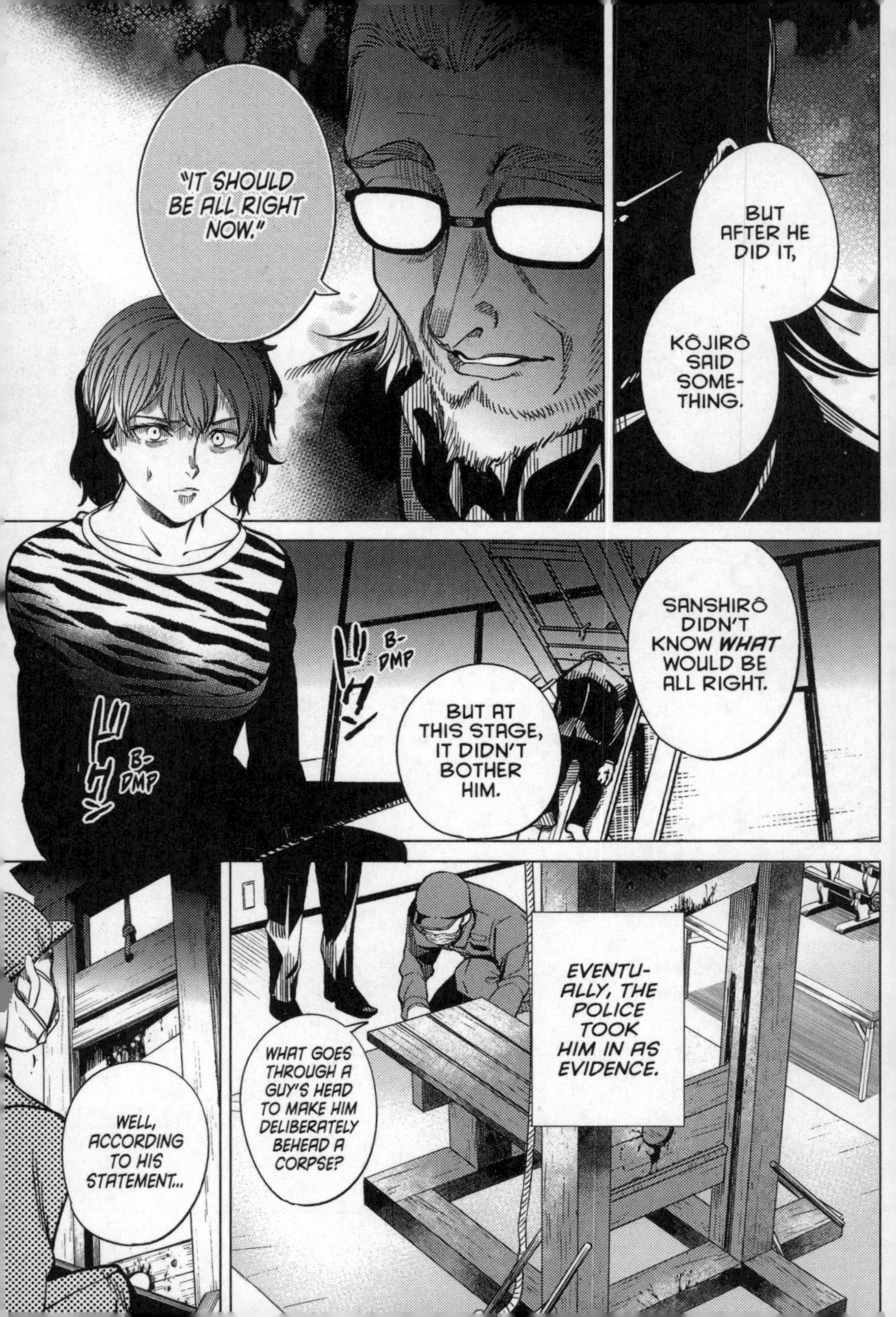
BUT AFTER HE DID IT,
KÔJIRÔ SAID SOMETHING.
"IT SHOULD BE ALL RIGHT NOW."
SANSHIRÔ DIDN'T KNOW *WHAT* WOULD BE ALL RIGHT.
B-DMP
BUT AT THIS STAGE, IT DIDN'T BOTHER HIM.
B-DMP
EVENTUALLY, THE POLICE TOOK HIM IN AS EVIDENCE.
WHAT GOES THROUGH A GUY'S HEAD TO MAKE HIM DELIBERATELY BEHEAD A CORPSE?
WELL, ACCORDING TO HIS STATEMENT...

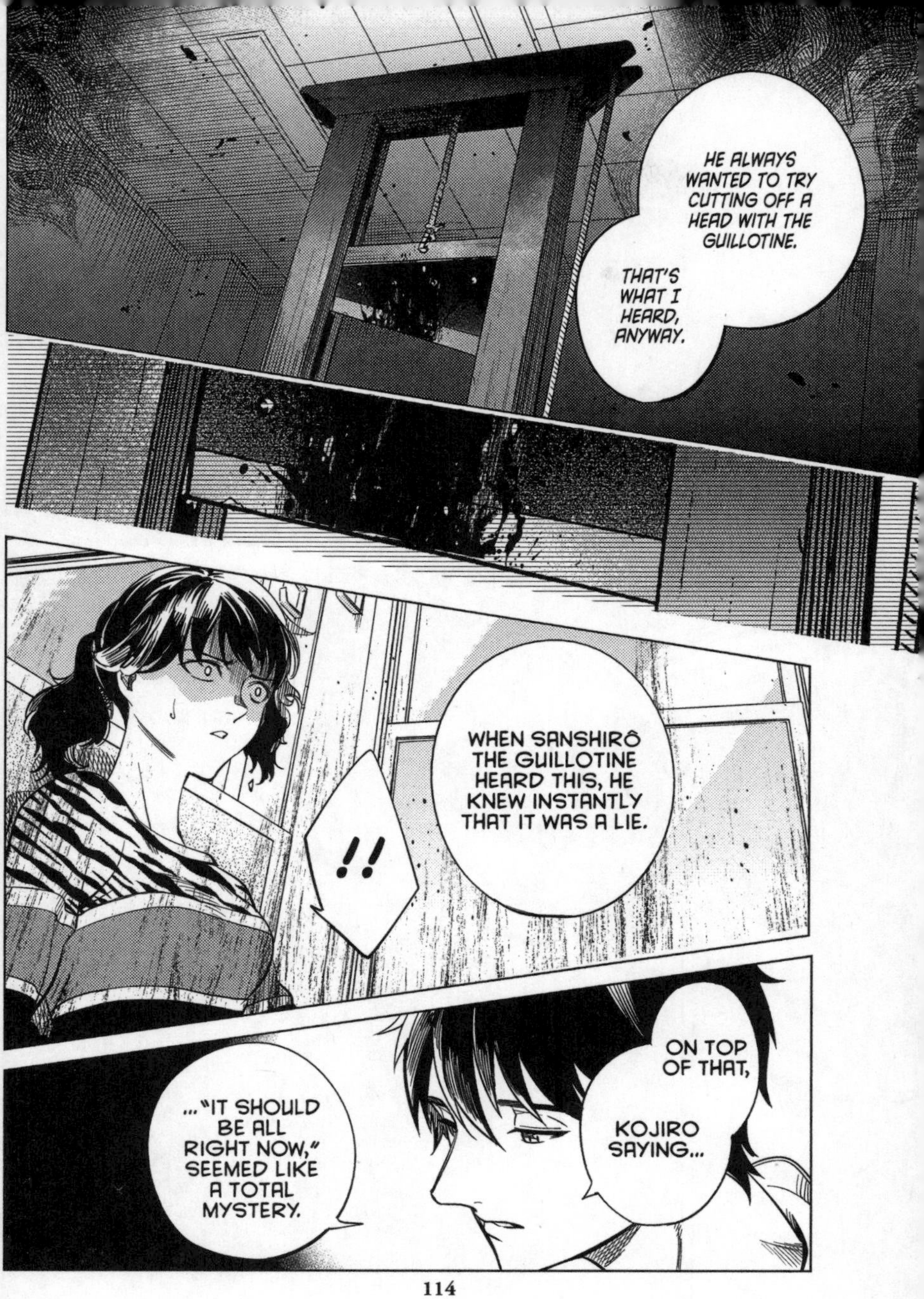
HE ALWAYS WANTED TO TRY CUTTING OFF A HEAD WITH THE GUILLOTINE.
THAT'S WHAT I HEARD, ANYWAY.
WHEN SANSHIRÔ THE GUILLOTINE HEARD THIS, HE KNEW INSTANTLY THAT IT WAS A LIE.
!!
ON TOP OF THAT,
KOJIRO SAYING...
..."IT SHOULD BE ALL RIGHT NOW," SEEMED LIKE A TOTAL MYSTERY.

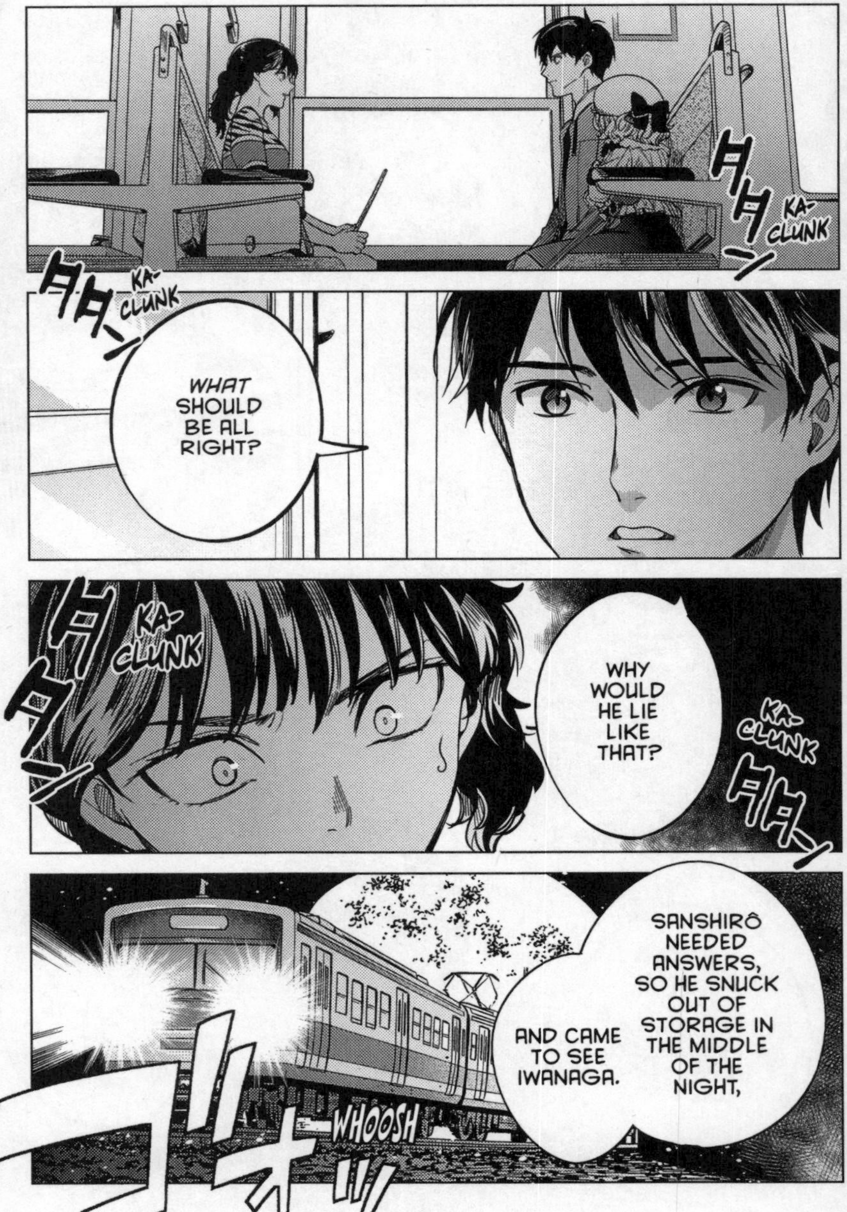
KA-CLUNK
WHAT SHOULD BE ALL RIGHT?
KA-CLUNK
KA-CLUNK
WHY WOULD HE LIE LIKE THAT?
KA-CLUNK
SANSHIRÔ NEEDED ANSWERS, SO HE SNUCK OUT OF STORAGE IN THE MIDDLE OF THE NIGHT,
AND CAME TO SEE IWANAGA.
WHOOSH

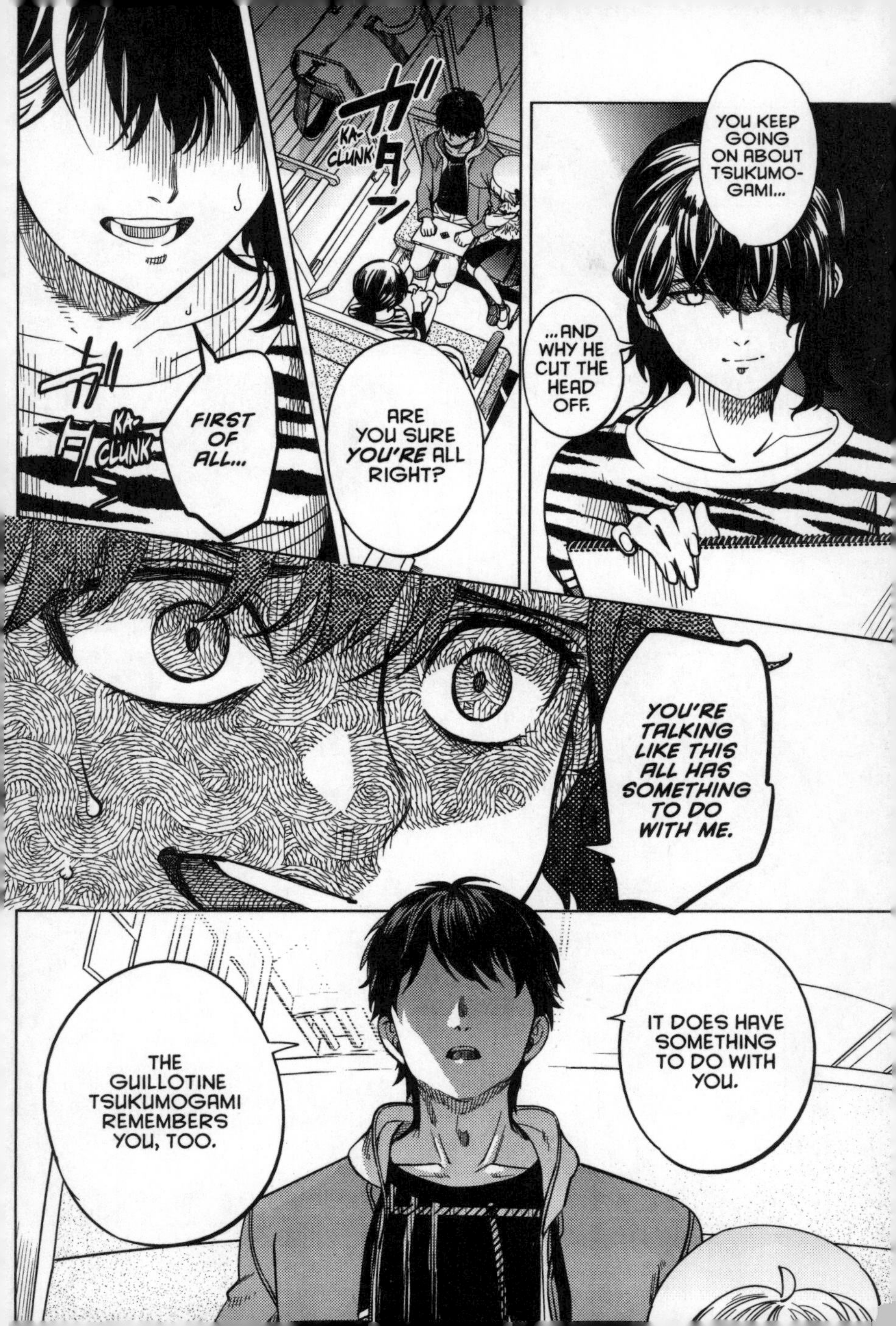
YOU KEEP GOING ON ABOUT TSUKUMOGAMI...
...AND WHY HE CUT THE HEAD OFF.
KA-CLUNK
ARE YOU SURE *YOU'RE* ALL RIGHT?
KA-CLUNK
FIRST OF ALL...
YOU'RE TALKING LIKE THIS ALL HAS SOMETHING TO DO WITH ME.
IT DOES HAVE SOMETHING TO DO WITH YOU.
THE GUILLOTINE TSUKUMOGAMI REMEMBERS YOU, TOO.

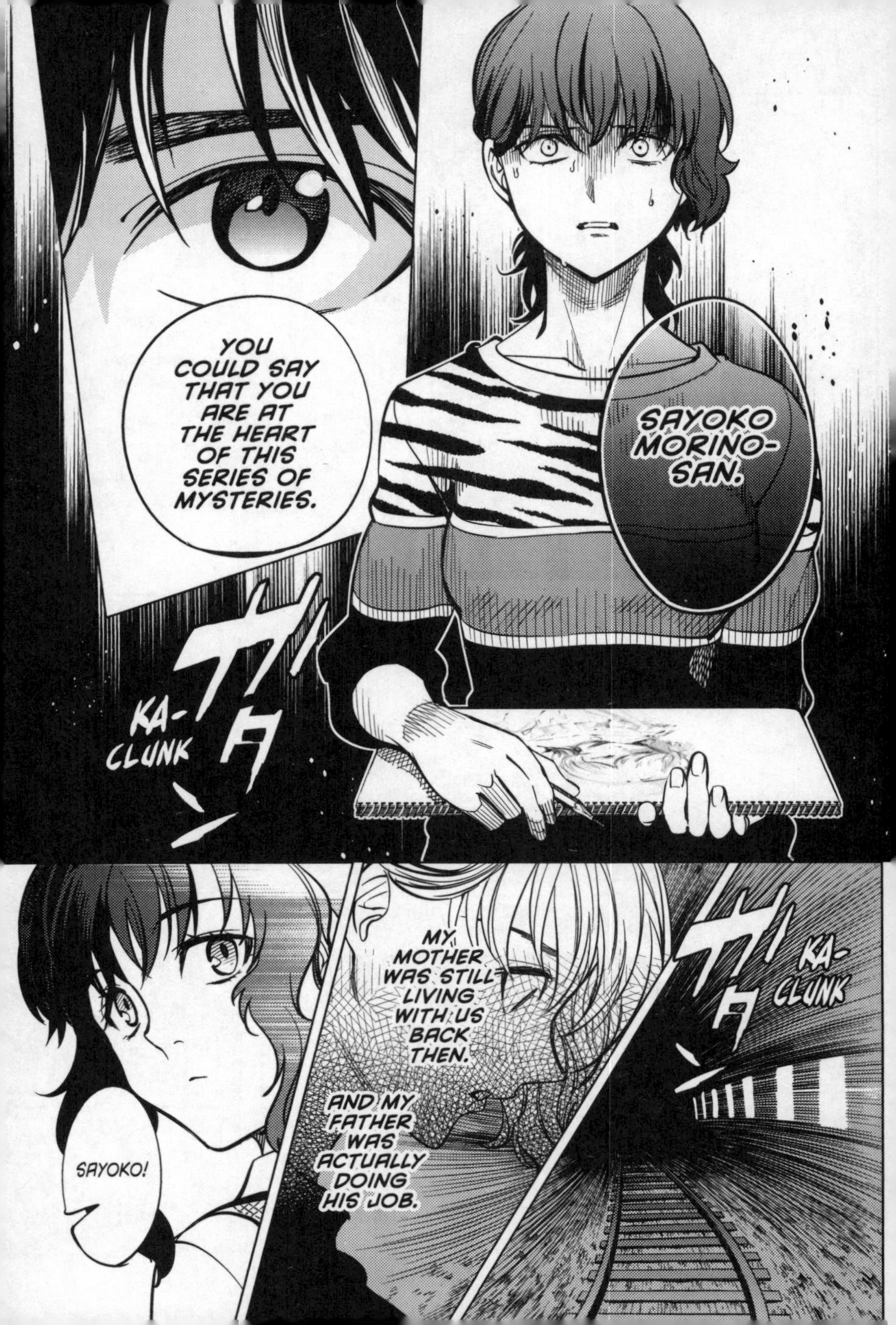
SAYOKO MORINO-SAN.
YOU COULD SAY THAT YOU ARE AT THE HEART OF THIS SERIES OF MYSTERIES.
KA-CLUNK
KA-CLUNK
MY MOTHER WAS STILL LIVING WITH US BACK THEN.
AND MY FATHER WAS ACTUALLY DOING HIS JOB.
SAYOKO!

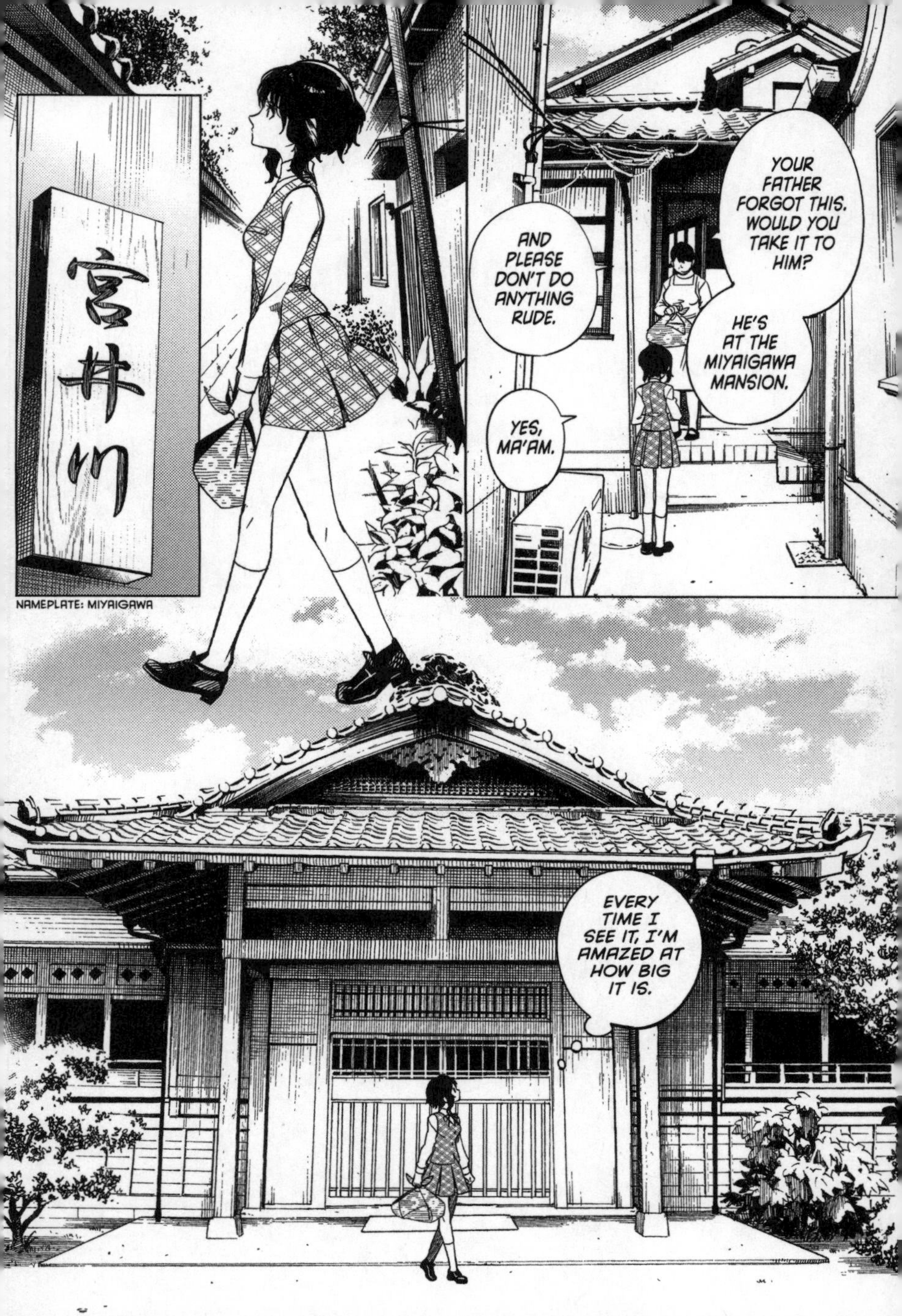
YOUR FATHER FORGOT THIS. WOULD YOU TAKE IT TO HIM?
HE'S AT THE MIYAIGAWA MANSION.
AND PLEASE DON'T DO ANYTHING RUDE.
YES, MA'AM.
宮井川
NAMEPLATE: MIYAIGAWA
EVERY TIME I SEE IT, I'M AMAZED AT HOW BIG IT IS.

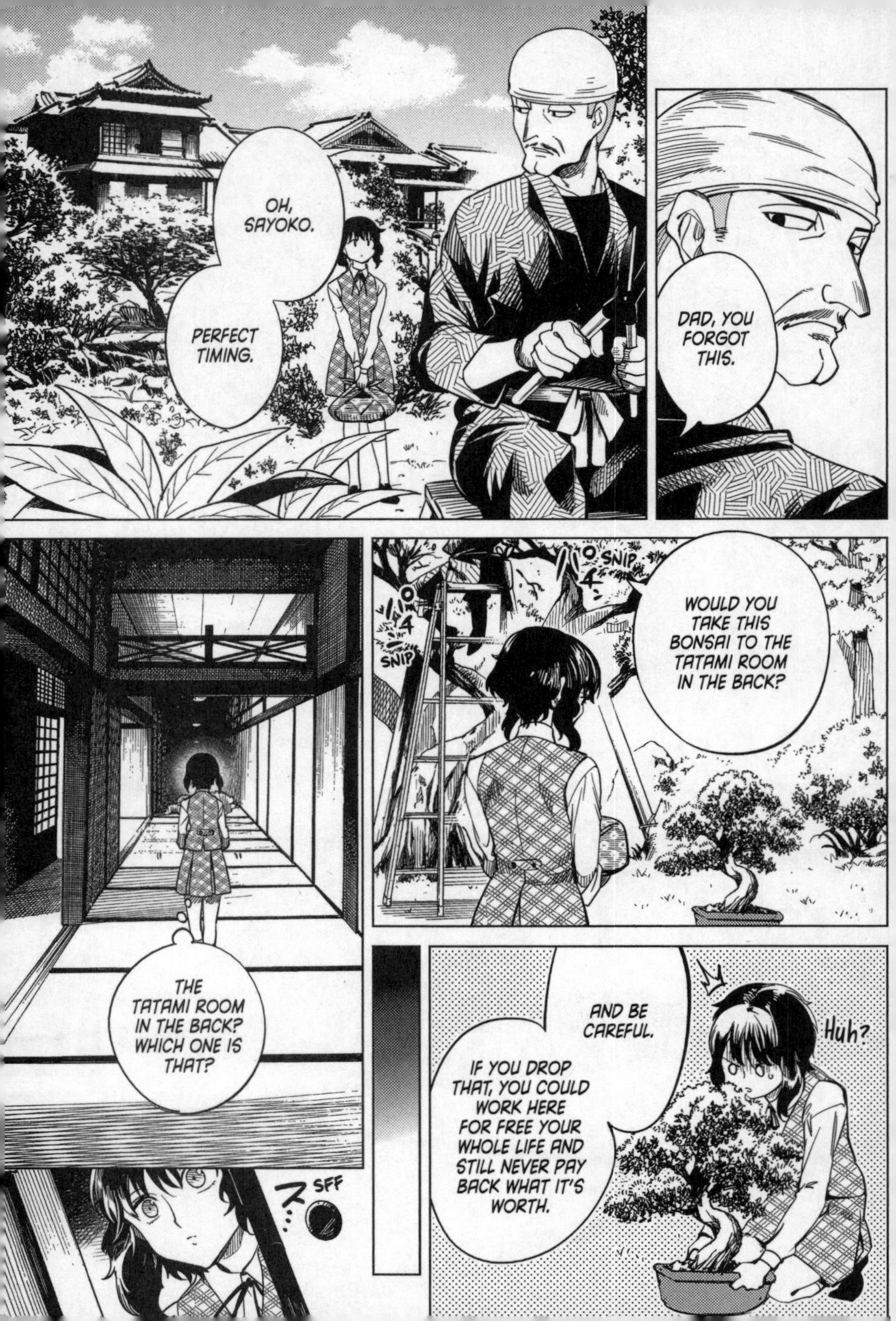
DAD, YOU FORGOT THIS.
OH, SAYOKO.
PERFECT TIMING.
SNIP
SNIP
WOULD YOU TAKE THIS BONSAI TO THE TATAMI ROOM IN THE BACK?
AND BE CAREFUL.
IF YOU DROP THAT, YOU COULD WORK HERE FOR FREE YOUR WHOLE LIFE AND STILL NEVER PAY BACK WHAT IT'S WORTH.
Huh?
THE TATAMI ROOM IN THE BACK? WHICH ONE IS THAT?
SFF

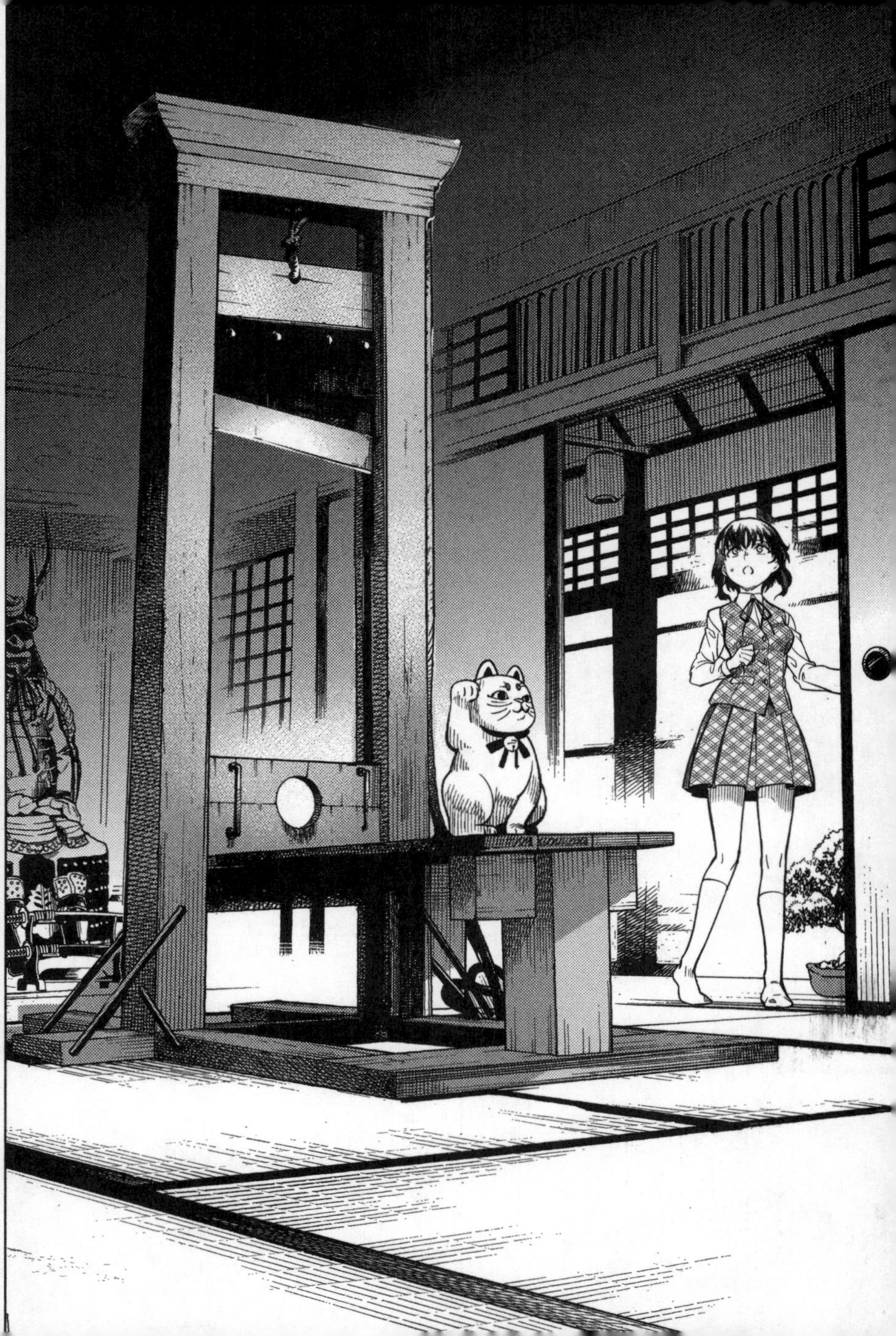

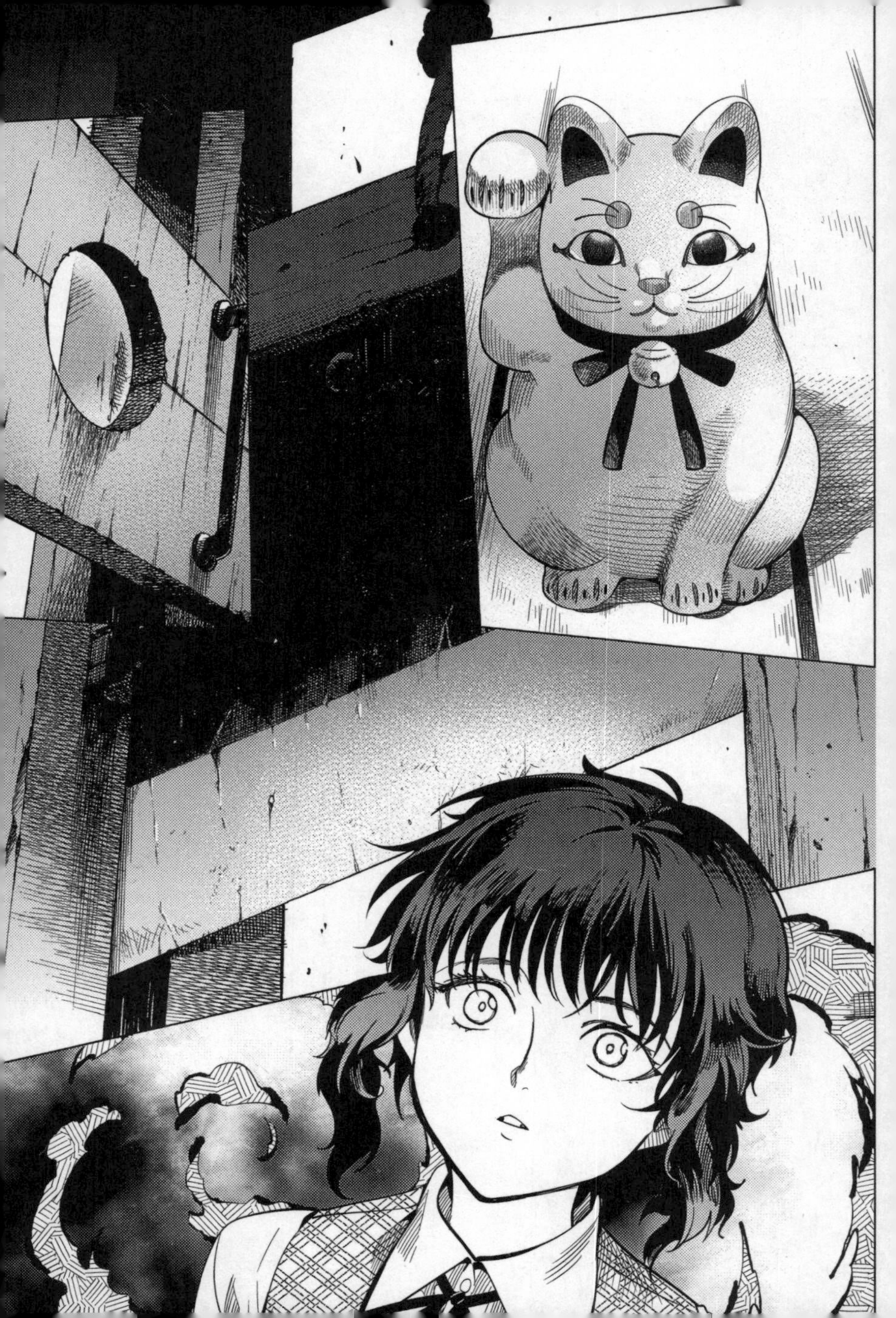

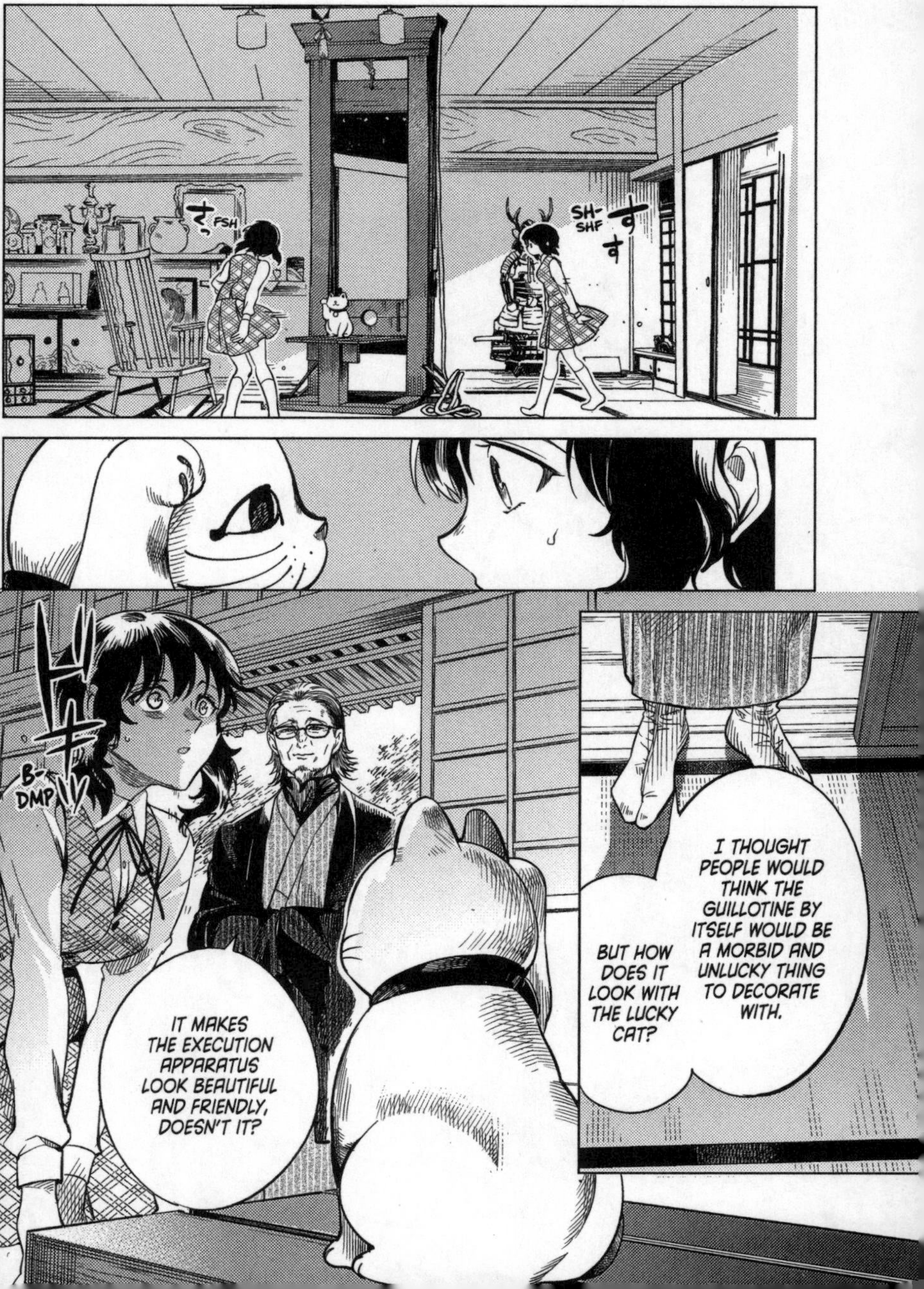
SH- SHF すす
さっ FSH
I THOUGHT PEOPLE WOULD THINK THE GUILLOTINE BY ITSELF WOULD BE A MORBID AND UNLUCKY THING TO DECORATE WITH.
BUT HOW DOES IT LOOK WITH THE LUCKY CAT?
B-DMP
IT MAKES THE EXECUTION APPARATUS LOOK BEAUTIFUL AND FRIENDLY, DOESN'T IT?

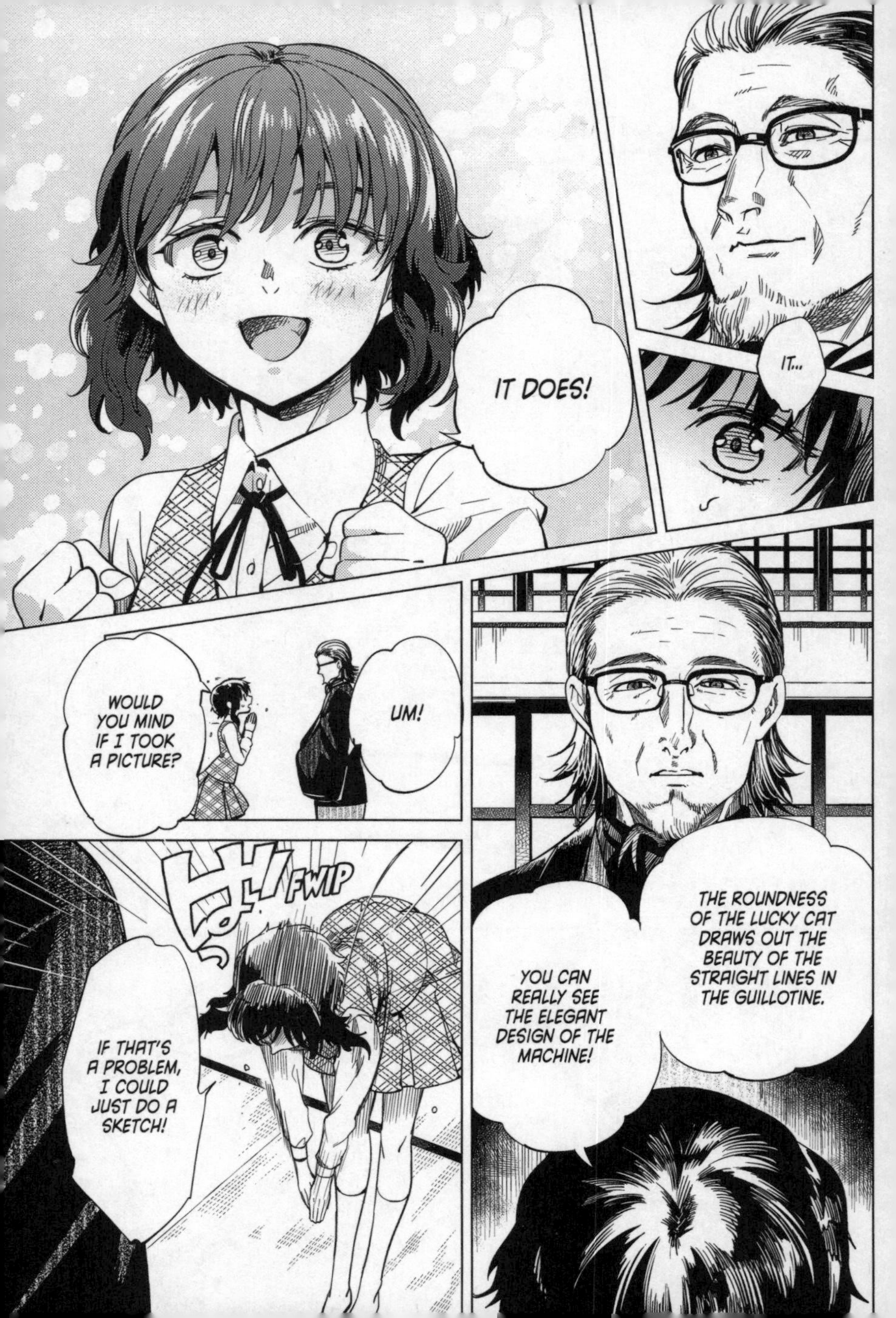
IT...
IT DOES!
THE ROUNDNESS OF THE LUCKY CAT DRAWS OUT THE BEAUTY OF THE STRAIGHT LINES IN THE GUILLOTINE.
YOU CAN REALLY SEE THE ELEGANT DESIGN OF THE MACHINE!
UM!
WOULD YOU MIND IF I TOOK A PICTURE?
FWIP
IF THAT'S A PROBLEM, I COULD JUST DO A SKETCH!

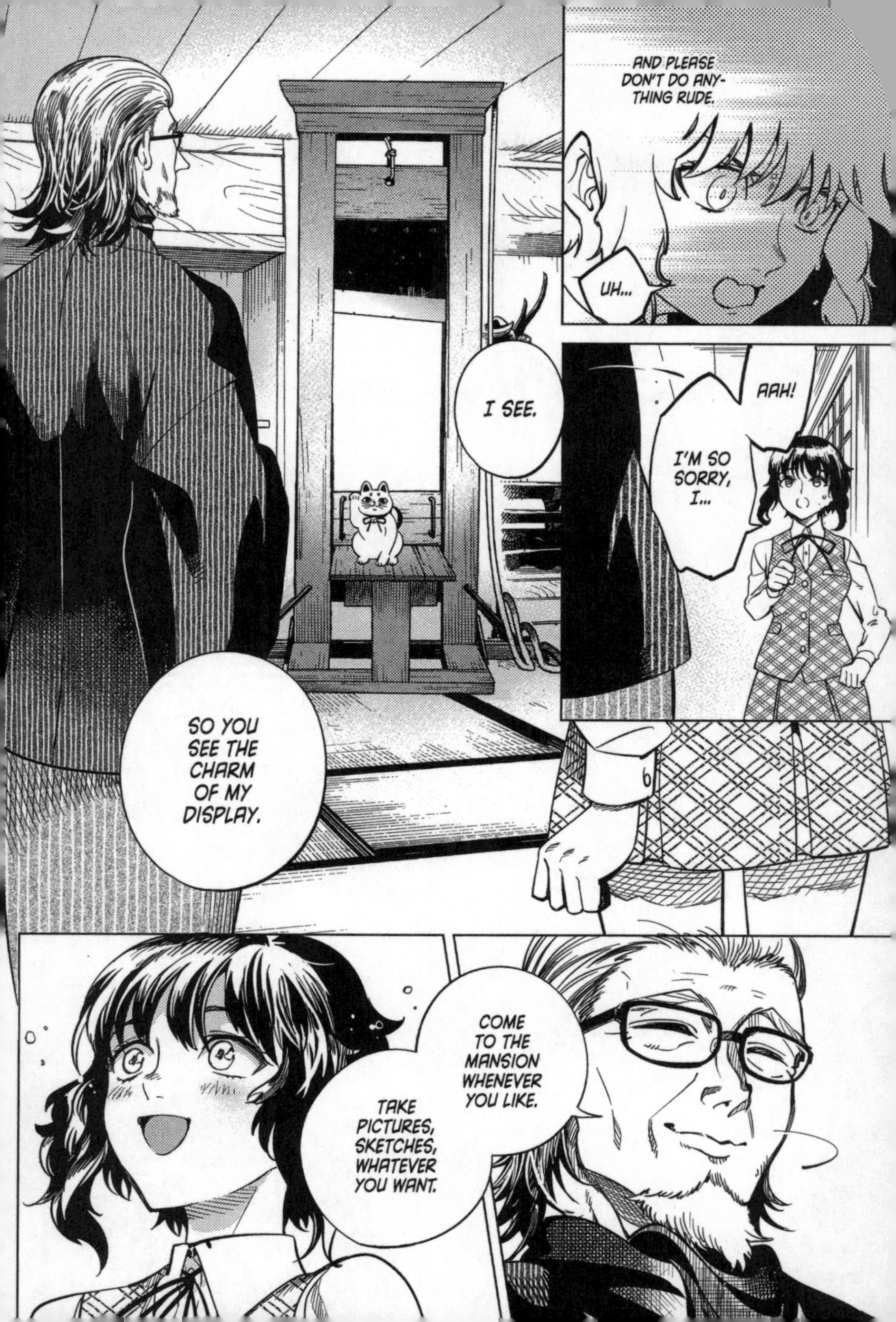
AND PLEASE DON'T DO ANY- THING RUDE.
UH...
AAH!
I'M SO SORRY, I...
I SEE.
SO YOU SEE THE CHARM OF MY DISPLAY.
COME TO THE MANSION WHENEVER YOU LIKE.
TAKE PICTURES, SKETCHES, WHATEVER YOU WANT.

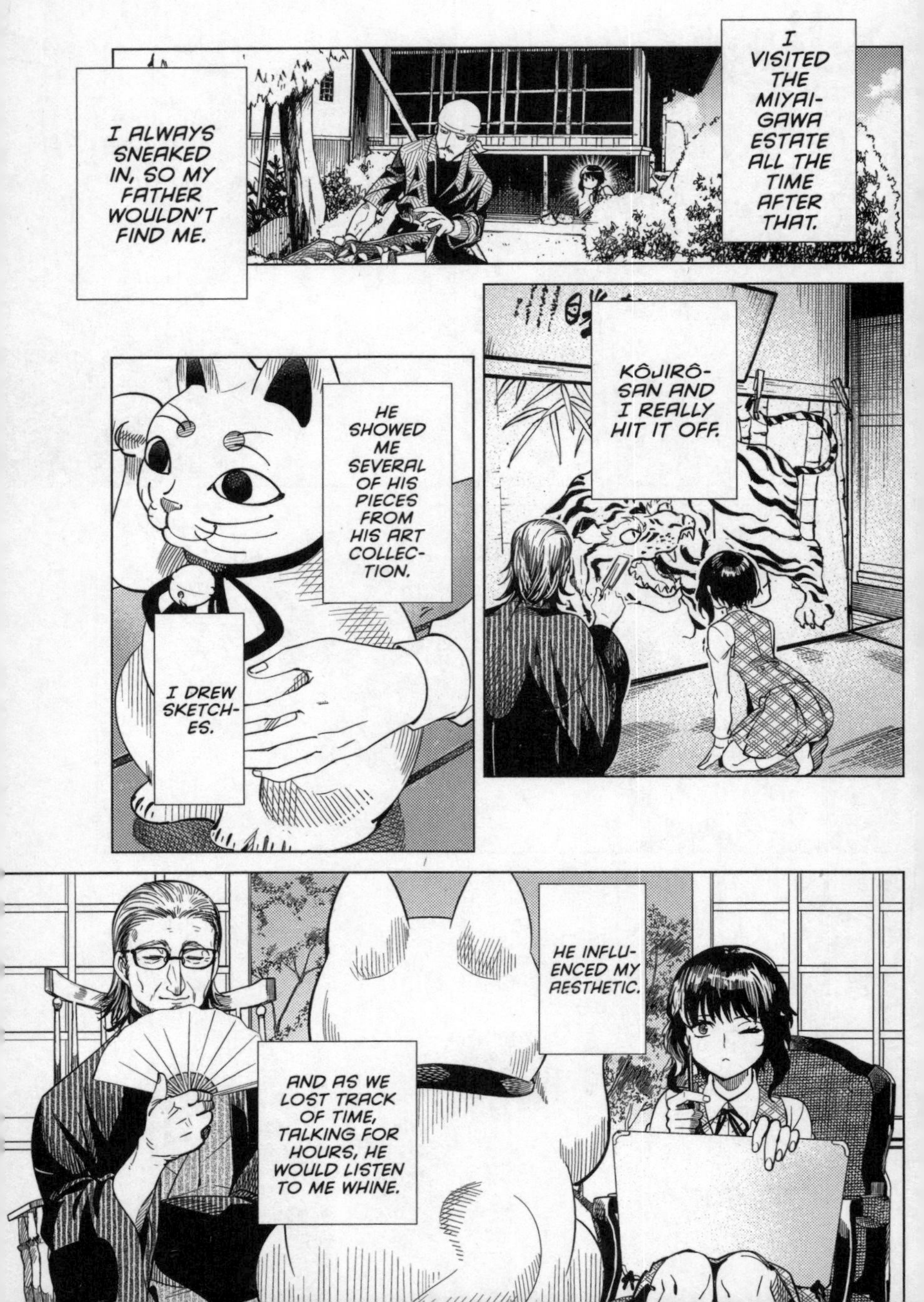
I VISITED THE MIYAI-GAWA ESTATE ALL THE TIME AFTER THAT.
I ALWAYS SNEAKED IN, SO MY FATHER WOULDN'T FIND ME.
KÔJIRÔ-SAN AND I REALLY HIT IT OFF.
HE SHOWED ME SEVERAL OF HIS PIECES FROM HIS ART COLLEC-TION.
I DREW SKETCH-ES.
HE INFLU-ENCED MY AESTHETIC.
AND AS WE LOST TRACK OF TIME, TALKING FOR HOURS, HE WOULD LISTEN TO ME WHINE.

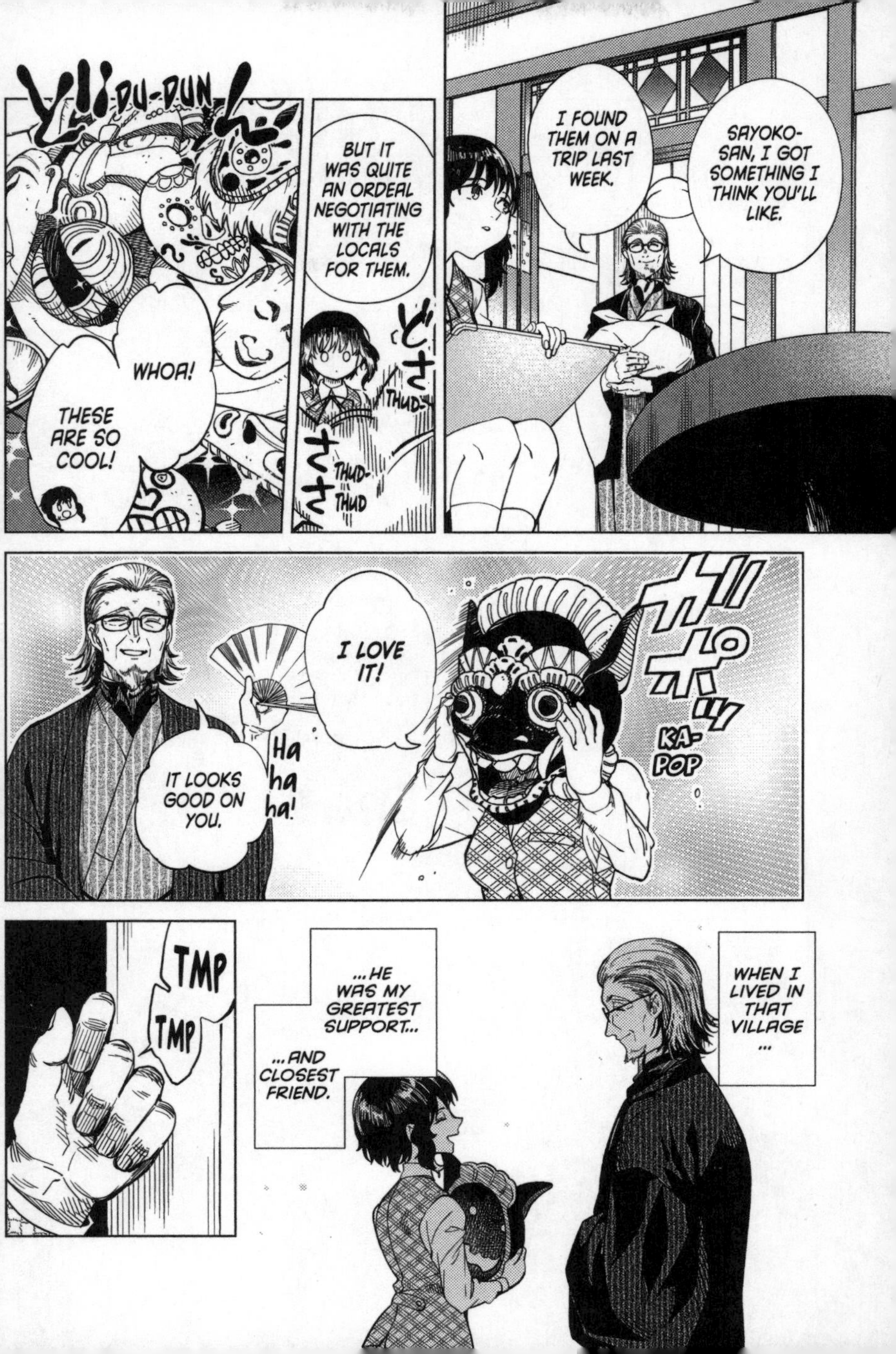
SAYOKO-SAN, I GOT SOMETHING I THINK YOU'LL LIKE.
I FOUND THEM ON A TRIP LAST WEEK.
BUT IT WAS QUITE AN ORDEAL NEGOTIATING WITH THE LOCALS FOR THEM.
どさ
THUD
THUD-THUD
DU-DUN
WHOA!
THESE ARE SO COOL!
KA-POP
I LOVE IT!
Ha ha ha!
IT LOOKS GOOD ON YOU.
WHEN I LIVED IN THAT VILLAGE ...
...HE WAS MY GREATEST SUPPORT...
...AND CLOSEST FRIEND.
TMP
TMP

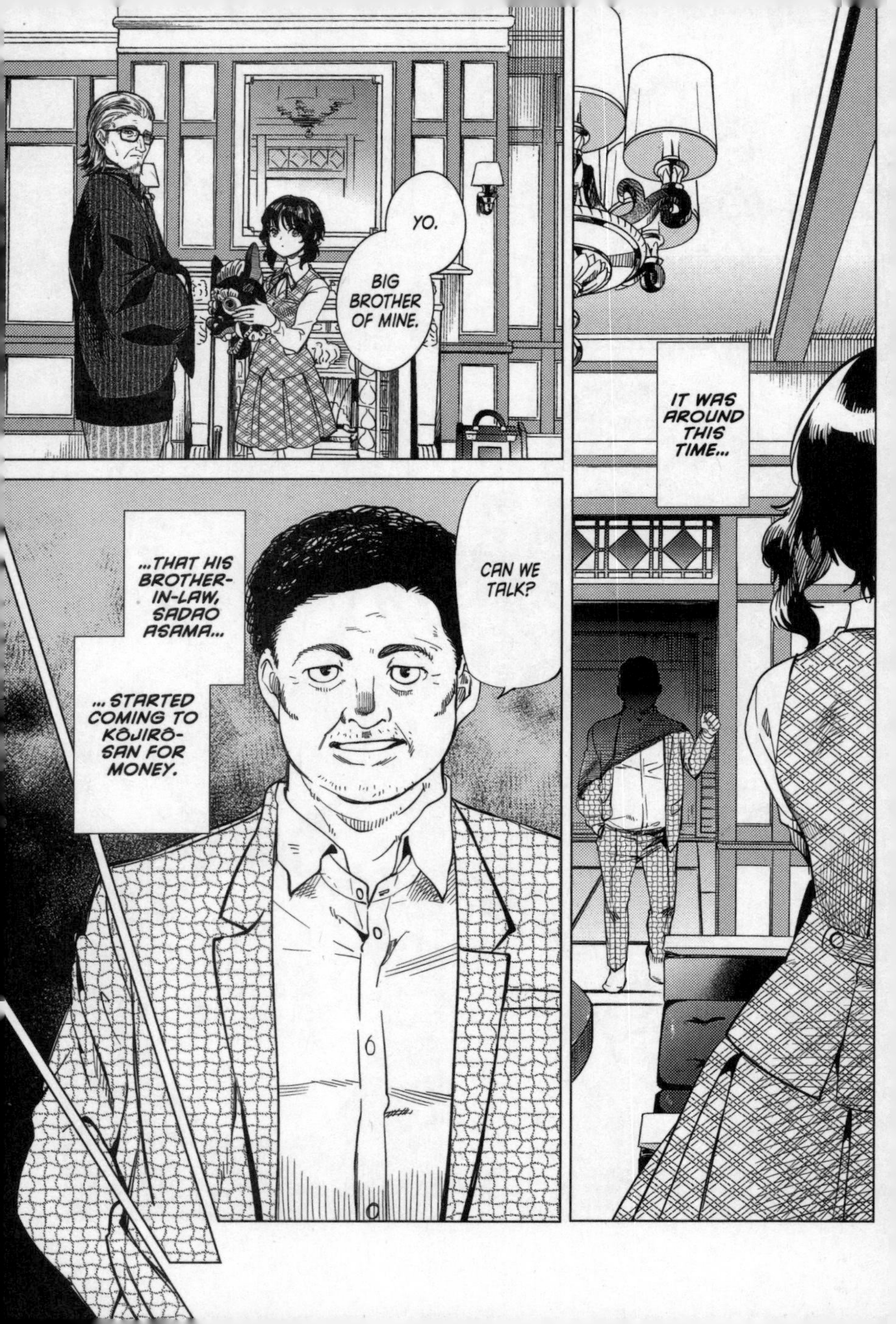
IT WAS AROUND THIS TIME...
YO.
BIG BROTHER OF MINE.
CAN WE TALK?
...THAT HIS BROTHER-IN-LAW, SADAO ASAMA...
...STARTED COMING TO KÔJIRÔ-SAN FOR MONEY.

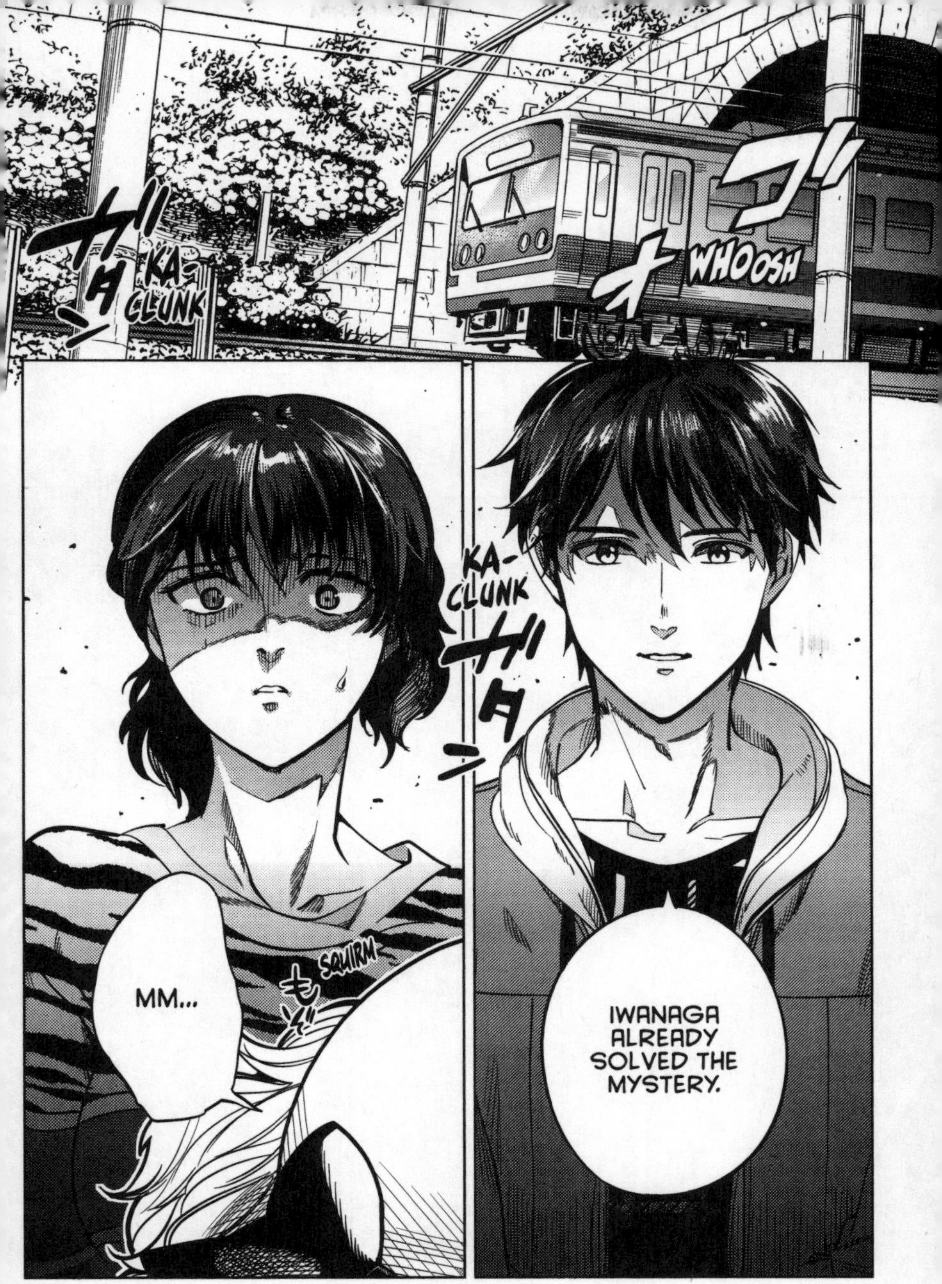
ゴオ
WHOOSH
ガタン
KA-CLUNK
IWANAGA ALREADY SOLVED THE MYSTERY.
ガタン
KA-CLUNK
もぞ
SQUIRM
MM...

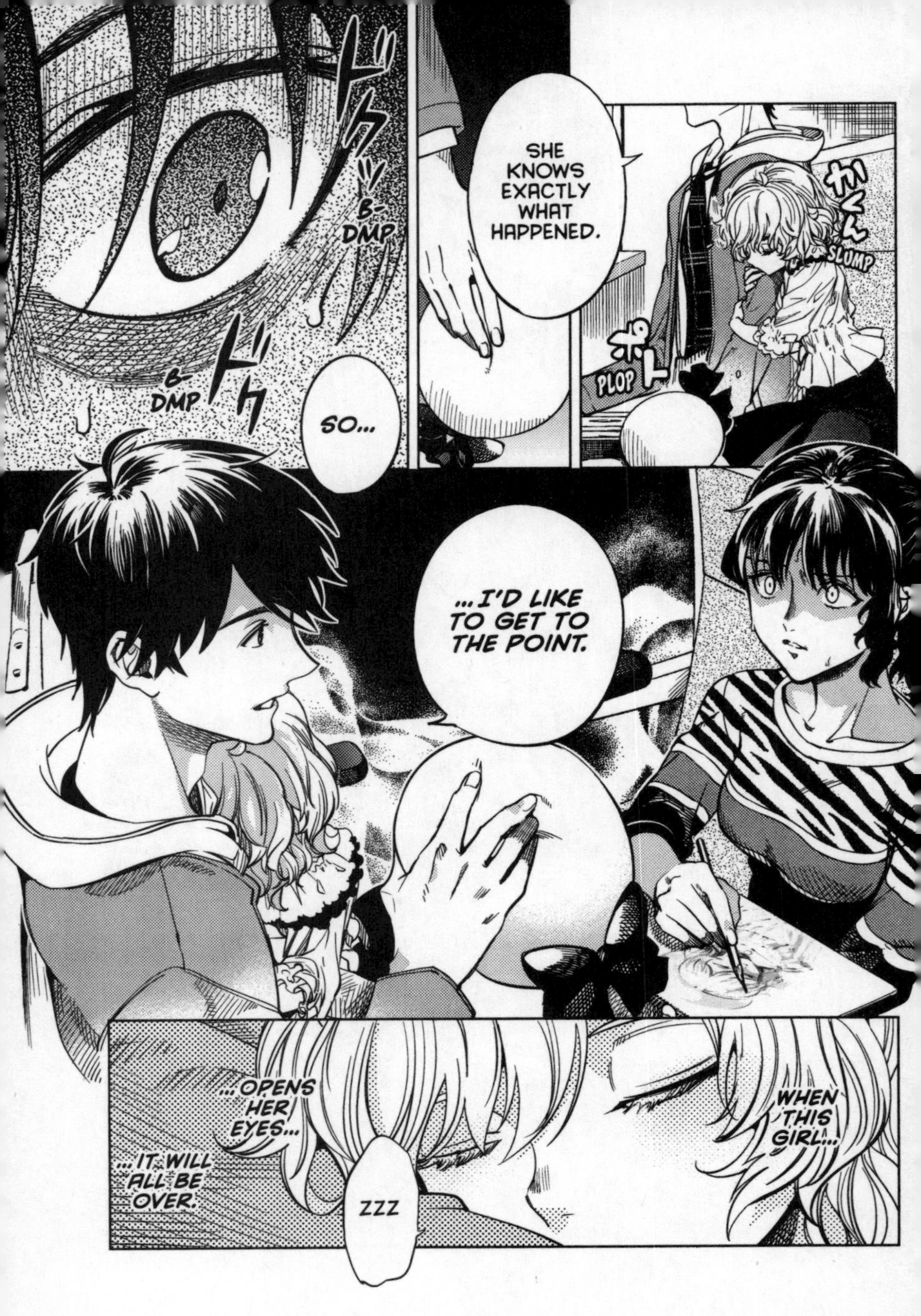
かくん
SLUMP
ポト
PLOP
SHE KNOWS EXACTLY WHAT HAPPENED.
B-DMP
B-DMP
SO...
...I'D LIKE TO GET TO THE POINT.
WHEN THIS GIRL...
...OPENS HER EYES...
...IT WILL ALL BE OVER.
ZZZ

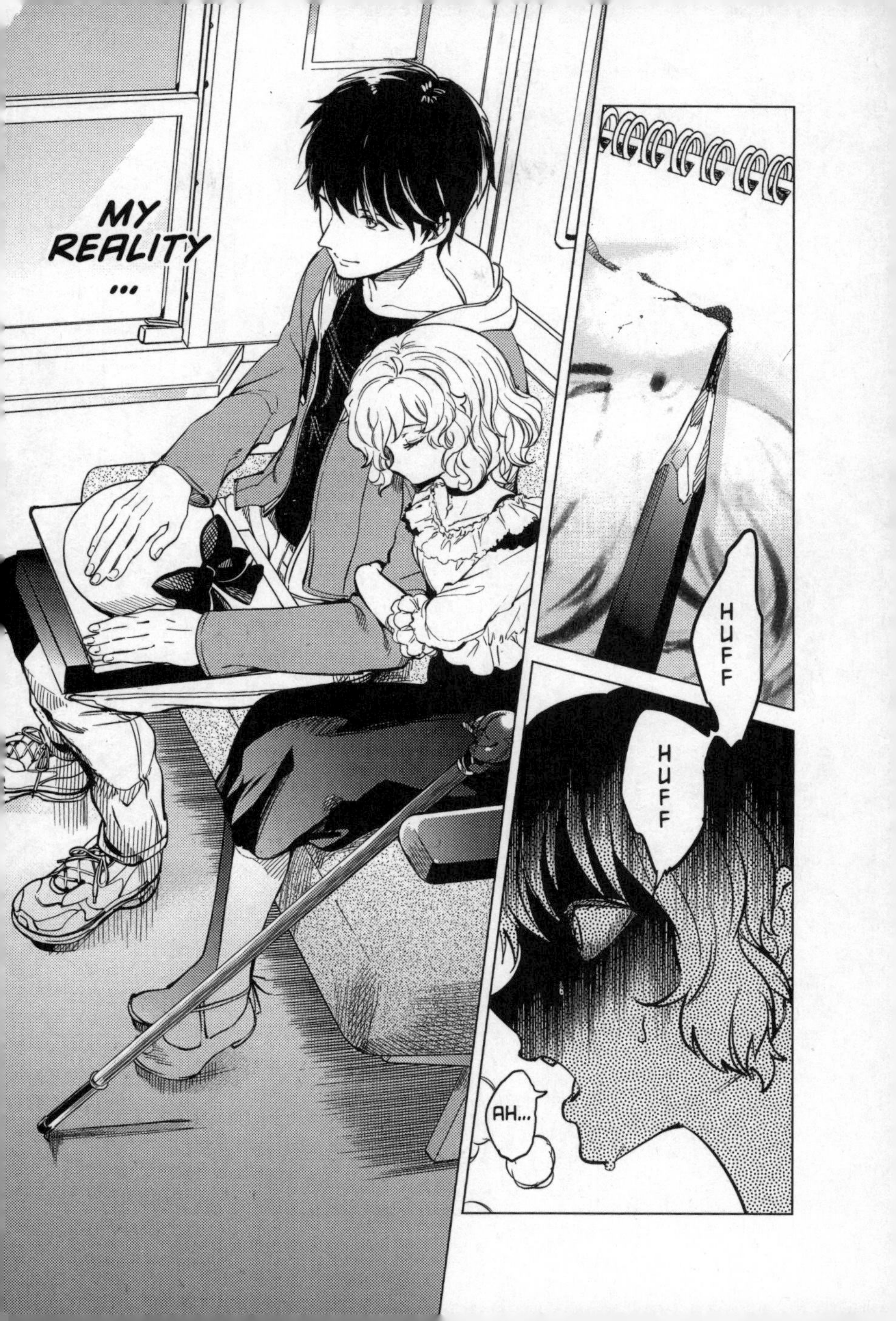
HUFF
HUFF
AH...
MY REALITY ...

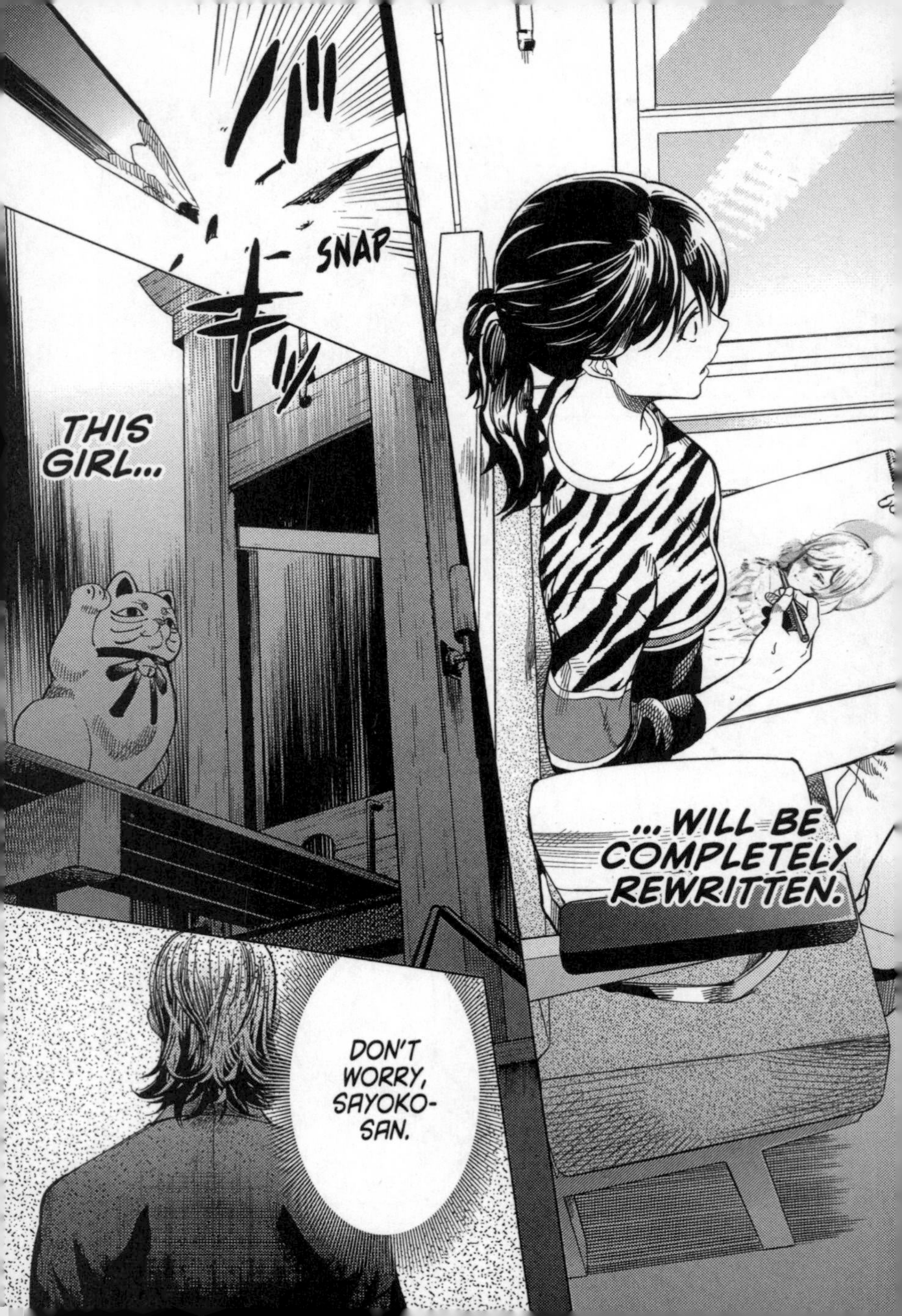
SNAP
THIS GIRL...
...WILL BE COMPLETELY REWRITTEN.
DON'T WORRY, SAYOKO-SAN.

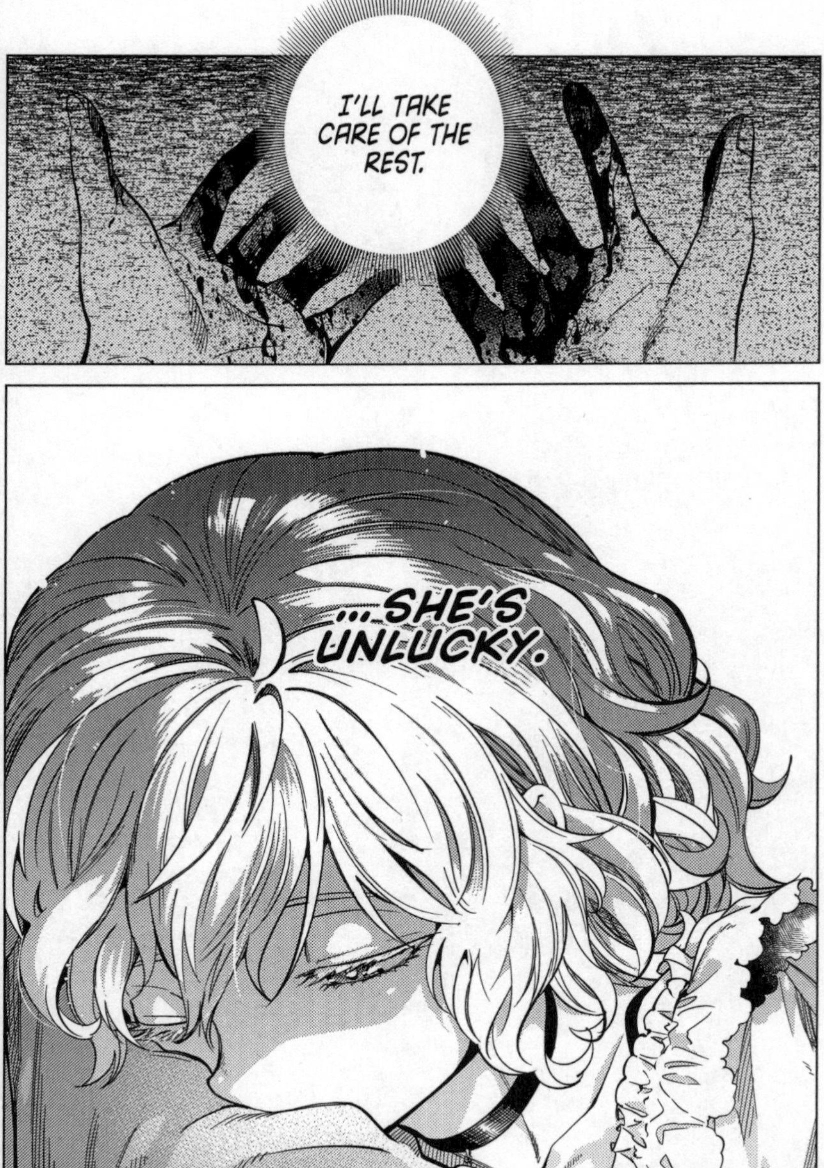
I'LL TAKE CARE OF THE REST.
...SHE'S UNLUCKY.

IN/SPECTRE

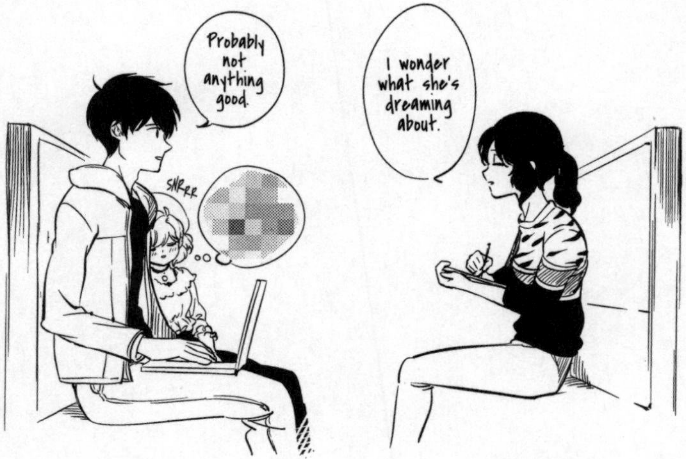
I wonder what she's dreaming about.
Probably not anything good.
SNRRR

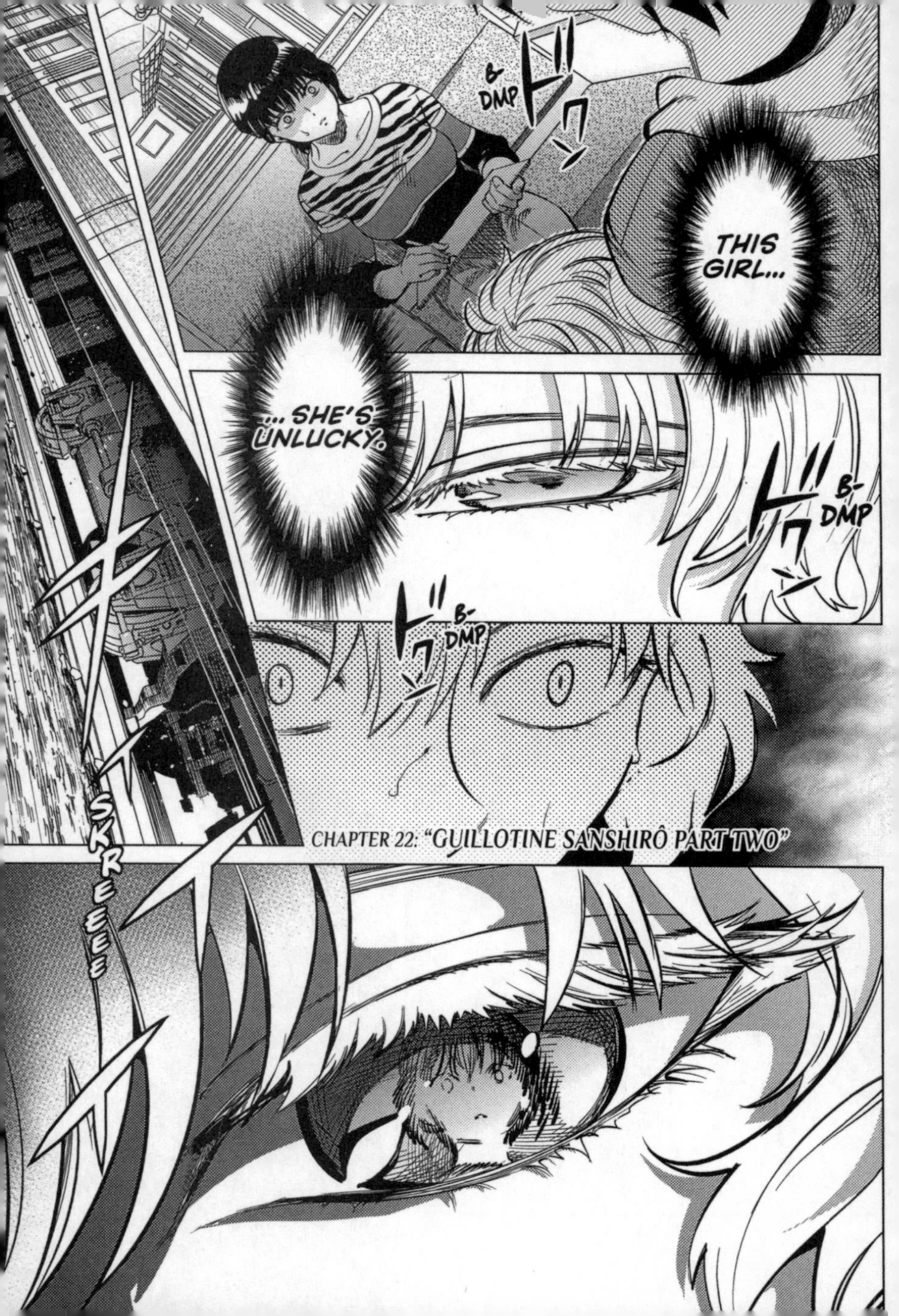
B-DMP
THIS GIRL...
B-DMP
...SHE'S UNLUCKY.
B-DMP
CHAPTER 22: "GUILLOTINE SANSHIRÔ PART TWO"
SKREEEE

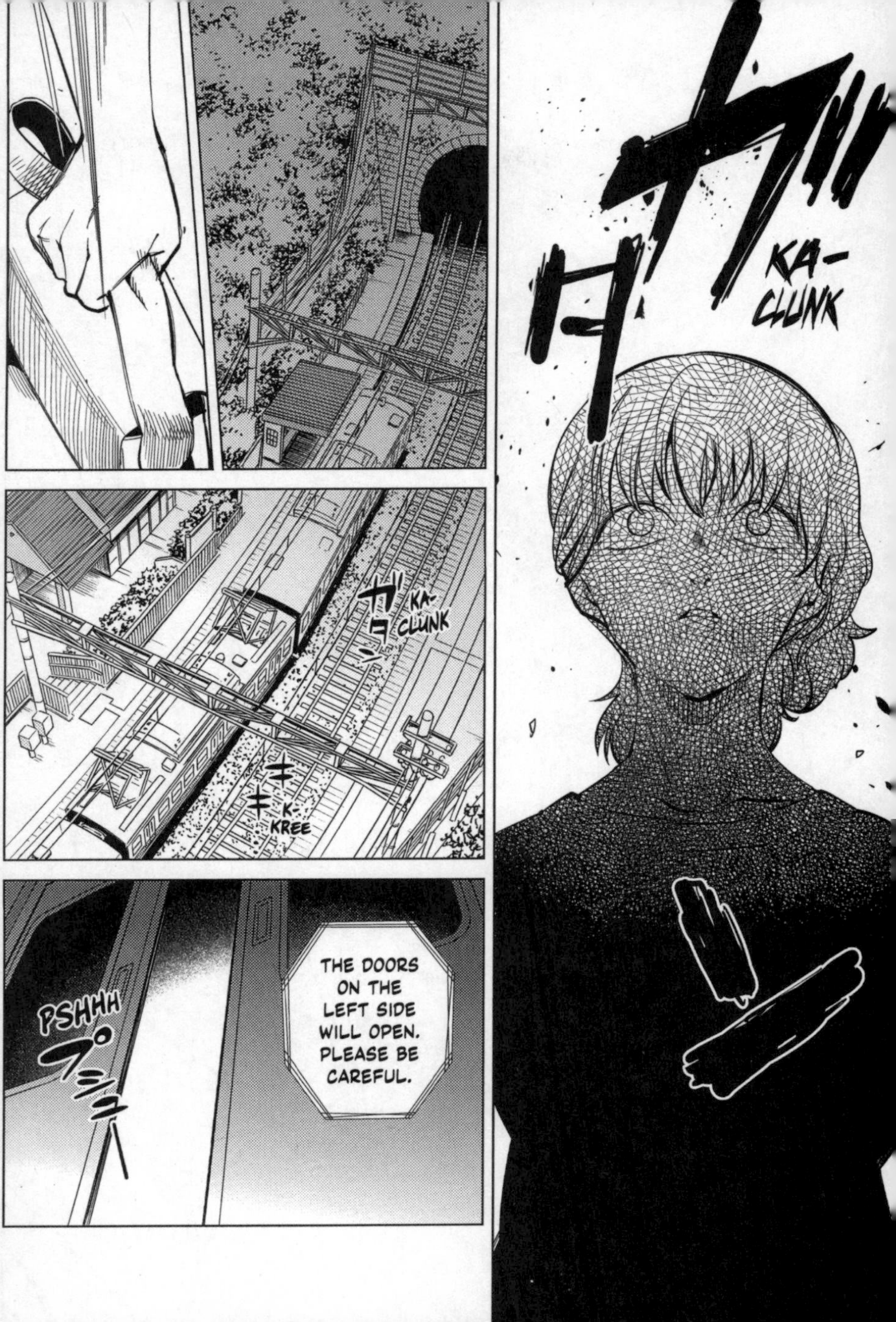
KA-CLUNK
KA-CLUNK
K-KREE
THE DOORS ON THE LEFT SIDE WILL OPEN. PLEASE BE CAREFUL.
PSHHH

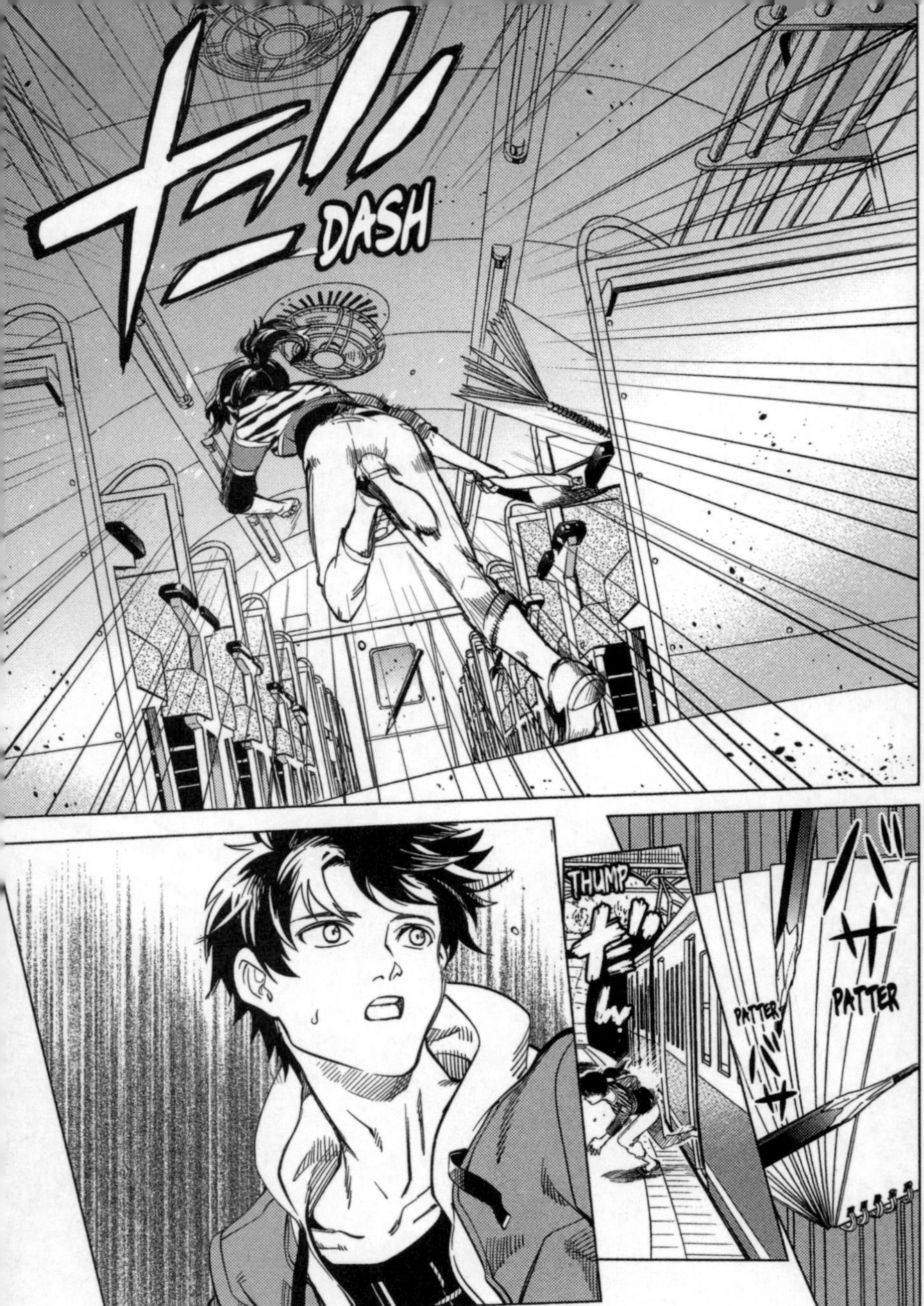
DASH
THUMP
PATTER
PATTER

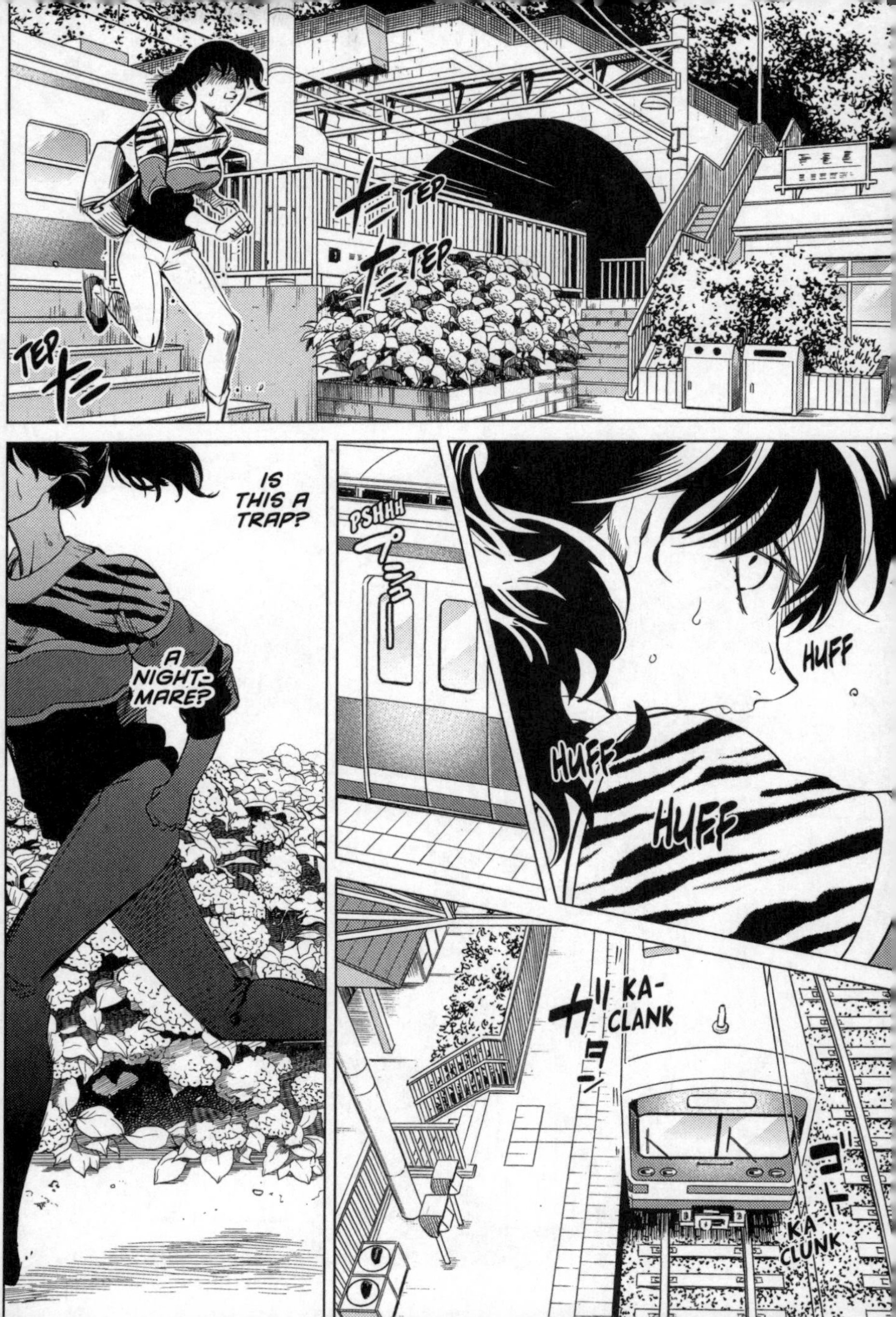

TEP
TEP
TEP
HUFF
HUFF
HUFF
PSHHH
KA-CLANK
KA-CLUNK
IS THIS A TRAP?
A NIGHT-MARE?

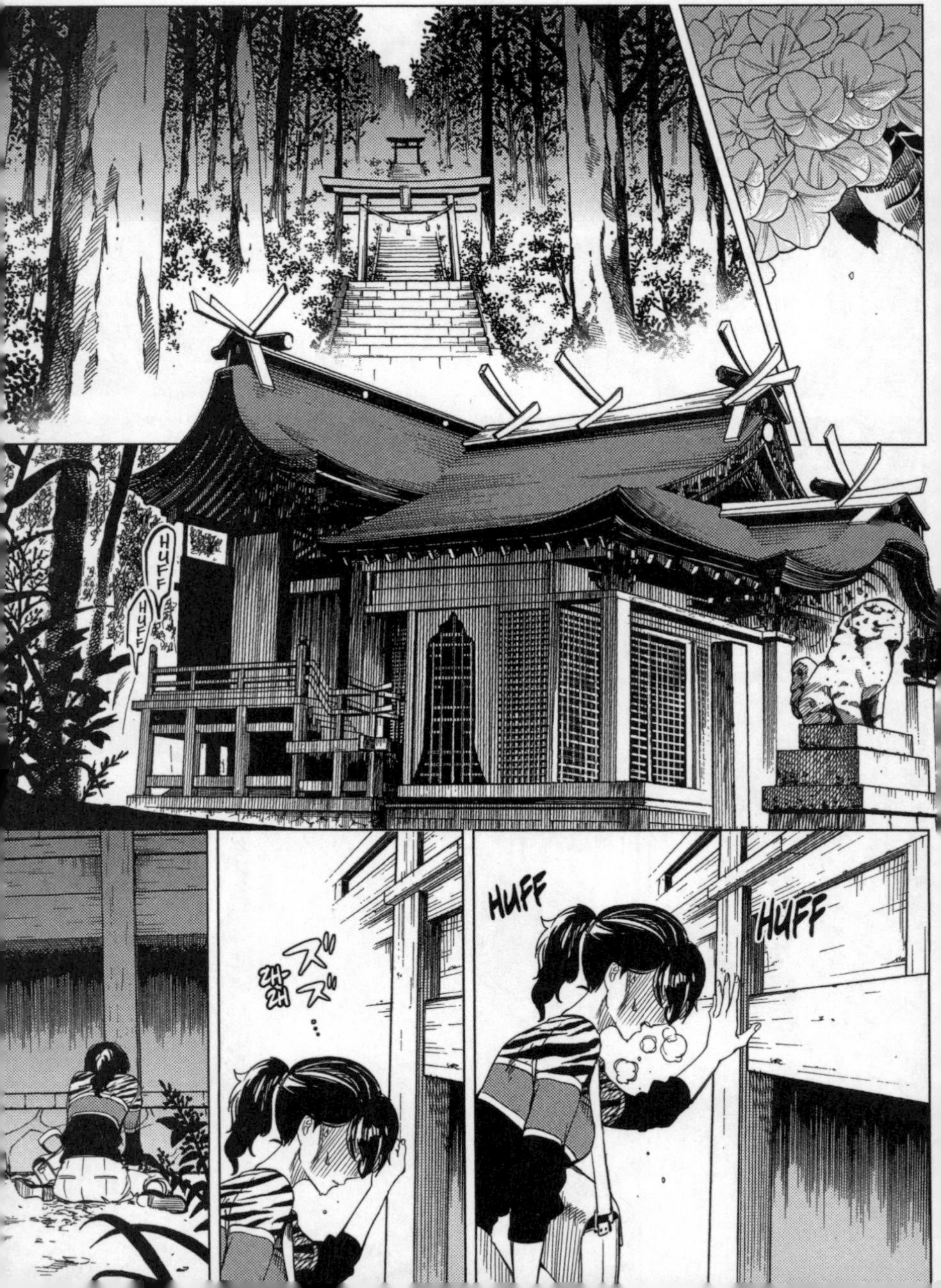
HUFF
HUFF
HUFF
HUFF
ズズ
ZH ZH...

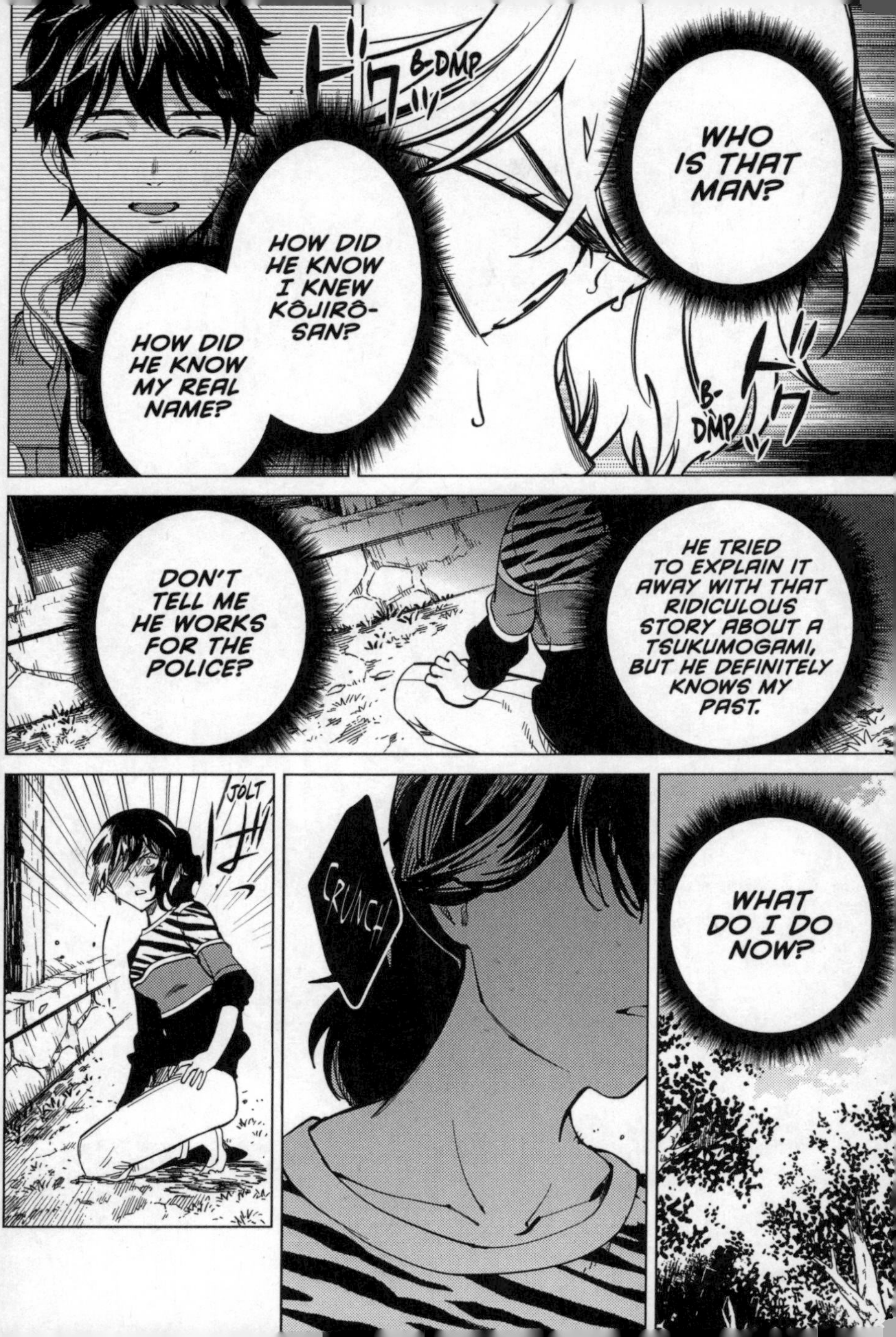
B-DMP
WHO IS THAT MAN?
B-DMP
HOW DID HE KNOW I KNEW KÔJIRÔ-SAN?
HOW DID HE KNOW MY REAL NAME?
HE TRIED TO EXPLAIN IT AWAY WITH THAT RIDICULOUS STORY ABOUT A TSUKUMOGAMI, BUT HE DEFINITELY KNOWS MY PAST.
DON'T TELL ME HE WORKS FOR THE POLICE?
WHAT DO I DO NOW?
CRUNCH
JOLT

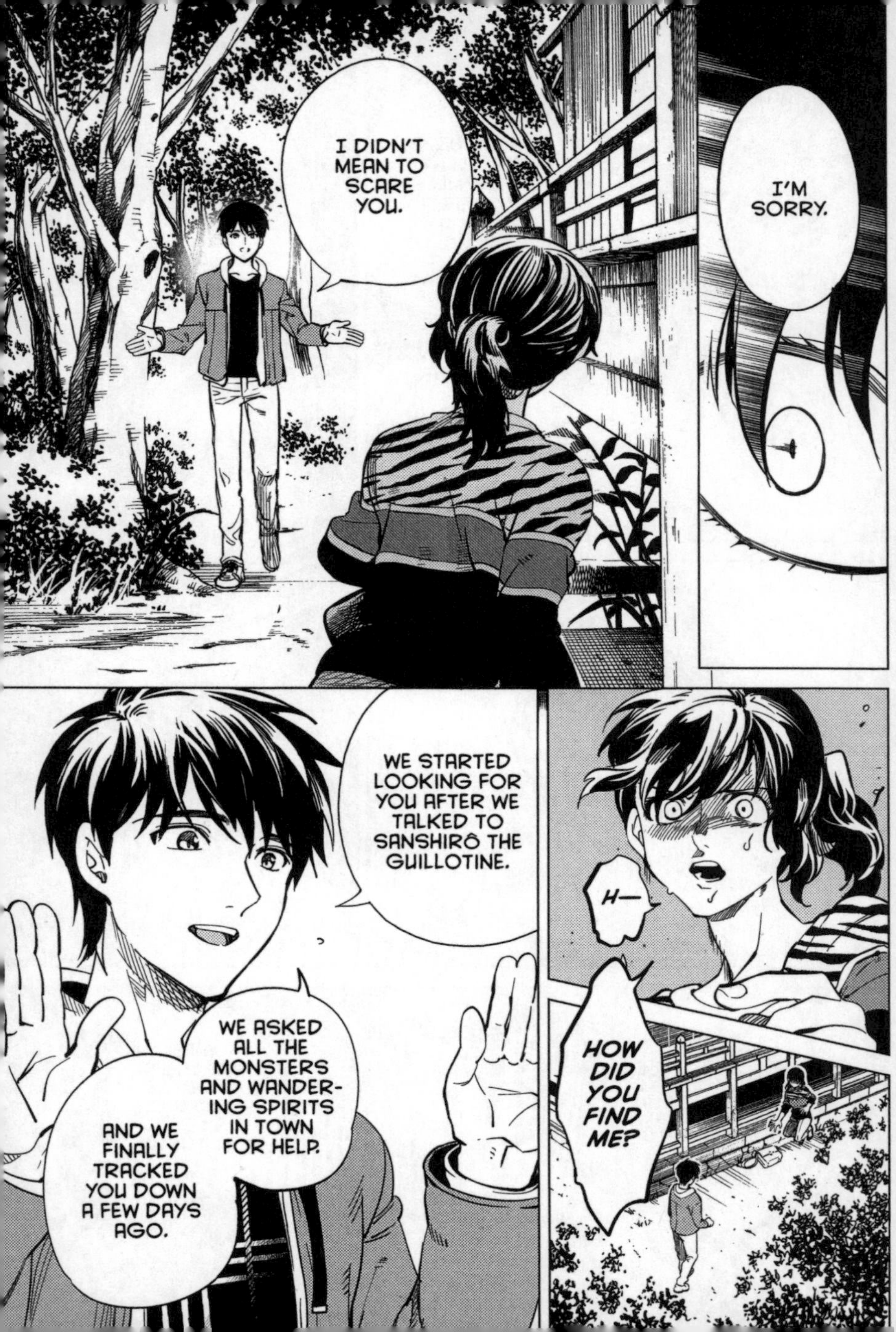
I'M SORRY.
I DIDN'T MEAN TO SCARE YOU.
H—
HOW DID YOU FIND ME?
WE STARTED LOOKING FOR YOU AFTER WE TALKED TO SANSHIRÔ THE GUILLOTINE.
WE ASKED ALL THE MONSTERS AND WANDER-ING SPIRITS IN TOWN FOR HELP.
AND WE FINALLY TRACKED YOU DOWN A FEW DAYS AGO.

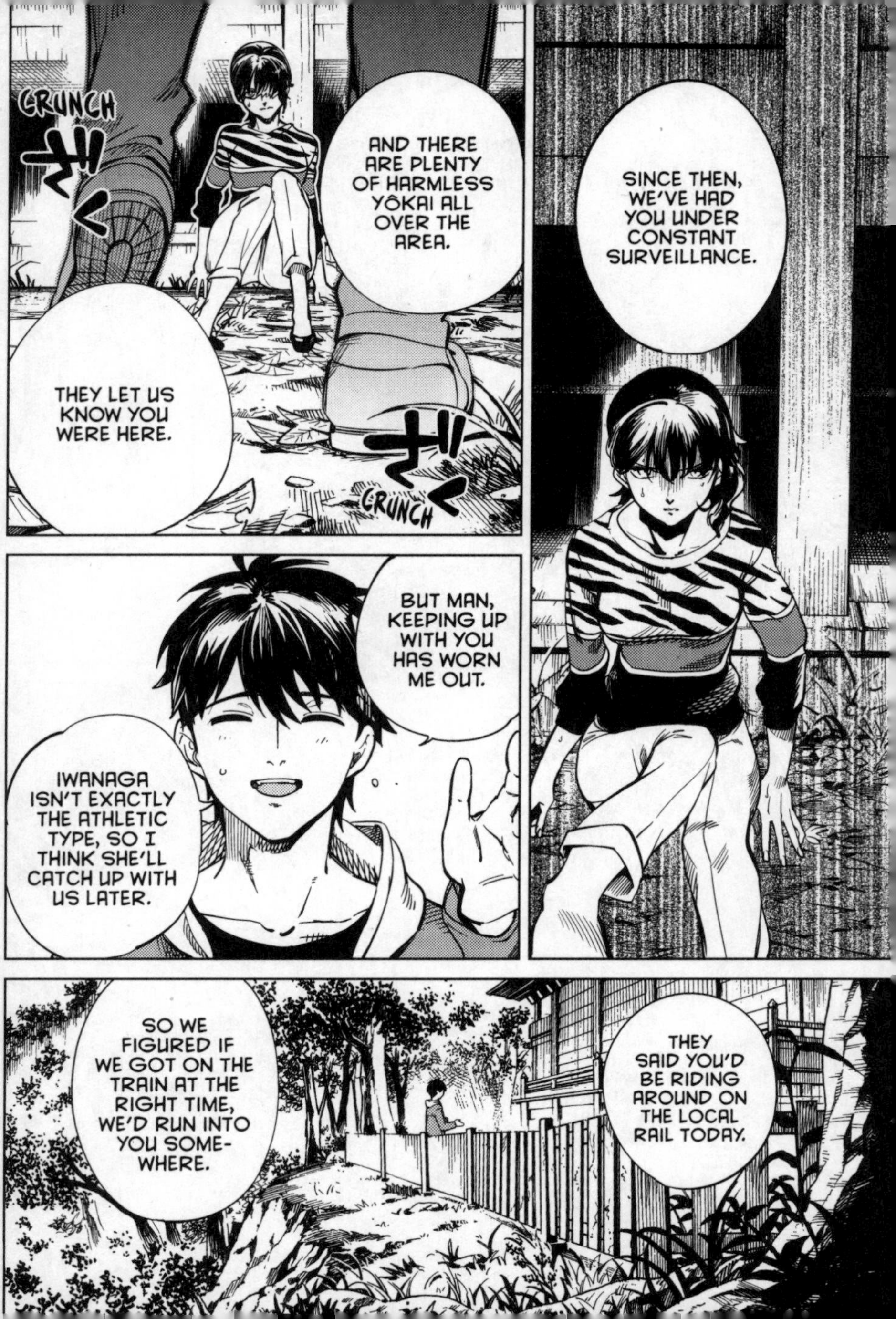
SINCE THEN, WE'VE HAD YOU UNDER CONSTANT SURVEILLANCE.
CRUNCH
AND THERE ARE PLENTY OF HARMLESS YÔKAI ALL OVER THE AREA.
THEY LET US KNOW YOU WERE HERE.
CRUNCH
BUT MAN, KEEPING UP WITH YOU HAS WORN ME OUT.
IWANAGA ISN'T EXACTLY THE ATHLETIC TYPE, SO I THINK SHE'LL CATCH UP WITH US LATER.
THEY SAID YOU'D BE RIDING AROUND ON THE LOCAL RAIL TODAY.
SO WE FIGURED IF WE GOT ON THE TRAIN AT THE RIGHT TIME, WE'D RUN INTO YOU SOME-WHERE.

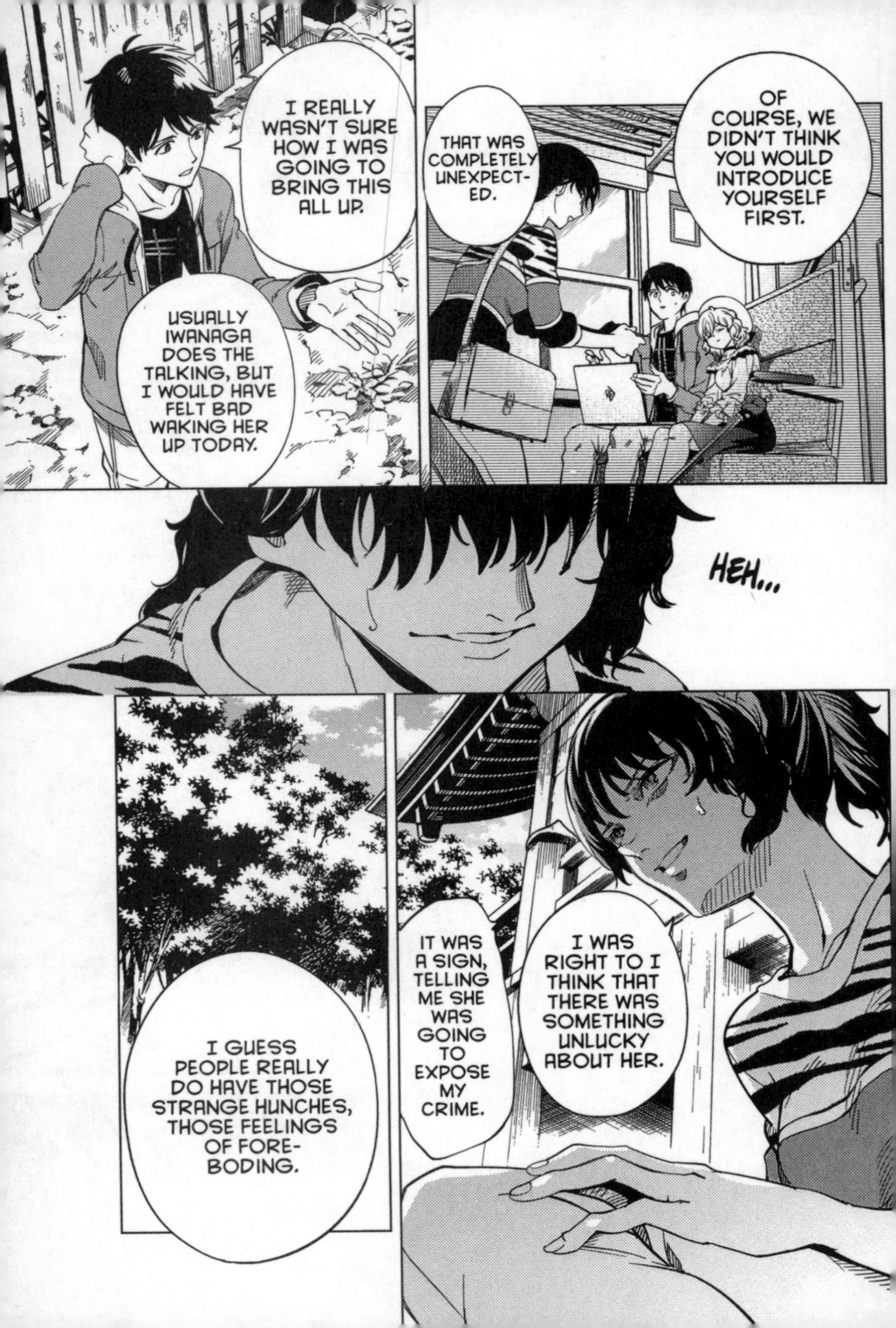
OF COURSE, WE DIDN'T THINK YOU WOULD INTRODUCE YOURSELF FIRST.
THAT WAS COMPLETELY UNEXPECT-ED.
I REALLY WASN'T SURE HOW I WAS GOING TO BRING THIS ALL UP.
USUALLY IWANAGA DOES THE TALKING, BUT I WOULD HAVE FELT BAD WAKING HER UP TODAY.
HEH...
I WAS RIGHT TO I THINK THAT THERE WAS SOMETHING UNLUCKY ABOUT HER.
IT WAS A SIGN, TELLING ME SHE WAS GOING TO EXPOSE MY CRIME.
I GUESS PEOPLE REALLY DO HAVE THOSE STRANGE HUNCHES, THOSE FEELINGS OF FORE-BODING.

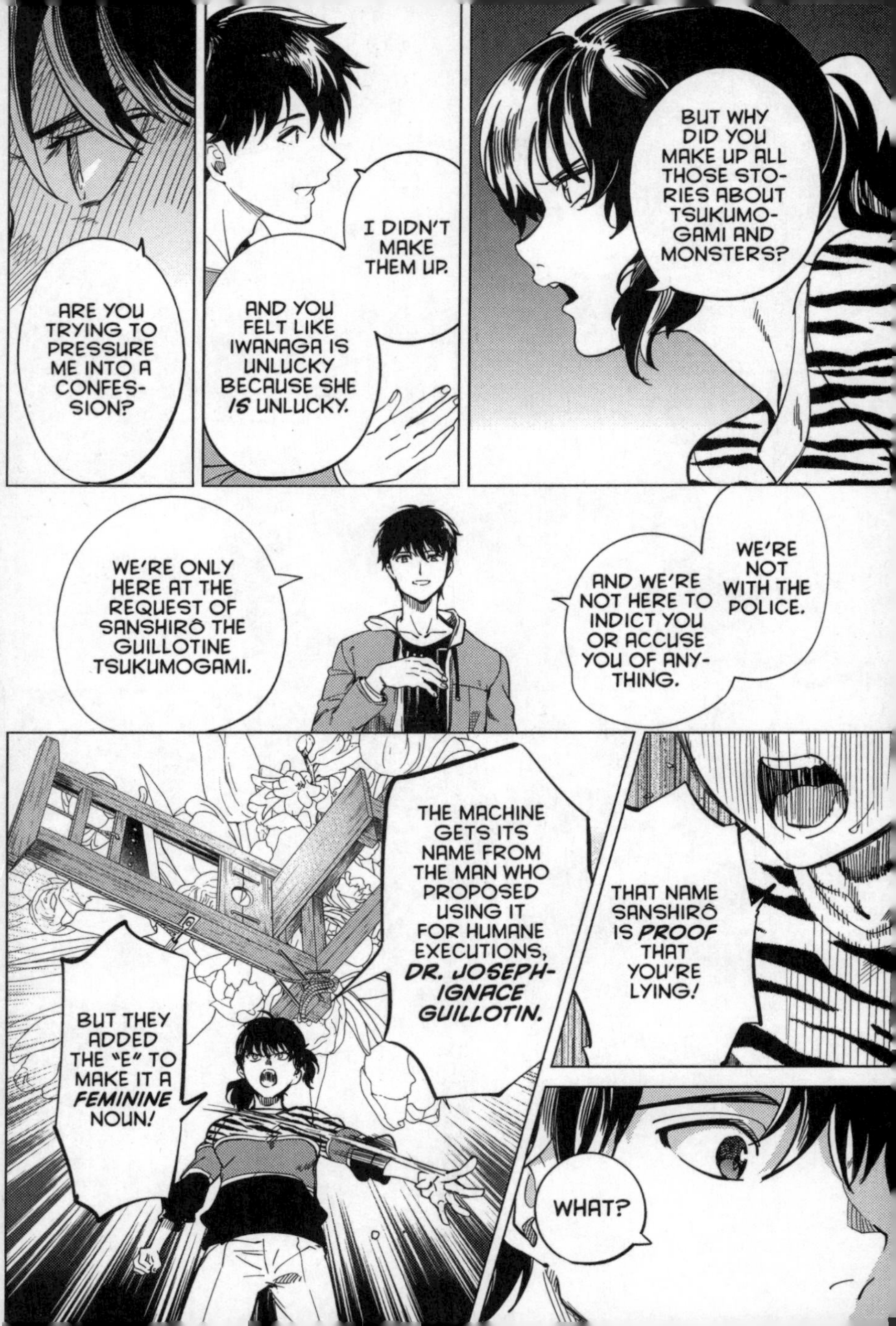
BUT WHY DID YOU MAKE UP ALL THOSE STORIES ABOUT TSUKUMOGAMI AND MONSTERS?
I DIDN'T MAKE THEM UP.
AND YOU FELT LIKE IWANAGA IS UNLUCKY BECAUSE SHE *IS* UNLUCKY.
ARE YOU TRYING TO PRESSURE ME INTO A CONFESSION?
WE'RE NOT WITH THE POLICE.
AND WE'RE NOT HERE TO INDICT YOU OR ACCUSE YOU OF ANYTHING.
WE'RE ONLY HERE AT THE REQUEST OF SANSHIRÔ THE GUILLOTINE TSUKUMOGAMI.
THAT NAME SANSHIRÔ IS *PROOF* THAT YOU'RE LYING!
WHAT?
THE MACHINE GETS ITS NAME FROM THE MAN WHO PROPOSED USING IT FOR HUMANE EXECUTIONS, ***DR. JOSEPH-IGNACE GUILLOTIN.***
BUT THEY ADDED THE "E" TO MAKE IT A ***FEMININE*** NOUN!

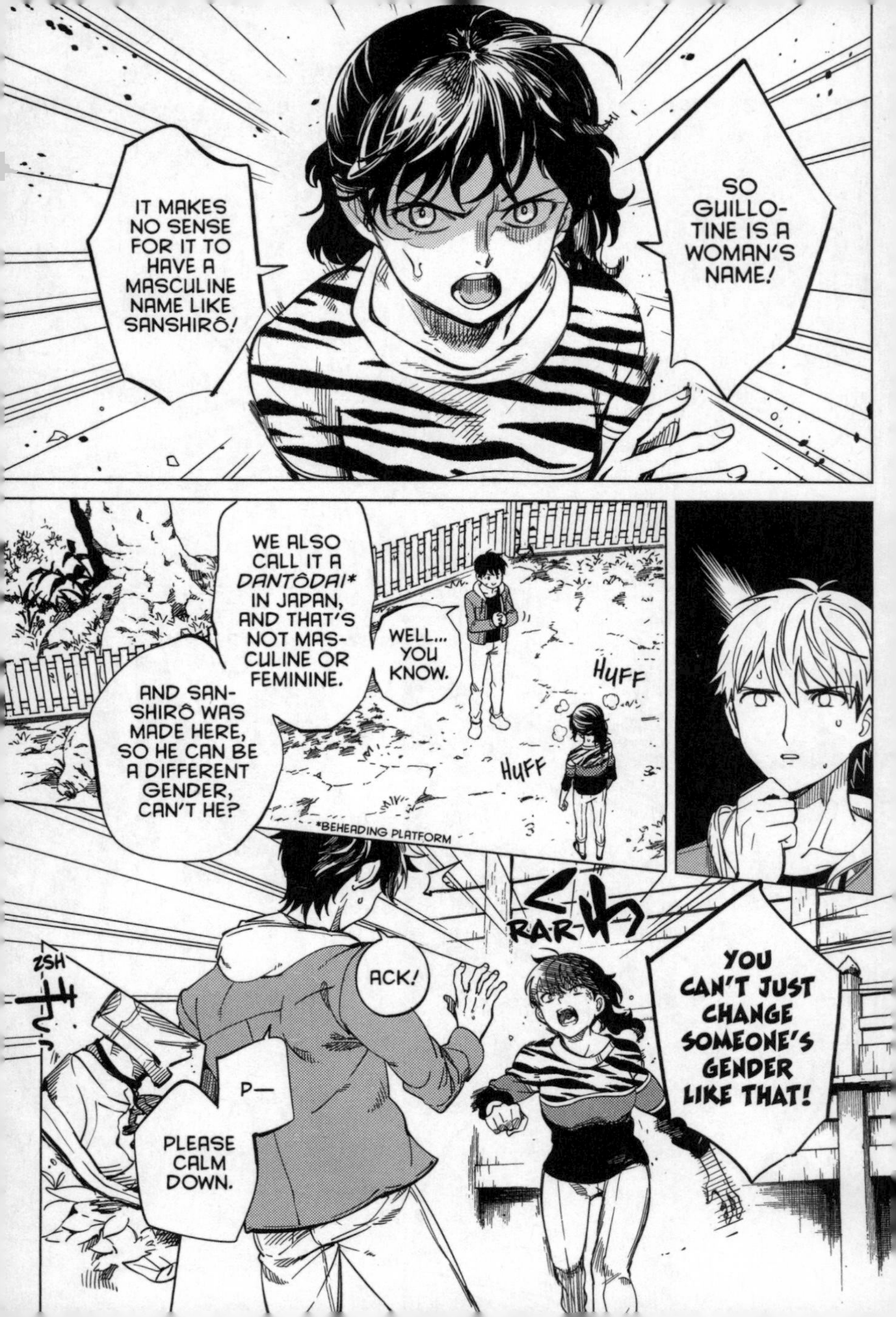
SO GUILLOTINE IS A WOMAN'S NAME!
IT MAKES NO SENSE FOR IT TO HAVE A MASCULINE NAME LIKE SANSHIRÔ!
WELL... YOU KNOW.
WE ALSO CALL IT A *DANTÔDAI** IN JAPAN, AND THAT'S NOT MASCULINE OR FEMININE.
HUFF
HUFF
AND SANSHIRÔ WAS MADE HERE, SO HE CAN BE A DIFFERENT GENDER, CAN'T HE?
*BEHEADING PLATFORM
RAR-K
YOU CAN'T JUST CHANGE SOMEONE'S GENDER LIKE THAT!
ACK!
P—
PLEASE CALM DOWN.
ZSH

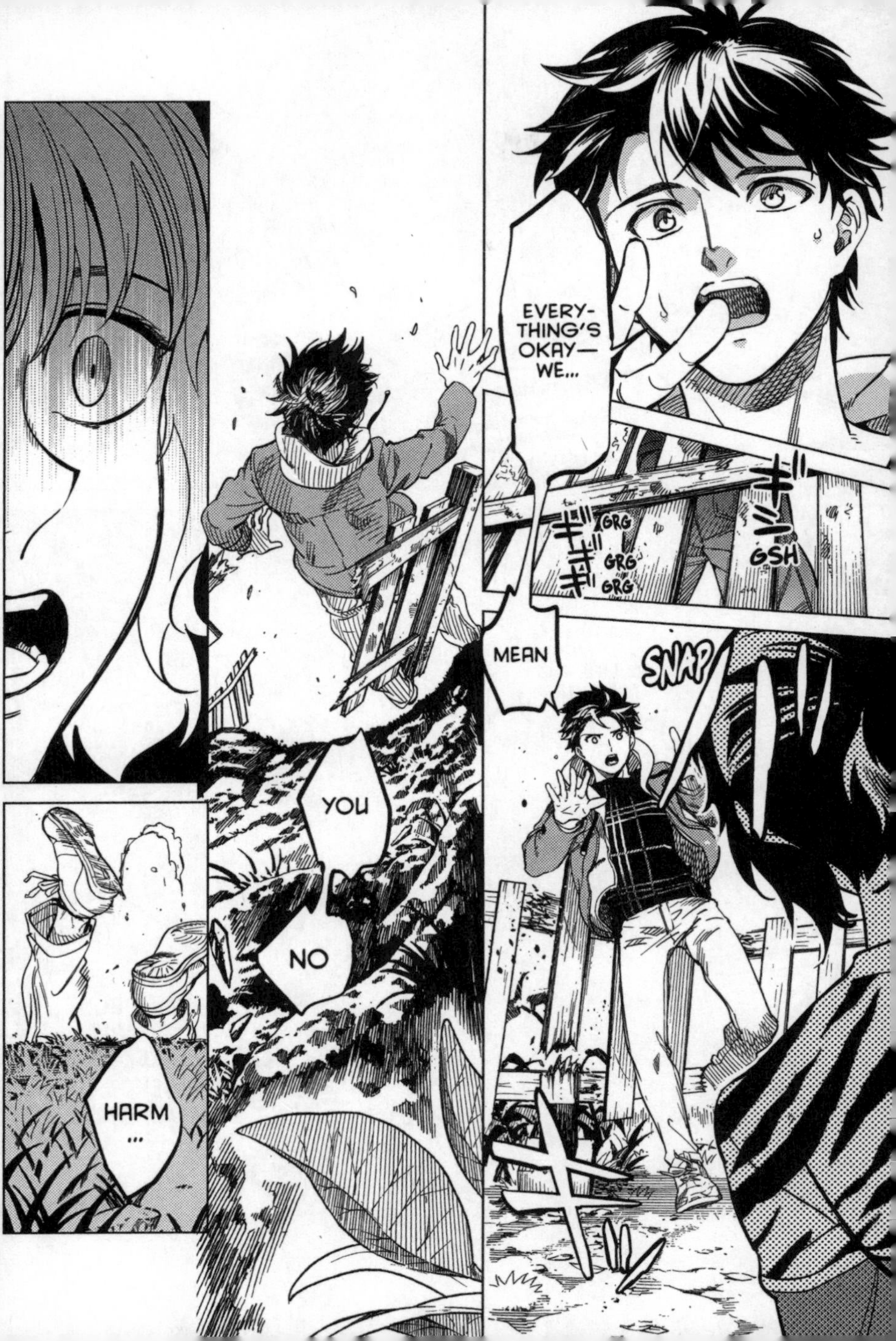
EVERY-THING'S OKAY—WE...
ギシ
GSH
ギギギ
GRG
GRG
GRG
MEAN
SNAP
YOU
NO
HARM
...

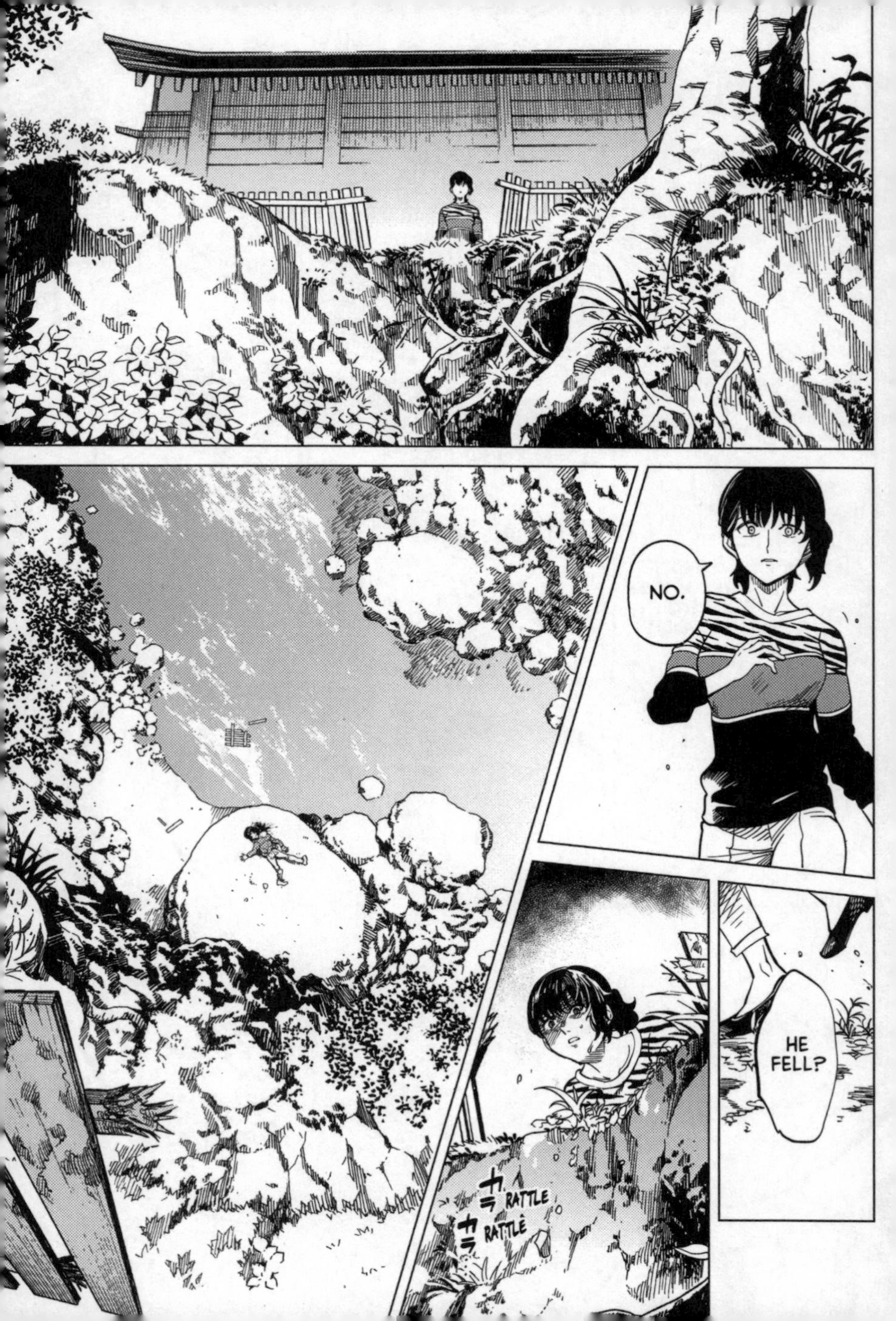
NO.
HE FELL?
カラ RATTLE
カラ RATTLE

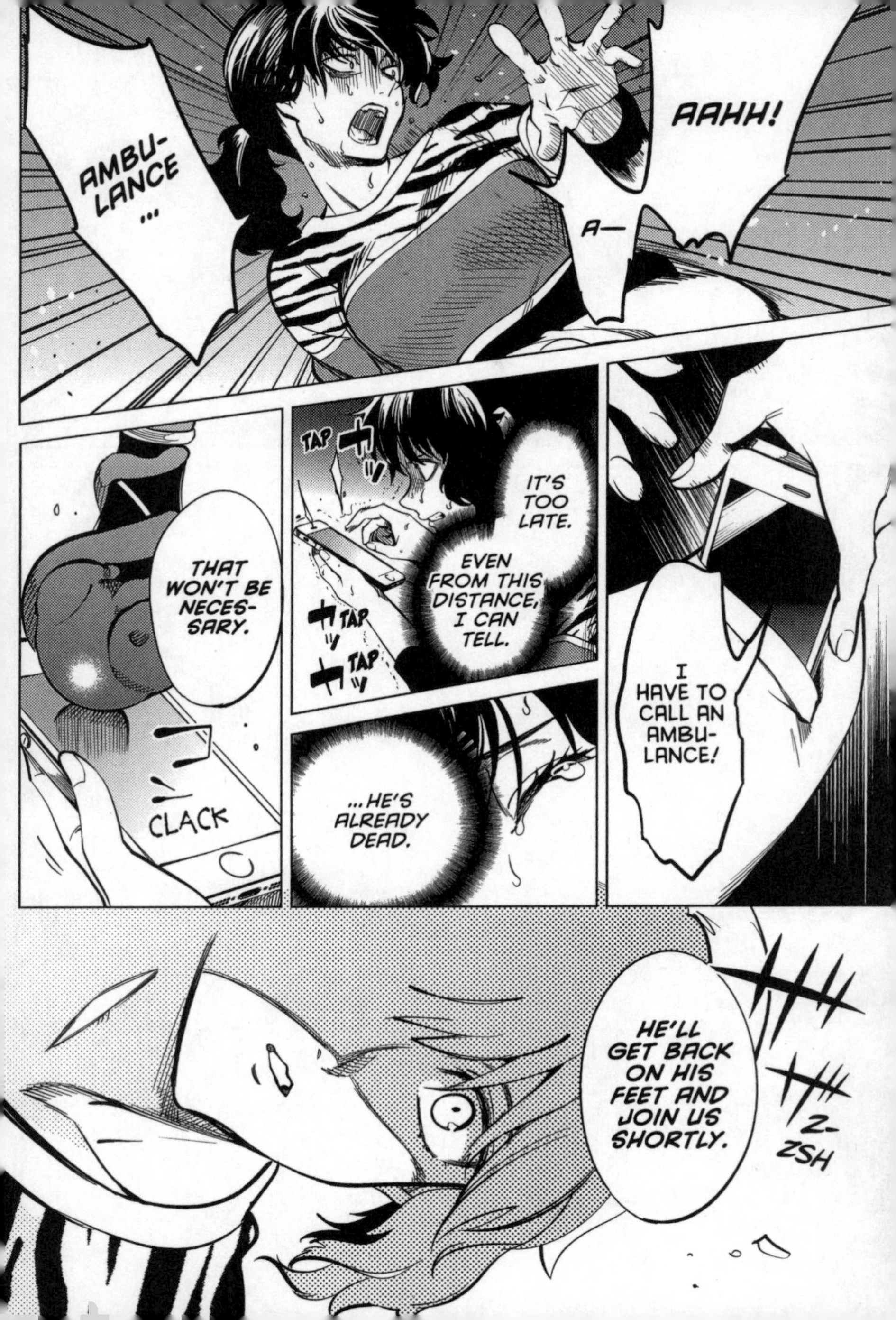
AAHH!
A—
AMBU-LANCE ...
I HAVE TO CALL AN AMBU-LANCE!
TAP
IT'S TOO LATE.
EVEN FROM THIS DISTANCE, I CAN TELL.
TAP
TAP
...HE'S ALREADY DEAD.
THAT WON'T BE NECES-SARY.
CLACK
Z-ZSH
HE'LL GET BACK ON HIS FEET AND JOIN US SHORTLY.

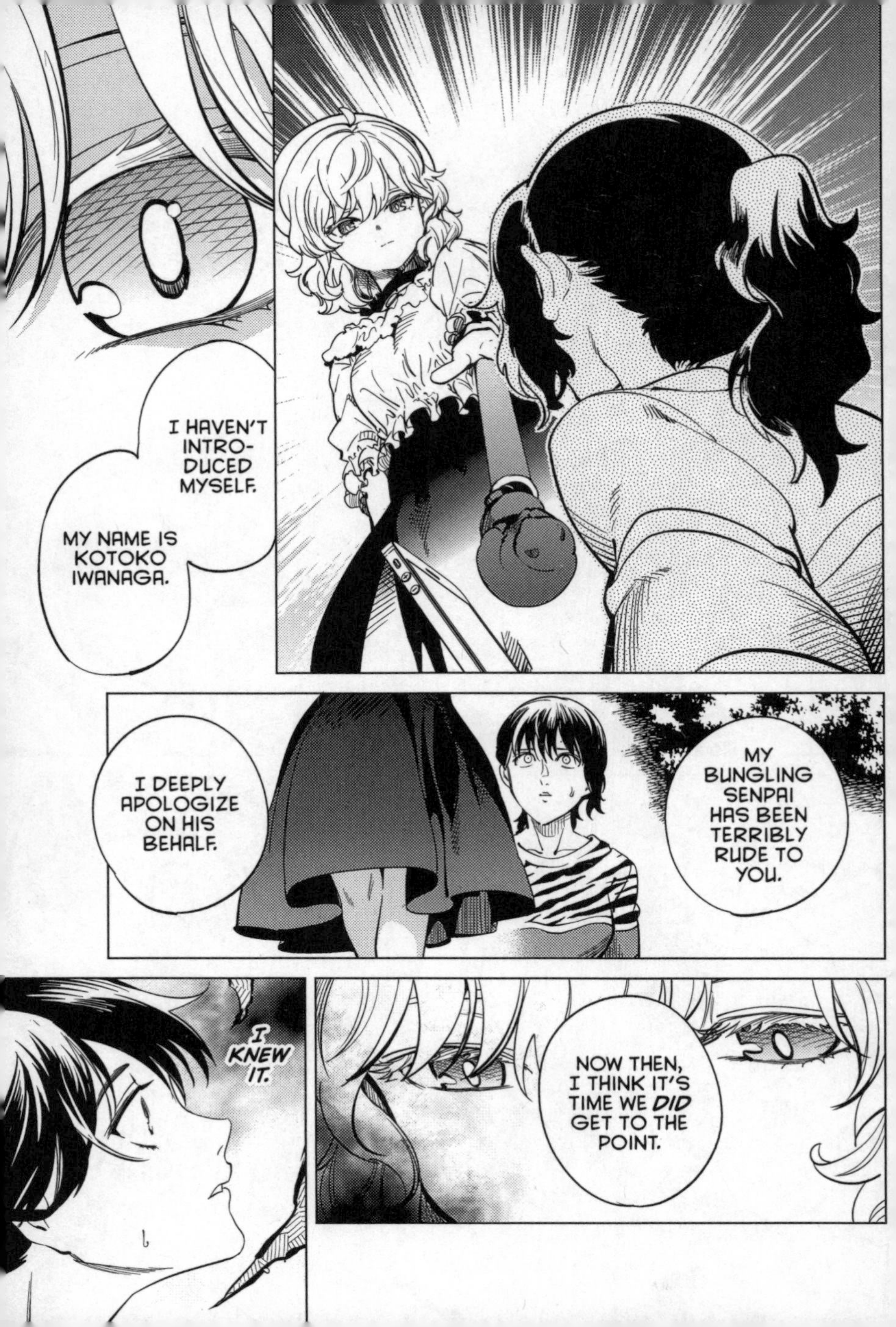
I HAVEN'T INTRO-DUCED MYSELF.
MY NAME IS KOTOKO IWANAGA.
MY BUNGLING SENPAI HAS BEEN TERRIBLY RUDE TO YOU.
I DEEPLY APOLOGIZE ON HIS BEHALF.
NOW THEN, I THINK IT'S TIME WE *DID* GET TO THE POINT.
I KNEW IT.

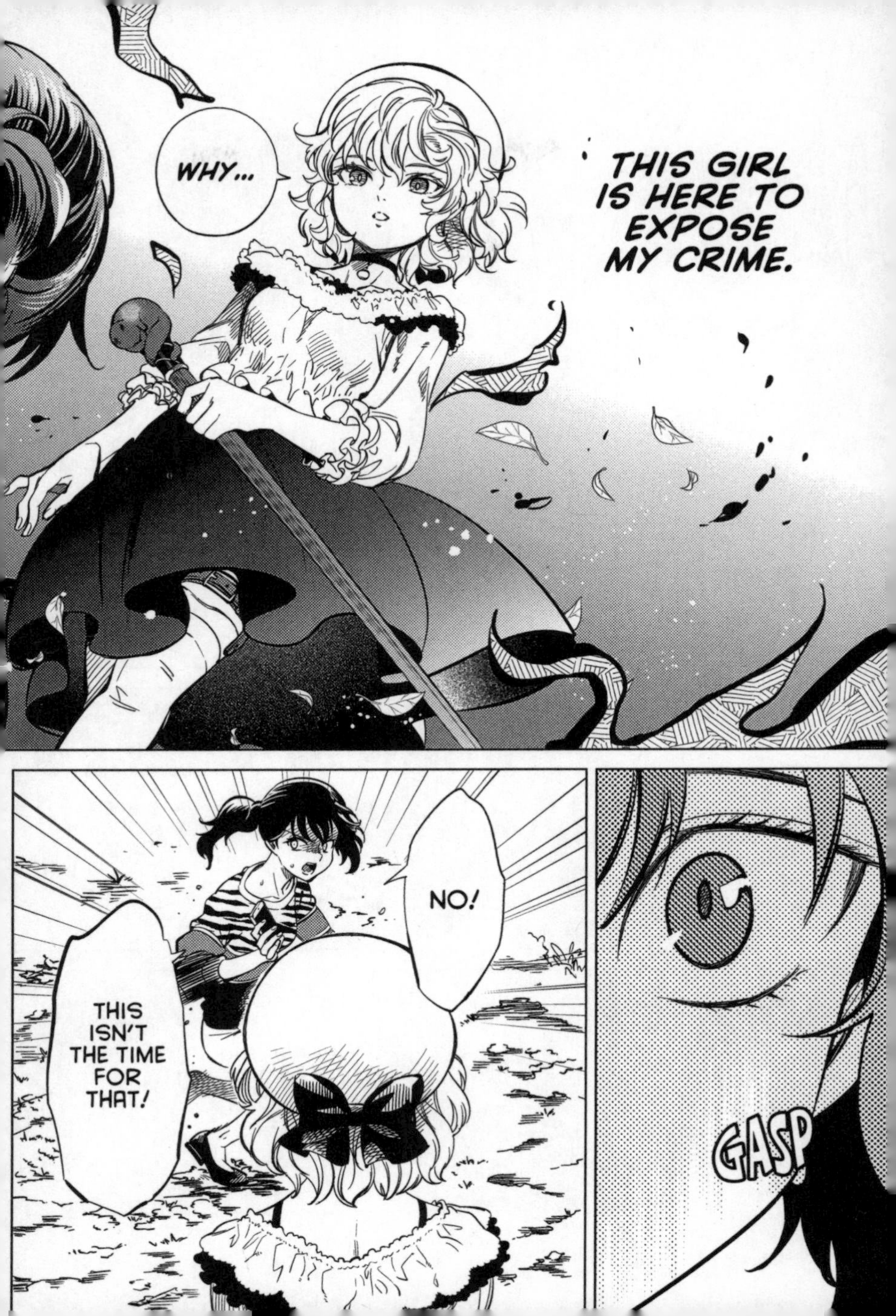
THIS GIRL IS HERE TO EXPOSE MY CRIME.
WHY...
GASP
NO!
THIS ISN'T THE TIME FOR THAT!

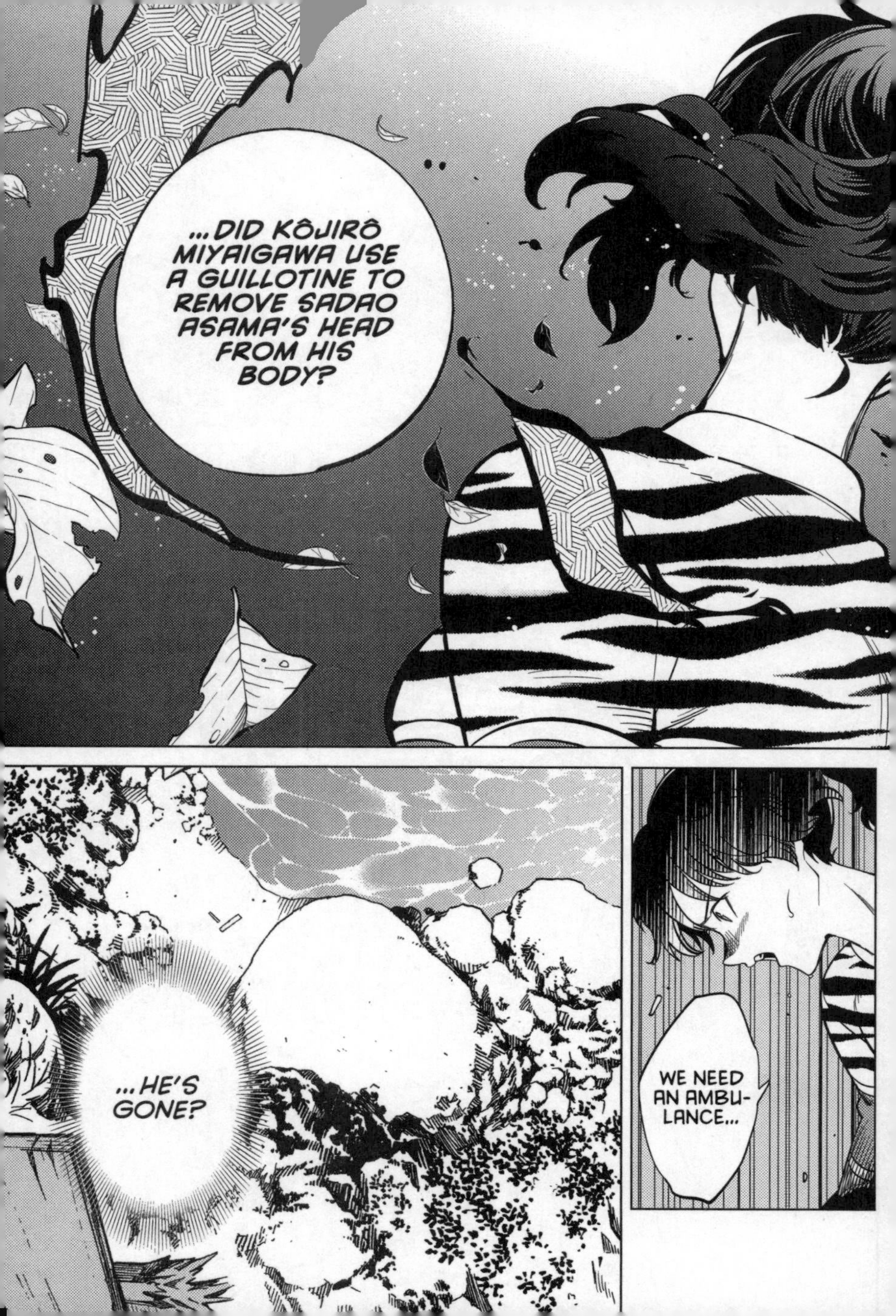
...DID KÔJIRÔ MIYAIGAWA USE A GUILLOTINE TO REMOVE SADAO ASAMA'S HEAD FROM HIS BODY?
WE NEED AN AMBU-LANCE...
...HE'S GONE?

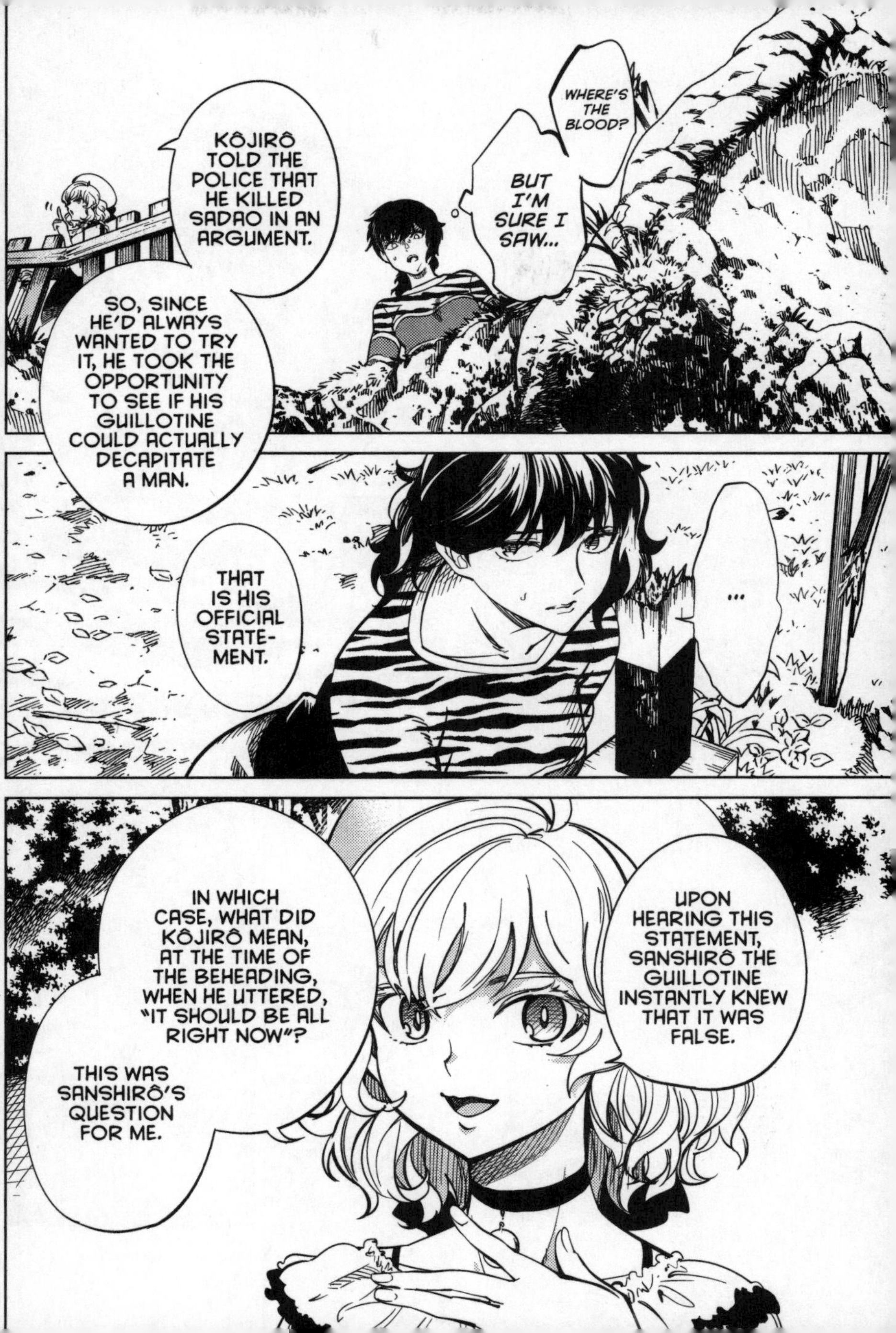
WHERE'S THE BLOOD?
BUT I'M SURE I SAW...
KÔJIRÔ TOLD THE POLICE THAT HE KILLED SADAO IN AN ARGUMENT.
SO, SINCE HE'D ALWAYS WANTED TO TRY IT, HE TOOK THE OPPORTUNITY TO SEE IF HIS GUILLOTINE COULD ACTUALLY DECAPITATE A MAN.
...
THAT IS HIS OFFICIAL STATEMENT.
UPON HEARING THIS STATEMENT, SANSHIRÔ THE GUILLOTINE INSTANTLY KNEW THAT IT WAS FALSE.
IN WHICH CASE, WHAT DID KÔJIRÔ MEAN, AT THE TIME OF THE BEHEADING, WHEN HE UTTERED, "IT SHOULD BE ALL RIGHT NOW"?
THIS WAS SANSHIRÔ'S QUESTION FOR ME.

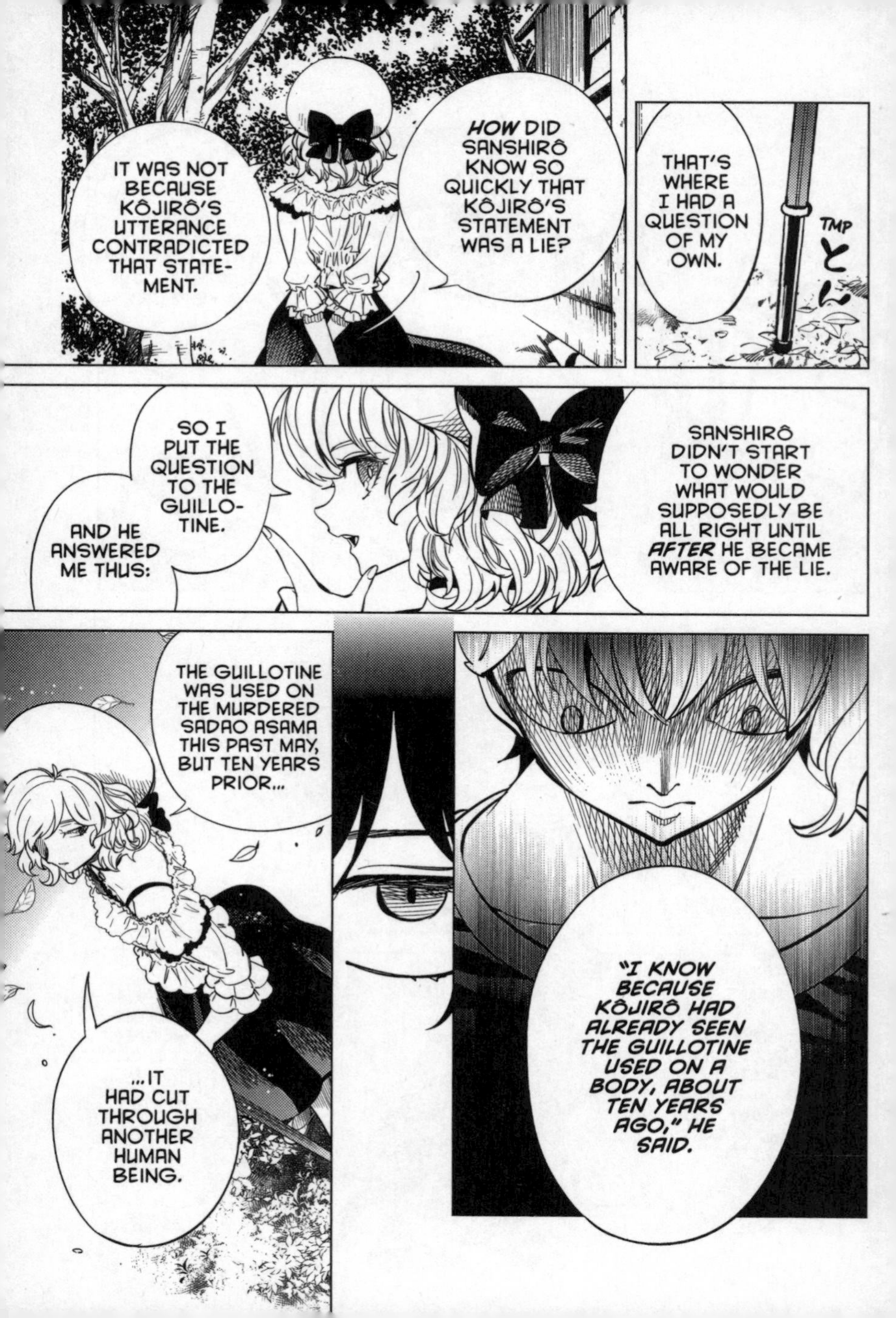
THAT'S WHERE I HAD A QUESTION OF MY OWN.
TMP
とん
HOW DID SANSHIRÔ KNOW SO QUICKLY THAT KÔJIRÔ'S STATEMENT WAS A LIE?
IT WAS NOT BECAUSE KÔJIRÔ'S UTTERANCE CONTRADICTED THAT STATEMENT.
SANSHIRÔ DIDN'T START TO WONDER WHAT WOULD SUPPOSEDLY BE ALL RIGHT UNTIL *AFTER* HE BECAME AWARE OF THE LIE.
SO I PUT THE QUESTION TO THE GUILLOTINE.
AND HE ANSWERED ME THUS:
"I KNOW BECAUSE KÔJIRÔ HAD ALREADY SEEN THE GUILLOTINE USED ON A BODY, ABOUT TEN YEARS AGO," HE SAID.
THE GUILLOTINE WAS USED ON THE MURDERED SADAO ASAMA THIS PAST MAY, BUT TEN YEARS PRIOR...
...IT HAD CUT THROUGH ANOTHER HUMAN BEING.

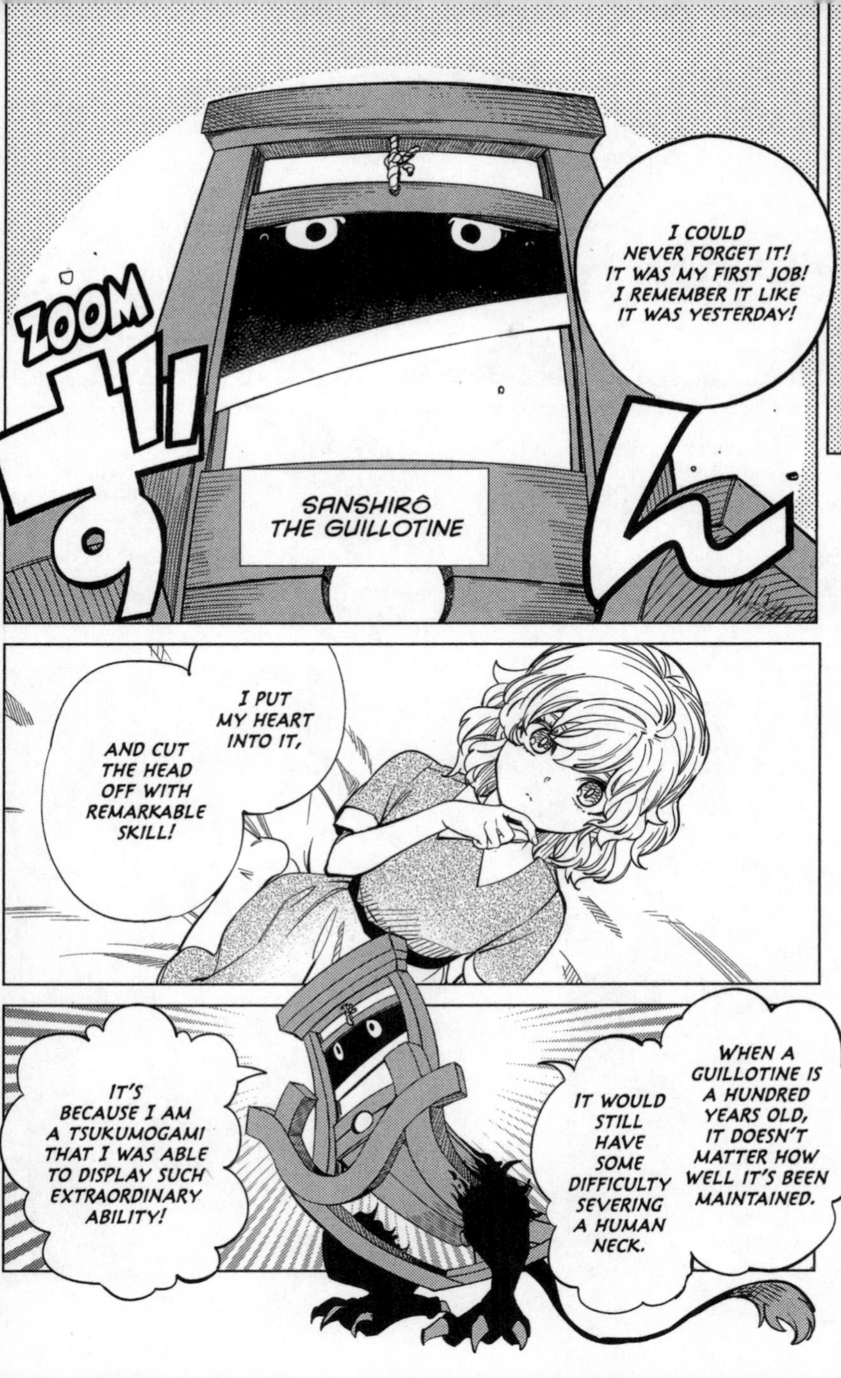
I COULD NEVER FORGET IT! IT WAS MY FIRST JOB! I REMEMBER IT LIKE IT WAS YESTERDAY!
ZOOM
SANSHIRÔ THE GUILLOTINE
I PUT MY HEART INTO IT,
AND CUT THE HEAD OFF WITH REMARKABLE SKILL!
WHEN A GUILLOTINE IS A HUNDRED YEARS OLD, IT DOESN'T MATTER HOW WELL IT'S BEEN MAINTAINED.
IT WOULD STILL HAVE SOME DIFFICULTY SEVERING A HUMAN NECK.
IT'S BECAUSE I AM A TSUKUMOGAMI THAT I WAS ABLE TO DISPLAY SUCH EXTRAORDINARY ABILITY!

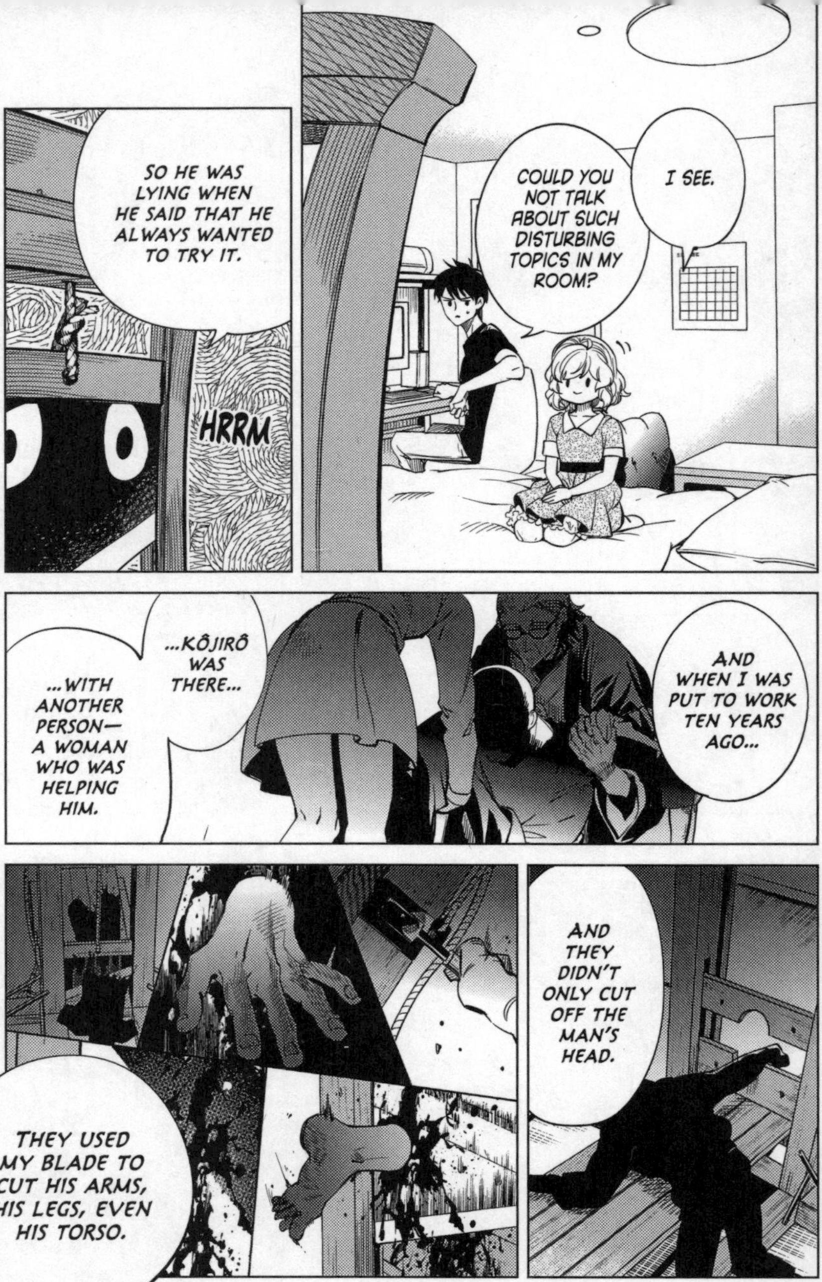
I SEE.
COULD YOU NOT TALK ABOUT SUCH DISTURBING TOPICS IN MY ROOM?
SO HE WAS LYING WHEN HE SAID THAT HE ALWAYS WANTED TO TRY IT.
HRRM
AND WHEN I WAS PUT TO WORK TEN YEARS AGO...
...KÔJIRÔ WAS THERE...
...WITH ANOTHER PERSON— A WOMAN WHO WAS HELPING HIM.
AND THEY DIDN'T ONLY CUT OFF THE MAN'S HEAD.
THEY USED MY BLADE TO CUT HIS ARMS, HIS LEGS, EVEN HIS TORSO.

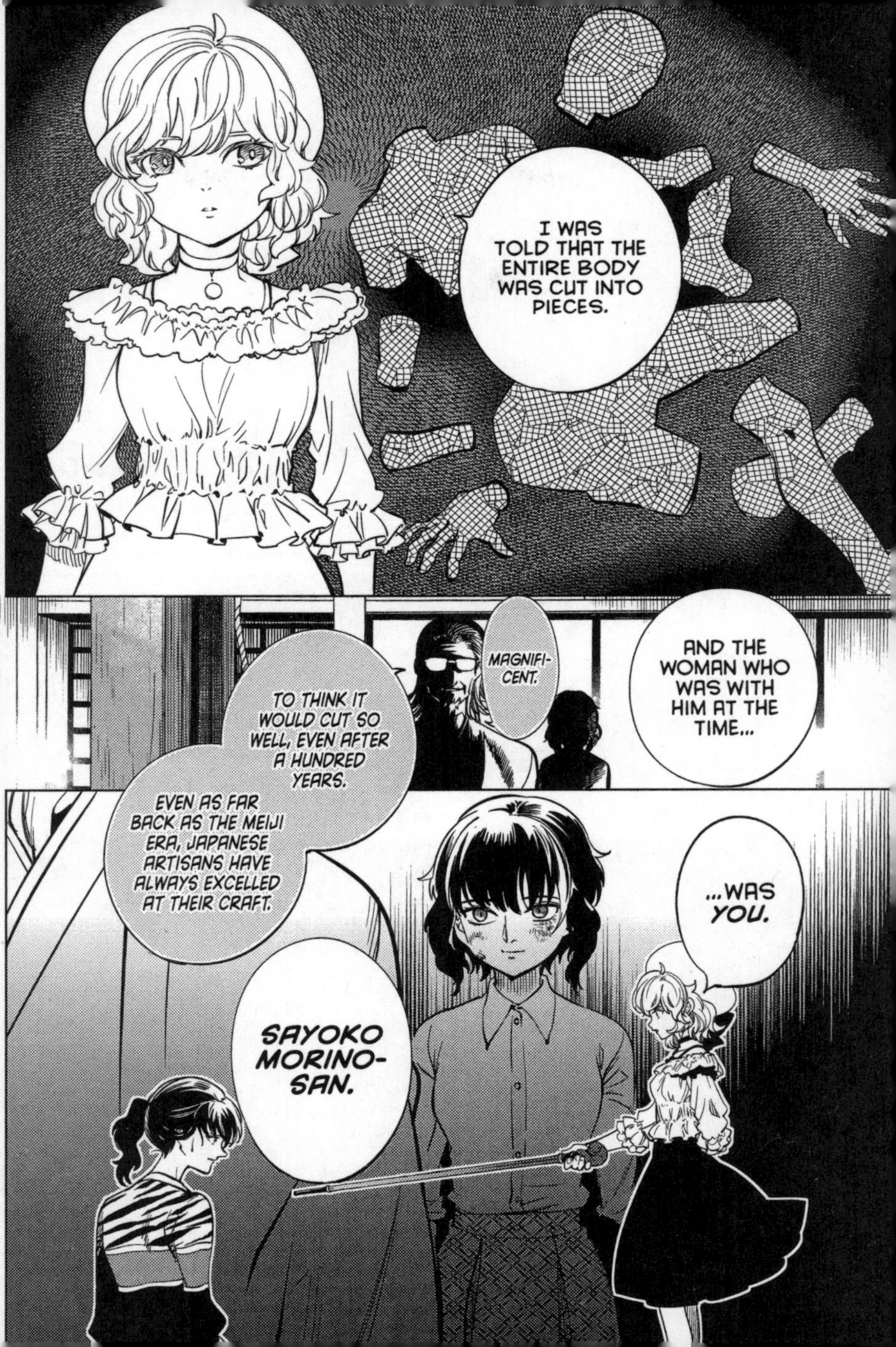
I WAS TOLD THAT THE ENTIRE BODY WAS CUT INTO PIECES.
AND THE WOMAN WHO WAS WITH HIM AT THE TIME...
MAGNIFI-CENT.
TO THINK IT WOULD CUT SO WELL, EVEN AFTER A HUNDRED YEARS.
EVEN AS FAR BACK AS THE MEIJI ERA, JAPANESE ARTISANS HAVE ALWAYS EXCELLED AT THEIR CRAFT.
...WAS *YOU.*
SAYOKO MORINO-SAN.

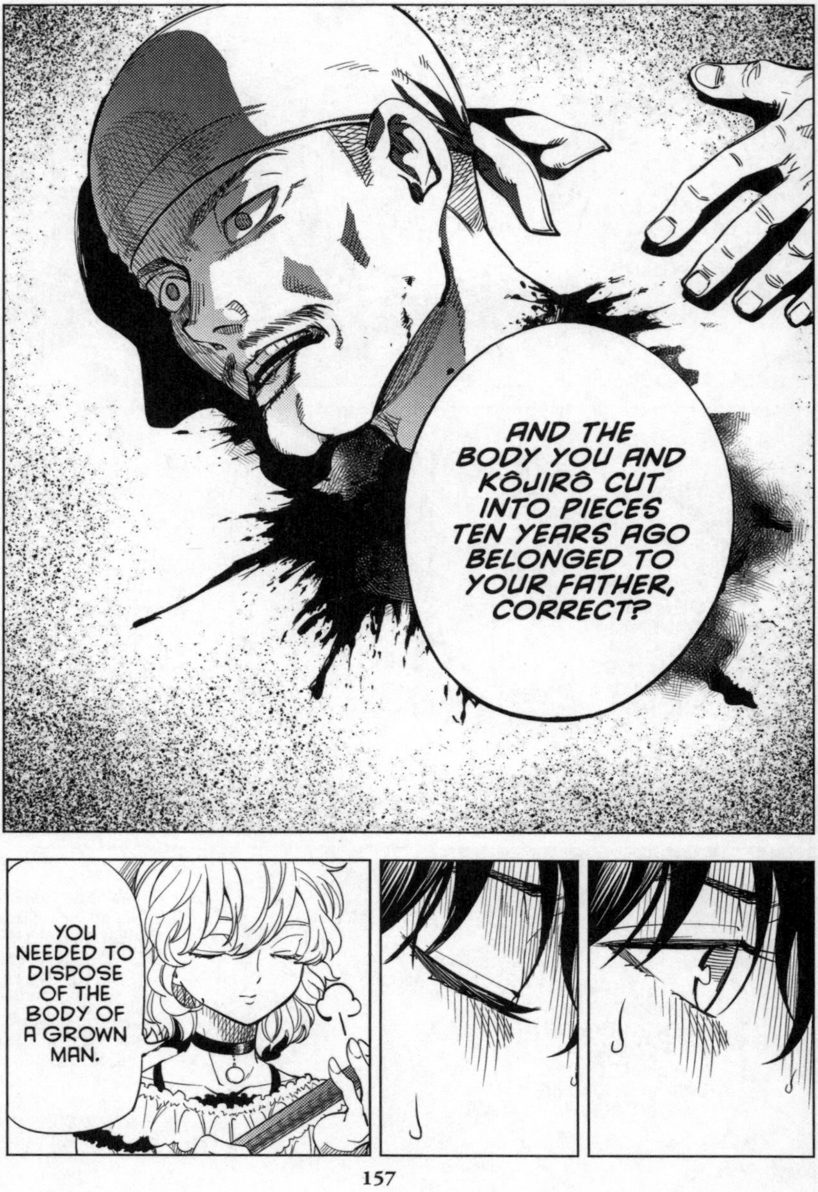
AND THE BODY YOU AND KÔJIRÔ CUT INTO PIECES TEN YEARS AGO BELONGED TO YOUR FATHER, CORRECT?
YOU NEEDED TO DISPOSE OF THE BODY OF A GROWN MAN.

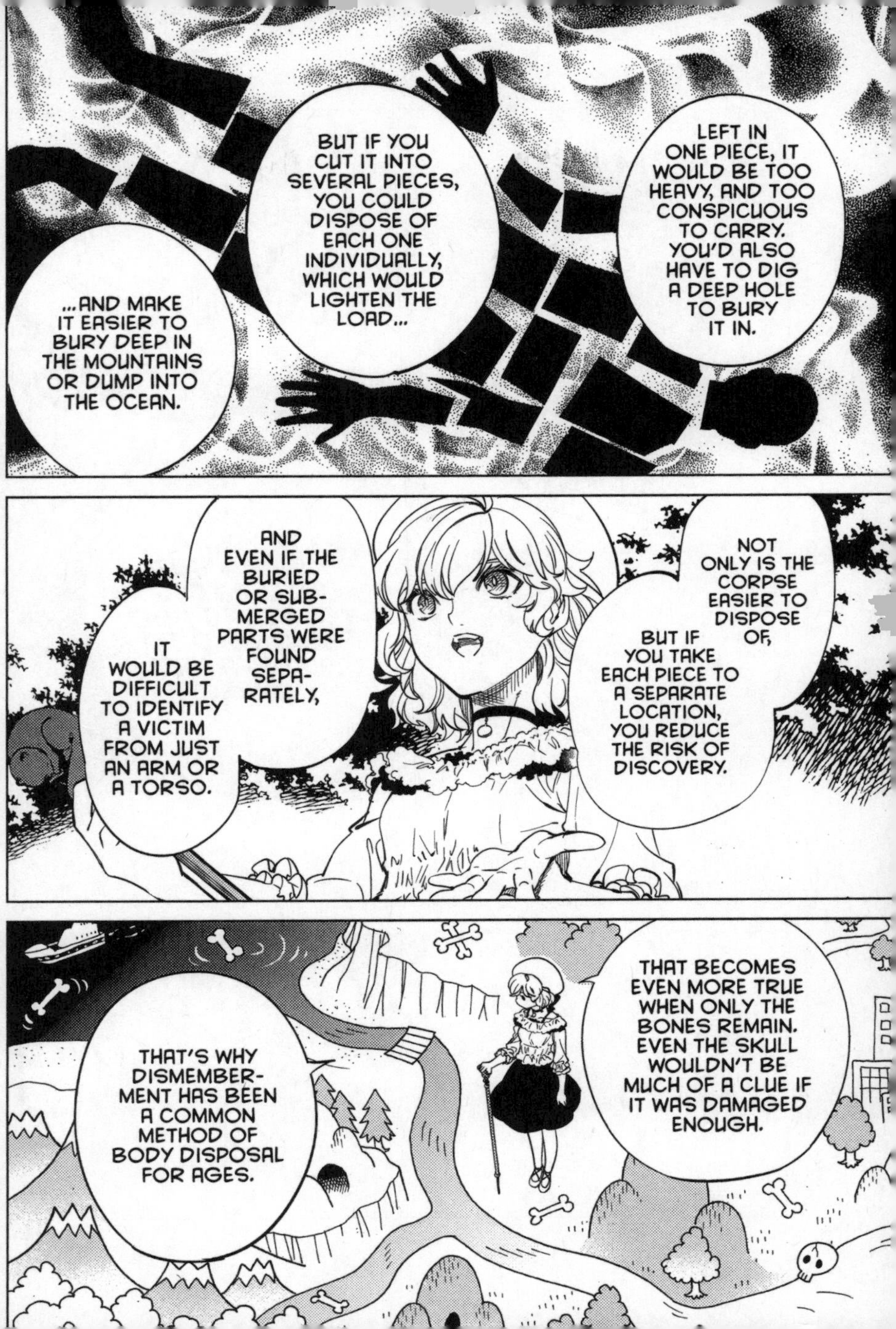
LEFT IN ONE PIECE, IT WOULD BE TOO HEAVY, AND TOO CONSPICUOUS TO CARRY. YOU'D ALSO HAVE TO DIG A DEEP HOLE TO BURY IT IN.
BUT IF YOU CUT IT INTO SEVERAL PIECES, YOU COULD DISPOSE OF EACH ONE INDIVIDUALLY, WHICH WOULD LIGHTEN THE LOAD...
...AND MAKE IT EASIER TO BURY DEEP IN THE MOUNTAINS OR DUMP INTO THE OCEAN.
NOT ONLY IS THE CORPSE EASIER TO DISPOSE OF,
BUT IF YOU TAKE EACH PIECE TO A SEPARATE LOCATION, YOU REDUCE THE RISK OF DISCOVERY.
AND EVEN IF THE BURIED OR SUB-MERGED PARTS WERE FOUND SEPA-RATELY,
IT WOULD BE DIFFICULT TO IDENTIFY A VICTIM FROM JUST AN ARM OR A TORSO.
THAT BECOMES EVEN MORE TRUE WHEN ONLY THE BONES REMAIN. EVEN THE SKULL WOULDN'T BE MUCH OF A CLUE IF IT WAS DAMAGED ENOUGH.
THAT'S WHY DISMEMBER-MENT HAS BEEN A COMMON METHOD OF BODY DISPOSAL FOR AGES.

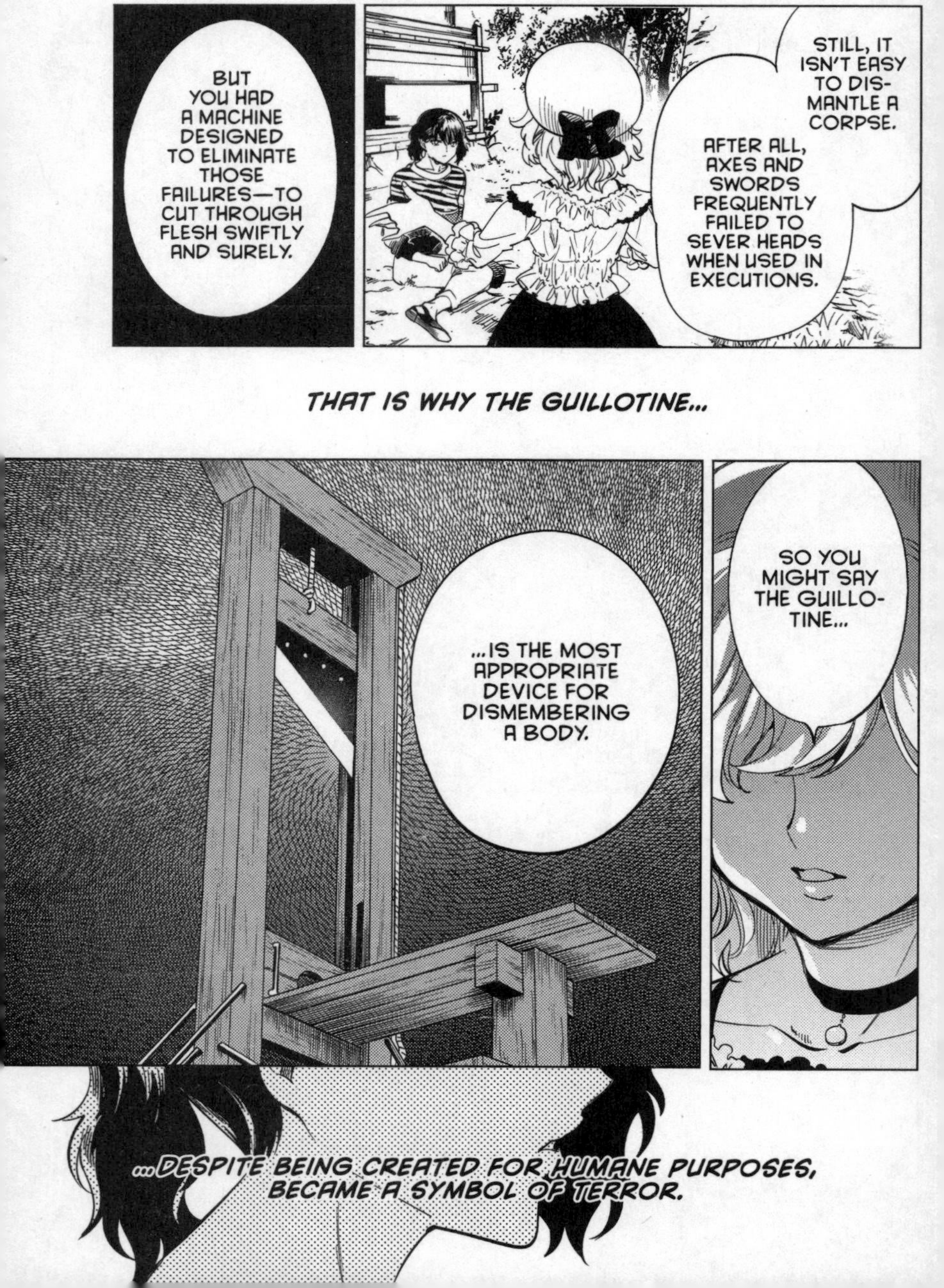
STILL, IT ISN'T EASY TO DIS-MANTLE A CORPSE.
AFTER ALL, AXES AND SWORDS FREQUENTLY FAILED TO SEVER HEADS WHEN USED IN EXECUTIONS.
BUT YOU HAD A MACHINE DESIGNED TO ELIMINATE THOSE FAILURES—TO CUT THROUGH FLESH SWIFTLY AND SURELY.
THAT IS WHY THE GUILLOTINE...
SO YOU MIGHT SAY THE GUILLO-TINE...
...IS THE MOST APPROPRIATE DEVICE FOR DISMEMBERING A BODY.
...DESPITE BEING CREATED FOR HUMANE PURPOSES, BECAME A SYMBOL OF TERROR.

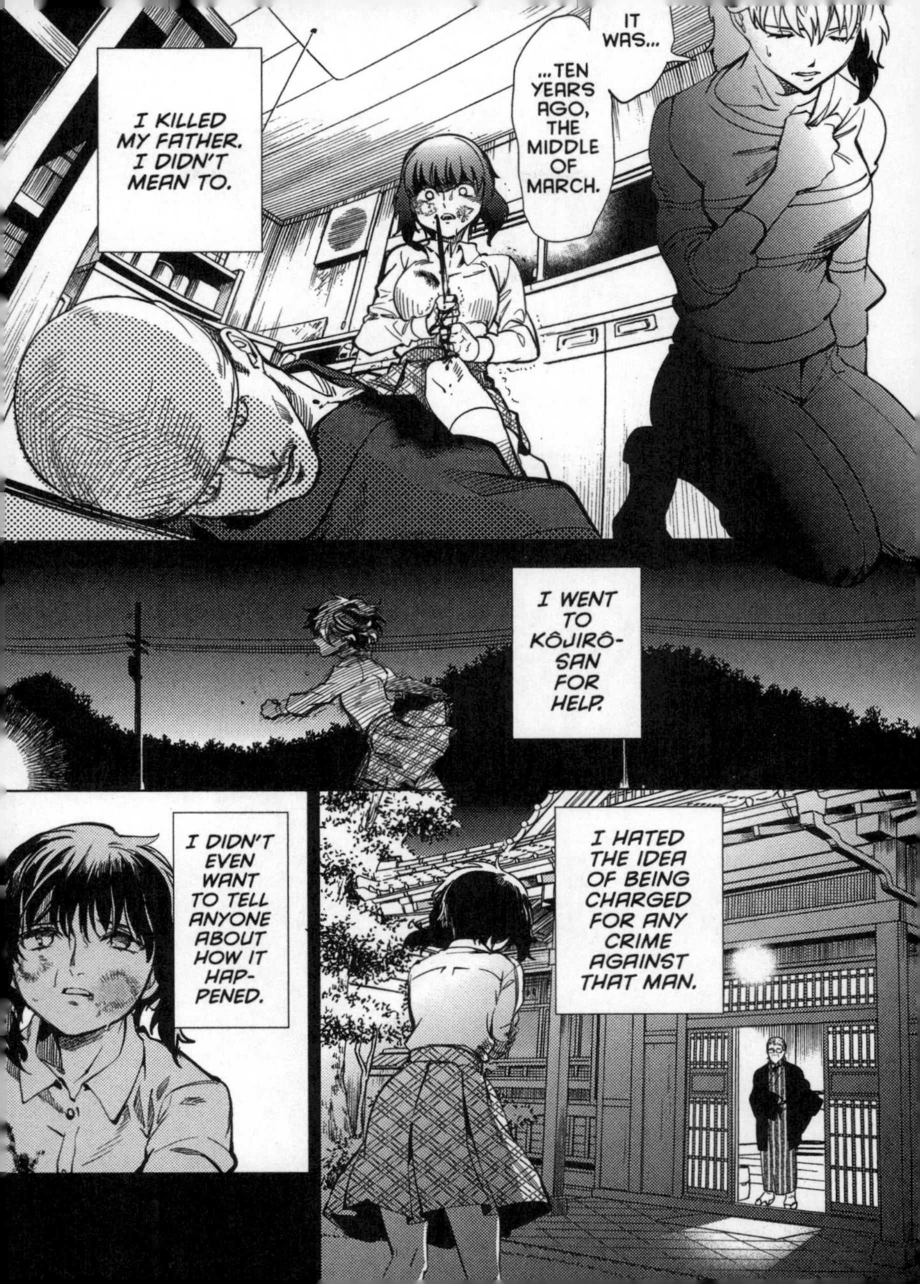
IT WAS...
...TEN YEARS AGO, THE MIDDLE OF MARCH.
I KILLED MY FATHER. I DIDN'T MEAN TO.
I WENT TO KÔJIRÔ-SAN FOR HELP.
I HATED THE IDEA OF BEING CHARGED FOR ANY CRIME AGAINST THAT MAN.
I DIDN'T EVEN WANT TO TELL ANYONE ABOUT HOW IT HAP-PENED.

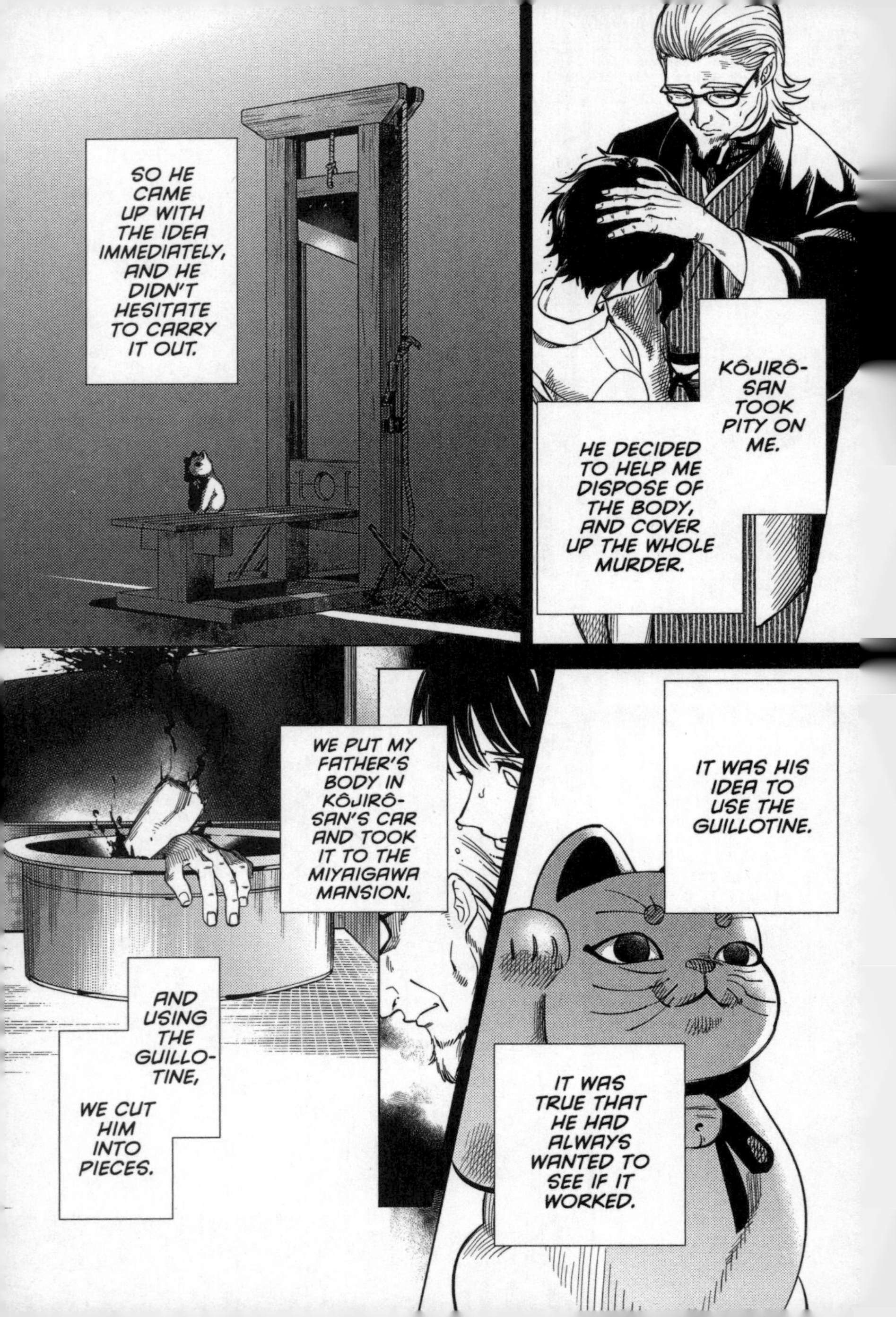
KÔJIRÔ-SAN TOOK PITY ON ME.
HE DECIDED TO HELP ME DISPOSE OF THE BODY, AND COVER UP THE WHOLE MURDER.
SO HE CAME UP WITH THE IDEA IMMEDIATELY, AND HE DIDN'T HESITATE TO CARRY IT OUT.
IT WAS HIS IDEA TO USE THE GUILLOTINE.
IT WAS TRUE THAT HE HAD ALWAYS WANTED TO SEE IF IT WORKED.
WE PUT MY FATHER'S BODY IN KÔJIRÔ-SAN'S CAR AND TOOK IT TO THE MIYAIGAWA MANSION.
AND USING THE GUILLOTINE,
WE CUT HIM INTO PIECES.

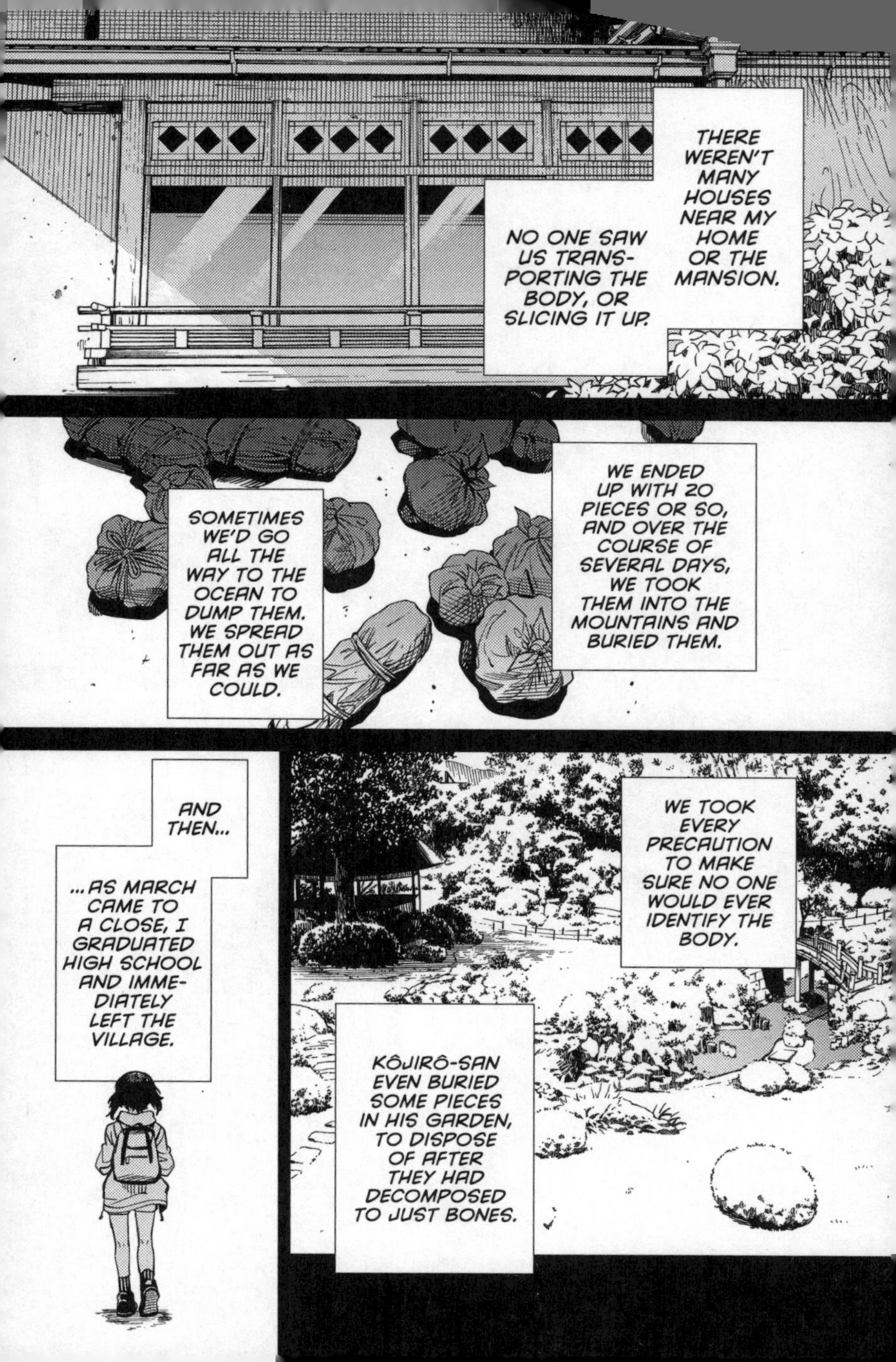
THERE WEREN'T MANY HOUSES NEAR MY HOME OR THE MANSION.
NO ONE SAW US TRANS-PORTING THE BODY, OR SLICING IT UP.
WE ENDED UP WITH 20 PIECES OR SO, AND OVER THE COURSE OF SEVERAL DAYS, WE TOOK THEM INTO THE MOUNTAINS AND BURIED THEM.
SOMETIMES WE'D GO ALL THE WAY TO THE OCEAN TO DUMP THEM. WE SPREAD THEM OUT AS FAR AS WE COULD.
WE TOOK EVERY PRECAUTION TO MAKE SURE NO ONE WOULD EVER IDENTIFY THE BODY.
KÔJIRÔ-SAN EVEN BURIED SOME PIECES IN HIS GARDEN, TO DISPOSE OF AFTER THEY HAD DECOMPOSED TO JUST BONES.
AND THEN...
...AS MARCH CAME TO A CLOSE, I GRADUATED HIGH SCHOOL AND IMME-DIATELY LEFT THE VILLAGE.

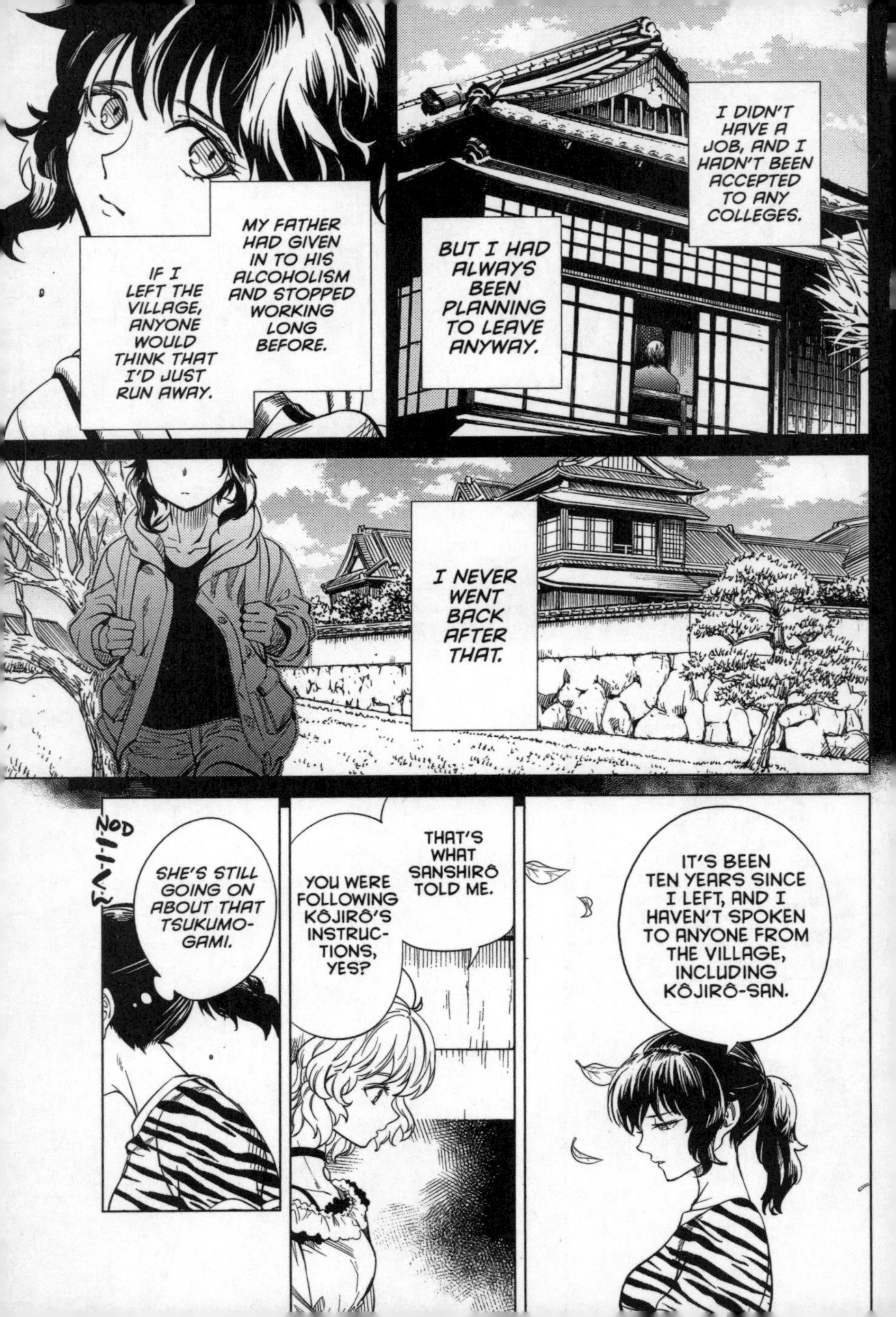
I DIDN'T HAVE A JOB, AND I HADN'T BEEN ACCEPTED TO ANY COLLEGES.
BUT I HAD ALWAYS BEEN PLANNING TO LEAVE ANYWAY.
MY FATHER HAD GIVEN IN TO HIS ALCOHOLISM AND STOPPED WORKING LONG BEFORE.
IF I LEFT THE VILLAGE, ANYONE WOULD THINK THAT I'D JUST RUN AWAY.
I NEVER WENT BACK AFTER THAT.
IT'S BEEN TEN YEARS SINCE I LEFT, AND I HAVEN'T SPOKEN TO ANYONE FROM THE VILLAGE, INCLUDING KÔJIRÔ-SAN.
YOU WERE FOLLOWING KÔJIRÔ'S INSTRUCTIONS, YES?
THAT'S WHAT SANSHIRÔ TOLD ME.
NOD
SHE'S STILL GOING ON ABOUT THAT TSUKUMO-GAMI.

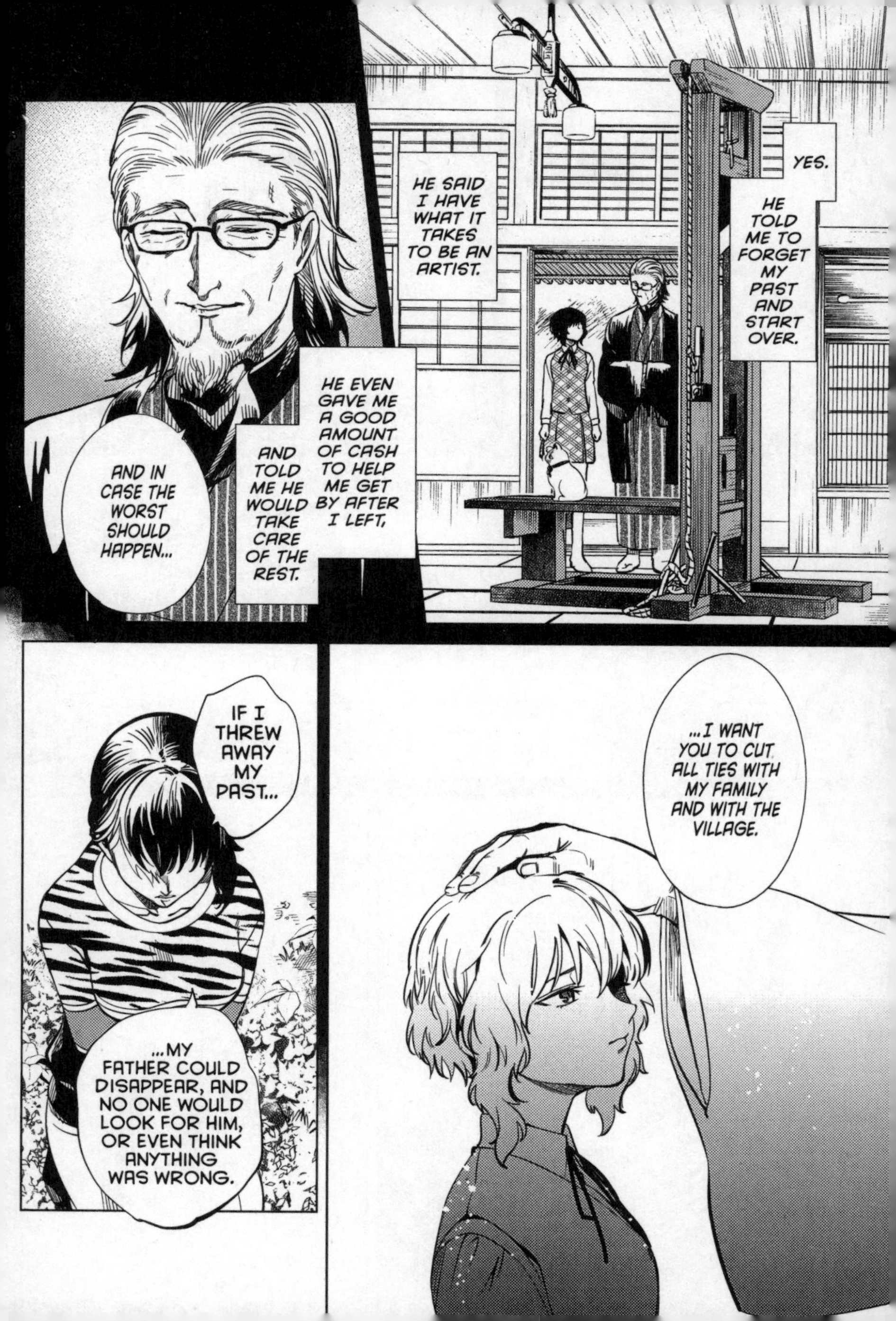
YES.
HE TOLD ME TO FORGET MY PAST AND START OVER.
HE SAID I HAVE WHAT IT TAKES TO BE AN ARTIST.
HE EVEN GAVE ME A GOOD AMOUNT OF CASH TO HELP ME GET BY AFTER I LEFT,
AND TOLD ME HE WOULD TAKE CARE OF THE REST.
AND IN CASE THE WORST SHOULD HAPPEN...
...I WANT YOU TO CUT ALL TIES WITH MY FAMILY AND WITH THE VILLAGE.
IF I THREW AWAY MY PAST...
...MY FATHER COULD DISAPPEAR, AND NO ONE WOULD LOOK FOR HIM, OR EVEN THINK ANYTHING WAS WRONG.

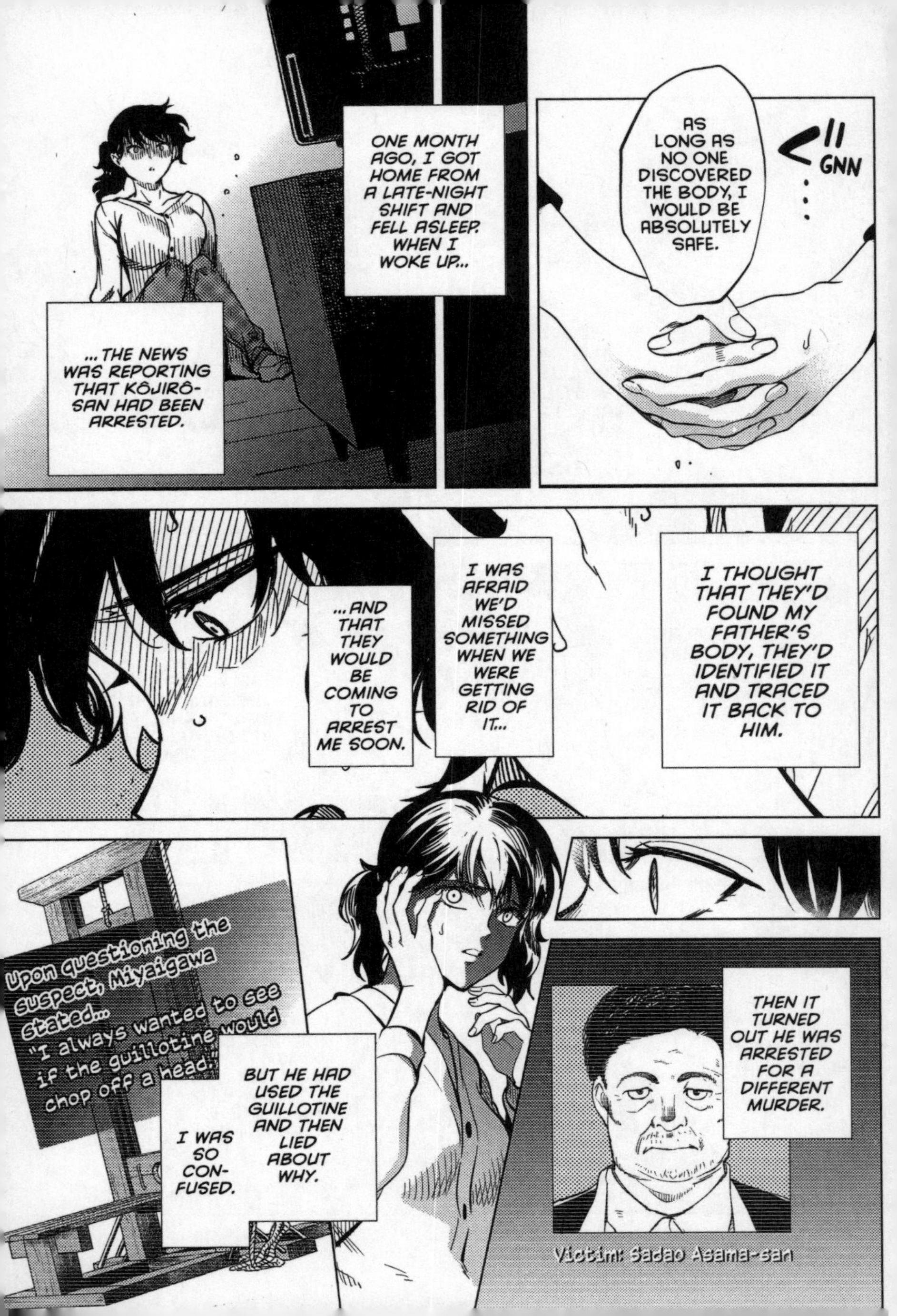
AS LONG AS NO ONE DISCOVERED THE BODY, I WOULD BE ABSOLUTELY SAFE.
GNN
ONE MONTH AGO, I GOT HOME FROM A LATE-NIGHT SHIFT AND FELL ASLEEP. WHEN I WOKE UP...
...THE NEWS WAS REPORTING THAT KÔJIRÔ-SAN HAD BEEN ARRESTED.
I THOUGHT THAT THEY'D FOUND MY FATHER'S BODY, THEY'D IDENTIFIED IT AND TRACED IT BACK TO HIM.
I WAS AFRAID WE'D MISSED SOMETHING WHEN WE WERE GETTING RID OF IT...
...AND THAT THEY WOULD BE COMING TO ARREST ME SOON.
THEN IT TURNED OUT HE WAS ARRESTED FOR A DIFFERENT MURDER.
Victim: Sadao Asama-san
Upon questioning the suspect, Miyaigawa stated... "I always wanted to see if the guillotine would chop off a head."
BUT HE HAD USED THE GUILLOTINE AND THEN LIED ABOUT WHY.
I WAS SO CON-FUSED.

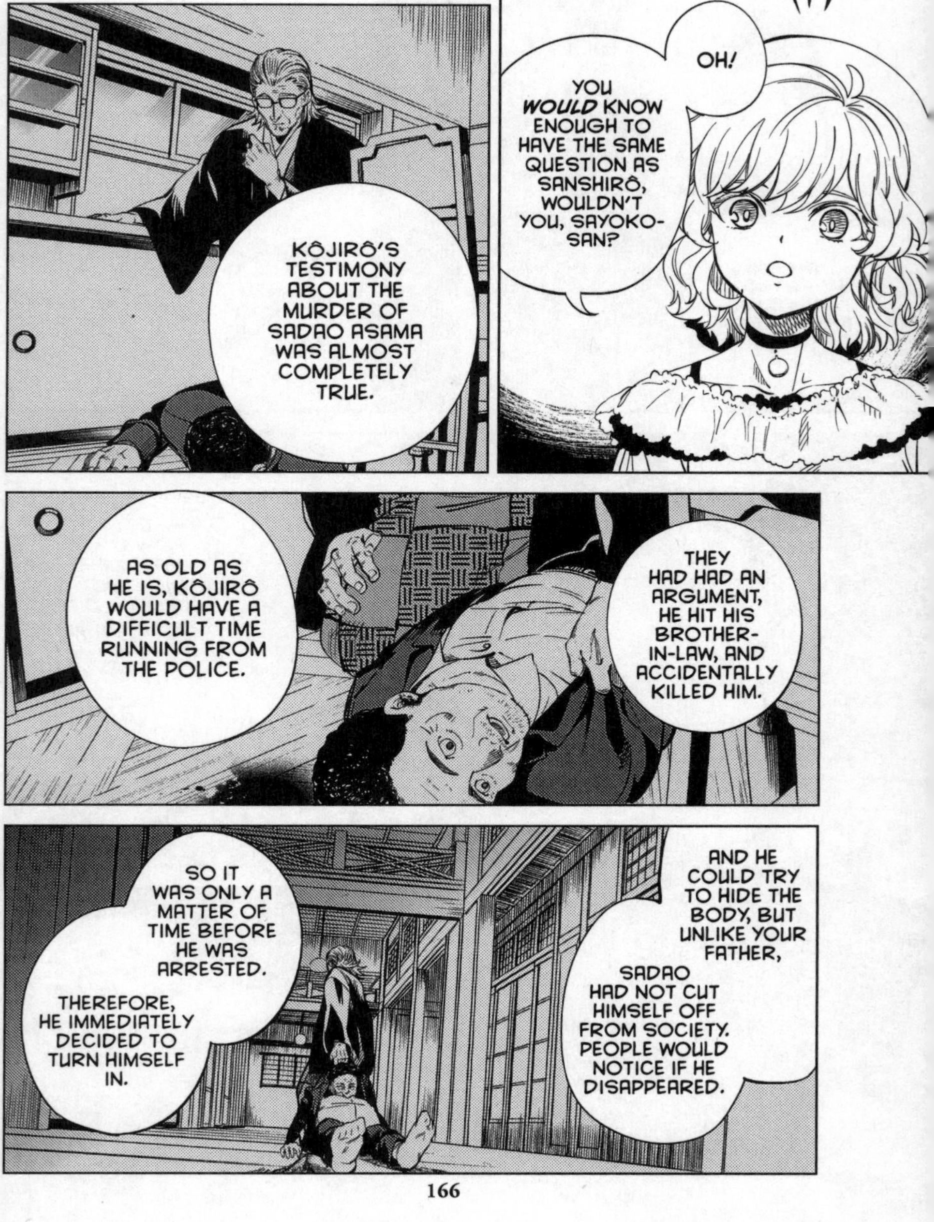
OH!
YOU *WOULD* KNOW ENOUGH TO HAVE THE SAME QUESTION AS SANSHIRÔ, WOULDN'T YOU, SAYOKO-SAN?
KÔJIRÔ'S TESTIMONY ABOUT THE MURDER OF SADAO ASAMA WAS ALMOST COMPLETELY TRUE.
THEY HAD HAD AN ARGUMENT, HE HIT HIS BROTHER-IN-LAW, AND ACCIDENTALLY KILLED HIM.
AS OLD AS HE IS, KÔJIRÔ WOULD HAVE A DIFFICULT TIME RUNNING FROM THE POLICE.
AND HE COULD TRY TO HIDE THE BODY, BUT UNLIKE YOUR FATHER,
SADAO HAD NOT CUT HIMSELF OFF FROM SOCIETY. PEOPLE WOULD NOTICE IF HE DISAPPEARED.
SO IT WAS ONLY A MATTER OF TIME BEFORE HE WAS ARRESTED.
THEREFORE, HE IMMEDIATELY DECIDED TO TURN HIMSELF IN.

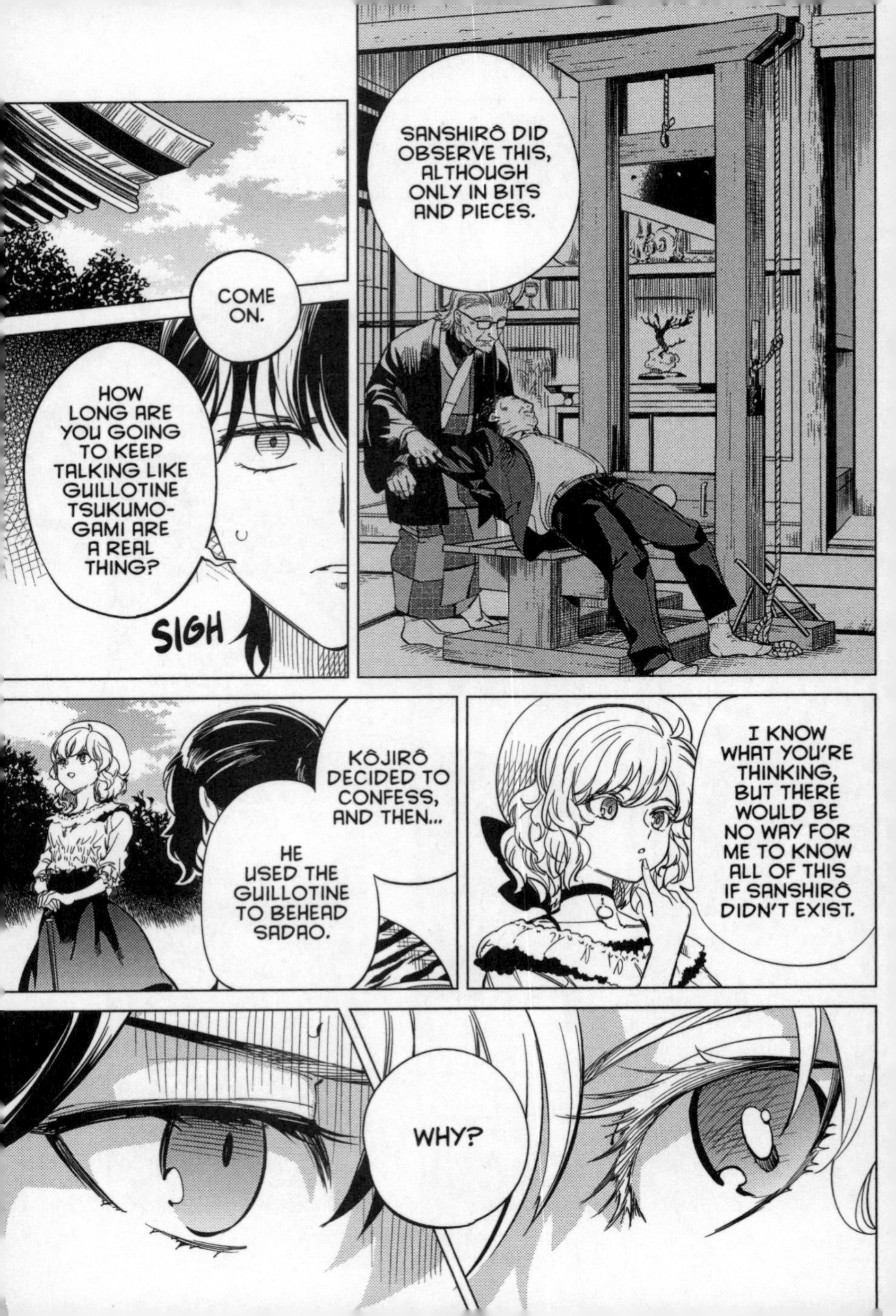
SANSHIRÔ DID OBSERVE THIS, ALTHOUGH ONLY IN BITS AND PIECES.
COME ON.
HOW LONG ARE YOU GOING TO KEEP TALKING LIKE GUILLOTINE TSUKUMO-GAMI ARE A REAL THING?
SIGH
I KNOW WHAT YOU'RE THINKING, BUT THERE WOULD BE NO WAY FOR ME TO KNOW ALL OF THIS IF SANSHIRÔ DIDN'T EXIST.
KÔJIRÔ DECIDED TO CONFESS, AND THEN...
HE USED THE GUILLOTINE TO BEHEAD SADAO.
WHY?

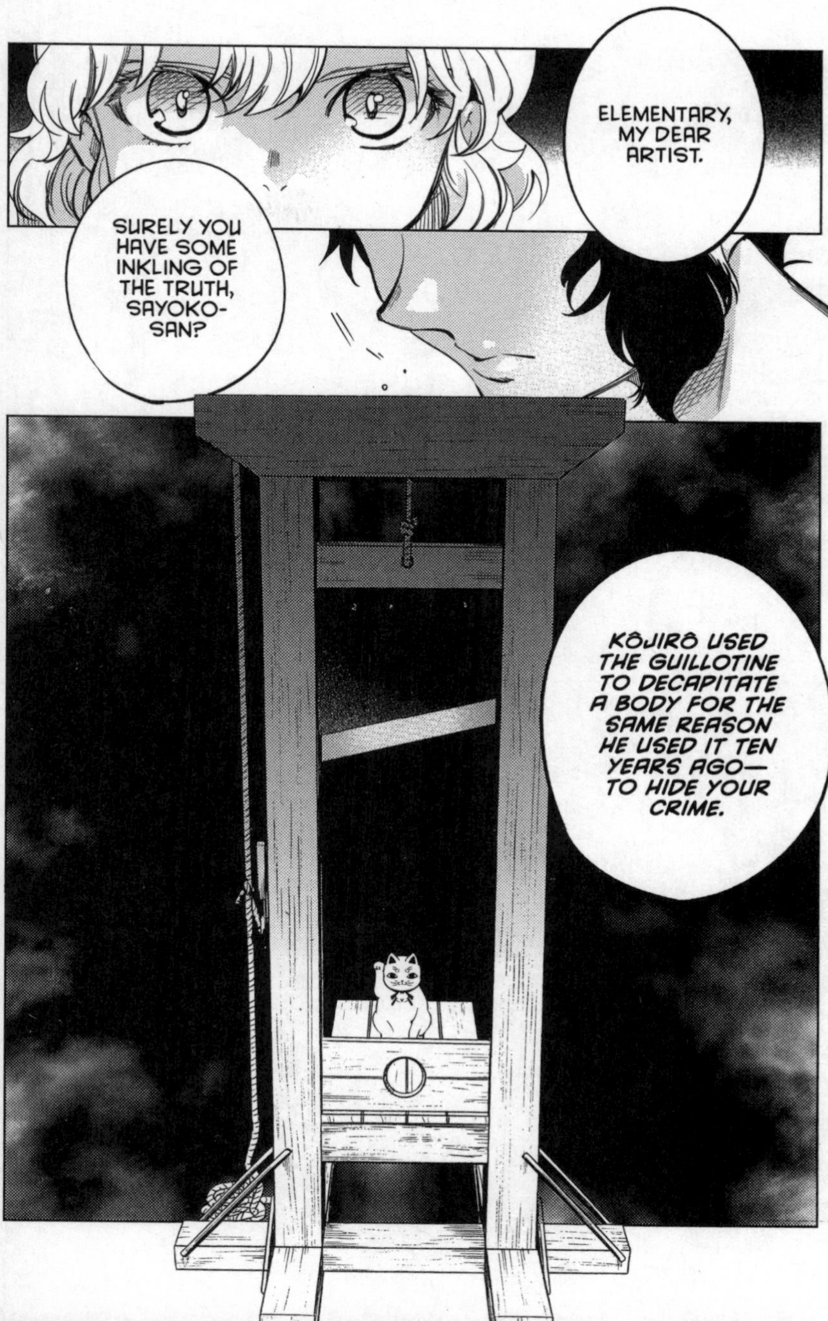
ELEMENTARY, MY DEAR ARTIST.
SURELY YOU HAVE SOME INKLING OF THE TRUTH, SAYOKO-SAN?
KÔJIRÔ USED THE GUILLOTINE TO DECAPITATE A BODY FOR THE SAME REASON HE USED IT TEN YEARS AGO— TO HIDE YOUR CRIME.

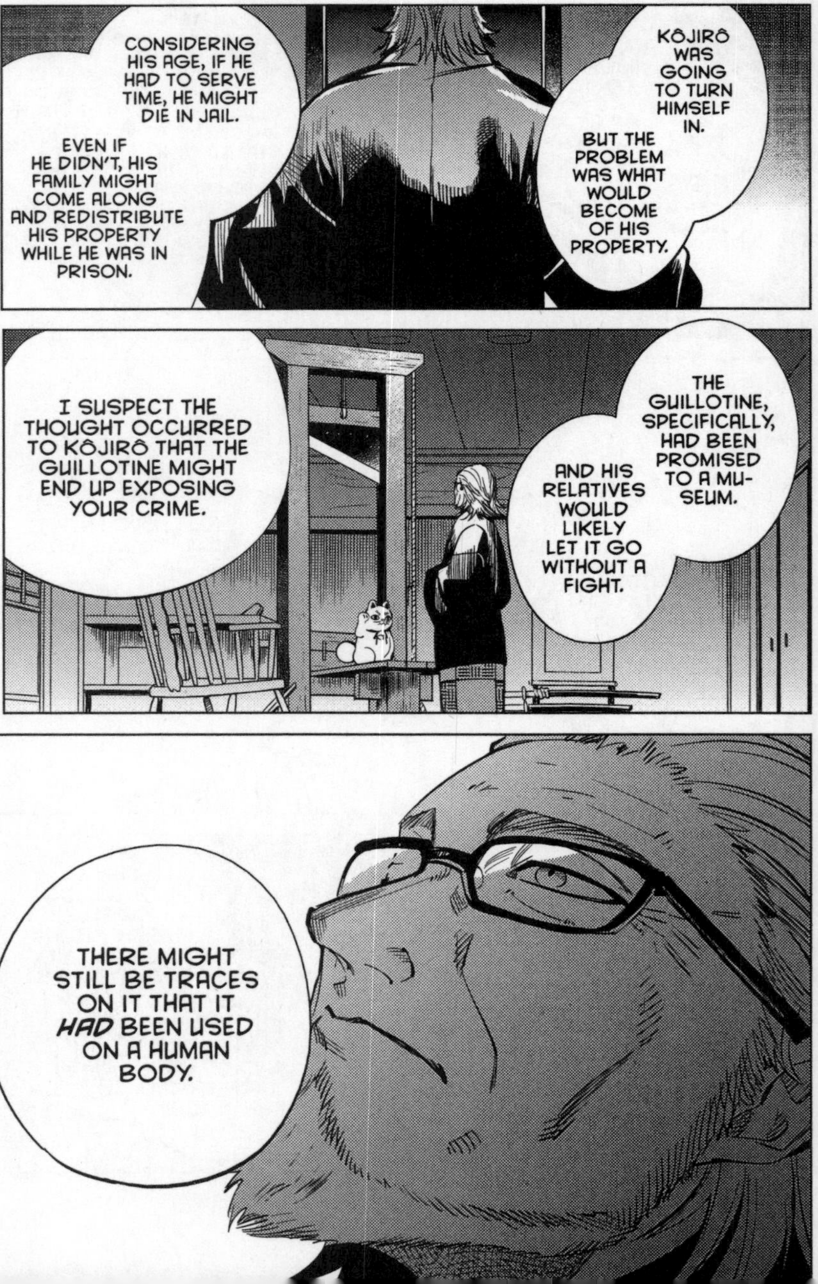
KÔJIRÔ WAS GOING TO TURN HIMSELF IN.
BUT THE PROBLEM WAS WHAT WOULD BECOME OF HIS PROPERTY.
CONSIDERING HIS AGE, IF HE HAD TO SERVE TIME, HE MIGHT DIE IN JAIL.
EVEN IF HE DIDN'T, HIS FAMILY MIGHT COME ALONG AND REDISTRIBUTE HIS PROPERTY WHILE HE WAS IN PRISON.
THE GUILLOTINE, SPECIFICALLY, HAD BEEN PROMISED TO A MU-SEUM.
AND HIS RELATIVES WOULD LIKELY LET IT GO WITHOUT A FIGHT.
I SUSPECT THE THOUGHT OCCURRED TO KÔJIRÔ THAT THE GUILLOTINE MIGHT END UP EXPOSING YOUR CRIME.
THERE MIGHT STILL BE TRACES ON IT THAT IT *HAD* BEEN USED ON A HUMAN BODY.

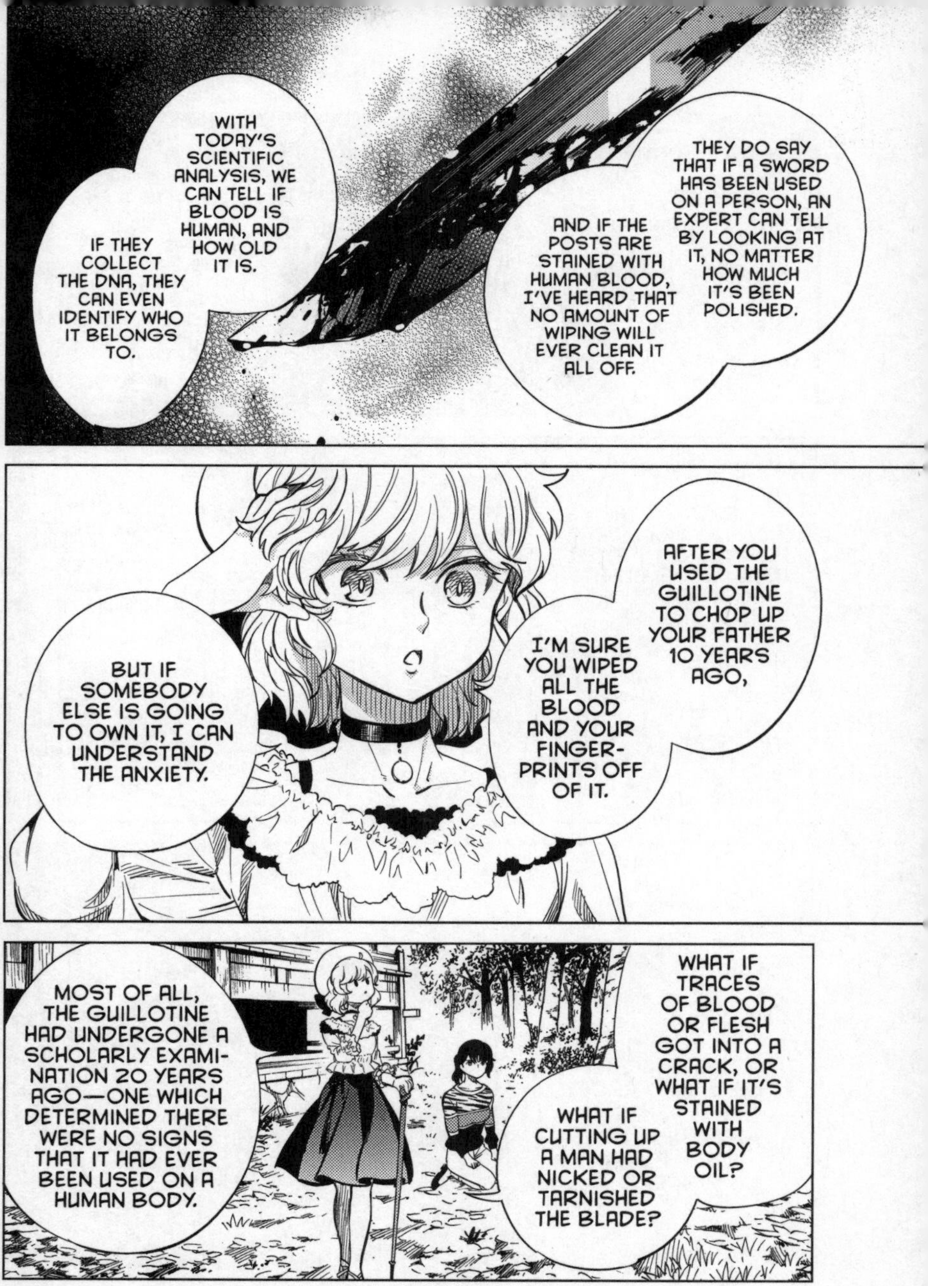
THEY DO SAY THAT IF A SWORD HAS BEEN USED ON A PERSON, AN EXPERT CAN TELL BY LOOKING AT IT, NO MATTER HOW MUCH IT'S BEEN POLISHED.
AND IF THE POSTS ARE STAINED WITH HUMAN BLOOD, I'VE HEARD THAT NO AMOUNT OF WIPING WILL EVER CLEAN IT ALL OFF.
WITH TODAY'S SCIENTIFIC ANALYSIS, WE CAN TELL IF BLOOD IS HUMAN, AND HOW OLD IT IS.
IF THEY COLLECT THE DNA, THEY CAN EVEN IDENTIFY WHO IT BELONGS TO.
AFTER YOU USED THE GUILLOTINE TO CHOP UP YOUR FATHER 10 YEARS AGO,
I'M SURE YOU WIPED ALL THE BLOOD AND YOUR FINGER-PRINTS OFF OF IT.
BUT IF SOMEBODY ELSE IS GOING TO OWN IT, I CAN UNDERSTAND THE ANXIETY.
WHAT IF TRACES OF BLOOD OR FLESH GOT INTO A CRACK, OR WHAT IF IT'S STAINED WITH BODY OIL?
WHAT IF CUTTING UP A MAN HAD NICKED OR TARNISHED THE BLADE?
MOST OF ALL, THE GUILLOTINE HAD UNDERGONE A SCHOLARLY EXAMI-NATION 20 YEARS AGO—ONE WHICH DETERMINED THERE WERE NO SIGNS THAT IT HAD EVER BEEN USED ON A HUMAN BODY.

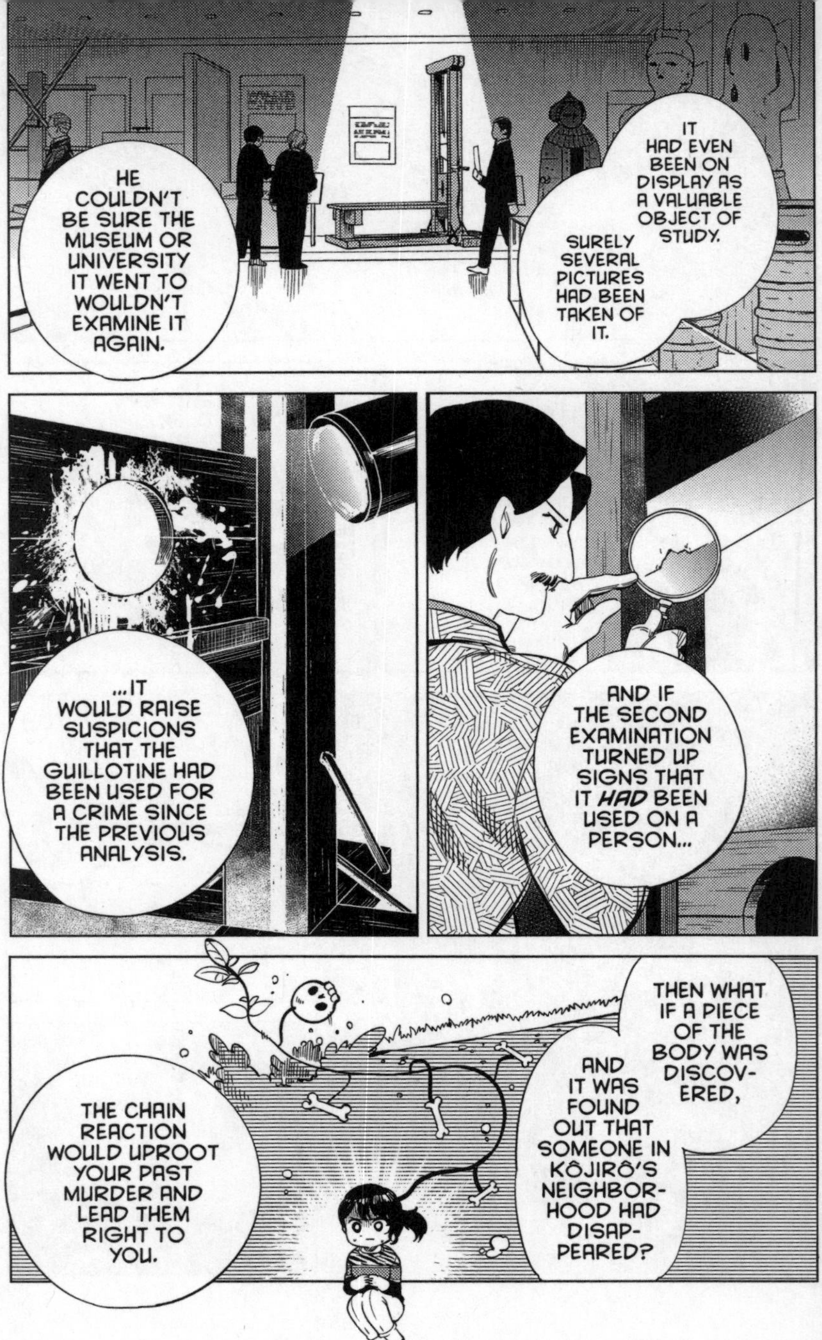
IT HAD EVEN BEEN ON DISPLAY AS A VALUABLE OBJECT OF STUDY.
SURELY SEVERAL PICTURES HAD BEEN TAKEN OF IT.
HE COULDN'T BE SURE THE MUSEUM OR UNIVERSITY IT WENT TO WOULDN'T EXAMINE IT AGAIN.
AND IF THE SECOND EXAMINATION TURNED UP SIGNS THAT IT *HAD* BEEN USED ON A PERSON...
...IT WOULD RAISE SUSPICIONS THAT THE GUILLOTINE HAD BEEN USED FOR A CRIME SINCE THE PREVIOUS ANALYSIS.
THEN WHAT IF A PIECE OF THE BODY WAS DISCOV-ERED,
AND IT WAS FOUND OUT THAT SOMEONE IN KÔJIRÔ'S NEIGHBOR-HOOD HAD DISAP-PEARED?
THE CHAIN REACTION WOULD UPROOT YOUR PAST MURDER AND LEAD THEM RIGHT TO YOU.

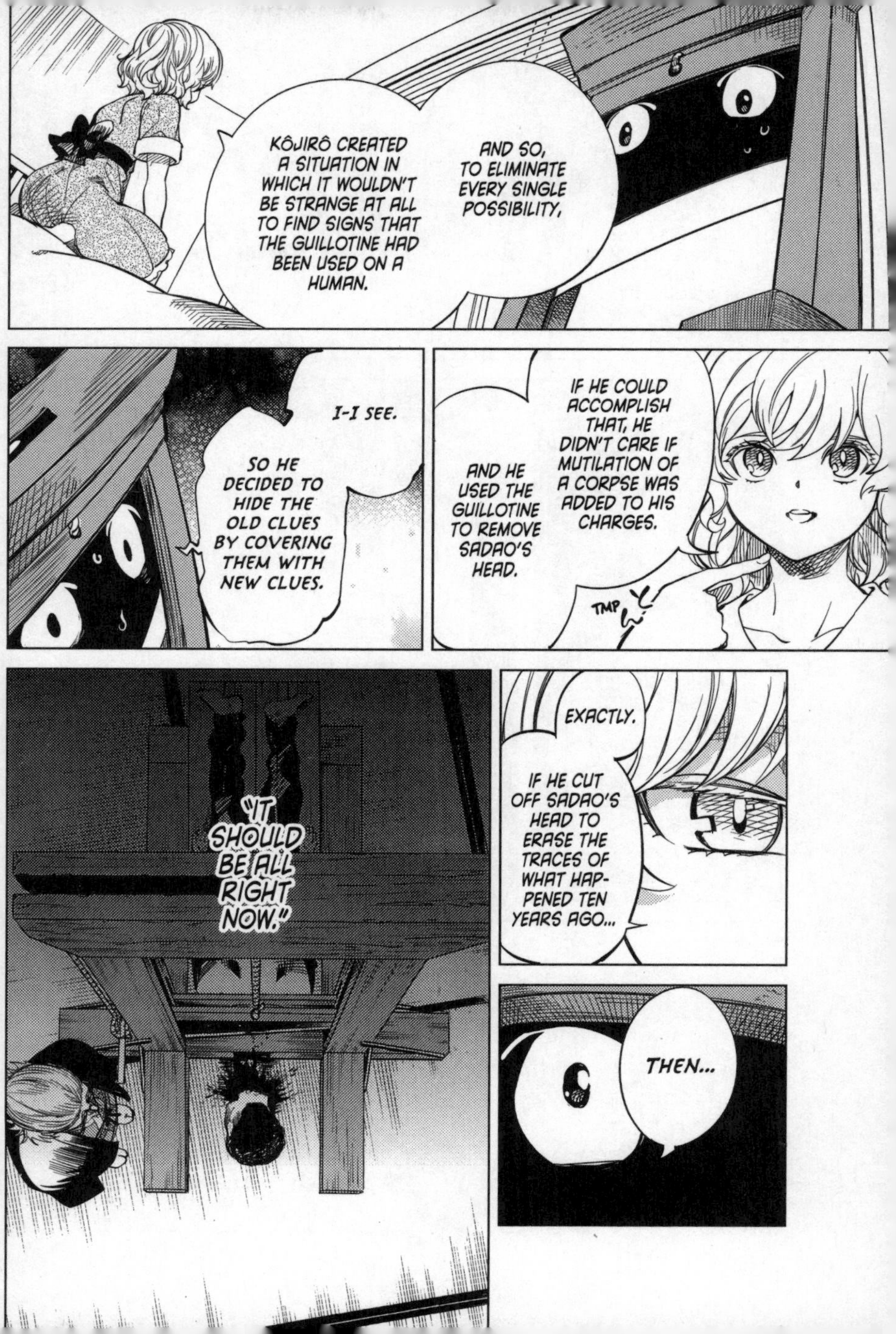
AND SO, TO ELIMINATE EVERY SINGLE POSSIBILITY,
KÔJIRÔ CREATED A SITUATION IN WHICH IT WOULDN'T BE STRANGE AT ALL TO FIND SIGNS THAT THE GUILLOTINE HAD BEEN USED ON A HUMAN.
IF HE COULD ACCOMPLISH THAT, HE DIDN'T CARE IF MUTILATION OF A CORPSE WAS ADDED TO HIS CHARGES.
AND HE USED THE GUILLOTINE TO REMOVE SADAO'S HEAD.
TMP
I-I SEE.
SO HE DECIDED TO HIDE THE OLD CLUES BY COVERING THEM WITH NEW CLUES.
EXACTLY.
IF HE CUT OFF SADAO'S HEAD TO ERASE THE TRACES OF WHAT HAP-PENED TEN YEARS AGO...
THEN...
"IT SHOULD BE ALL RIGHT NOW."

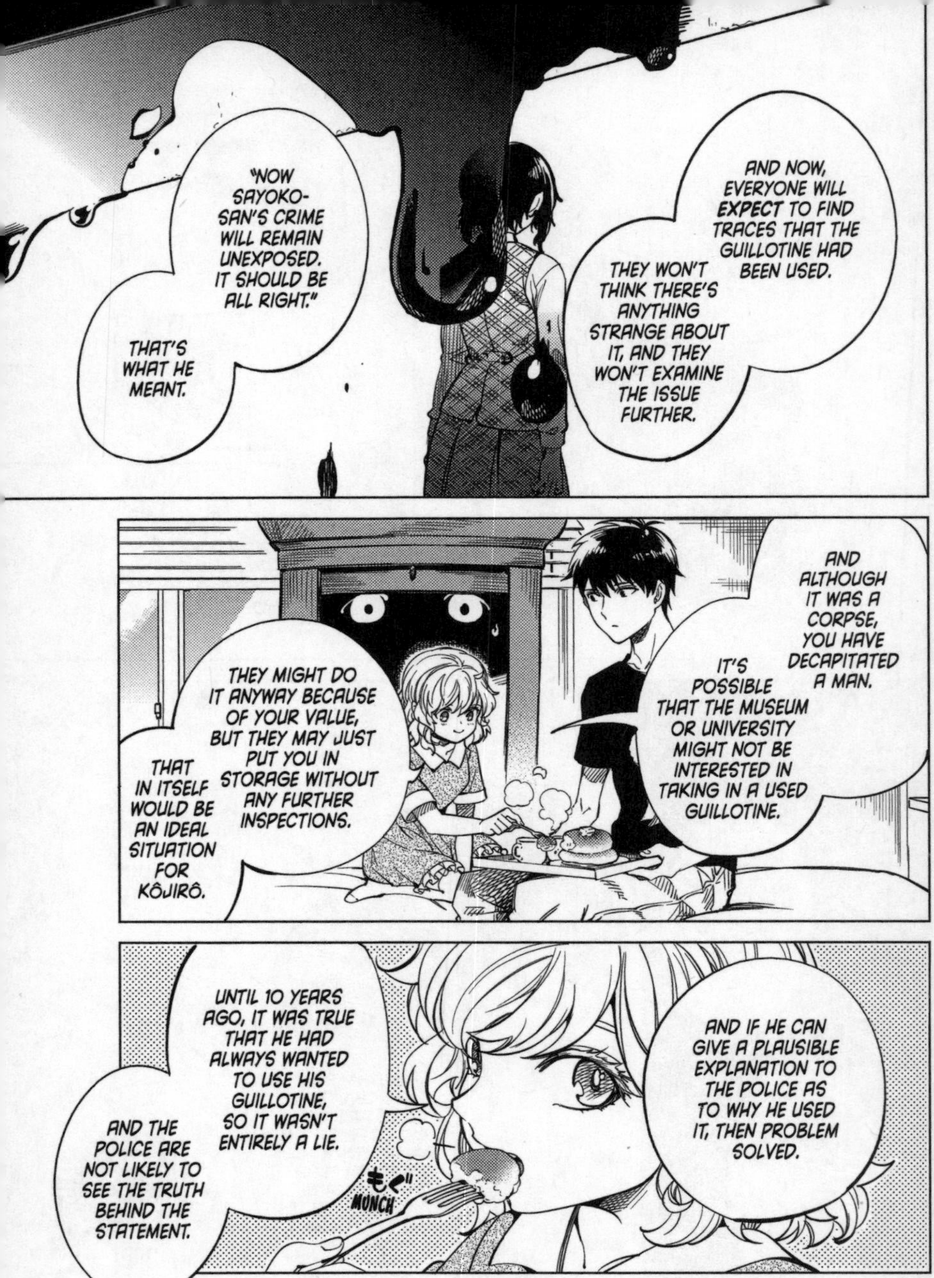
AND NOW, EVERYONE WILL EXPECT TO FIND TRACES THAT THE GUILLOTINE HAD BEEN USED.
THEY WON'T THINK THERE'S ANYTHING STRANGE ABOUT IT, AND THEY WON'T EXAMINE THE ISSUE FURTHER.
"NOW SAYOKO-SAN'S CRIME WILL REMAIN UNEXPOSED. IT SHOULD BE ALL RIGHT."
THAT'S WHAT HE MEANT.
AND ALTHOUGH IT WAS A CORPSE, YOU HAVE DECAPITATED A MAN.
IT'S POSSIBLE THAT THE MUSEUM OR UNIVERSITY MIGHT NOT BE INTERESTED IN TAKING IN A USED GUILLOTINE.
THEY MIGHT DO IT ANYWAY BECAUSE OF YOUR VALUE, BUT THEY MAY JUST PUT YOU IN STORAGE WITHOUT ANY FURTHER INSPECTIONS.
THAT IN ITSELF WOULD BE AN IDEAL SITUATION FOR KÔJIRÔ.
AND IF HE CAN GIVE A PLAUSIBLE EXPLANATION TO THE POLICE AS TO WHY HE USED IT, THEN PROBLEM SOLVED.
UNTIL 10 YEARS AGO, IT WAS TRUE THAT HE HAD ALWAYS WANTED TO USE HIS GUILLOTINE, SO IT WASN'T ENTIRELY A LIE.
AND THE POLICE ARE NOT LIKELY TO SEE THE TRUTH BEHIND THE STATEMENT.
もぐ
MUNCH

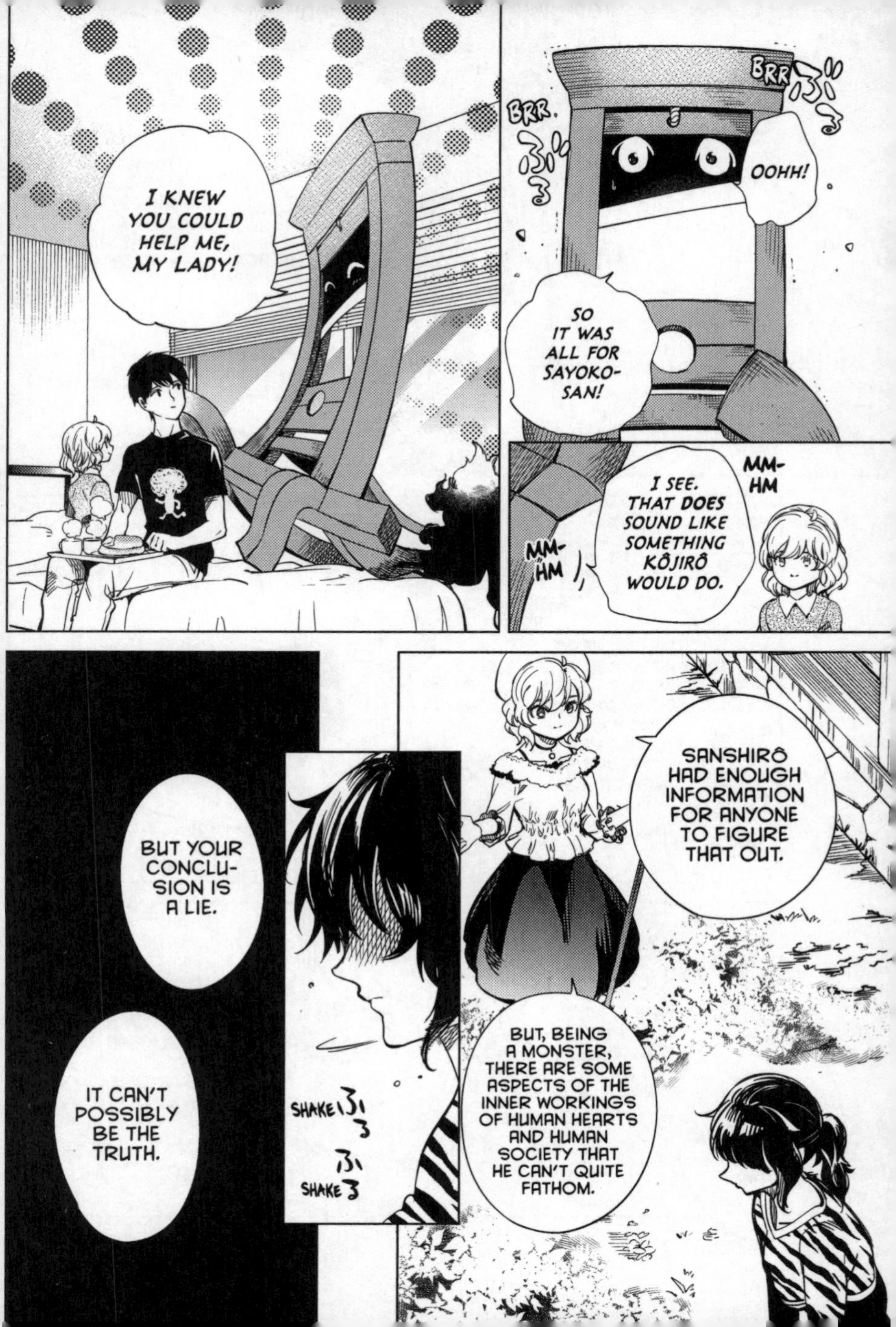
BRR ぶる
BRR. ぶる
OOHH!
SO IT WAS ALL FOR SAYOKO-SAN!
MM-HM
I SEE. THAT DOES SOUND LIKE SOMETHING KÔJIRÔ WOULD DO.
MM-HM
I KNEW YOU COULD HELP ME, MY LADY!
SANSHIRÔ HAD ENOUGH INFORMATION FOR ANYONE TO FIGURE THAT OUT.
BUT, BEING A MONSTER, THERE ARE SOME ASPECTS OF THE INNER WORKINGS OF HUMAN HEARTS AND HUMAN SOCIETY THAT HE CAN'T QUITE FATHOM.
SHAKE ふる
SHAKE ふる
BUT YOUR CONCLUSION IS A LIE.
IT CAN'T POSSIBLY BE THE TRUTH.

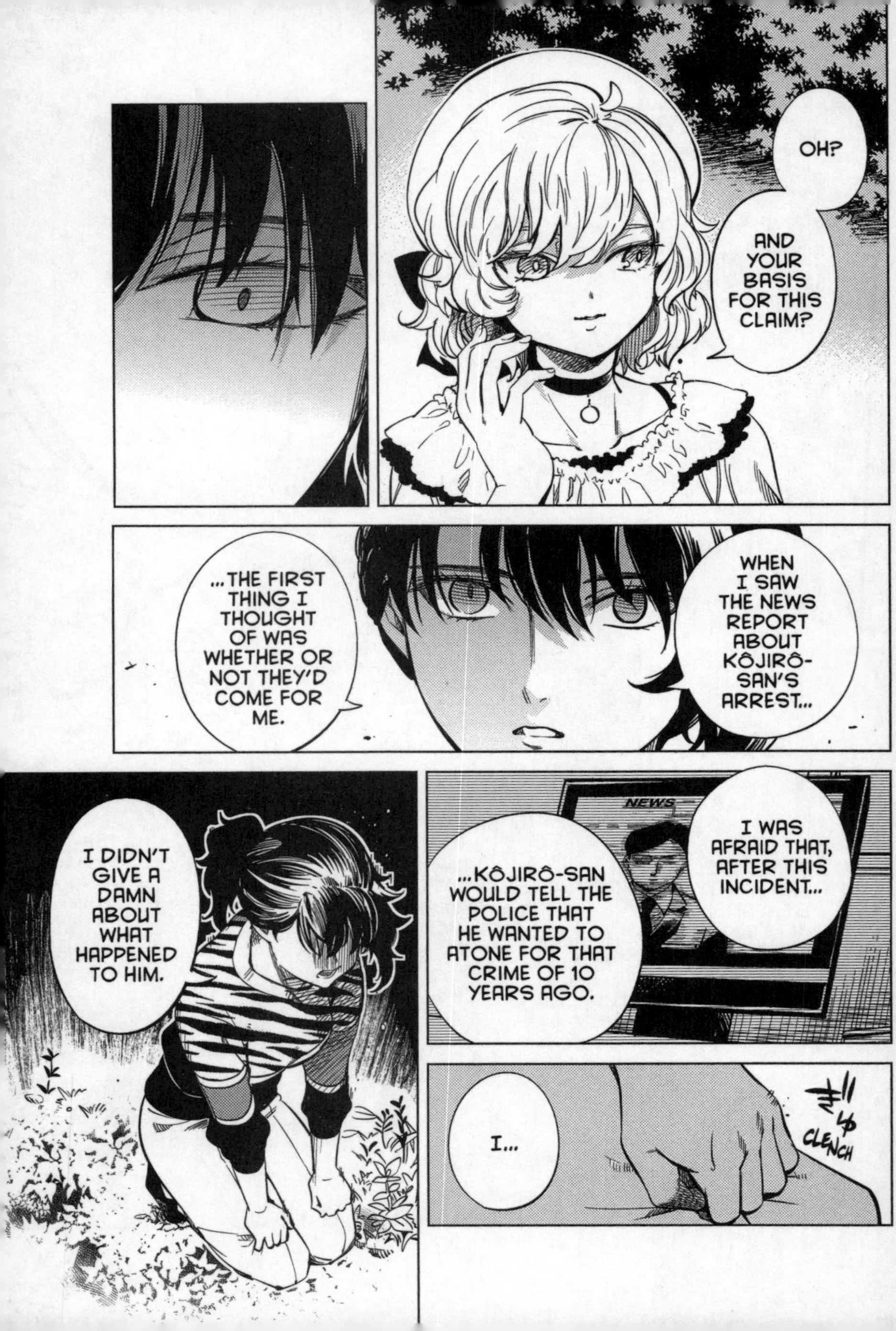
OH?
AND YOUR BASIS FOR THIS CLAIM?
WHEN I SAW THE NEWS REPORT ABOUT KÔJIRÔ-SAN'S ARREST...
...THE FIRST THING I THOUGHT OF WAS WHETHER OR NOT THEY'D COME FOR ME.
NEWS
I WAS AFRAID THAT, AFTER THIS INCIDENT...
...KÔJIRÔ-SAN WOULD TELL THE POLICE THAT HE WANTED TO ATONE FOR THAT CRIME OF 10 YEARS AGO.
きゅ
CLENCH
I...
I DIDN'T GIVE A DAMN ABOUT WHAT HAPPENED TO HIM.

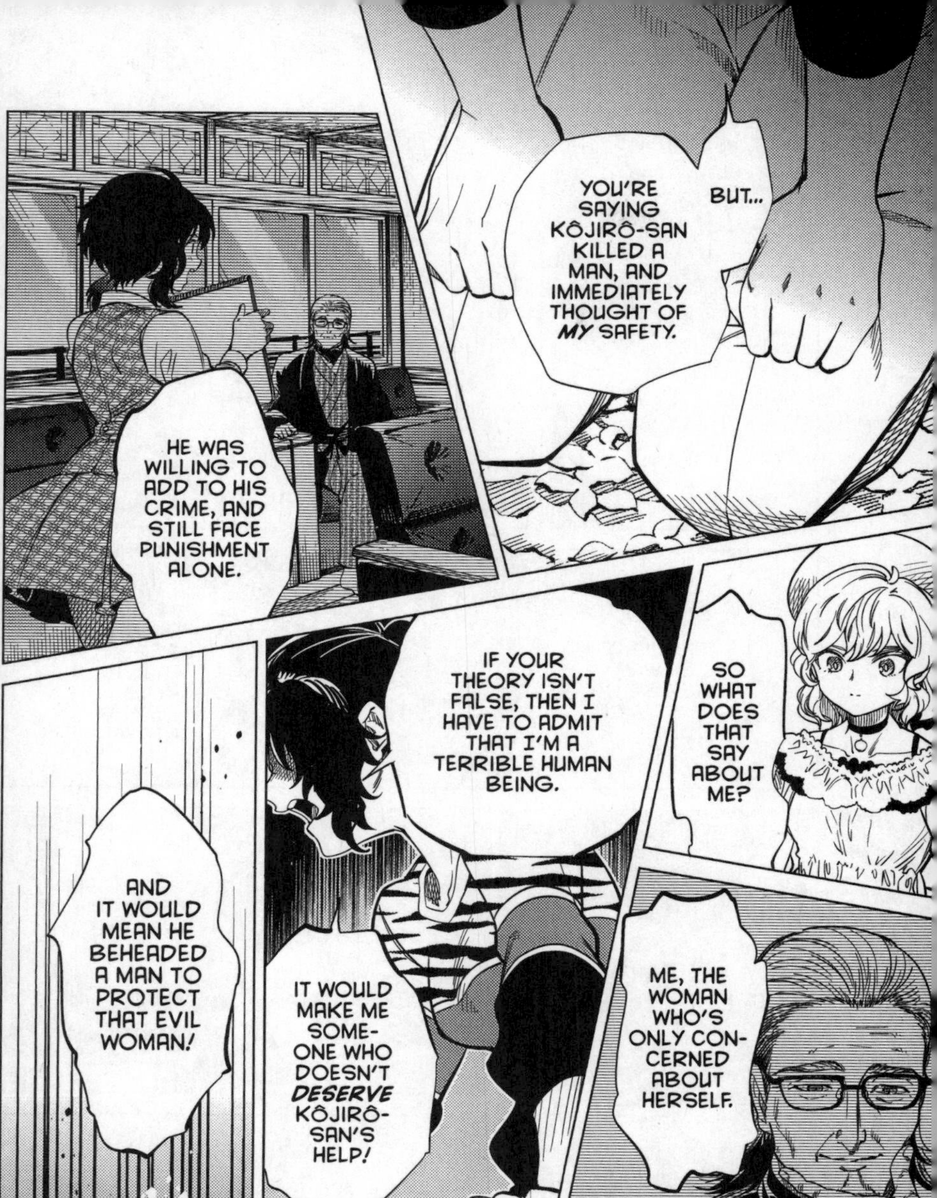
BUT...
YOU'RE SAYING KÔJIRÔ-SAN KILLED A MAN, AND IMMEDIATELY THOUGHT OF *MY* SAFETY.
HE WAS WILLING TO ADD TO HIS CRIME, AND STILL FACE PUNISHMENT ALONE.
SO WHAT DOES THAT SAY ABOUT ME?
ME, THE WOMAN WHO'S ONLY CON-CERNED ABOUT HERSELF.
IF YOUR THEORY ISN'T FALSE, THEN I HAVE TO ADMIT THAT I'M A TERRIBLE HUMAN BEING.
IT WOULD MAKE ME SOME-ONE WHO DOESN'T ***DESERVE*** KÔJIRÔ-SAN'S HELP!
AND IT WOULD MEAN HE BEHEADED A MAN TO PROTECT THAT EVIL WOMAN!

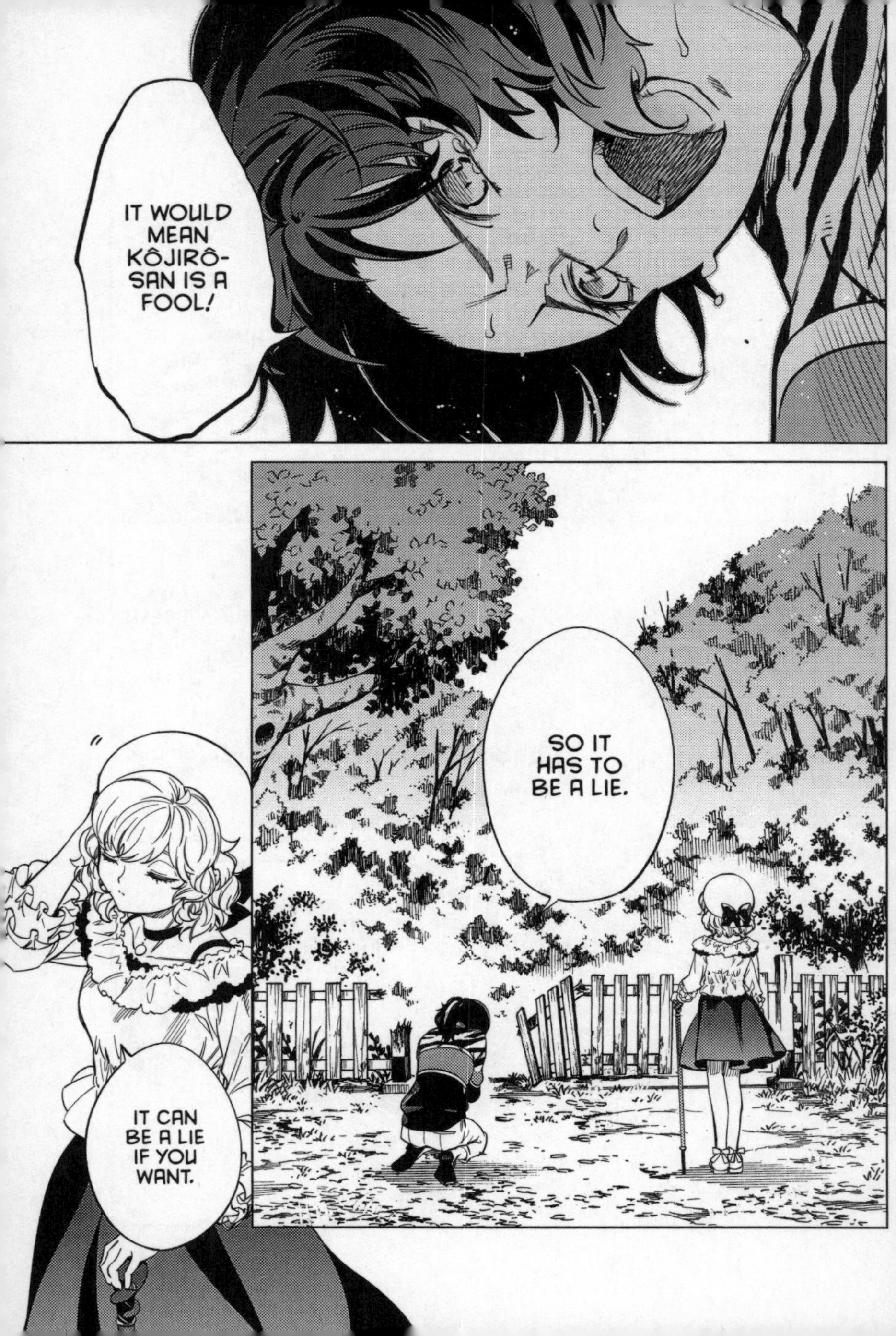
IT WOULD MEAN KÔJIRÔ-SAN IS A FOOL!
SO IT HAS TO BE A LIE.
IT CAN BE A LIE IF YOU WANT.

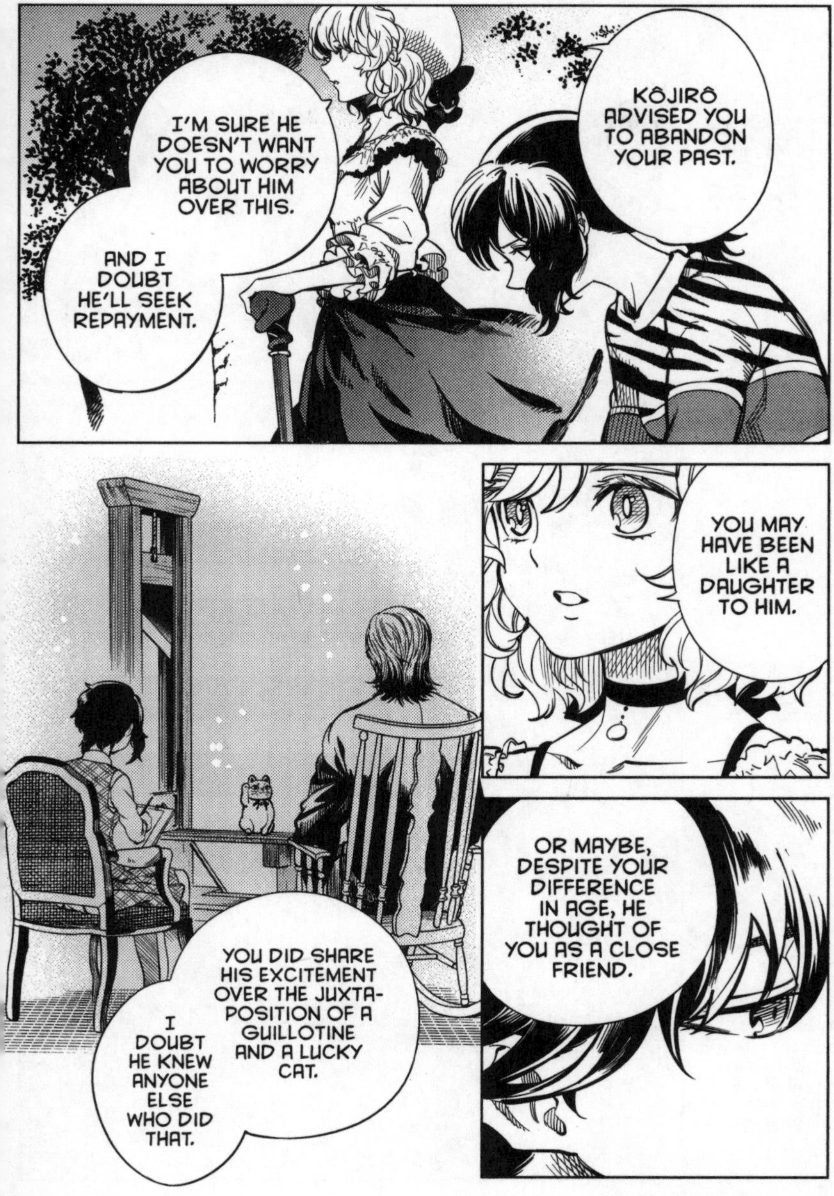
KÔJIRÔ ADVISED YOU TO ABANDON YOUR PAST.
I'M SURE HE DOESN'T WANT YOU TO WORRY ABOUT HIM OVER THIS.
AND I DOUBT HE'LL SEEK REPAYMENT.
YOU MAY HAVE BEEN LIKE A DAUGHTER TO HIM.
OR MAYBE, DESPITE YOUR DIFFERENCE IN AGE, HE THOUGHT OF YOU AS A CLOSE FRIEND.
YOU DID SHARE HIS EXCITEMENT OVER THE JUXTA-POSITION OF A GUILLOTINE AND A LUCKY CAT.
I DOUBT HE KNEW ANYONE ELSE WHO DID THAT.

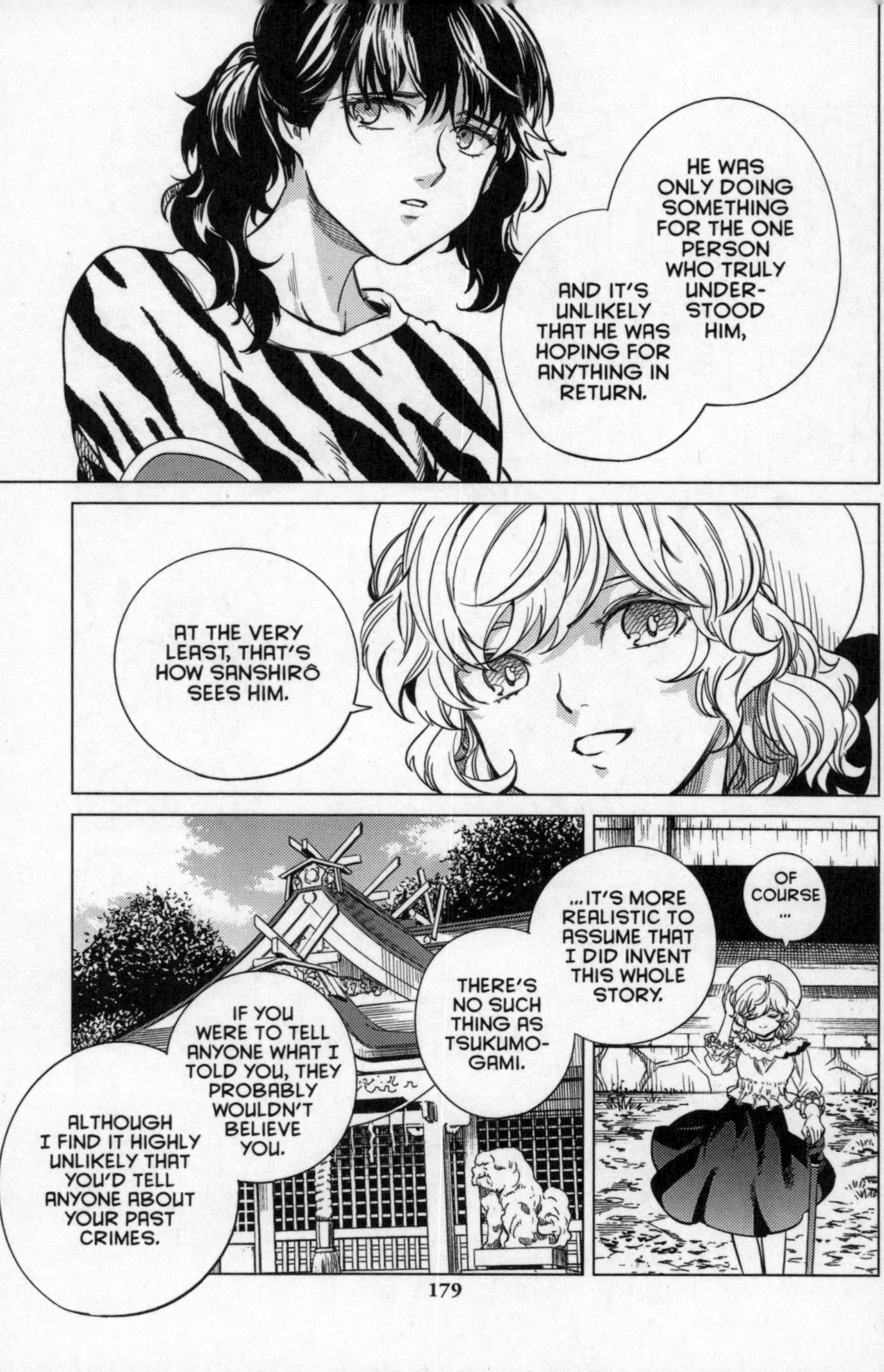
HE WAS ONLY DOING SOMETHING FOR THE ONE PERSON WHO TRULY UNDER-STOOD HIM,
AND IT'S UNLIKELY THAT HE WAS HOPING FOR ANYTHING IN RETURN.
AT THE VERY LEAST, THAT'S HOW SANSHIRÔ SEES HIM.
OF COURSE ...
THERE'S NO SUCH THING AS TSUKUMO-GAMI.
...IT'S MORE REALISTIC TO ASSUME THAT I DID INVENT THIS WHOLE STORY.
IF YOU WERE TO TELL ANYONE WHAT I TOLD YOU, THEY PROBABLY WOULDN'T BELIEVE YOU.
ALTHOUGH I FIND IT HIGHLY UNLIKELY THAT YOU'D TELL ANYONE ABOUT YOUR PAST CRIMES.

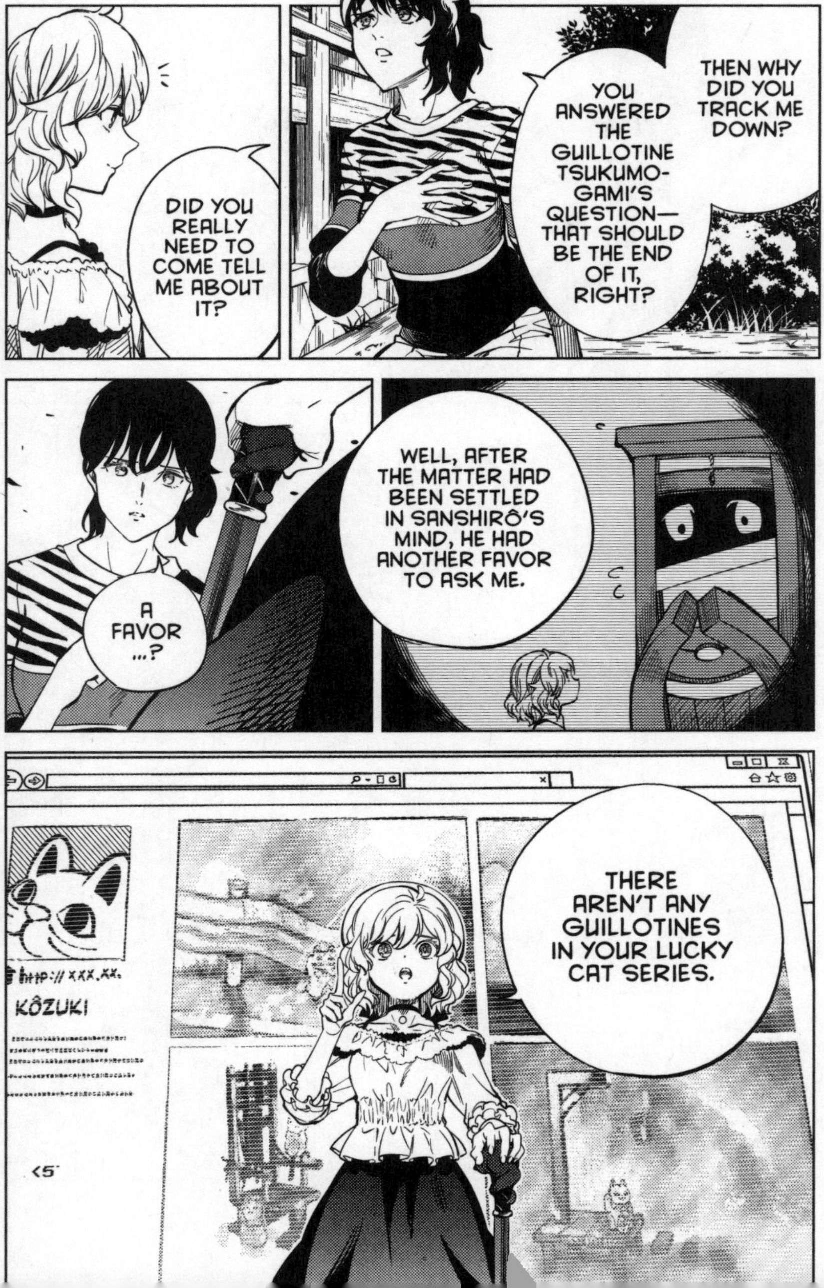
THEN WHY DID YOU TRACK ME DOWN?
YOU ANSWERED THE GUILLOTINE TSUKUMO-GAMI'S QUESTION—THAT SHOULD BE THE END OF IT, RIGHT?
DID YOU REALLY NEED TO COME TELL ME ABOUT IT?
WELL, AFTER THE MATTER HAD BEEN SETTLED IN SANSHIRÔ'S MIND, HE HAD ANOTHER FAVOR TO ASK ME.
A FAVOR ...?
THERE AREN'T ANY GUILLOTINES IN YOUR LUCKY CAT SERIES.
KÔZUKI

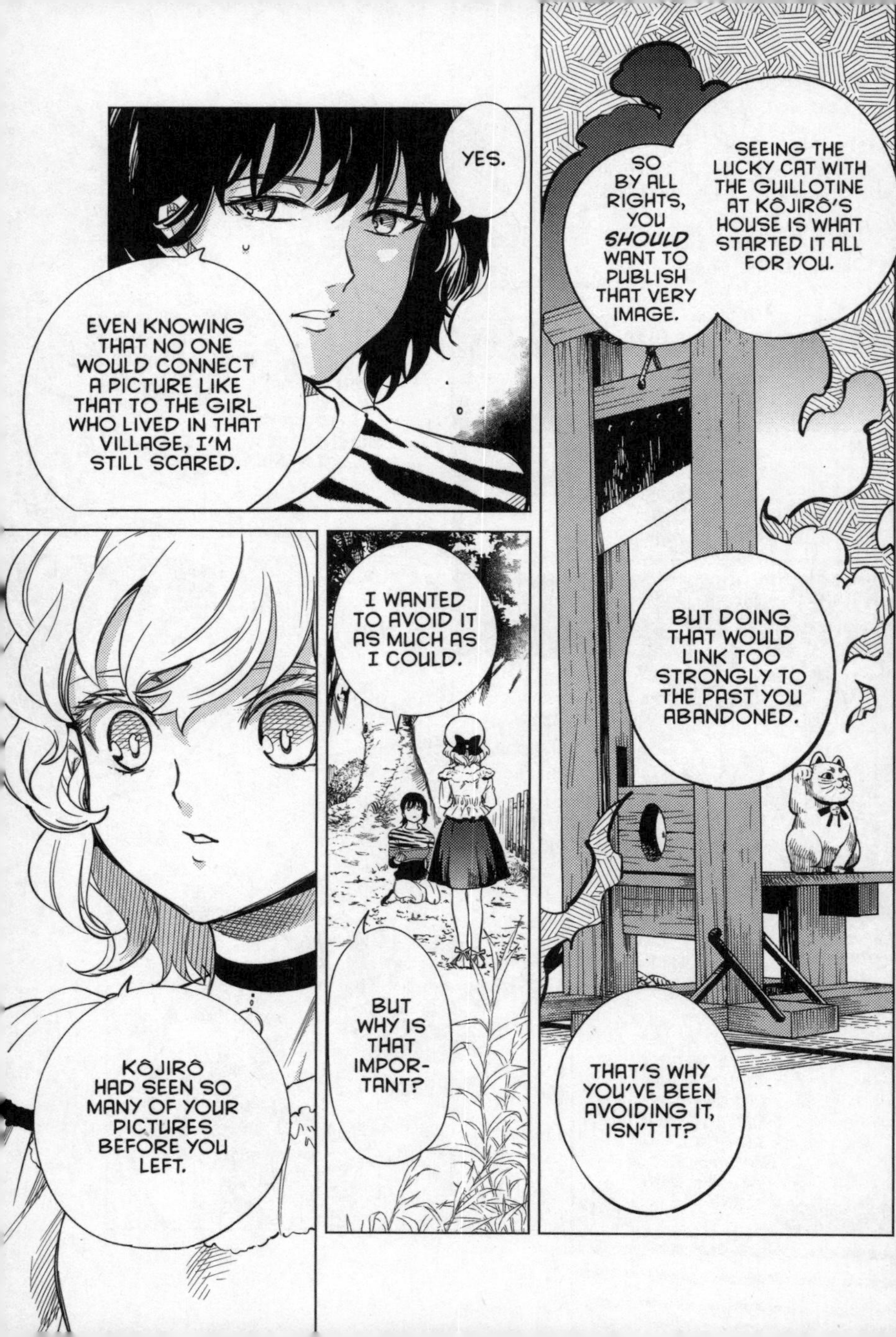
SEEING THE LUCKY CAT WITH THE GUILLOTINE AT KÔJIRÔ'S HOUSE IS WHAT STARTED IT ALL FOR YOU.
SO BY ALL RIGHTS, YOU *SHOULD* WANT TO PUBLISH THAT VERY IMAGE.
BUT DOING THAT WOULD LINK TOO STRONGLY TO THE PAST YOU ABANDONED.
THAT'S WHY YOU'VE BEEN AVOIDING IT, ISN'T IT?
YES.
EVEN KNOWING THAT NO ONE WOULD CONNECT A PICTURE LIKE THAT TO THE GIRL WHO LIVED IN THAT VILLAGE, I'M STILL SCARED.
I WANTED TO AVOID IT AS MUCH AS I COULD.
BUT WHY IS THAT IMPOR-TANT?
KÔJIRÔ HAD SEEN SO MANY OF YOUR PICTURES BEFORE YOU LEFT.

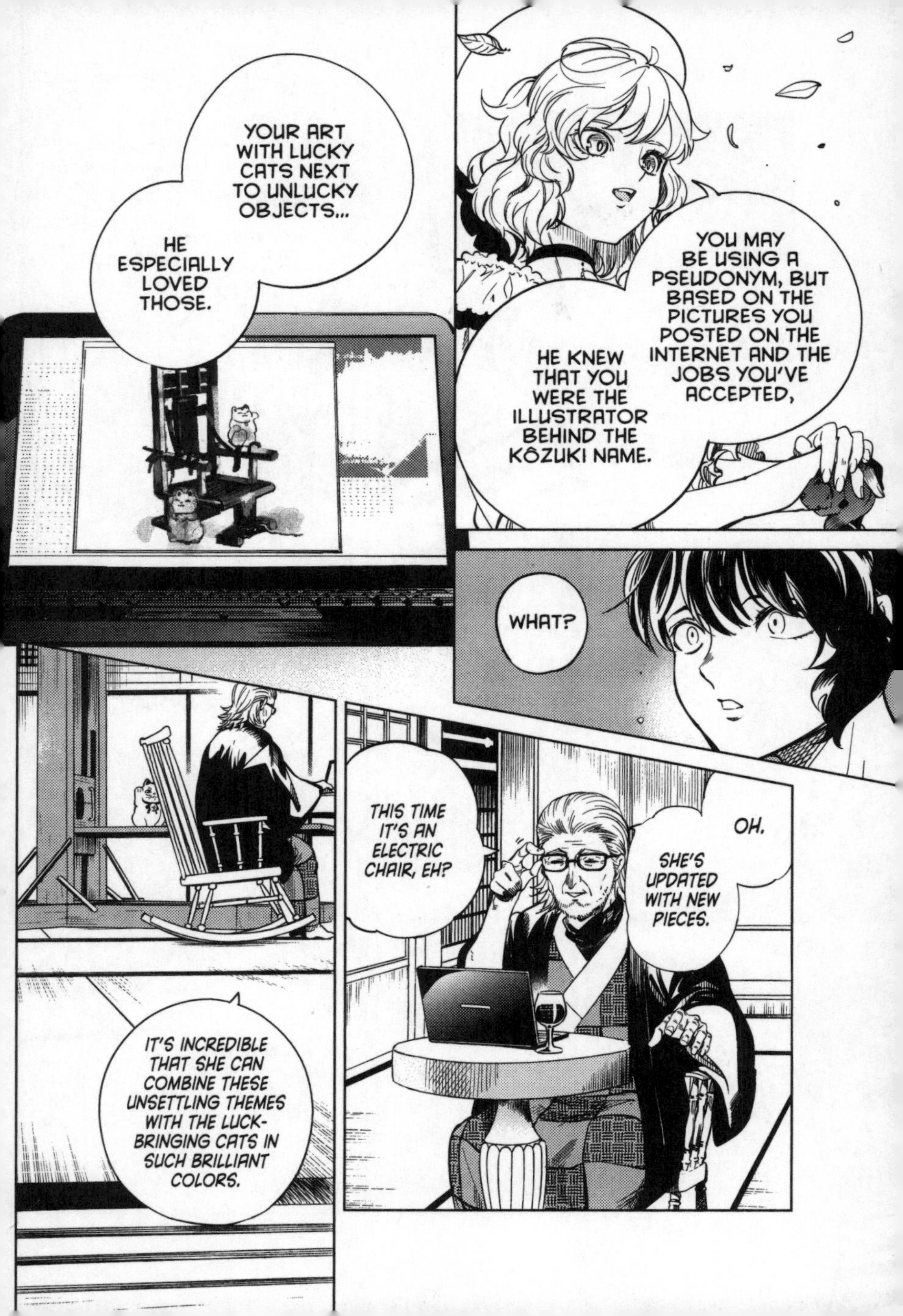
YOU MAY BE USING A PSEUDONYM, BUT BASED ON THE PICTURES YOU POSTED ON THE INTERNET AND THE JOBS YOU'VE ACCEPTED,
HE KNEW THAT YOU WERE THE ILLUSTRATOR BEHIND THE KÔZUKI NAME.
YOUR ART WITH LUCKY CATS NEXT TO UNLUCKY OBJECTS...
HE ESPECIALLY LOVED THOSE.
WHAT?
OH.
SHE'S UPDATED WITH NEW PIECES.
THIS TIME IT'S AN ELECTRIC CHAIR, EH?
IT'S INCREDIBLE THAT SHE CAN COMBINE THESE UNSETTLING THEMES WITH THE LUCK-BRINGING CATS IN SUCH BRILLIANT COLORS.

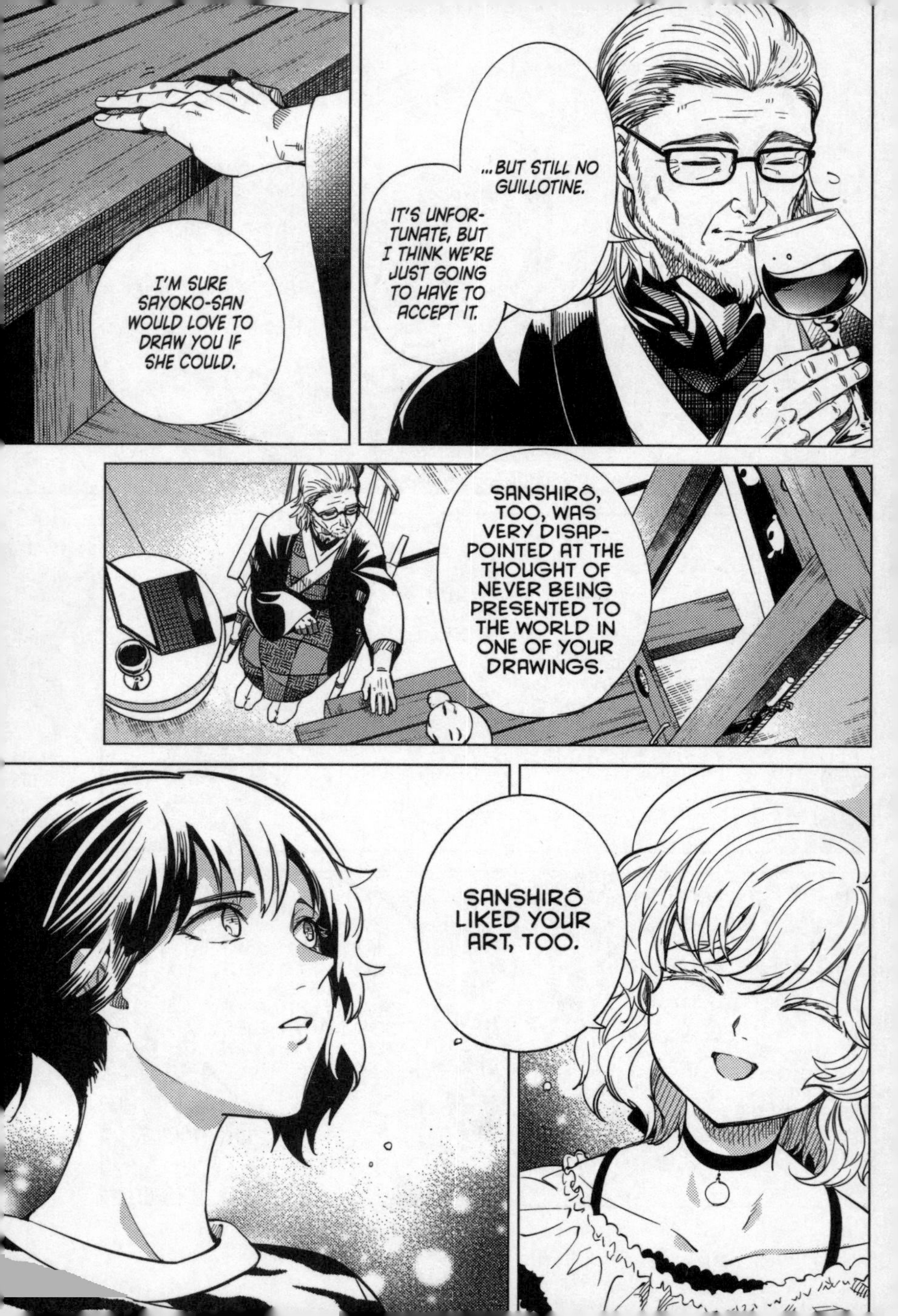
...BUT STILL NO GUILLOTINE.
IT'S UNFORTUNATE, BUT I THINK WE'RE JUST GOING TO HAVE TO ACCEPT IT.
I'M SURE SAYOKO-SAN WOULD LOVE TO DRAW YOU IF SHE COULD.
SANSHIRÔ, TOO, WAS VERY DISAPPOINTED AT THE THOUGHT OF NEVER BEING PRESENTED TO THE WORLD IN ONE OF YOUR DRAWINGS.
SANSHIRÔ LIKED YOUR ART, TOO.

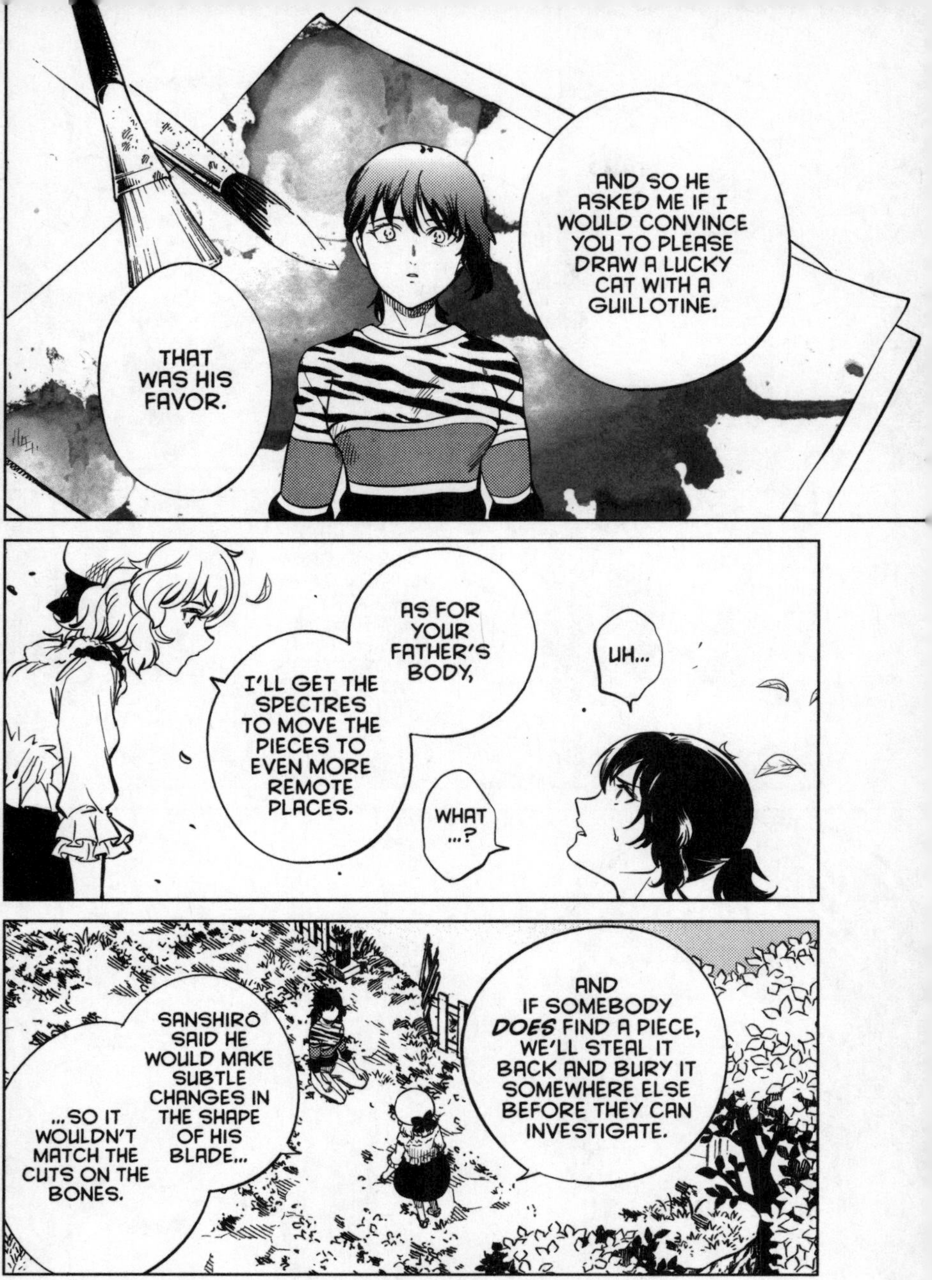
AND SO HE ASKED ME IF I WOULD CONVINCE YOU TO PLEASE DRAW A LUCKY CAT WITH A GUILLOTINE.
THAT WAS HIS FAVOR.
UH...
AS FOR YOUR FATHER'S BODY,
I'LL GET THE SPECTRES TO MOVE THE PIECES TO EVEN MORE REMOTE PLACES.
WHAT ...?
AND IF SOMEBODY *DOES* FIND A PIECE, WE'LL STEAL IT BACK AND BURY IT SOMEWHERE ELSE BEFORE THEY CAN INVESTIGATE.
SANSHIRÔ SAID HE WOULD MAKE SUBTLE CHANGES IN THE SHAPE OF HIS BLADE...
...SO IT WOULDN'T MATCH THE CUTS ON THE BONES.

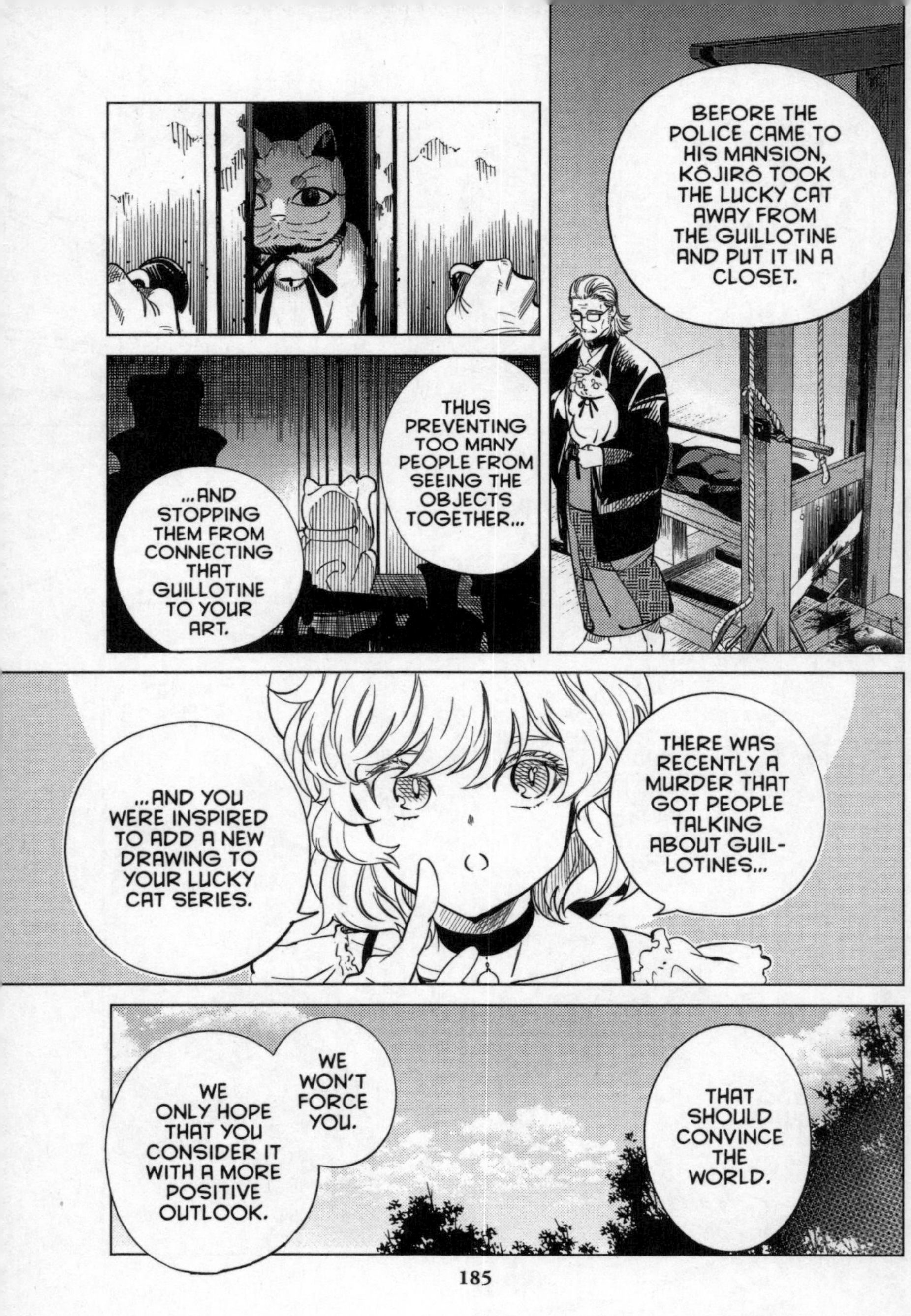
BEFORE THE POLICE CAME TO HIS MANSION, KÔJIRÔ TOOK THE LUCKY CAT AWAY FROM THE GUILLOTINE AND PUT IT IN A CLOSET.
THUS PREVENTING TOO MANY PEOPLE FROM SEEING THE OBJECTS TOGETHER...
...AND STOPPING THEM FROM CONNECTING THAT GUILLOTINE TO YOUR ART.
THERE WAS RECENTLY A MURDER THAT GOT PEOPLE TALKING ABOUT GUIL-LOTINES...
...AND YOU WERE INSPIRED TO ADD A NEW DRAWING TO YOUR LUCKY CAT SERIES.
THAT SHOULD CONVINCE THE WORLD.
WE WON'T FORCE YOU.
WE ONLY HOPE THAT YOU CONSIDER IT WITH A MORE POSITIVE OUTLOOK.

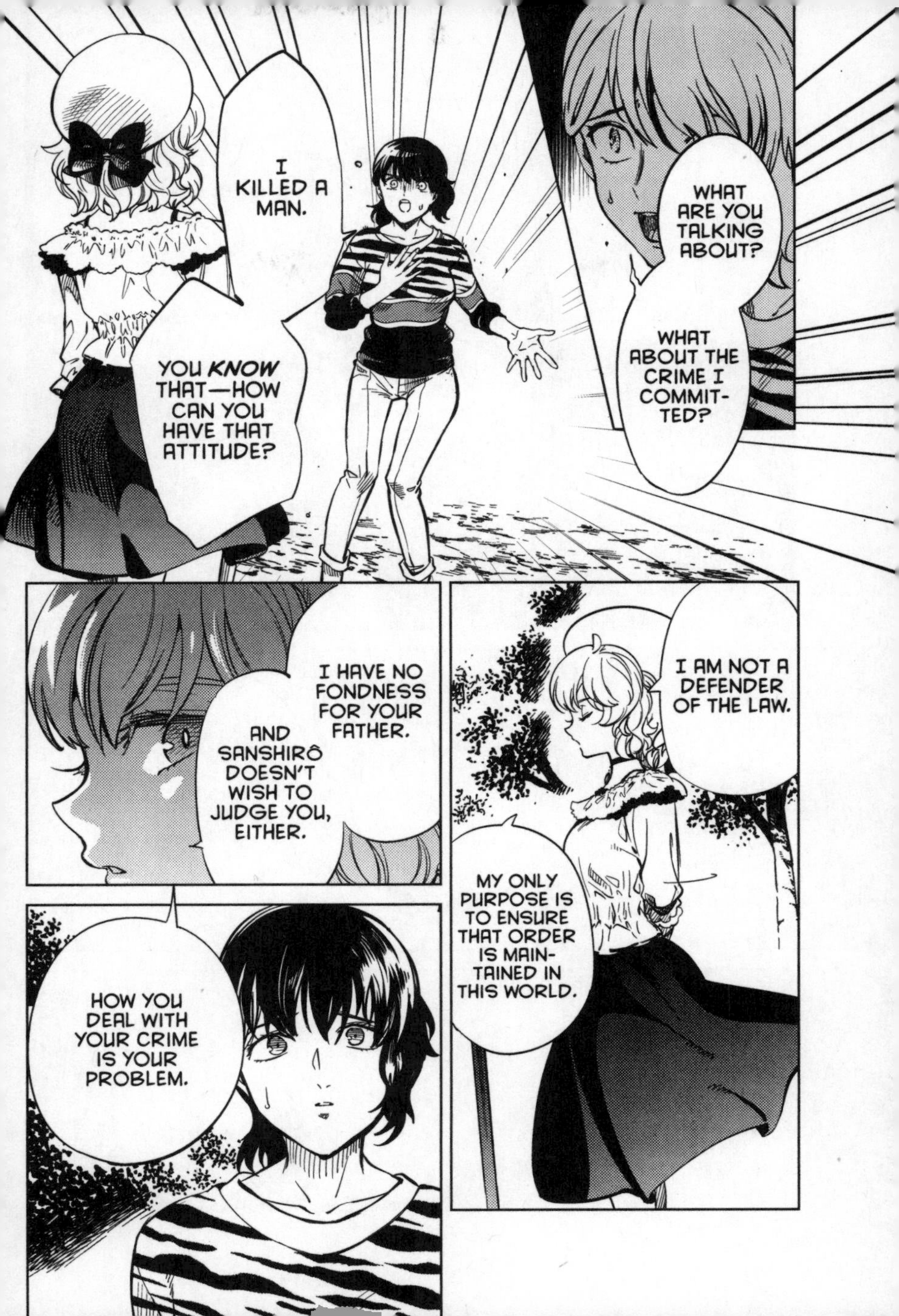
WHAT ARE YOU TALKING ABOUT?
WHAT ABOUT THE CRIME I COMMITTED?
I KILLED A MAN.
YOU *KNOW* THAT—HOW CAN YOU HAVE THAT ATTITUDE?
I AM NOT A DEFENDER OF THE LAW.
MY ONLY PURPOSE IS TO ENSURE THAT ORDER IS MAINTAINED IN THIS WORLD.
I HAVE NO FONDNESS FOR YOUR FATHER.
AND SANSHIRÔ DOESN'T WISH TO JUDGE YOU, EITHER.
HOW YOU DEAL WITH YOUR CRIME IS YOUR PROBLEM.

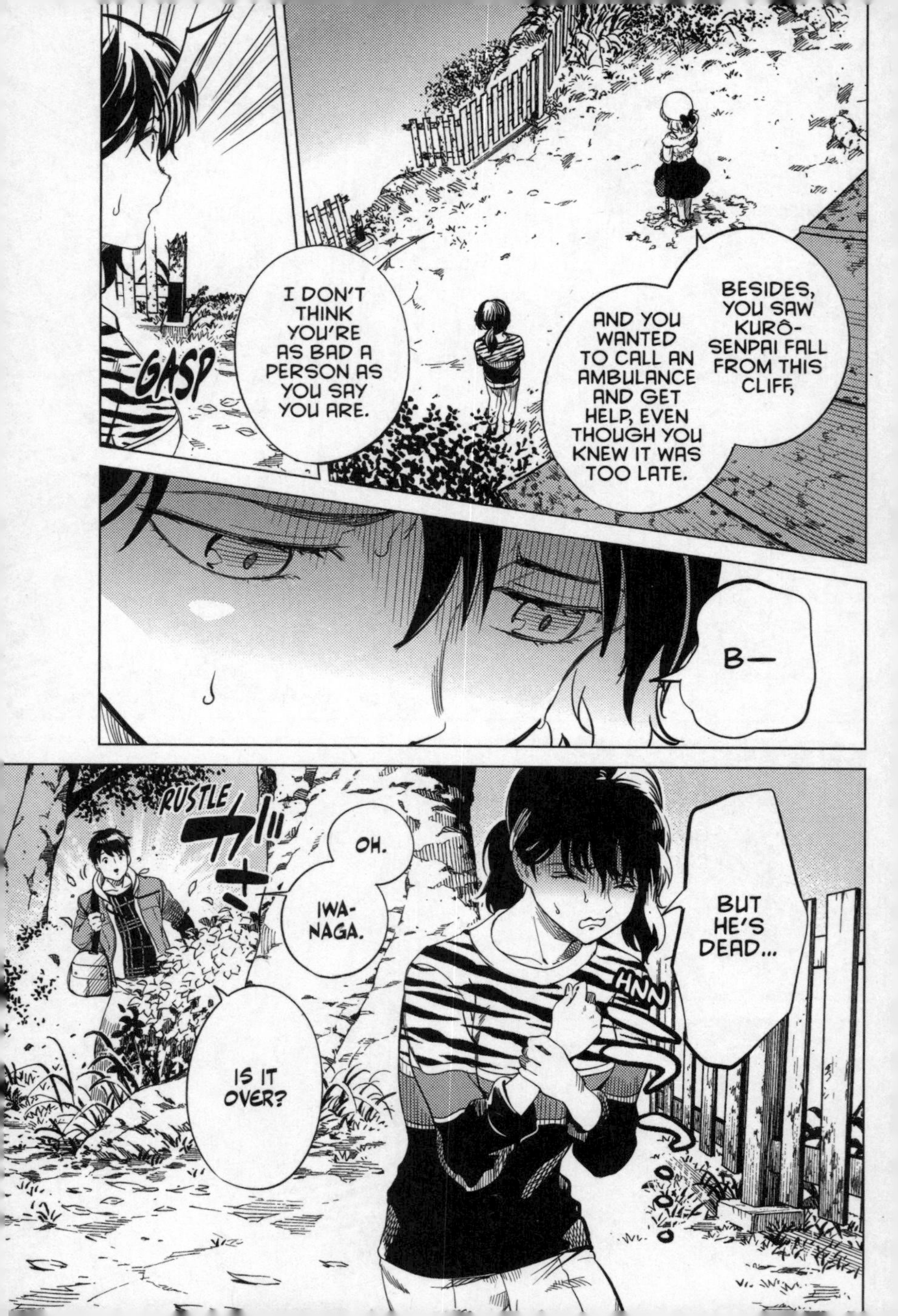
BESIDES, YOU SAW KURÔ-SENPAI FALL FROM THIS CLIFF,
AND YOU WANTED TO CALL AN AMBULANCE AND GET HELP, EVEN THOUGH YOU KNEW IT WAS TOO LATE.
I DON'T THINK YOU'RE AS BAD A PERSON AS YOU SAY YOU ARE.
GASP
B—
BUT HE'S DEAD...
HNN
RUSTLE
OH.
IWA-NAGA.
IS IT OVER?

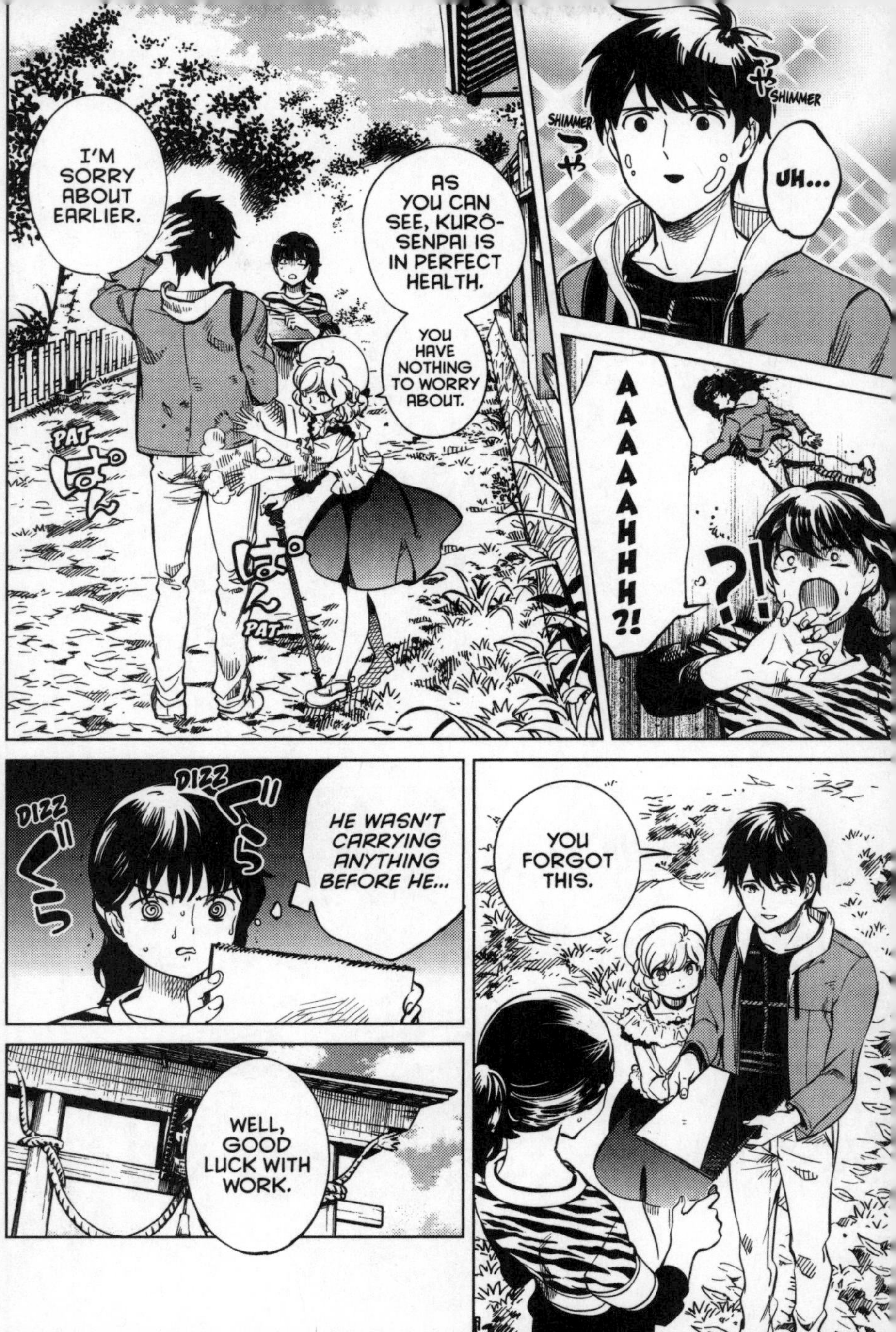
SHIMMER
SHIMMER
UH...
AAAAAHHHH?!
?!
AS YOU CAN SEE, KURÔ-SENPAI IS IN PERFECT HEALTH.
YOU HAVE NOTHING TO WORRY ABOUT.
I'M SORRY ABOUT EARLIER.
PAT
PAT
YOU FORGOT THIS.
HE WASN'T CARRYING ANYTHING BEFORE HE...
DIZZ
DIZZ
WELL, GOOD LUCK WITH WORK.

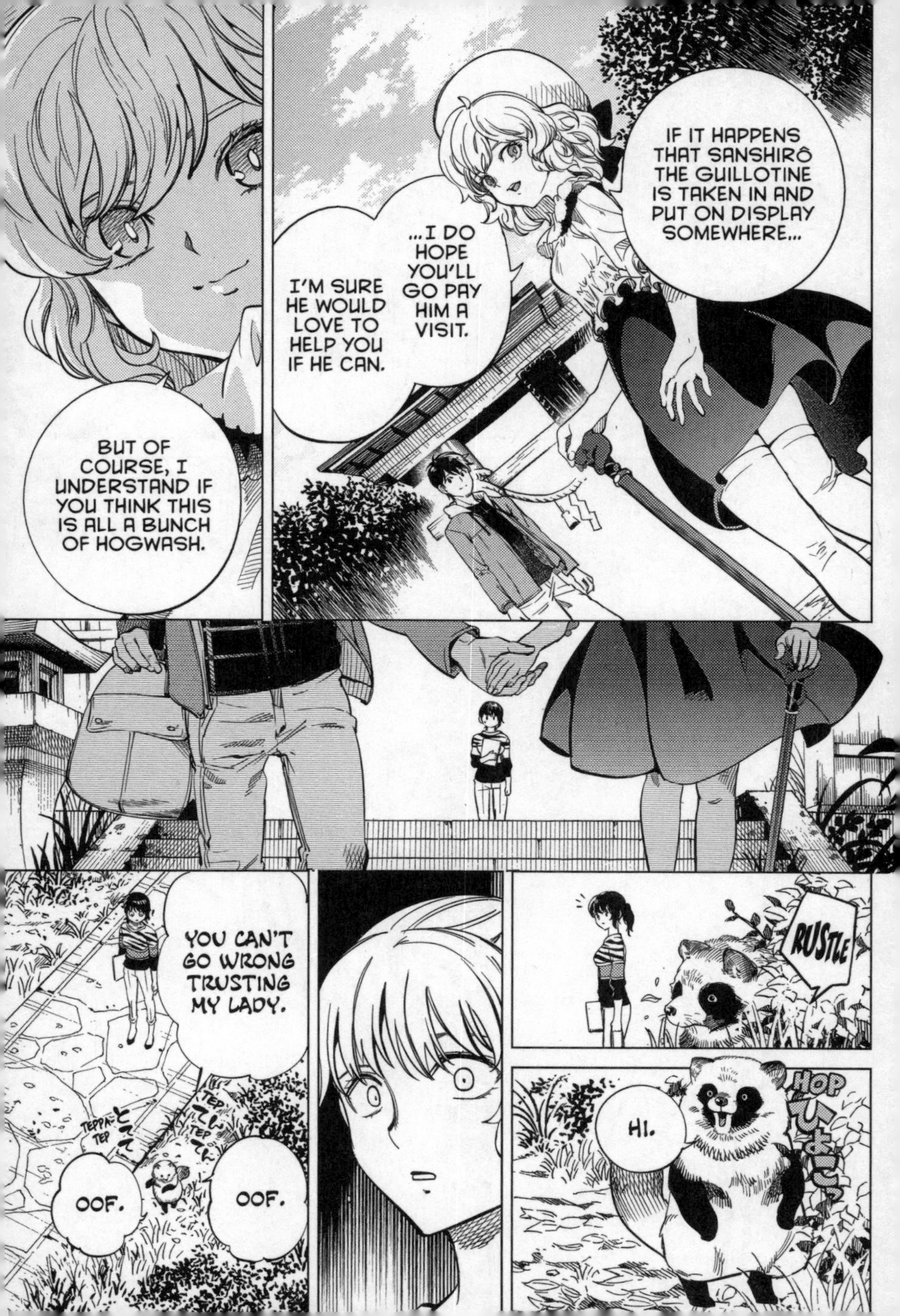
IF IT HAPPENS THAT SANSHIRÔ THE GUILLOTINE IS TAKEN IN AND PUT ON DISPLAY SOMEWHERE...
...I DO HOPE YOU'LL GO PAY HIM A VISIT.
I'M SURE HE WOULD LOVE TO HELP YOU IF HE CAN.
BUT OF COURSE, I UNDERSTAND IF YOU THINK THIS IS ALL A BUNCH OF HOGWASH.
RUSTLE
HI.
HOP
YOU CAN'T GO WRONG TRUSTING MY LADY.
TEP TEP
TEPPA-TEP
OOF.
OOF.

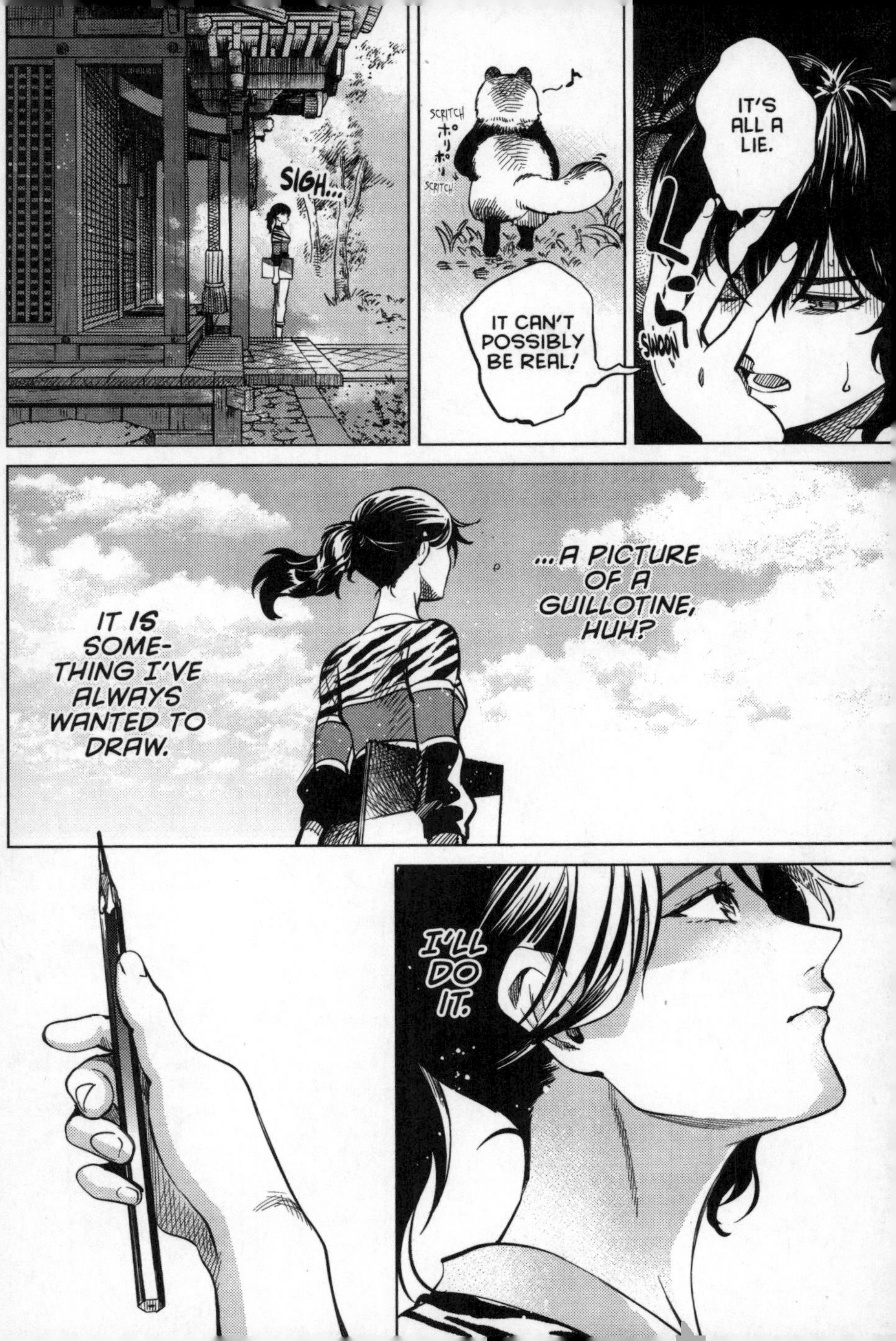
IT'S ALL A LIE.
SWOON
IT CAN'T POSSIBLY BE REAL!
SCRITCH
ポリポリ
SCRITCH
SIGH...
...A PICTURE OF A GUILLOTINE, HUH?
IT IS SOMETHING I'VE ALWAYS WANTED TO DRAW.
I'LL DO IT.

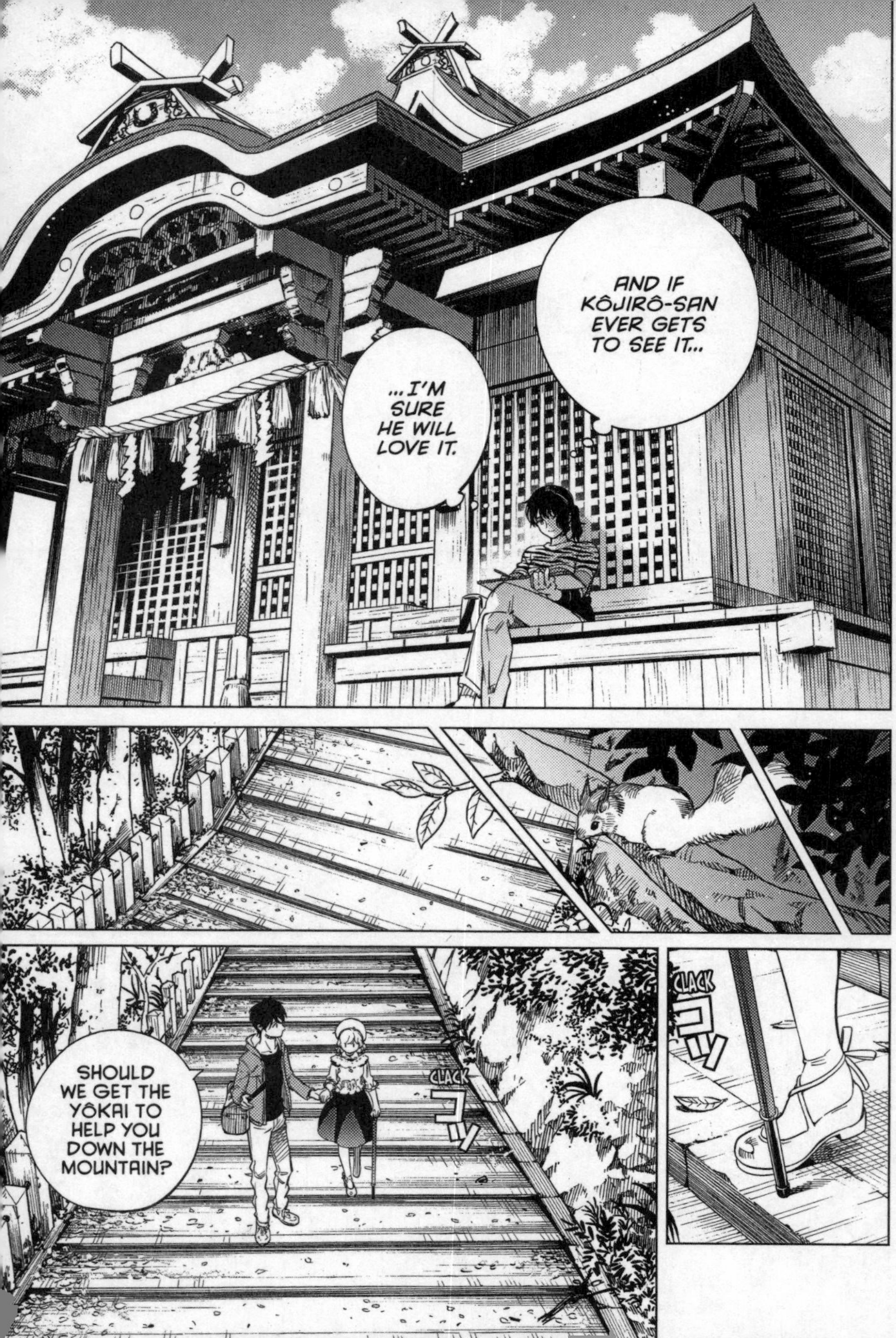
AND IF KÔJIRÔ-SAN EVER GETS TO SEE IT...
...I'M SURE HE WILL LOVE IT.
CLACK
コツ
CLACK
コツ
SHOULD WE GET THE YÔKAI TO HELP YOU DOWN THE MOUNTAIN?

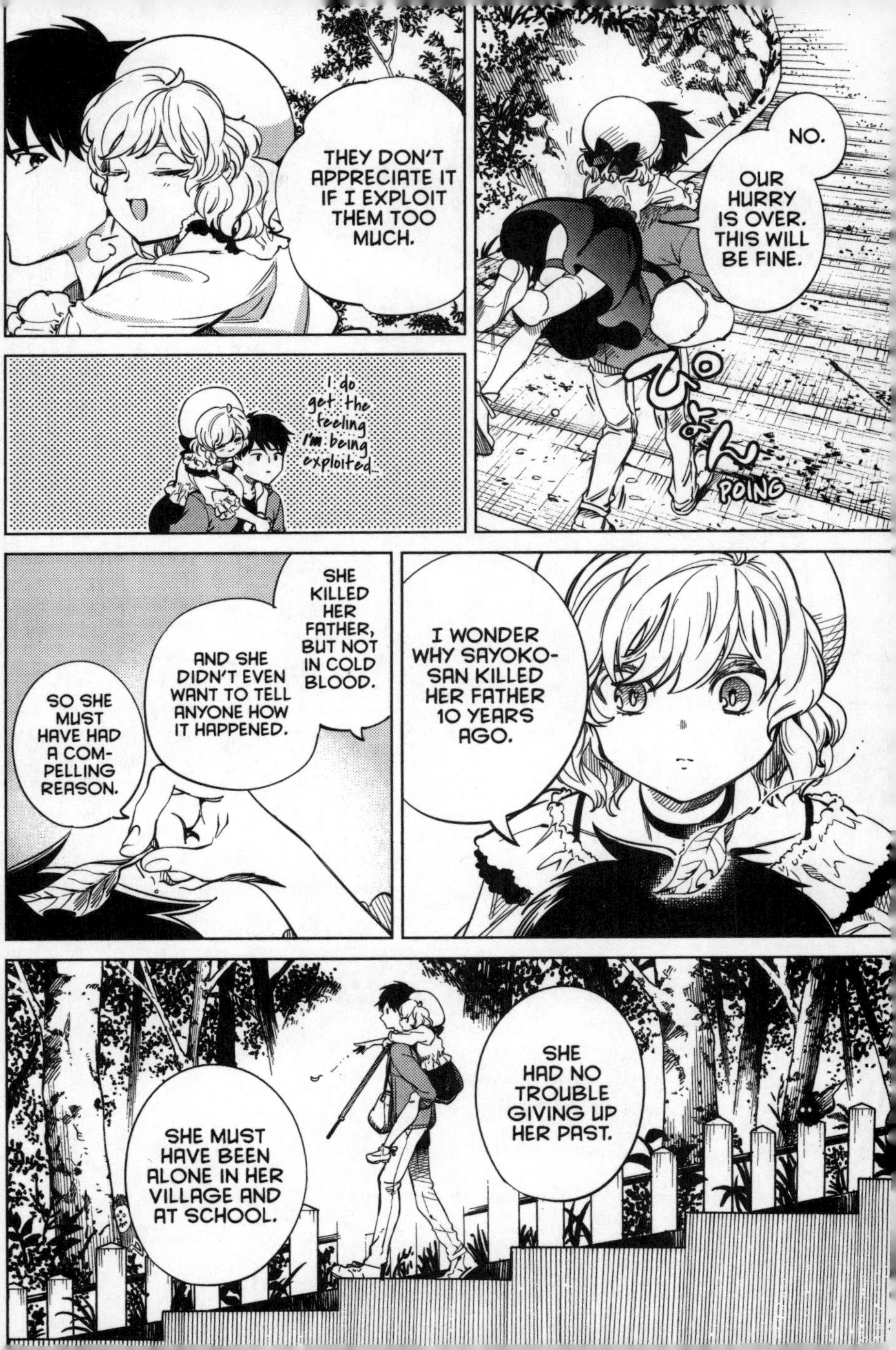
NO.
OUR HURRY IS OVER. THIS WILL BE FINE.
ぴょん
POING
THEY DON'T APPRECIATE IT IF I EXPLOIT THEM TOO MUCH.
I do get the feeling I'm being exploited.
I WONDER WHY SAYOKO-SAN KILLED HER FATHER 10 YEARS AGO.
SHE KILLED HER FATHER, BUT NOT IN COLD BLOOD.
AND SHE DIDN'T EVEN WANT TO TELL ANYONE HOW IT HAPPENED.
SO SHE MUST HAVE HAD A COM-PELLING REASON.
SHE HAD NO TROUBLE GIVING UP HER PAST.
SHE MUST HAVE BEEN ALONE IN HER VILLAGE AND AT SCHOOL.

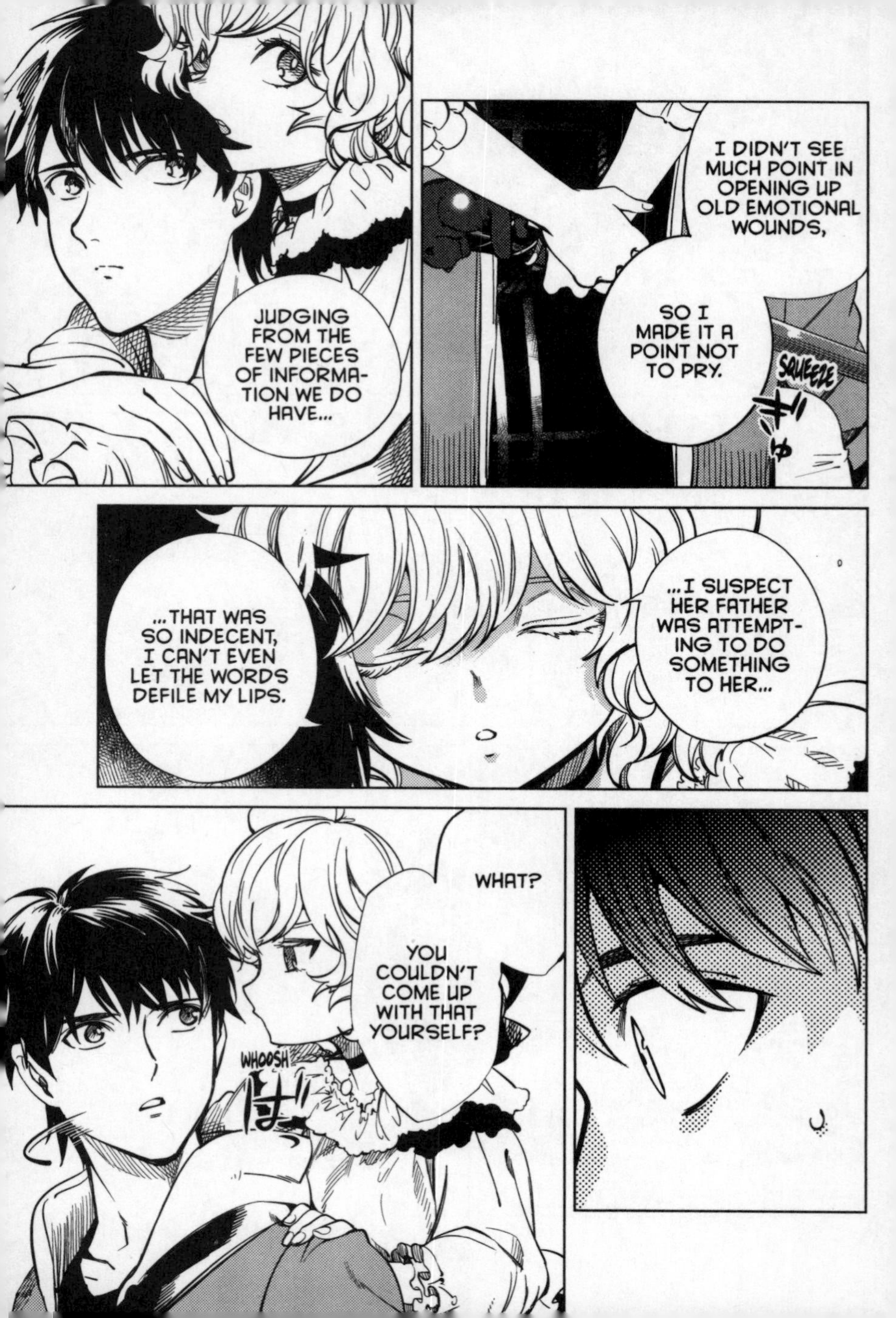
I DIDN'T SEE MUCH POINT IN OPENING UP OLD EMOTIONAL WOUNDS,
SO I MADE IT A POINT NOT TO PRY.
SQUEEZE
JUDGING FROM THE FEW PIECES OF INFORMATION WE DO HAVE...
...I SUSPECT HER FATHER WAS ATTEMPTING TO DO SOMETHING TO HER...
...THAT WAS SO INDECENT, I CAN'T EVEN LET THE WORDS DEFILE MY LIPS.
WHAT?
YOU COULDN'T COME UP WITH THAT YOURSELF?
WHOOSH

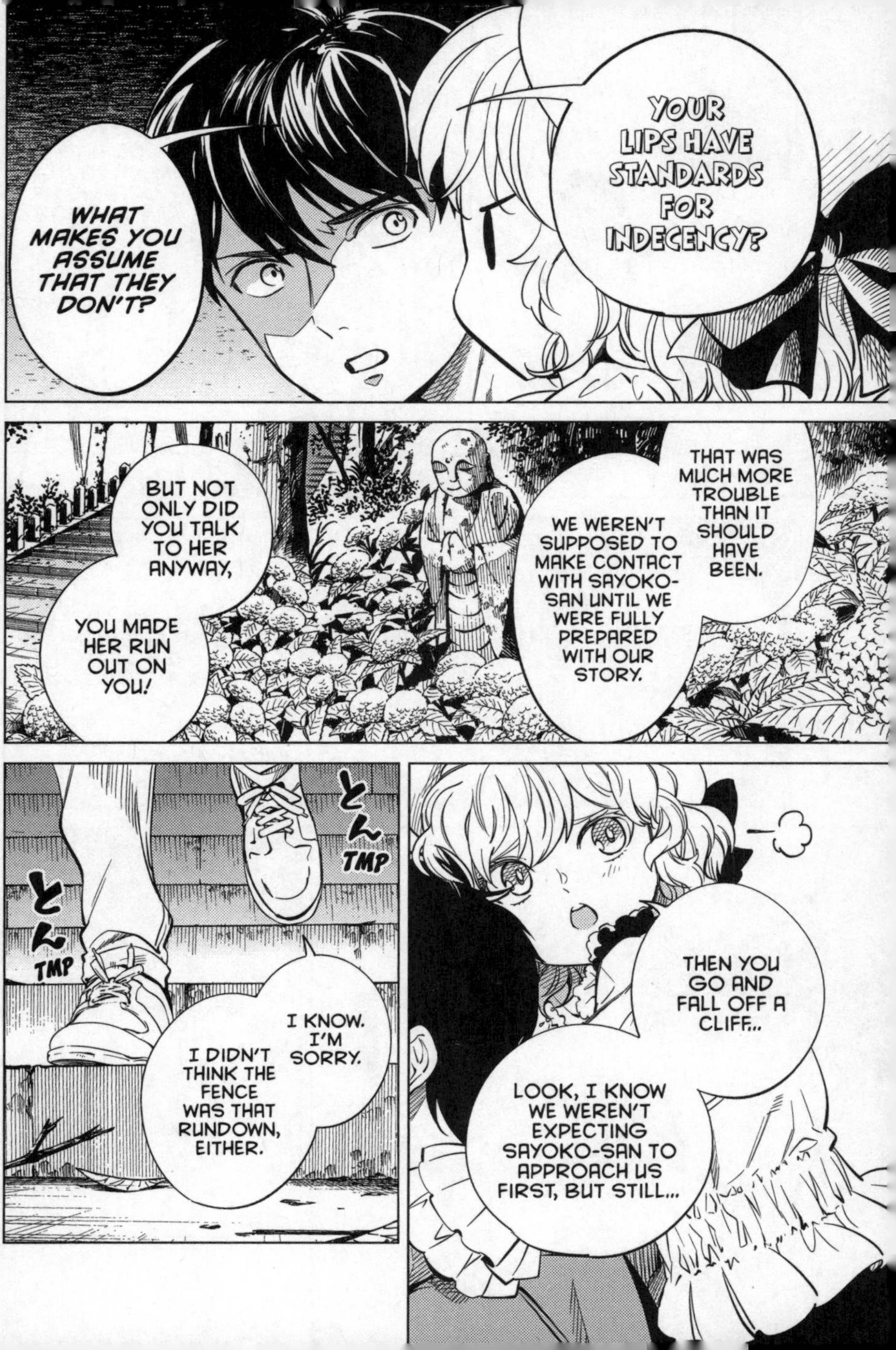
YOUR LIPS HAVE STANDARDS FOR INDECENCY?
WHAT MAKES YOU ASSUME THAT THEY DON'T?
THAT WAS MUCH MORE TROUBLE THAN IT SHOULD HAVE BEEN.
WE WEREN'T SUPPOSED TO MAKE CONTACT WITH SAYOKO-SAN UNTIL WE WERE FULLY PREPARED WITH OUR STORY.
BUT NOT ONLY DID YOU TALK TO HER ANYWAY,
YOU MADE HER RUN OUT ON YOU!
THEN YOU GO AND FALL OFF A CLIFF...
LOOK, I KNOW WE WEREN'T EXPECTING SAYOKO-SAN TO APPROACH US FIRST, BUT STILL...
とん
TMP
とん
TMP
I KNOW. I'M SORRY.
I DIDN'T THINK THE FENCE WAS THAT RUNDOWN, EITHER.

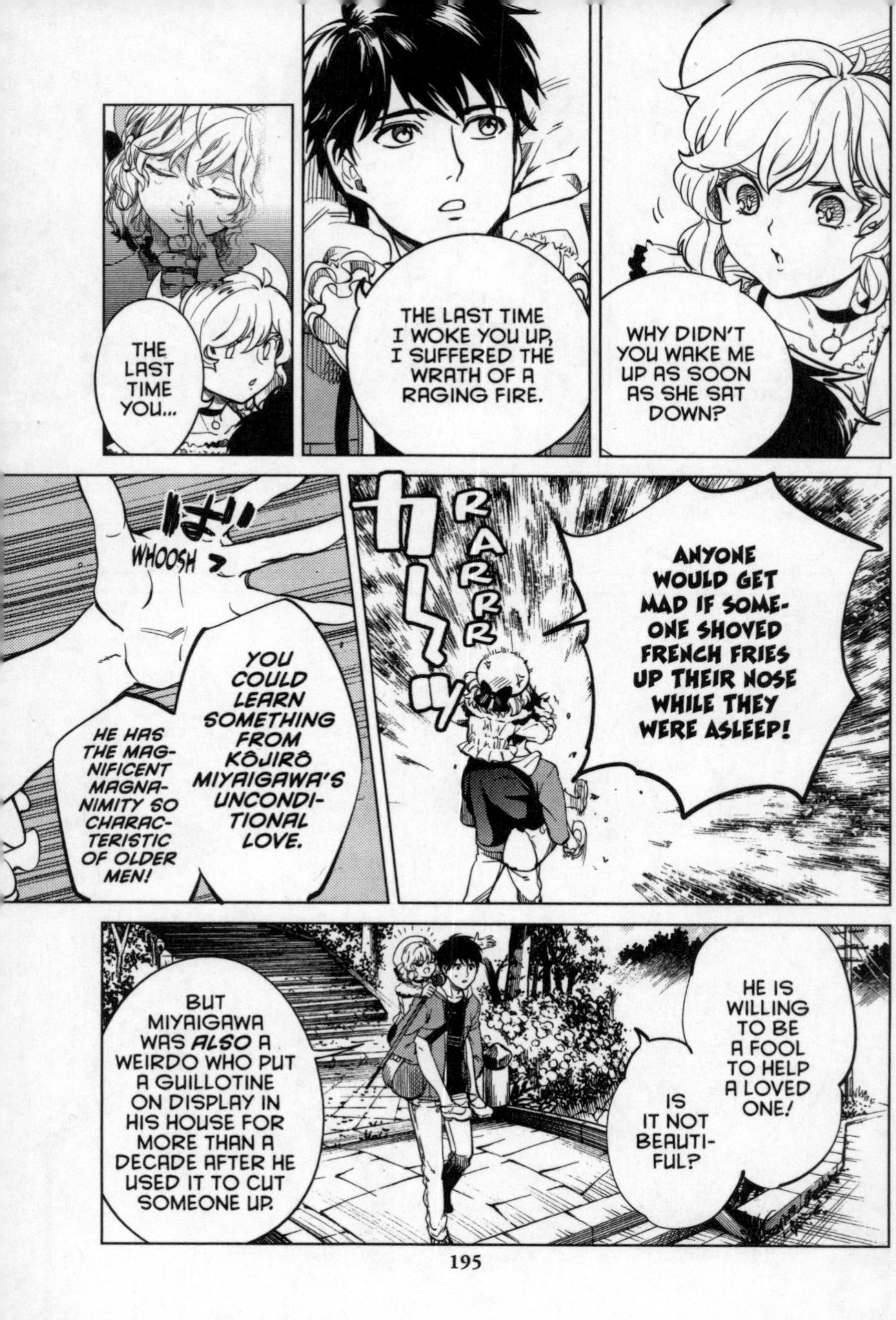
WHY DIDN'T YOU WAKE ME UP AS SOON AS SHE SAT DOWN?
THE LAST TIME I WOKE YOU UP, I SUFFERED THE WRATH OF A RAGING FIRE.
THE LAST TIME YOU...
RARRR
ANYONE WOULD GET MAD IF SOME-ONE SHOVED FRENCH FRIES UP THEIR NOSE WHILE THEY WERE ASLEEP!
WHOOSH
YOU COULD LEARN SOMETHING FROM KÔJIRÔ MIYAIGAWA'S UNCONDITIONAL LOVE.
HE HAS THE MAGNIFICENT MAGNANIMITY SO CHARACTERISTIC OF OLDER MEN!
HE IS WILLING TO BE A FOOL TO HELP A LOVED ONE!
IS IT NOT BEAUTIFUL?
BUT MIYAIGAWA WAS *ALSO* A WEIRDO WHO PUT A GUILLOTINE ON DISPLAY IN HIS HOUSE FOR MORE THAN A DECADE AFTER HE USED IT TO CUT SOMEONE UP.

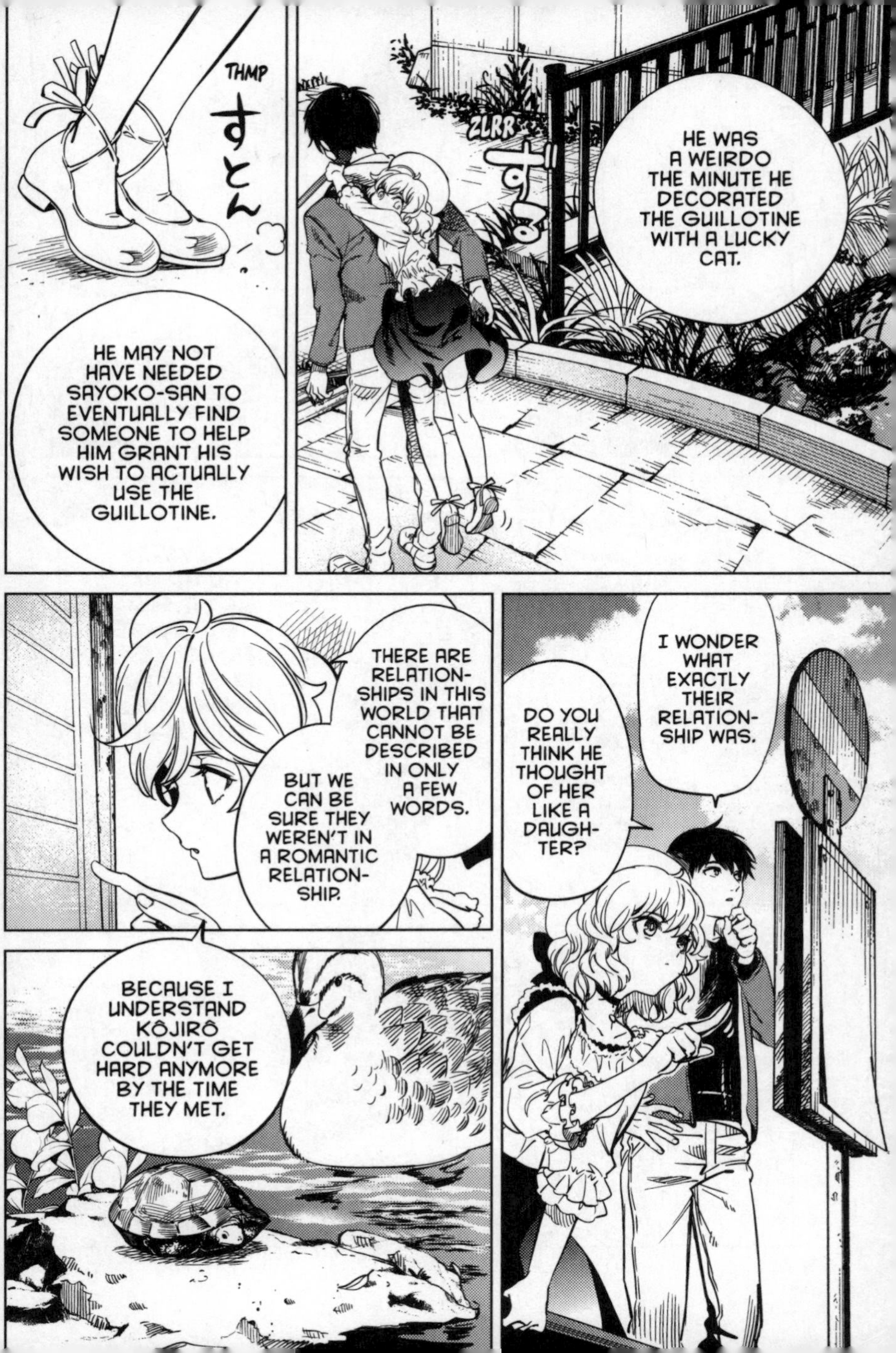
ZLRR
ずる
HE WAS A WEIRDO THE MINUTE HE DECORATED THE GUILLOTINE WITH A LUCKY CAT.
THMP
すとん
HE MAY NOT HAVE NEEDED SAYOKO-SAN TO EVENTUALLY FIND SOMEONE TO HELP HIM GRANT HIS WISH TO ACTUALLY USE THE GUILLOTINE.
I WONDER WHAT EXACTLY THEIR RELATION-SHIP WAS.
DO YOU REALLY THINK HE THOUGHT OF HER LIKE A DAUGH-TER?
THERE ARE RELATION-SHIPS IN THIS WORLD THAT CANNOT BE DESCRIBED IN ONLY A FEW WORDS.
BUT WE CAN BE SURE THEY WEREN'T IN A ROMANTIC RELATION-SHIP.
BECAUSE I UNDERSTAND KÔJIRÔ COULDN'T GET HARD ANYMORE BY THE TIME THEY MET.

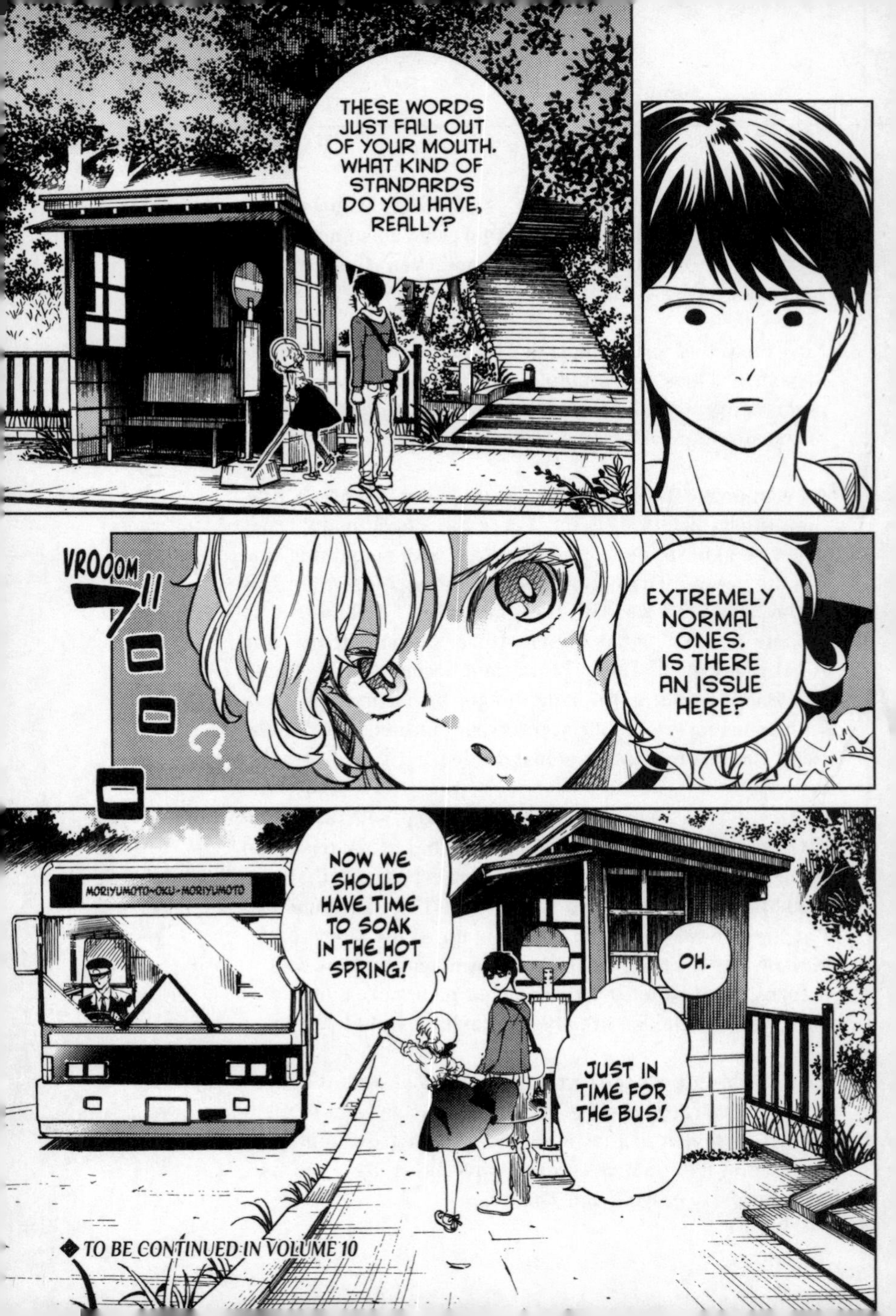
THESE WORDS JUST FALL OUT OF YOUR MOUTH. WHAT KIND OF STANDARDS DO YOU HAVE, REALLY?
EXTREMELY NORMAL ONES. IS THERE AN ISSUE HERE?
VROOOM
?
OH.
JUST IN TIME FOR THE BUS!
NOW WE SHOULD HAVE TIME TO SOAK IN THE HOT SPRING!
MORIYUMOTO-OKU-MORIYUMOTO
◆ TO BE CONTINUED IN VOLUME 10

A Discussion of Titles from the Author

I'm the author, Kyo Shirodaira. And this is Volume Nine. This will be the third volume that takes an episodic format. It should be okay to read this volume even if you haven't read the others.

Now then, this volume has an episode entitled "Guillotine Sanshirô." Titles really should be something that catch the reader's eye, create a clear image of the contents or mood of the story, and leave an impression on the memory.

If I wait until after I write the story to come up with a title, then it gets pretty difficult. There have been many times when I'd agonize over it, and end up with something that has me going, "There might be something better, but this is the best I can do with the time I have." That's true of Volume Seven's "What the Guardian Serpent Heard" and "Lucky Day at the Unagi Restaurant." Sometimes I choose a title, and I end up thinking I might be surprisingly okay with exposing it to public scrutiny, but nothing I do can get rid of the feeling that I had just settled.

Contrariwise, sometimes I think a story with a certain title could be interesting, and write that story based on the title, and in those cases, I never worry about that title later. "Guillotine Sanshirô" is one title I can get behind. But then I have a hard time coming up with a story that actually fits the title, and sometimes no matter how well it turns out, I wonder if there might be a more suitable story for the title, so I really just can't be satisfied.

Also, when a title is too distinctive, or is weird for the sake of being weird, it can be overly aggressive, and readers will either love it or they'll hate it. When I grow up, I want to be confident enough to use simple titles like *The Cask, The Birds, Face, Wall,* and *The Rasp.*

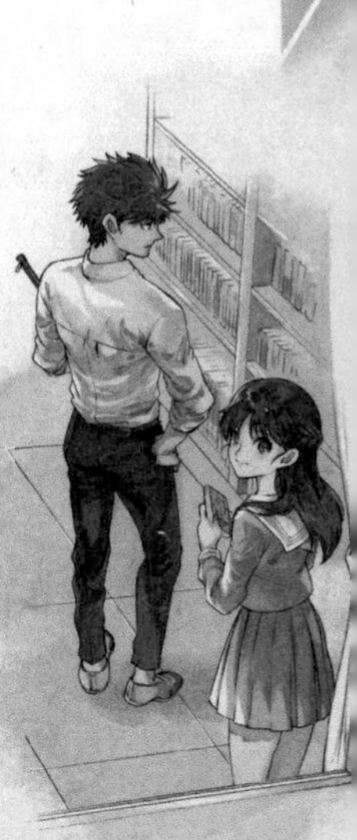

But these days, the distinctive titles are easier to find in an internet search, and with simple titles, you run the risk of them getting mixed up with another title that has the same word in it. It's a difficult balance.

And as for the series' original (Japanese) title, *Invented Inference,* I came up with that at an early stage, along with the story itself. It was concise and distinct, and it fit with the story, so I was satisfied with it. But now that it's a manga and it just keeps going, I wish I could go back in time and tell my past self, "Don't call it that. You can't put 'invented' and 'inference' together, it just makes things complicated. Call it *The Immortal Boy and the Little Rich Girl* or *The Invincible Kotoko Iwanaga,* or something else that makes it sound like a comedy, and then you won't have people accusing it of not being a mystery."

Well, even if I could do that, it would cause a time paradox, and that would complicate things, too.

A certain someone will be returning in the next volume, and we plan to return the story to the grander scheme of things. I hope that I can give it a new kind of twist, even for a mystery series.

Well, I hope you will read the next volume.

Kyo Shirodaira

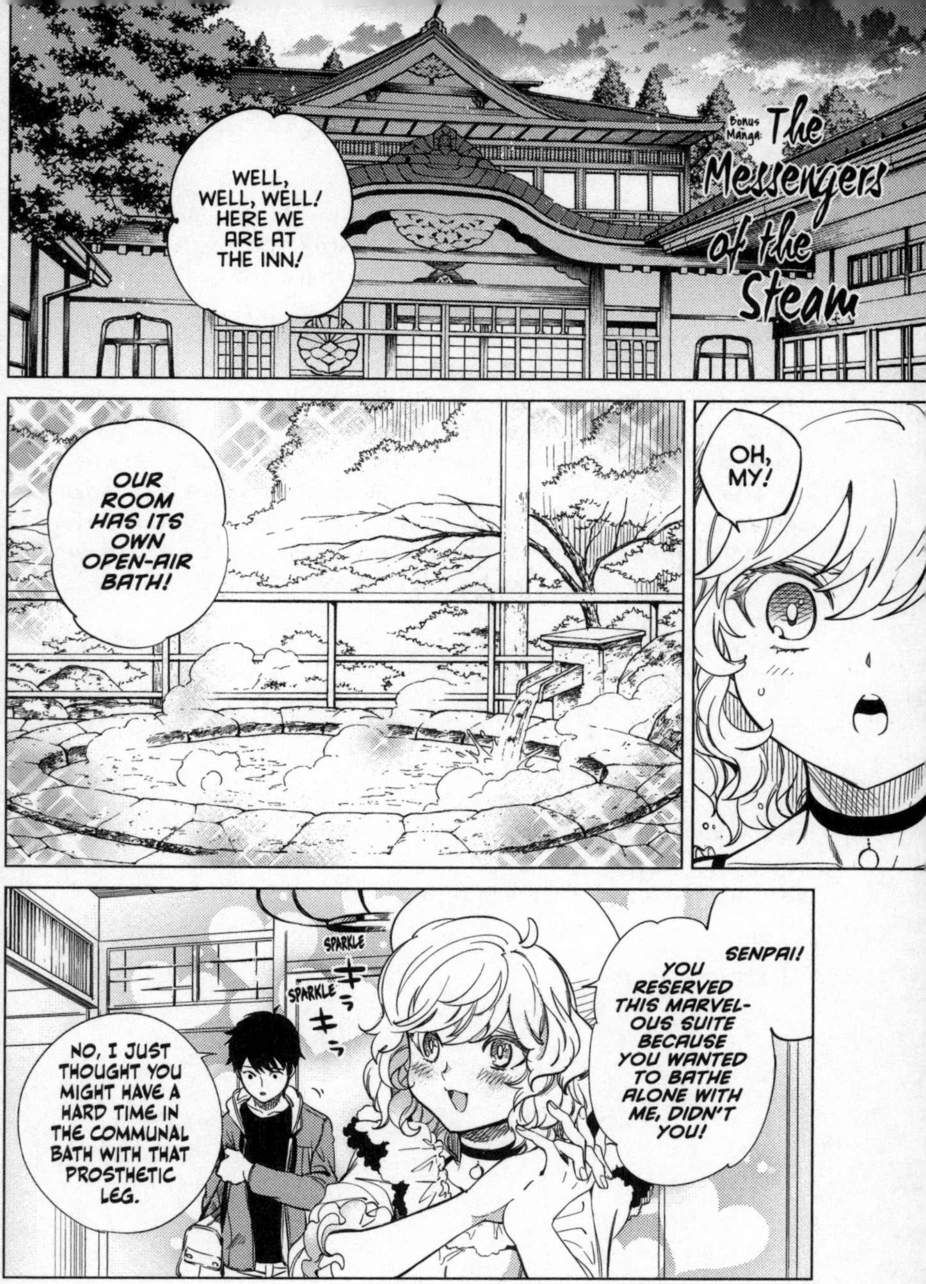
Bonus Manga: The Messengers of the Steam
WELL, WELL, WELL! HERE WE ARE AT THE INN!
OH, MY!
OUR ROOM HAS ITS OWN OPEN-AIR BATH!
SENPAI!
YOU RESERVED THIS MARVEL-OUS SUITE BECAUSE YOU WANTED TO BATHE ALONE WITH ME, DIDN'T YOU!
SPARKLE
キラ
SPARKLE
キラ
NO, I JUST THOUGHT YOU MIGHT HAVE A HARD TIME IN THE COMMUNAL BATH WITH THAT PROSTHETIC LEG.

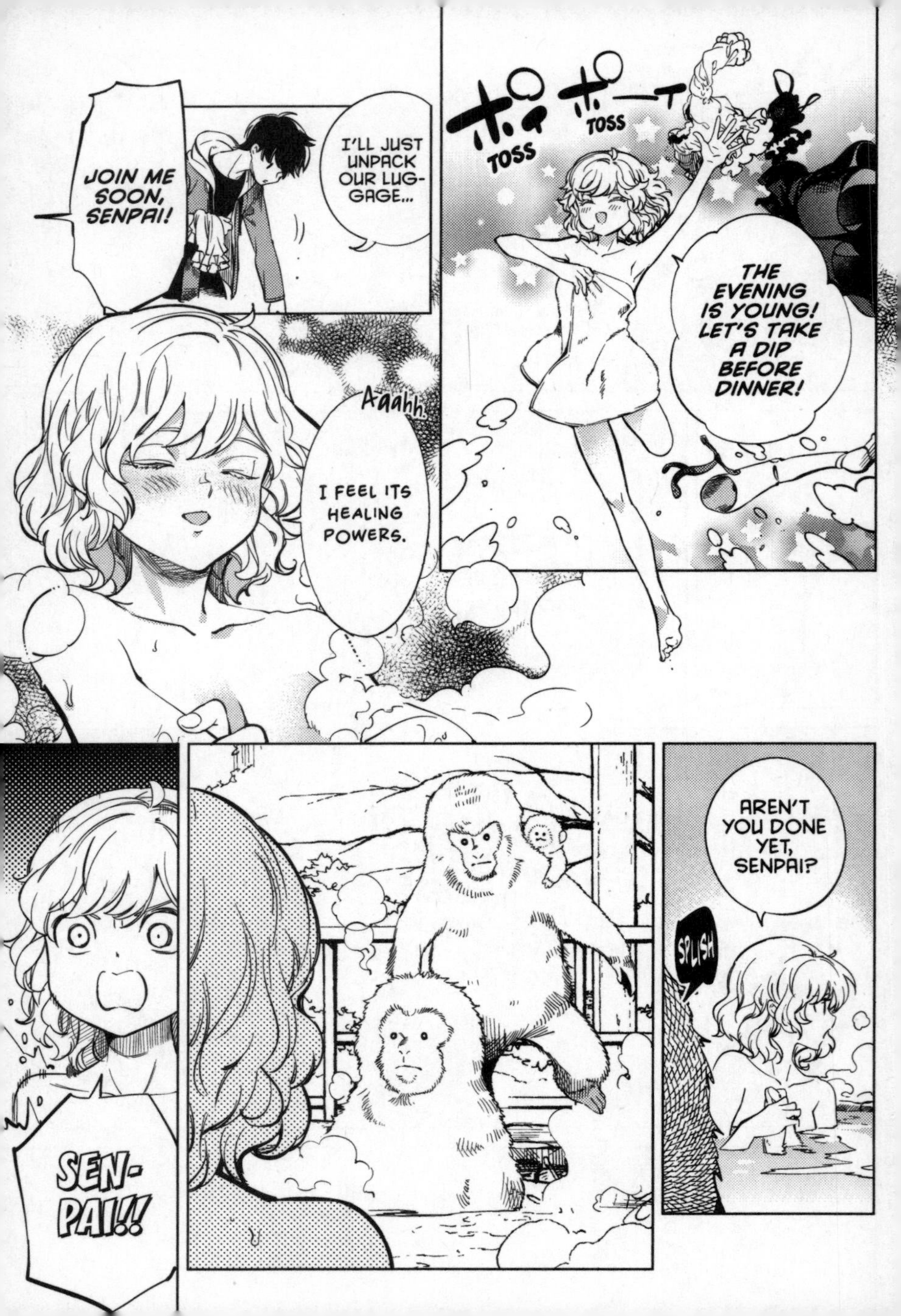
ポイ
TOSS
ポーイ
TOSS
THE EVENING IS YOUNG! LET'S TAKE A DIP BEFORE DINNER!
JOIN ME SOON, SENPAI!
I'LL JUST UNPACK OUR LUG-GAGE...
Aaahh.
I FEEL ITS HEALING POWERS.
AREN'T YOU DONE YET, SENPAI?
SPLISH
SEN-PAI!!

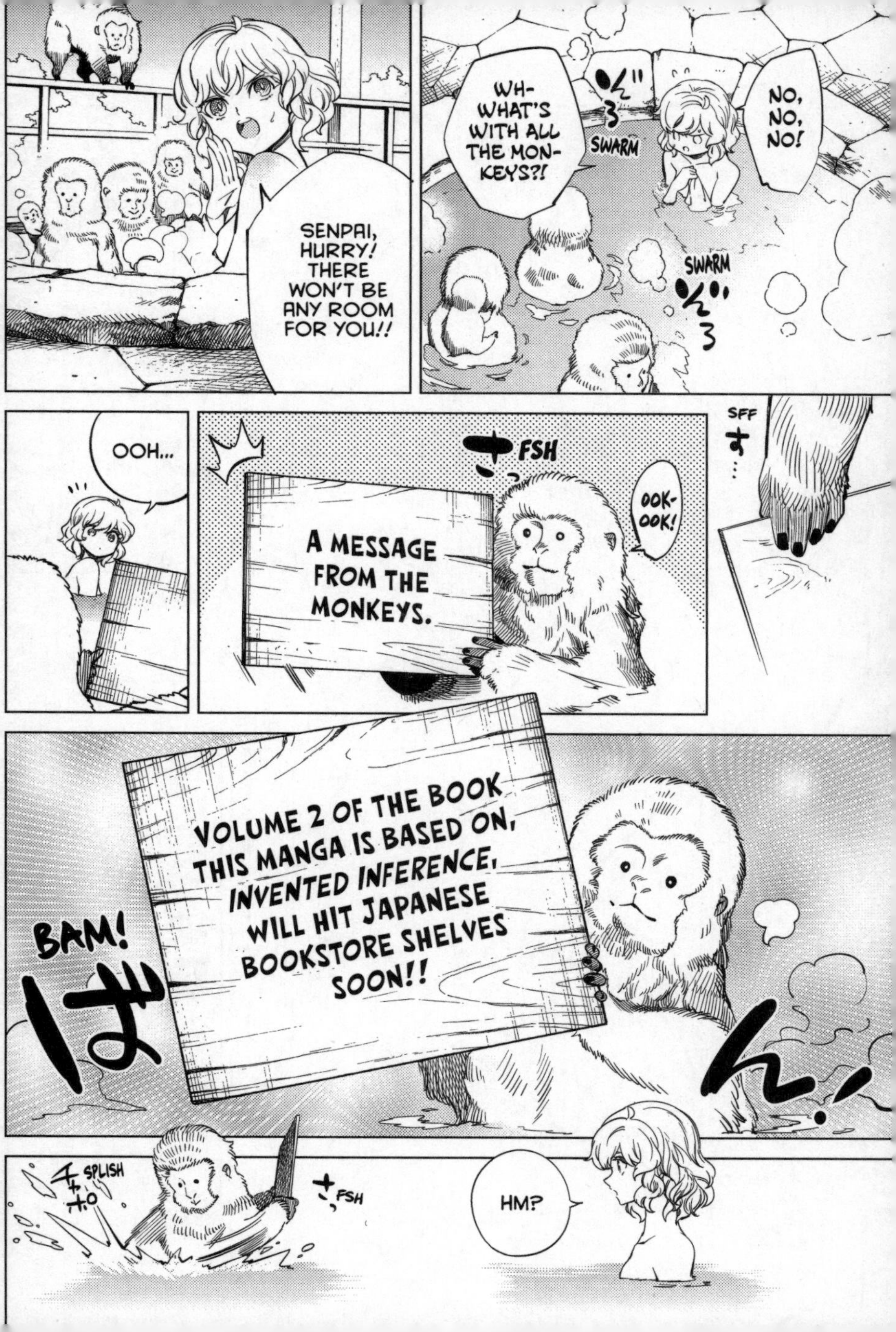
NO, NO, NO!
WH-WHAT'S WITH ALL THE MON-KEYS?!
SWARM
SWARM
SENPAI, HURRY! THERE WON'T BE ANY ROOM FOR YOU!!
SFF
OOK-OOK!
FSH
A MESSAGE FROM THE MONKEYS.
OOH...
VOLUME 2 OF THE BOOK THIS MANGA IS BASED ON, INVENTED INFERENCE, WILL HIT JAPANESE BOOKSTORE SHELVES SOON!!
BAM!
HM?
FSH
SPLISH

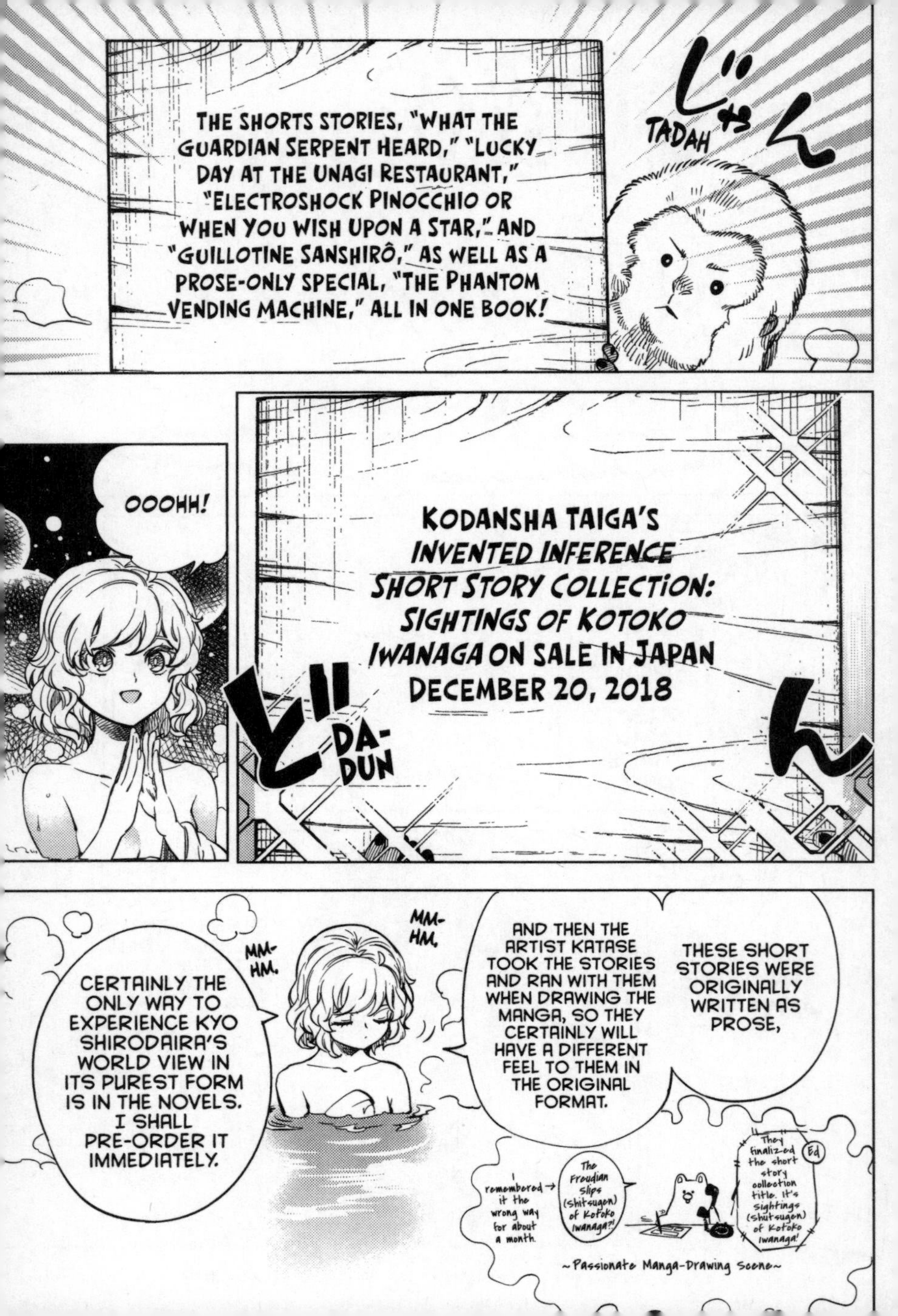

TADAH
THE SHORTS STORIES, "WHAT THE GUARDIAN SERPENT HEARD," "LUCKY DAY AT THE UNAGI RESTAURANT," "ELECTROSHOCK PINOCCHIO OR WHEN YOU WISH UPON A STAR," AND "GUILLOTINE SANSHIRÔ," AS WELL AS A PROSE-ONLY SPECIAL, "THE PHANTOM VENDING MACHINE," ALL IN ONE BOOK!
KODANSHA TAIGA'S *INVENTED INFERENCE SHORT STORY COLLECTION: SIGHTINGS OF KOTOKO IWANAGA* ON SALE IN JAPAN DECEMBER 20, 2018
DA-DUN
OOOHH!
THESE SHORT STORIES WERE ORIGINALLY WRITTEN AS PROSE,
AND THEN THE ARTIST KATASE TOOK THE STORIES AND RAN WITH THEM WHEN DRAWING THE MANGA, SO THEY CERTAINLY WILL HAVE A DIFFERENT FEEL TO THEM IN THE ORIGINAL FORMAT.
MM-HM.
MM-HM.
CERTAINLY THE ONLY WAY TO EXPERIENCE KYO SHIRODAIRA'S WORLD VIEW IN ITS PUREST FORM IS IN THE NOVELS. I SHALL PRE-ORDER IT IMMEDIATELY.
Ed
They finalized the short story collection title. It's Sightings (Shutsugen) of Kotoko Iwanaga!
The Freudian Slips (Shitsugen) of Kotoko Iwanaga?!
I remembered it the wrong way for about a month.
~Passionate Manga-Drawing Scene~

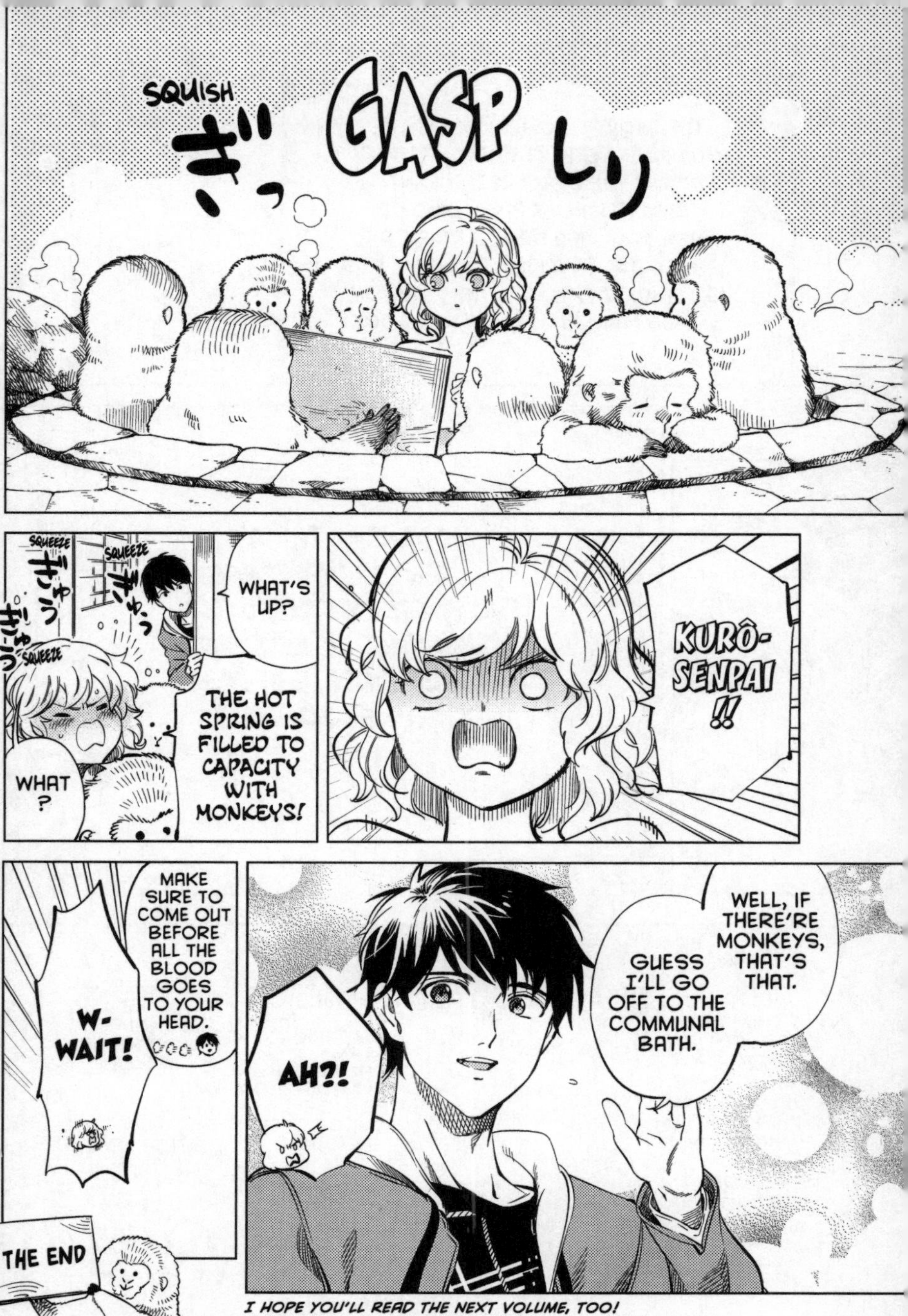
しり
GASP
SQUISH
ぎっ
KURÔ-SENPAI!!
WHAT'S UP?
SQUEEZE
ぎゅう
SQUEEZE
ぎゅう
SQUEEZE
ぎゅう
THE HOT SPRING IS FILLED TO CAPACITY WITH MONKEYS!
WHAT?
WELL, IF THERE'RE MONKEYS, THAT'S THAT.
GUESS I'LL GO OFF TO THE COMMUNAL BATH.
AH?!
MAKE SURE TO COME OUT BEFORE ALL THE BLOOD GOES TO YOUR HEAD.
W-WAIT!
THE END

I HOPE YOU'LL READ THE NEXT VOLUME, TOO!
STAFF: ASAI, SHIMAMEGURI, UMI, EDITOR: O-GAWA, T-DA

TRANSLATION NOTES

Already June, page 4

While June is a very, very late time of year to someone in the United States school system (so late that they might as well not bother trying to get more club members), in Japan the school year starts in April. It's late enough that a club would have a hard time recruiting, as most students will have already decided how to spend their time after school, but not so late that adding to their numbers would be pointless.

Dans in judo and kendo, page 8

Dan ranks in Japanese martial arts are the ones that come after the *kyû*, or beginning, ranks. In judo, this means that Manabu has a black belt, although the degree of black belt is not stated. He has made it to a similarly high level in kendo (Japanese fencing), but kendo doesn't use belts to show ranks.

The go-home club, page 9

In Japan, almost every student in school is in a club (at some schools, it's required). Usually, the clubs are divided into two categories: *undôbu*, or athletic clubs (including all the sports teams), and *bunkabu*, or culture clubs (including art, music, literature, etc.). There is one final category of clubs, and that's the category for people who haven't joined any club—the *kitakubu*, or go-home club. Members of this club use their extracurricular time to go home.

Japanese cross, page 91

As the reader may expect, the Japanese cross was used for crucifixion, but Japan had its own unique version of the punishment. After parading the condemned through town on horseback, the executioners would tie him to the cross, or *haritsukedai*, and spear him from both sides before delivering a final blow to the throat.

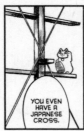

YOU EVEN HAVE A JAPANESE CROSS.

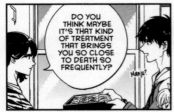

DO YOU THINK MAYBE IT'S THAT KIND OF TREATMENT THAT BRINGS YOU SO CLOSE TO DEATH SO FREQUENTLY?
Manju?

Onsen manju, page 105

Manju are a kind Japanese dumpling, with a sweet red bean filling. At hot spring resorts, tourists can buy *onsen manju*, or "hot spring dumplings," which are made with wheat flour and brown sugar.

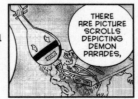

THERE ARE PICTURE SCROLLS DEPICTING DEMON PARADES,

Biwa and koto, page 108

These are both types of traditional Japanese musical instruments. The biwa is a type of lute (any string instrument with a neck), and the koto is a plucked stringed instrument, where 13 strings are stretched over a wooden body.

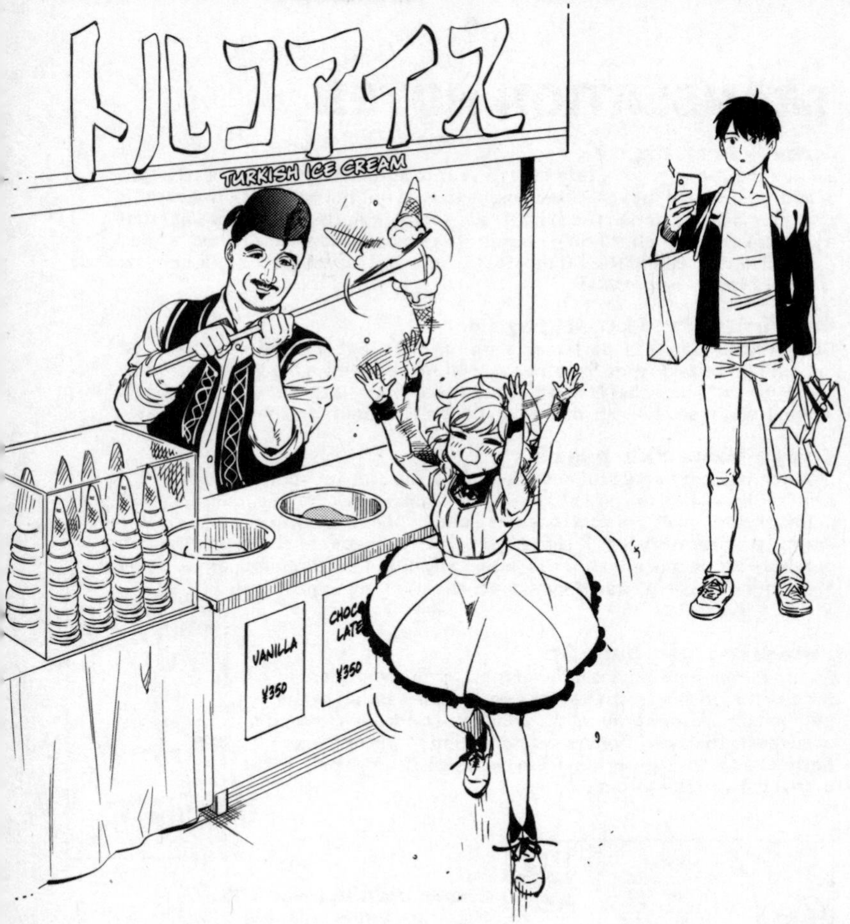
トルコアイス
TURKISH ICE CREAM
VANILLA
¥350
CHOCO
LATE
¥350

Kotoko Iwanaga, teased at the Turkish ice cream stand.

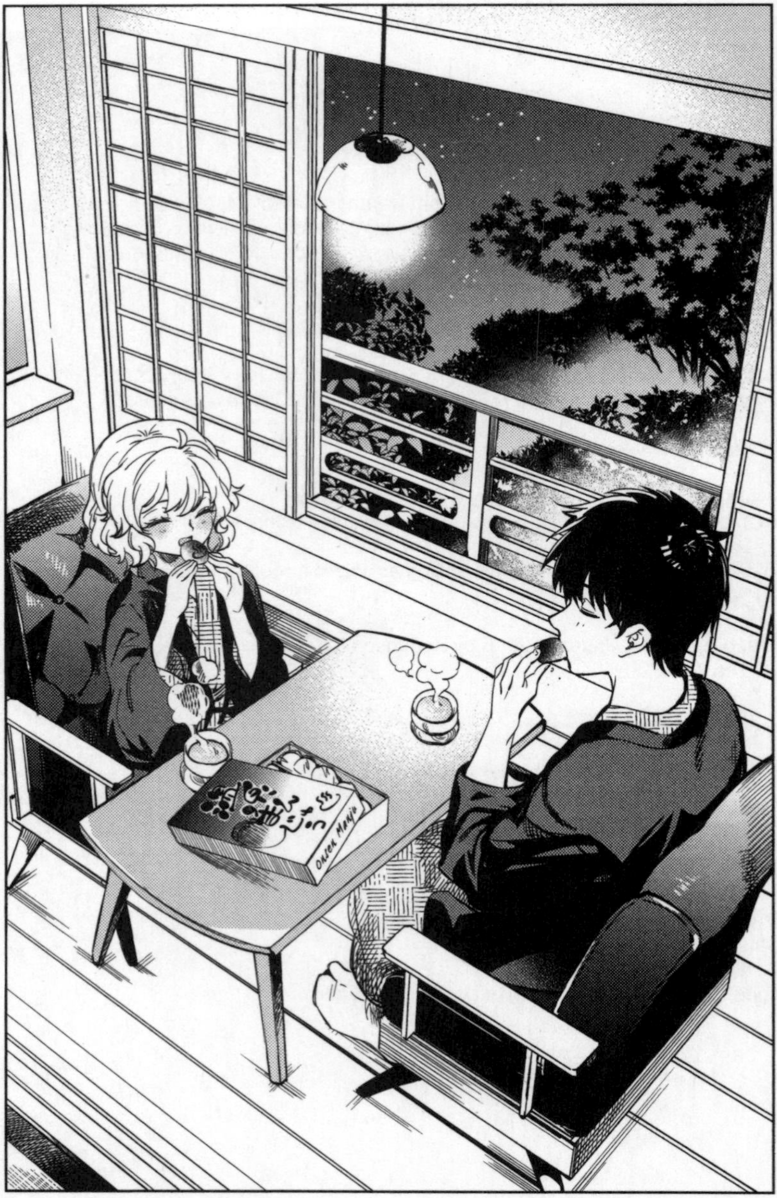
Onsen Manju

In/Spectre volume 9 is a work of fiction. Names, characters, places, and incidents are the products of the author's imagination or are used fictitiously. Any resemblance to actual events, locales, or persons, living or dead, is entirely coincidental.

A Kodansha Comics Trade Paperback Original.

Published in the United States by Kodansha Comics,
an imprint of Kodansha USA Publishing, LLC, New York.

Publication rights for this English edition arranged through Kodansha Ltd., Tokyo.

First published in Japan in 2018 by Kodansha Ltd., Tokyo, as *Kyokou Suiri* volume 9.

ISBN 978-1-63236-670-2

Printed in the United States of America.

www.kodanshacomics.com

9 8 7 6 5 4 3 2

Translation: Alethea Nibley & Athena Nibley
Lettering: Lys Blakeslee
Editing: Ajani Oloye
Kodansha Comics edition cover design: Phil Balsman